Praise for Wedlock

'*Wedlock* is the best biogr[illegible] It's gripping, ad[illegible] *Mail on Sunday*

'This torrent of a biography sweeps the reader along . . . Mary's prolonged, audacious struggle to extricate herself from this marriage is a match for Hollywood' *Independent*

'Moore has meticulously const[illegible] more compelling tale' *Gu*[illegible]

'Moore makes a[illegible]

'Mesmerising . . . [illegible]gorously researched' *Fin*[illegible]

'Gallops headlong towards an unbelievably tense denouement which any work of Hollywood fiction would struggle to match' *Scotland on Sunday*

'Wendy Moore delivers the full ghastliness with brilliant panache' *Daily Express*

'*Wedlock* is serious, perceptive, thoughtful and – by no means least – compulsively readable' *Washington Post*

'This splendid book, well researched and richly detailed, is as gripping as a novel' *Daily Telegraph*

'Moore unravels in meticulous detail the story of how one man beat, abused and finally cowed one of the most famous aristocrats of the day' *The Times*

'Moore, mistress of suspense, writes in the gripping language of a thriller . . . This book has it all – the blackest of villains, the strangest friendship, kidnap, abortions, riches and all completely true' *Observer*

Wendy Moore is a writer and journalist. Her work has been published in a range of newspapers and magazines, including the *Times* and *Sunday Telegraph*, and has won several awards. Her first book, *The Knife Man*, was critically acclaimed and shortlisted for both the Saltire and Marsh biography awards. She lives in south London with her husband and two children.

By Wendy Moore

The Knife Man
Wedlock

WEDLOCK

How Georgian Britain's Worst Husband Met His Match

WENDY MOORE

PHOENIX

For Mum and Dad
In celebration of more than fifty years
of marital harmony

A PHOENIX PAPERBACK

First published in Great Britain in 2009
by Weidenfeld & Nicolson
This paperback edition published in 2010
by Phoenix,
an imprint of Orion Books Ltd
Orion House, 5 Upper St Martin's Lane
London, WC2H 9EA

An Hachette UK company

5 7 9 10 8 6 4

A CIP catalogue record for this book
is available from the British Library.

ISBN 978-0-7538-2825-0

Typeset by Input Data Services Ltd, Bridgwater, Somerset

Printed and bound in the Great Britain by Clays Ltd, St Ives plc

The Orion Publishing Group's policy is to use papers that
are natural, renewable and recyclable products and
made from wood grown in sustainable forests. The logging
and manufacturing processes are expected to conform to
the environmental regulations of the country of origin.

www.orionbooks.co.uk

Contents

Who can say that I had not a right to use *any* stratagem in this matter of love? Or, why say love? I wanted the wealth of the lady.

William Makepeace Thackeray, *The Memoirs of Barry Lyndon, Esq.*

1
An Affair of Honour

London, 13 January 1777

Settling down to read his newspaper by the candlelight illuminating the dining room of the Adelphi Tavern, John Hull anticipated a quiet evening. Having opened five years earlier, as an integral part of the vast riverside development designed by the Adam brothers, the Adelphi Tavern and Coffee House had established a reputation for its fine dinners and genteel company. Many an office worker like Hull, a clerk at the Government's Salt Office, sought refuge from the clamour of the nearby Strand in the tavern's first-floor dining room with its elegant ceiling panels depicting Pan and Bacchus in pastel shades. On a Monday evening in January, with the day's work behind him, Hull could expect to read his journal undisturbed.

At first, when he heard the two loud bangs, at about 7 p.m., Hull assumed they were caused by a door slamming downstairs. A few minutes later, there was no mistaking the sound of clashing swords.[1] Throwing aside his newspaper, Hull ran down the stairs and tried to open the door to the ground-floor parlour. Finding it locked, and growing increasingly alarmed at the violent clatter from within, he shouted for waiters to help him force the door. Finally bursting into the room, Hull could dimly make out two figures fencing furiously in the dark. Reckless as to his own safety, the clerk grabbed the sword arm of the nearest man, thrust himself between the two duellists and insisted that they lay down their swords. Even so, it was several more minutes before he could persuade the first swordsman to yield his weapon.

It was not a moment too soon. The man who had reluctantly surrendered his sword now fell swooning to the floor and, in the light of candles brought by servants, a large bloodstain could be seen seeping across his waistcoat. A cursory examination by Hull convinced him that the man was gravely injured. 'I think there were three wounds in his right breast, and one upon his sword arm,' he would later attest. The second duellist, although less seriously wounded, was bleeding from a gash to his thigh. With no time to be lost, servants were despatched to summon medical aid. They returned with a physician, named John Scott, who ran a dispensary from his house nearby, and a surgeon, one Jessé Foot, who lived in a neighbouring street. Both concurred with Hull's amateur opinion, agreeing that the collapsed man had suffered a serious stab wound where his opponent's sword had run through his chest from right to left – presumably on account of the fencers standing sideways on – as well as a smaller cut to his abdomen and a scratch on his sword arm. Dishevelled and deathly pale, his shirt and waistcoat opened to bare his chest, the patient sprawled in a chair as the medical men tried to revive him with smelling salts, water and wine, and to staunch the bleeding by applying a poultice. Whatever benefit the pair may have bestowed by this eminently sensible first aid was almost certainly reversed when they cut open a vein in their patient's arm to let blood, the customary treatment for almost every ailment. Unsurprisingly, given the weakening effect of this further loss of blood, no sooner had the swordsman revived than he fainted twice more. It was with some justification, therefore, that the two medics pronounced their patient's injuries might well prove fatal. The discovery of two discarded pistols, still warm from having been fired, suggested that the outcome could easily have been even more decisive. With his life declared to be hanging by a thread, the fading duellist now urged his erstwhile adversary to flee the tavern – taking pains to insist that he had acquitted himself honourably – and even offered his own carriage for the getaway.

This was sound advice, for duels of honour had been repeatedly condemned or banned since the custom had first been imported from continental Europe to Britain in the early seventeenth century. Anyone participating in such a trial of combat risked being charged with murder, and subsequently hanged, should their opponent die, while those who took the role of seconds, whose job was to ensure fair play, could be charged as accomplices to murder. Yet such legal deterrents had done little to discourage reckless gallants bent on settling a dispute of honour. Far from declining under threat of prosecution, duelling had not only endured but flourished spectacularly in the eighteenth century. During the reign of George III, from 1760 to 1820, no fewer than 172 duels would be fought in which 69 men died and 96 were wounded. When Lord Byron, great-uncle of the poet, killed his cousin William Chaworth in a petty argument about poaching in 1765, the baron was charged with manslaughter and only escaped the death sentence by virtue of his status as a peer. The gradual replacement of swords by pistols in the later eighteenth century inevitably put the participants at greater risk of fatal injury, assuming that these frequently inaccurate firearms hit their mark. John Wilkes, the radical politician, only survived a duel in 1763 because his assailant's bullet was deflected by a coat button. As the fashion for settling scores by combat grew, so the perverse rules of etiquette surrounding duelling had become more convoluted to the extent that rule books, such as the *Twenty-six Commandments* published in Ireland in 1777, were produced in an attempt to guide combatants through the ritualistic maze.

Yet for all the legal prohibition, the deadly game had not only grown in popularity but was also widely tolerated. During George III's long reign only eighteen cases were ever brought to trial; just seven participants were found guilty of manslaughter and three of murder, and only two suffered execution. This lax approach by authority was scarcely surprising, given that during the same period duels were fought by two prime ministers – William Petty Shelburne and William Pitt the Younger – and a leader of the opposition, Charles James Fox. Public opinion largely condoned the practice too. The pre-eminent literary figure Samuel Johnson argued that a gentleman who was challenged to a duel could legitimately fight in self-defence.[2] Indeed, most members of the aristocracy and gentry firmly believed that once a challenge had been laid down, a gentleman was honour-bound to accept. Yet despite the very real risk that he might swing on the gallows at Tyburn on account of the condition of his opponent, the second duellist in the Adelphi Tavern declined the offer of escape. Certainly, the wound to his thigh meant that he was in little shape to run. Moreover, he was too well known to hide for long.

As the parlour filled with friends and onlookers, including the two seconds belatedly arriving on the scene, many recognised the fashionably attired figure of the apparent victor of the contest as the Reverend Henry Bate.[3] Although attempted murder was hardly compatible with his vows to the Church, the 31-year-old parson had already established something of a reputation for bravado. Educated at Oxford, although he left without taking a degree, Bate had initially joined the army where he acquired valuable skills in combat. But he promptly swapped his military uniform for a clerical gown when his father died and the young Bate succeeded to his living as rector of North Fambridge in Essex. Before long he had added the curacy of Hendon, a sleepy hamlet north of London, to his ecclesiastical duties. Comfortably well-off but socially ambitious, Bate's impeccably groomed figure was a more familiar sight in the coffee-houses and theatres of London than in the pulpits of his village churches. Indeed, it was for his literary, rather than his religious, works that Bate was famed.

Friendly with David Garrick, the playwright and theatre manager, Bate had written several farces and comic operas which had met with moderate acclaim. He employed his pen to much greater effect, however, as editor of the *Morning Post*. Set up as a rival to the *Morning Chronicle* in 1772, the *Post* had helped transform the face of the press with its lively, pugnacious style, in sharp contrast to the dull and pompous approach of its competitors. Since his appointment as editor two years previously, Bate had consolidated his journal's reputation for fearlessly exposing scandal in public and private life, boosting circulation as a result. Taking full advantage of the recent hard-won freedom for journalists to report debates in Parliament, the *Post* took equal liberties in revealing details of the intrigues and excesses of Georgian society's rich and famous, the so-called *bon ton*. Although strategically placed dashes obscured the names of the miscreants, the identities of well-known celebrities of their day, such as Lord D—re and Lady J—sey, were easily guessed by their friends and enemies over the breakfast table.

At a time when the importance of the press in defending

a constitutional democracy was rapidly becoming recognised, as well as its potential for abusing that freedom, Bate stood out as the most notorious editor of all. Flamboyant and domineering – some would say bullying – Bate had recently seen off a facsimile rival of the *Post* in characteristic style, by leading a noisy procession of drummers and trumpeters marching through Piccadilly. Horace Walpole, the remorseless gossip, was appalled at the scene, which he watched from his window and described in full to a friend. 'A solemn and expensive masquerade exhibited by a clergyman in defence of daily scandal against women of the first rank, in the midst of a civil war!' he blustered.[4] Samuel Johnson, as a fellow hack, at least gave Bate credit for his 'courage' as a journalist, if not for his merit, when pressed by his friend and biographer James Boswell. This was something of a back-handed compliment, however, since as Johnson explained: 'We have more respect for a man who robs boldly on the highway, than for a fellow who jumps out of a ditch, and knocks you down behind your back.'[5]

Acclaimed then, if not universally admired, as a vigorous defender of press freedom, Bate had also established a reputation for his physical combative skills. A well-publicised disagreement some four years previously at Vauxhall, the popular pleasure gardens on the south of the Thames, had left nobody in doubt of his courage. Leaping to the defence of an actress friend who was being taunted by four uncouth revellers, Bate had accepted a challenge by one of the party to a duel the following day. When the challenger slyly substituted a professional boxer of Herculean proportions, Bate gamely stripped to the waist and squared up. Although much the smaller of the two pugilists, the parson proceeded to pummel the boxer into submission within fifteen minutes, mashing his face 'into a jelly' without suffering a single significant blow himself. The episode, which was naturally reported fully in the *Morning Post*, earned Bate the nickname 'the Fighting Parson'. Having established his credentials both for bravery and combat skills, the Reverend Bate was plainly not a man to pick an argument with. Oddly this had not deterred his opponent at the Adelphi.

A relative newcomer to London society, the defeated duellist was seemingly a stranger to everyone in the tiny parlour with the exception of his opponent and his tardy second. Although he was now sprawled in a chair under the ministrations of his medical attendants, it was plain that the man was uncommonly tall by eighteenth-century standards and slenderly built. The surgeon Foot, meeting him for the first time, would later estimate his height at more than five feet ten inches – a commanding five inches above the average Georgian.[6] Despite a prominent hooked nose, his face was strikingly handsome, with small, piercing eyes under thick dark eyebrows and thin but sensuous lips. His obvious authority and bearing betrayed his rank as an officer in the King's Army, while his softly spoken brogue revealed his Anglo-Irish descent. And for all his life-threatening injuries, he exuded a charisma that held the entire room in thrall. His name was gleaned by the gathered party as Captain Andrew Robinson Stoney. And it was he, it now emerged, who had provoked the duel.

With the identity of the duellists established, details of the circumstances leading to their fateful meeting quickly unfolded and were subsequently confirmed in a report of events agreed between the combatants for the press.[7] In providing this statement, attributing neither guilt nor blame, the duellists were complying with contemporary rules of duelling conduct. But as their version of events made plain, most of the circumstances surrounding the Adelphi duel had flouted all the accepted principles of duelling behaviour. Meeting at night rather than in the cold light of day (traditionally at dawn), staging their duel inside a busy city venue rather than a remote location outdoors, and fighting without their seconds (who should have been present to promote reconciliation), were all strictly contrary to the rules. Yet the pretext for their fight to the death was entirely typical of duels which had been conducted since medieval knights had first engaged in the lists. The honour of a woman, it emerged, was at the crux of the dispute.

In the perverse code of honour which governed duelling, any form of insult to a woman was to be regarded by a man whose protection she enjoyed as the gravest possible outrage. According to the *Twenty-six Commandments*, for example, such an insult should be treated as 'by one degree a greater offence than if given to the gentleman personally'. So while women were by convention almost always absent from duels, shielded from the horror of bloodshed and gore, their reputation or wellbeing was frequently at the very core of the ritual. Indeed, for some women, it might be said, the prospect of being fought over by two hot-blooded rivals could be quite intoxicating to the extent that duels were sometimes encouraged even if their consequences were later regretted.

There was no doubt, in the case of the duel at the Adelphi, that the reputation of the woman in question had been grossly impugned. Since early December 1776, readers of Bate's *Morning Post* had read with mounting interest reports of the amorous exploits of the Countess of Strathmore. Despite having only recently shed her widow's mourning costume, the young countess had been spotted in her carriage riding through St James's Park engaged in a passionate argument with Captain Stoney, the *Post* had revealed.[8] Fuelling his readers' titillation and moral outrage, the newspaper's anonymous correspondent had speculated on whether the wealthy widow would bestow her favours on the Irish soldier or on a rival suitor, a Scottish entrepreneur called George Gray who had recently brought home a small fortune from India. Even more scandalously, the *Post* suggested, the countess might find herself in the 'arms of her F—n', a thinly disguised reference to her own footman. Less than two weeks later, readers spluttered into their morning coffee as the *Post* divulged that the countess had broken with her 'long-favoured-paramour' – presumably Gray – then announced the following morning that she was planning to elope with him abroad. The New Year brought no reprieve as the newspaper's revelations continued apace.

If the upstanding readers of the *Post* were in any doubt as to the impropriety of the countess's conduct, this was briskly swept aside by a concurrent series of articles, in the form of a curious exchange of letters, which alternately condemned and defended her behaviour. Written under a variety of pseudonyms, one side accused the countess of betraying the memory of her late husband, the Earl of Strathmore, whose death she was said to have greeted with 'cold indifference', and of forsaking her five young children, in her blatant exploits with her various suitors. Whether or not the countess, in exasperation at the intrusion of the press into her private affairs, had then provoked the duel to defend her honour was a matter of conjecture. One member of her household in London's fashionable Grosvenor Square would later claim that the countess had declared that 'the man who would call upon the Editor of that Paper, and revenge her cause upon him, should have both her hand and her heart'.[9] Certainly, by the middle of January 1777, the Irish army officer Stoney had taken it upon himself to act – in Bate's words – as the 'Countess of Strathmore's champion'.

Not surprisingly, given the vindictive nature of the articles attacking both the countess and himself, Stoney had initially written to Bate demanding to know the identity of the writers. Somewhat more surprisingly, Bate had responded by insisting he did not know. In truth, this was not unlikely. The lurid interest in the sexual misdemeanours of Georgian celebrities had spawned a highly organised industry in gossip-mongering. Certain newspapers even provided secret post boxes so that anyone with salacious information could deposit their claims directly with the printers without being identified. The printers were then conveniently unable to reveal the identity of the writers, while newspaper editors frequently had neither sight nor supervision of such material prior to publication. Although publishing such inflammatory accusations, without the least effort to check their veracity, raised the serious prospect of being sued for libel, publishers often considered that the boost in their circulation figures justified that risk.

Bate's protestations of ignorance, coupled with his profuse apologies, did little to mollify Stoney, however, who took the somewhat progressive view that an editor should take responsibility for the material published in his newspaper. Bate had therefore little option but to agree to a meeting with the irate soldier, which took place, according to their record of events, on the evening of Friday 10 January in the Turk's Head Coffee-house in the Strand. Here, in the convivial atmosphere of the fuggy coffee-house, Bate had managed to convince Stoney that he had been innocent of any involvement in the attacks and further promised to ensure that no more insults would appear. And so when Stoney opened the *Post* the following morning to read yet further revelations about the countess's love life he was apoplectic. The latest article, which reported that 'the Countess of

Grosvenor-Square, is frequently made happy by the visits (tho' at different periods) of the bonny, tho' *almost expended Scot*, and the Irish widower', seemed almost calculated to incense him. Immediately, Stoney dashed off a further letter to Bate demanding his right 'to vindicate the dignity of a Gentleman' by seeking satisfaction in the traditional manner. He concluded by naming an old army friend, Captain Perkins Magra, as his second who would arrange events.

Still Bate blustered and prevaricated. In the flurry of letters that flew back and forth across the city that weekend, all faithfully reproduced in the jointly agreed record, accusations and counter-accusations grew more and more heated. When finally he was denounced as a 'coward and a scoundrel', Bate had little alternative but to accept Stoney's challenge. On Monday 13 January, therefore, Bate had consulted his own ex-army buddy, the rather dubious Captain John Donellan, who had recently been dismissed from service in India and had taken up a post as master of ceremonies at the Pantheon assembly rooms in Oxford Street. Already accused of various financial irregularities while serving with the East India Company, Donellan would eventually be hanged for poisoning his wife's brother to get his hands on her family's riches.[10] Agreeing to stand as Bate's second, Donellan had lent the parson his sword, which Bate hid under his great-coat. That afternoon Bate had sent Stoney a final letter, which ended resignedly: 'I find myself compelled to go so far armed, in the event at least, as to be able to defend myself, and since nothing can move you from your sanguinary purposes – as you seemed resolved, that either my life or my gown shall be the sacrifice of your groundless revenge – in the name of God pursue it!'

Having dined out on Monday afternoon, Bate had set off apprehensively just after 6 p.m. to walk the dimly lit streets to his home, one of the new Adelphi houses in Robert Street, his friend's sword held ready beneath his coat. Turning off the bustling Strand into Adam Street, he was passing the doorway of the Adelphi Tavern when the towering figure of Stoney loomed towards him, seized him by the shoulder and forced him inside. Still protesting that he did not wish to fight, the 'Fighting Parson' had reluctantly accompanied the Irishman into the ground-floor parlour where Stoney once more demanded he reveal the names of the writers of the offending articles. On Bate's insistence that he did not know, the soldier had declared: 'Then, Sir, you must give me immediate satisfaction!'

In the sputtering light of candles, Stoney's valet brought in a case containing a pair of pistols which had been purchased that day from the shop of Robert Wogdon, London's most celebrated gunsmith.[11] From his premises in the Haymarket since the early 1770s, Wogdon had produced exquisitely crafted duelling pistols renowned for their lightness, speed and – above all – deadly accuracy. A duel being now unavoidable and the death of one or both duellists probable, both men sent word to summon their seconds. Stoney despatched his valet to locate Captain Magra, while Bate sent a hurried note to find his friend Donellan. When neither of these fellows had appeared after some considerable delay, and with Bate becoming increasingly anxious to escape, Stoney had abruptly locked the parlour door, stuffed the keyhole with paper and placed a screen in front of it. Opening the case of Wogdon's pistols he had ordered Bate to choose his weapon. When the parson refused first fire, Stoney immediately snatched up a pistol and took aim. But for all his military training, the proximity of his target and the precision accuracy of Wogdon's guns, his bullet had merely pierced the parson's hat and smashed into the mirror behind, which shattered on impact. Returning fire, according to duelling procedure, Bate's aim was equally askew – or equally well judged – for his bullet apparently ripped through Stoney's coat and waistcoat without so much as grazing his opponent's skin.

Still thirsty for blood, Stoney had insisted that they now draw swords. Only when blood had been spilled, according to duelling law, could honour be said to have been satisfied. As Stoney charged towards him with his sword outstretched, Bate deflected the weapon and speared his opponent right through the chest, according to the agreed testimony. So fierce was the ensuing combat in the expiring candlelight that Bate's borrowed sword had been bent almost double, at which point Stoney had decently allowed him to straighten it. And although he was now bleeding profusely and severely weakened by his injuries, Stoney had insisted on continuing the fight in the dark until at length the door had burst open and Hull had tumbled into the room. Quickly taking in the scene dimly reflected in the broken mirror, Hull and the other rescuers were in little doubt that they had only just prevented a catastrophe.

Later publishing his own version of what he described as the 'late affair of honour' in *The Gazetteer and New Daily Advertiser*, Hull had declared his surprise, given the darkness of the room and the ferocity of the fencing, that 'one of the combatants were not absolutely killed on the spot'. It was a sentiment with which the two medical men, Foot and Scott, readily agreed. In a joint statement published in the same newspaper, in which they described their patients' injuries in detail, the pair attested that Stoney's chest wound had 'bled very considerably'. They concluded 'we have every reason to believe, that the rencontre must have determined *fatally*, had not the interposition of the gentlemen who broke into the room put an end to it'. Indeed, as Foot helped the ailing Stoney into his carriage and rode with him back to the officer's apartment at St James's Coffee House in nearby St James's Street, his professional concern was so great that he insisted on stopping en route in Pall Mall at the house of the celebrated surgeon Sir Caesar Hawkins for further medical assistance. One of the most popular surgeons in London, numbering George III among his patients, the elderly Hawkins visited Stoney in his rooms two hours later. Although he did not personally examine the wounds, merely checking over the patient as he languished in bed, Hawkins would later add his own testimony as to the severity of the duellist's injuries. Four respectable witnesses, therefore, had all testified to the life-threatening nature of Stoney's wounds. It was scarcely surprising then, given the captain's plight, that the object of his reckless venture should visit her hero the very next day.

Steeped in the romantic literature of eighteenth-century Britain, few women could have failed to be moved by the actions of a handsome young captain who had leapt to defend their honour with the ultimate act of chivalry. Mary Eleanor Bowes, the 27-year-old Dowager Countess of Strathmore, was no exception. Indeed, as an accomplished writer of fashionably lyrical literature herself – her five-act tragic play, which itself featured a duel, had been well-received and her poems were admired by friends – there could be little doubt that the countess would respond to such a sacrifice with passion. And so, after sending her hero a gushing letter of gratitude the following morning, the anxious countess arrived at St James's Coffee House later that day to deliver her thanks in person.

Bustling into Stoney's apartment, the countess was

understandably distressed at the sight of the stricken soldier who lay groaning in bed, his face 'deadly white'.[12] The surgeon, Jessé Foot, still faithfully tending his patient, was touched by the scene, which he later described. Wearing a loose, low-cut dress, which showed off her small figure and ample bust to best advantage, the countess rushed to comfort Stoney. Although her greatest asset, her luxuriant dark brown hair, was almost certainly hidden beneath the customary powdered grey wig, the young widow had lively, wide eyes in a pretty, fair-complexioned face with a determined chin. She appeared, recalled Foot, 'in very fine health' while her cheeks 'glowed with all the warmth of a gay widow'. Her rosy countenance heightened by her obvious agitation, the countess drew close as the soldier informed her that his injuries were mortal, a diagnosis swiftly confirmed by Foot. Apparently weakened by his lethal wounds, the Irishman delivered his news 'in a very low Tone of Voice', the countess would later recall, while he appeared to be 'in great Torture'.[13] Aghast to hear of her champion's impending demise, the countess seized the sword Stoney had used in his ordeal and insisted on taking it home to place beneath her pillow. 'She seemed poor silly soul! as if she blessed the duel,' Foot later remarked, 'and blessed every body about it, for the sake of the precious prize the contest brought her.'[14] Such pity might have seemed rather misplaced, given the life of seamless extravagance the countess had enjoyed so far.

The only daughter of one of the most successful entrepreneurs in Georgian times, the northern coal magnate George Bowes, Mary Eleanor had become the richest heiress in Britain – some said Europe – at the age of eleven when her father died.[15] Having led a life of pleasure since her earliest years, she had continued to indulge her fine taste for expensive jewellery, lavish costumes and generous entertaining after her marriage to the Earl of Strathmore on her eighteenth birthday. And since the earl's premature death less than a year before, she had enjoyed more liberty than ever to pursue her extravagant lifestyle as well as her twin interests in science and the arts.

Educated to an unusually high standard by her doting father, Mary Eleanor had established a modest reputation for her literary efforts and was fluent in several languages. More significantly, she had won acclaim in the almost exclusively male-dominated world of science as a knowledgeable and accomplished botanist. Encouraged by senior figures in the Royal Society, she had stocked her extensive gardens and hothouses with exotic plants from around the globe and was even now planning to finance an expedition to bring back new species from southern Africa. According to Foot, not often given to praise, she was simply 'the most intelligent female botanist of the age'.[16]

If her stupendous fortune had brought her material pleasures and intellectual gifts, a life of unremitting flattery and indulgence had not helped the countess to develop a shrewd awareness of character. Beset by eager suitors and fawning admirers since her husband's death, the merry widow had enjoyed flirting and cavorting with little discrimination. Now that a respectable period of mourning for her first husband was coming to an end, however, she had turned her mind to finding a suitable new partner for herself and a dependable stepfather to her five young children. Having proved himself a faithful companion and an athletic lover for almost a year, George Gray seemed a reasonable choice. A rakish entrepreneur, in the mould of her beloved father, 39-year-old Gray had returned from India four years previously. A flamboyant man about town, friendly with James Boswell and the playwright Samuel Foote, Gray shared her appetite for fine living and her love of literature. His unpopularity with her late husband's family, anxious to deter fortune hunters from squandering her children's inheritance, only made him more alluring. And so in a secret ceremony in St Paul's Cathedral six months previously, the countess had pledged to marry Gray – a commitment then regarded as legally binding.

The arrival in town that same summer of the charming and handsome Irish soldier, Andrew Robinson Stoney, had piqued Mary Eleanor's interest. Yet for all his passionate declarations, she had not been swayed from her commitment to her Scottish lover and plans for Gray and the countess to elope and marry abroad were well in hand by the beginning of 1777. Now that she saw her young Irish admirer lying close to death from his battle to defend her reputation, however, she found her emotions in turmoil. When Stoney begged her to grant him one final request before his impending death, she felt it would have been heartless to refuse.[17] Elated at the real-life drama in which she found herself, and reluctant to deny herself the tragically romantic ending which must surely unfold, Mary Eleanor agreed to her dying hero's request: to marry him before he expired. At a time when marriage was laughably easy to enter into but well nigh impossible to end, her decision may have seemed reckless. Yet what harm could possibly ensue from marrying a poor dying soldier who would shortly make her a widow again? She even commemorated the mournful occasion in verse.

Unmov'd Maria saw the splendid suite
Of rival captives sighing at her feet,
Till in her cause his sword young Stoney drew,
And to avenge, the gallant wooer flew!

Bravest among the brave! – and first to prove
By death! or conquests! who best knew to love![18]

But pale and faint the wounded lover lies,
While more than pity fills Maria's eyes!
In her soft breast, where passion long had strove,
Resistless sorrow fix'd the reign of love!
'Dear youth,' she cries, 'we meet no more to part!
Then take thy honour's due – my bleeding heart!'

Three days later, on 17 January 1777, Mary Eleanor Bowes, the Countess of Strathmore, married Andrew Robinson Stoney, in St James's Church, Piccadilly.[19] Borne to the church on a makeshift bed, Stoney made his vows at the altar doubled in pain. Mary Eleanor's footman, George Walker, and Stoney's friend and financial advisor, William Davis, were the witnesses. And it seemed to the small gathering watching the ceremony that it could only be a matter of days before the groom returned to the church – in a wooden casket. Convinced of her new husband's imminent demise, the countess felt no need to reveal to him two quite devastating secrets. And for her part, Mary Eleanor was about to discover some surprising facts about 'Captain' Stoney.

2

Downright Girlishness

Gibside, County Durham, 1757

From the moment that she was tall enough to peep over the windowsills of Gibside Hall, the infant Mary Eleanor had been confronted by the sight of a majestic stone column rising before her eyes. Begun in the year after her birth in 1749 as a potent symbol of her ageing father's wealth, power and – not least – virility, the Column to Liberty had gained in feet as Mary grew in inches. By her eighth birthday in 1757, it soared a staggering 140 feet, making it the second tallest column in Britain after Wren's Monument commemorating the Great Fire of London. At last the finishing touches could be added. As Mary laboured over her lessons indoors, a shed was raised to the summit, providing shelter for the sculptor who scaled the wooden scaffolding to carve the figure of Lady Liberty at the top. Finally unveiled later that year, the twelve-foot crowning statue, covered in gold leaf, represented not only an uncompromising belief in individual liberty over state interference but also an inspiring vision of female power and independence. It was a sight that the young Mary Eleanor would not forget.

Long before her birth, great things had been anticipated of Mary Eleanor Bowes. Her father, George Bowes, had unexpectedly inherited his family's estates in County Durham and Yorkshire, with their extensive coal deposits, at the age of twenty-one, after the sudden deaths of his two elder brothers. The Bowes family had been powerful landowners in the north-east since Sir Adam Bowes, a high-ranking lawyer, was granted land at Streatlam, near Barnard Castle, in southern County Durham in the fourteenth century. Sir Adam's descendants had increased their property and influence through well-judged marital alliances with wealthy local families and through loyal service to the Crown. Sir George Bowes had escorted Mary Queen of Scots to imprisonment in Bolton Castle, Yorkshire, in 1568 and remained a staunch supporter of Elizabeth I the following year when the Catholic Earls of Northumberland and Westmorland launched their failed Northern Rebellion. Holding Barnard Castle against the rebels for a crucial eleven days, Sir George was 'the surest pyllore the queen's majesty had in these parts' according to Lord Burghley, Elizabeth's chief advisor. His great-grandson, Sir William Bowes, who was elected MP for County Durham five times, brought the family further wealth through his marriage to heiress Elizabeth Blakiston in 1691. When Sir William died in 1706, Lady Bowes was left not only to bring up their four sons and four daughters on her own but also to manage the vast coal-rich estate of Gibside, on the southern bank of the River Derwent, which she inherited from her own father in 1713. She achieved both with aplomb, handling disputes within the local coal trade with shrewd determination while patiently guiding her eldest son, William. Spending most of his time in London, the ungrateful heir neglected his country seat while upbraiding his mother, 'surely you don't think me such a fool as to prefer the Charms of a stupid, dull, Country Life, to the pleasures of the Town'.[1] When William died unmarried at the age of twenty-four in 1721, and his ill-tempered brother Thomas followed him to the grave within a year, it was the third son George who came into possession of the Bowes–Blakiston estate.

Dynamic, tall and good-looking, George Bowes had run away from home at the age of eighteen to buy himself a commission as a captain in a cavalry regiment using money given to him by his mother for an entirely different purpose.[2] Army life did nothing to cool Bowes's intractable temper or his zest for life. At six feet tall, with expressive grey eyes in an open, oval-shaped face, Bowes presented both a formidable figure and a pleasing countenance. He was, according to his daughter Mary Eleanor, 'uncommonly handsome' and a 'great rake in his youth'. Yet while he shared the fiery temper and forceful temperament of his two elder brothers, unlike them George Bowes shouldered his responsibilities as a landowner, employer and public figure. Abandoning his brief army career, he took up his seat at Gibside Hall, which he preferred to gloomy Streatlam Castle, and grasped the reins of the family's coal business with customary zeal. His youthful reputation for aggressive business tactics earned him the nickname 'The Count' from one rival, while another called him 'the Csar'. Yet Bowes also demonstrated a keen appreciation of the arts as well as a flair for romance.

Soon after inheriting his estate, at the age of twenty-three Bowes married fourteen-year-old Eleanor Verney following a passionate courtship which began when she was only ten. The posthumous daughter of Thomas Verney, Eleanor was heiress to the considerable wealth of her grandfather, the Dean of Windsor. By the age of thirteen, she was renowned for her beauty and her learning. A tiny book of her poetry, copied out in miniature copperplate handwriting, survives to this day.[3] Undoubtedly, the marriage negotiations had initially been prompted by financial motives on the part of Bowes and possibly his mother, in common with the vast majority of marriages between prosperous landed families in the early eighteenth century. By the time the marriage neared settlement, however, Bowes was helplessly in love with the beguiling Eleanor.

Mostly kept apart from the object of his fascination by distance and propriety, Bowes plied her mother with letters that professed his 'great Respect & love' for her 'Beautiful Daughter'.[4] Eventually allowed to address the captivating Eleanor directly, Bowes gushed, 'I conjure you thus to ease a Heart full of You, & tell you with the utmost sincerity I love you above all things'. As thirteen-year-old Eleanor responded with cool formality, describing the trivia of her daily life, Bowes could hardly restrain his impatience: 'Dear Madam, I am not able to bear the cruel absence from my angel any longer without having recourse to Pen & Paper for relief of my tortur'd heart which can at present find no other way to ease its self.' At last, with the cumbersome financial details settled, the wedding took place on 1 October 1724, shortly after Eleanor turned fourteen.[5] Her youth itself was no bar to the marriage – twelve was the minimum marrying age for girls and fourteen for boys – but the couple had waited until Eleanor was old enough to receive her inheritance. Bowes was finally united with his adored child bride – in every sense. In one loving letter to his 'Nelly', when Bowes was away on business, he ended with the jaunty postscript: 'I assure you that I found my Bed very cold last night for want of my Companion.'

Just two and a half months after the wedding, Eleanor died suddenly, probably from one of the many infectious diseases that stalked eighteenth-century Britain. Bowes was devastated. He poured out his grief in frenzied letters to Mrs Verney confessing that his loss had made him doubt his faith and lose his reason. All his future happiness, he wept, had depended on his young bride, whom he described as 'the most accomplish'd of her Sex'. Although many promising Georgian relationships ended in premature death, Eleanor's sudden demise was considered sufficiently tragic to merit the attentions of not one but two acclaimed literary minds. The poet and travel writer Lady Mary Wortley Montagu revealed her jaundiced view of marriage in a poem written on the day of Eleanor's death which began: 'Hail, happy bride, for thou art truly blest!/Three months of rapture, crown'd with endless rest.' Fellow writer Mary Astell, who is thought to have penned her response at the same social event, blamed marriage itself – or lust at least – for the young bride's early death, with the words: 'Lost when the fatal Nuptial Knot was tie'd,/Your Sun declin'd, when you became a Bride./A soul refin'd, like your's soar'd above/The gross Amusements of low, Vulgar love.'[6] Bereft of his love, vulgar or otherwise, George Bowes escorted his wife's corpse to its burial at Westminster Abbey, after which he was forced to repay her dowry with interest.[7] It took him a full nineteen years to recover sufficiently from his grief to consider remarriage. In the meantime, he threw himself into improving his estate at Gibside and transforming the coal industry.

With the abundant coal seams running beneath his Durham and Yorkshire estates, Bowes was literally sitting on a fortune. His marriage settlement with Eleanor Verney had named as many as forty collieries owned by the Bowes family in County Durham alone. For the men, and boys as young as seven, who hewed and hauled the coal in precarious, gas-filled tunnels and the women who sorted the coal at the surface, it was hazardous and unpleasant but – for the men at least – well-paid work. For the colliery owners like Bowes coal was big business. In eighteenth-century Britain, with industry mushrooming and urban populations burgeoning, coal was in sharp demand, with Durham coal particularly prized. By the middle of the century, almost two million tons of coal were being produced annually by north-eastern coalfields – nearly half the national output – and most of this was shipped to London, which by now was Europe's biggest city. The process was highly convoluted. Coal-owners like Bowes, with collieries close to the Tyne and its tributary the Derwent, transported their coal in horse-drawn trucks on wooden rails – forerunners of the railways – to quays or 'staithes' which lined the river banks. From here, the coal was loaded on to small boats, known as 'keels', then rowed downriver to the mouth of the Tyne where it was hauled on to seagoing colliers for the two-week voyage down the coast to London. Once it arrived in the Thames estuary, the coal was loaded on to river-going vessels called 'lighters', and then transferred to members of the Woodmongers Company who enjoyed a monopoly on its sale in London. With each change of transport, the coal changed hands – going through four expensive and closely controlled transactions which hiked up its price each time.

Frustrated at the lack of control over their hard-won product, several of the powerful north-eastern coal-owners seized the initiative. Setting aside for once his disputes with his neighbours, in 1726 Bowes joined forces with four other major coal-owners from the region to forge the Grand Alliance. By co-operating in buying land, limiting supply and sharing profits, the allies formed an effective monopoly which controlled virtually all coal production in the north-east. The cartel would dominate the British coal industry for the rest of the century. When Bowes was elected MP for County Durham in 1727, a seat he would hold for the rest of his life, he used his lobbying power to promote the partners' interests, spending the five or six months each winter when Parliament met lodging in the capital. With the immense profits his coal produced, supplemented by rents from the many farms on his Durham and Yorkshire estates, Bowes invested in stocks and shares, property, ships, racehorses and art. Any surplus was ploughed into improving his beloved rural retreat of Gibside.

It was not until 1743, at the age of forty-two, that George Bowes felt ready to form a new romantic alliance. In March, he blamed a delay in writing to a friend on a 'Fair Lady' whom he hoped to 'persuade to come into the North this Summer'.[8] Still a handsome man though by now somewhat corpulent, Bowes had evidently not lost his courting skills, for in June he married Mary Gilbert, sole heiress to her father Edward Gilbert's idyllic country estate of St Paul's Walden Bury in Hertfordshire. Some twenty years Bowes's junior, Mary brought a sizeable dowry, or marriage 'portion', worth £20,000 – equivalent to more than £3m today.[9] It is probable that the marriage was largely one of convenience, bringing together two ancient landed families in the hope of providing an heir for both. Although their partnership proved companionable enough, Mary would always stand in the shadow of her formidable husband and the ghost of her adored predecessor – Bowes's 'favourite first wife' in the words of Mary Eleanor. If she were ever tempted to forget her forerunner, there were no less than six portraits of 'the first Mrs Bowes' hanging at Gibside, including one in the second Mrs Bowes's bedroom, to remind her.

Hard-working and pious, Mary Bowes devoted herself to managing the family's several large households, while steadfastly supporting her husband in his busy public and private life. Proving herself a capable businesswoman, she managed the family's voluminous accounts and large domestic staff, at Gibside each summer, in London every winter, and at their rented house in Yorkshire which served as a staging point between the two. Settling the numerous bills for food, travel, clothing, medicine, servants' wages and family entertainment with meticulous efficiency, she gave George Bowes his 'pocket expenses' and paid for his barbers' fees, while dispensing generous sums to charity.

The couple had been married six years, and had doubtless given up all hope of an heir, by the time Mary Bowes gave birth to a daughter on 24 February 1749. Since it was the parliamentary season and the household was ensconced in London, the baby was born at the family's rented home in affluent Upper Brook Street, delivered by one of society's favourite 'man midwives', Dr Francis Sandys. Baptised a month later in London's most fashionable church, St George's in Hanover Square, the baby was named Mary Eleanor, in homage both to her dutiful mother and to her father's beloved first wife.[10] Bowes hoped that she would combine the attributes of both.

Immediately, George Bowes had grand designs for Mary Eleanor's future. If she was not born literally with a silver spoon in her mouth, her doting father was quick to remedy that absence, purchasing a candlestick and spoon 'for the Child' from a London silversmith within weeks of her birth.[11] After the customary four weeks' lying-in for Mrs Bowes, during which time Mary Eleanor was breastfed by a wet-nurse, the family packed up the house in London and undertook the arduous two-day journey north by coach. Accompanied by her nurse and proud parents, baby Mary Eleanor was conveyed to her family seat with the pomp normally associated with a royal progress. When the family stopped overnight at Ledstone, their halfway home in Yorkshire, bells were rung to announce her birth. As the entourage continued on to Darlington, Durham, Gateshead and finally Gibside, villagers, servants and neighbours were left in no doubt as to the importance of the tiny girl's arrival. Church bells pealed and coins tinkled into the hands of the poor at every stop along the route.

If anyone suspected that for all his show of celebration, Bowes might secretly have yearned for a son to continue the family's ancient name, they could see no signs of disappointment. One friend, Captain William FitzThomas, congratulated Bowes on his daughter's birth while bluntly expressing the prevailing misogyny of the times. 'What tho' it be'nt a Boy, the same materials will produce one,' he encouraged lustily, adding by way of compensation that 'at least your Blood, if not your name will be transmitted to Posterity'. Another well-wisher was rather more tactful, remarking that if nothing else, Mary Eleanor's birth presented the opportunity for an advantageous marriage which might mend the wrangles that continued between coal-owners despite their compact. Such an alliance would be 'the liklyest way to put an end to all Disputes' he suggested, adding pointedly: 'Never did young Lady come into this world with more good wishes from all Ranks and Conditions of Men, Women & Children'.[12]

Indeed, daughters blessed with large dowries were often deemed more valuable in the competitive Georgian marriage market than sons. Aristocratic mothers fell over themselves to secure a daughter from a wealthy middle-class family for their needy heirs. Describing such arranged marriages as 'Smithfield bargains', the writer Hester Chapone exclaimed sardonically, 'so much ready money for so much land, and my daughter flung in into the bargain!'[13] But after decades of waiting for an heir, the prospect of handing over his daughter and his hard-earned profits to another prominent family held little attraction for Bowes. He had no intention of moderating his ambitions for his long-awaited offspring, just because she happened to be the wrong sex. Adamant that his baby girl would not only perpetuate his bloodline but would also continue the family name, he made a new will just before Mary Eleanor's first birthday. Accordingly, the document named her as the sole heir to his vast estate and stipulated that any future husband must change his name to Bowes.[14] Insisting that a man should take his wife's surname was not completely unprecedented – one of Bowes's coal partners, Sir Sydney Montagu, had been forced to adopt his bride's name of Wortley – but it was still highly irregular, and much resented, in Georgian Britain.

Learning to crawl across the thickly carpeted rooms of Gibside Hall, taking her first steps in the thousand-acre gardens, Mary Eleanor Bowes – as she would remain all her life – began to explore the glorious rural retreat she would one day inherit. It was a work still in progress. Bowes had made only cosmetic alterations to the draughty Jacobean mansion, built by his Blakiston great-great-grandfather at the beginning of the seventeenth century, with the arms of James I still emblazoned above the door. Perched on a ledge above the Derwent, the imposing three-storey seventy-roomed house turned its back to the river – the conduit of Bowes's wealth – and instead faced south across the landscaped parkland which Bowes was slowly transforming. Within the spacious main rooms, lit by tall mullioned windows, the toddling Mary Eleanor negotiated bulky pieces of mahogany and oak furniture while Bowes's valuable collection of silverware, china, art and books was kept carefully beyond her reach. More than 300 pictures adorned the walls of the house, with 119 lining the staircase alone, including works by Rubens, Raphael and Hogarth. Since both her mother and father were avid readers, the library held more than a thousand volumes, from seventeenth-century classics such as Dryden's *Virgil* and Milton's *Works*, to contemporary writings on science, law and architecture, as well as novels by Fielding and Smollett. But no sooner had Mary Eleanor learned to walk than she found her explorations thwarted. When she was sixteen months old, her mother bought a pair of 'leading strings' – reins – in an effort to harness her wanderings and a year later steel bars were fixed across the nursery fireplace. But if her mother sought to restrain her daughter's free spirit indoors, outside Mary Eleanor was free to roam. That same summer, one of the estate carpenters fashioned 'a Set of little Chaise Wheels for Miss Bowes' – presumably a small cart to be pulled by a pony – in which she could trundle around the gardens.[15]

Determined to build himself a country seat to rival any in the land, Bowes had started landscaping his estate twenty years earlier. Although he had consulted some of the best known landscape gardeners of the era, the resulting mixture of romantic swathes of woodland and natural-looking contours, made popular by designers such as Capability Brown, combined with formal straight walks and long rides, fashionable from an earlier age, was essentially his own vision. A new driveway, carved out between 1738 and 1740, drew visitors towards the house along a sweeping road that threaded between the trees, affording views of intriguing architectural structures on the way. Bowes had commissioned Daniel Garrett, one of the north-east's most successful architects, to build a 'banqueting house' in his signature Gothic style from 1741 to 1745. First glimpsed through the trees, as visitors navigated the drive, the fanciful one-storey building sat overlooking an octagonal pond and across to the valley beyond. Used for intimate concerts where guests were offered light refreshments, rather than full-blown banquets – since it possessed only a small kitchen – the banqueting house provided an ideal viewing point for Bowes's improvements.

Continuing down the precipitous drive, visitors arrived at a stately building in the latest Palladian style, which could easily have served as fine accommodation for any country gentleman. This was where Bowes kept his horses. Designed by Garrett to resemble a two-storey villa with five bays, work on the stable block was finished by 1751, when Mary Eleanor was two. She may well have watched as the twenty or so horses were led into their stalls and she doubtless sat in one of the family's several coaches as it was driven into the central courtyard. Naturally enough, as a former captain in the cavalry, Bowes had a passionate interest in horses. Having introduced fox-hunting into the county in 1738, he had expanded the stud he had inherited from his father at Streatlam. His horse Cato won the Newcastle Races, which were run each year on the city's Town Moor, in 1753.[16]

At last, as they swept around a final bend on the tortuous driveway, guests would arrive at a broad grassed terrace in front of Gibside Hall. This impressive avenue, which stretched half a mile in either direction, was known as the Grand or Great Walk. Bordered by young elms, the Grand Walk had taken estate labourers three years to dig, level and turf, working entirely by hand. As soon as the avenue was finished, in the year after Mary Eleanor's birth, Bowes had set his mind to his grandest project, the Column to Liberty, which would stand at the walk's north-eastern end to provide his tenants, workers and neighbours with a powerful reminder of his own towering importance over their lives. Workmen had begun boring a hole for the foundations in September 1750. The following month Bowes consulted Capability Brown, who had built a similar edifice at Stowe a few years earlier. After detailing precise measurements of the 115-feet-high octagonal column at Stowe, Brown offered to design a similar model for Gibside and to 'put you in a way that you will be sure to have your Building stand'.[17] Bowes never took up Brown's proposal but he promptly ordered his own architect, probably Garrett, to design a column which would be taller, grander and sport a bigger statue than the one at Stowe.

Built from local stone, the column rose falteringly over the next seven years. One visitor in 1753, Edward Montagu, who had inherited a relative's collieries near Newcastle, was suitably impressed after dining at Gibside that summer. Surveying the half-built column, rising on its square pedestal, he informed his wife, the literary hostess Elizabeth Montagu: 'Mr Bowes is at present upon a work of great magnificence, which is the erecting a column of above 140 feet high. This, as far as I know, may be the largest that ever was erected by a subject in this Island, and may yield to nothing but the Monument in London.'[18] When Daniel Garrett died that same year, work on the column halted temporarily but resumed the following June with James Paine, who took over many of Garrett's contracts, assuming its supervision. The Swedish traveller Reinhold Angerstein, who visited Gibside in 1754 as part of a six-year fact-finding expedition around Europe, watched in awe as the great slabs of stone were winched to the top of the rising column, sheathed in its wooden scaffolding. Having toured Bowes's mines, railways and staithes, as well as his 'splendid park' with its 'magnificent buildings', Angerstein was so inspired by the sheer human effort put into building Bowes's monument, that he sat down to draw it.[19] A little too susceptible to his host's self-aggrandisement, Angerstein noted that the project was expected to cost £4,000. In fact, the final bill would come to an only slightly less remarkable £1,600.

It was only as the great column reached its completion that Bowes settled on the form of the statue that would grace its summit. Angerstein had recorded that the column would be dedicated to Minerva, the Roman goddess of wisdom, medicine, commerce, soldiers, art and music – which conveniently encompassed most of Bowes's interests. Still undecided, in 1756 Bowes visited St Paul's Cathedral and St George's Church in Bloomsbury looking for inspiration.[20] Whether in a fit of nationalistic fervour or as an expression of his radical Whig sympathies, he settled on the figure of Liberty the following year. At a time when the words of 'Rule Britannia' had only recently been set to music as a patriotic anthem, the figure of Liberty was a powerful icon, celebrating as it did the traditional rights of Britons within a constitutional monarchy.

Having approved the final design, depicting Lady Liberty holding the 'staff of maintenance' and the 'cap of liberty' – traditionally also held aloft by Britannia – Bowes ordered the final stones to be hauled to the top. Labourers watched as Christopher Richardson, a sculptor from Doncaster, climbed the scaffolding to his makeshift shed at the summit, and the figure slowly began to take shape.

Growing up amid the perpetual thrill of concert parties, dinners, hunts, electioneering rallies and a stream of admiring visitors at Gibside – and in the heady social spin of London each winter – Mary Eleanor soon acquired a taste for being the centre of attention. She was already at the hub of her parents' privileged world. When she caught measles in London just after her third birthday in 1752, both parents were understandably frantic. Measles was only one of a plethora of common childhood killers – along with mumps, scarlet fever, diphtheria, smallpox and whooping cough – which meant that more than half of babies born in London in the mid-1700s never reached their fifth birthdays.[21] For nearly two weeks, as Mary feverishly battled the disease, servants took shifts sitting with her night and day while her parents consulted an apothecary and a physician for advice. Despite their attentions – the apothecary bled the three-year-old twice according to medical custom – Mary Eleanor pulled through.

Returning to the fresh country air of Gibside, Mary Bowes gave thanks for her daughter's recovery with gifts to the poor while her husband lavished a chair, silver buckles and 'playthings' on his precious only child. Having nearly lost their daughter to one virulent disease, it was not surprising that they took precautions against an even more deadly one a few years later. At six, Mary Eleanor was inoculated against smallpox by a surgeon in London using the contemporary technique of jabbing her arm with some live smallpox virus taken from the pustules of an infected patient. The method had been imported to Britain in the 1720s by Lady Mary Wortley Montagu – in the face of initially strong medical opposition – after she had observed the practice in Turkey. Although still highly risky, both for the patient and for anyone they came into contact with, the inoculation did confer future immunity and had become highly popular by the mid-eighteenth century. Immediately after her inoculation, Mary Eleanor was whisked into quarantine for four weeks; there were further alms for the poor on her recovery.

Cosseted from disease, indulged with toys and treats, clothed in the finest fashions and fed on the choicest foods, it is little wonder that Mary Eleanor grew up headstrong and precocious. Waited on by a fleet of servants from the moment she awoke in her nursery bed until the second her eyelids drooped at night, she quickly learned how to attain whatever she wanted. While her mother attempted to inculcate a sense of humility and charity into her growing daughter, giving her money to distribute to the poor on their journeys north, her father would slip her a guinea pocket money – equivalent to a quarter of their kitchen maid's annual wage. If her reserved, thrifty mother demonstrated the attributes of the ideal female in eighteenth-century Britain, this made little impact on the impulsive Mary Eleanor. Far more compelling was the example of her flamboyant and brash father with his talent for the grand gesture and determination to accomplish whatever he set his mind to. One contemporary would later insist that Mary had been 'spoiled by overindulgence, ruined by overkindness, and corrupted by over caresses'.[22] Yet her childhood was by no means a life of unending indolence. For just as much as his beloved Gibside, George Bowes regarded his daughter as a project for improvement.

From the beginning, Bowes was determined that his only daughter should receive the education normally enjoyed by the most privileged sons of the aristocracy. Mary Eleanor would later recall that 'he brought me up with a view to my being as accomplished at thirteen, as his favourite first wife was at that age, in every kind of learning, except Latin.'[23] Initially under the guiding eye of a governess, closely supervised by Bowes, Mary learned to read and write. By the age of four she could read fluently and was proudly paraded at social gatherings to recite by heart passages from the Bible, verse by Milton and elegies from Ovid. 'At four years old I could read uncommonly well,' Mary later wrote, 'and was kept tight to it, made to get many things off by heart.' With her father encouraging 'an insatiable thirst for all kinds of knowledge', Mary Eleanor was well on her way to becoming what she later described as 'a prodigy of learning'.

At a time when the education of girls, even in wealthy families, was restricted to the acquisition of social graces and accomplishments such as dancing, needlework, painting and music, Bowes's approach was a rare and enlightened one.

Children's education had become a popular topic for debate, with children being considered as individuals in their own right, with specific needs, for the first time. But discussion centred mainly on the appropriate education for boys, fuelling the growth of public boarding schools, the popularity of universities and enthusiasm for sending sons on the 'grand tour' of Europe.

Since no respectable profession was open to upper-class girls, and they were essentially being groomed for marriage, few parents saw any point in wasting time and money on improving their daughters' minds. Indeed, learned women were often viewed as objects of ridicule, if not scorn, since they offended the idealised image of the acquiescent, passive female. 'Nothing, I think, is more disagreeable than Learning in a Female,' declared Thomas Sherlock, the Bishop of London, while Lord Bath blamed the headaches suffered by the poet and classicist Elizabeth Carter on her devotion to learning.[24] Lady Mary Wortley Montagu confessed to 'stealing' her education, by surreptitiously studying Latin when her family believed she was reading 'nothing but romances'. Writing to her own daughter, Lady Bute, in 1753 she urged that her granddaughter should enjoy a similarly advanced education since 'learning (if she has a real taste for it) will not only make her contented but happy in it'.[25] But equally she recommended that her granddaughter should 'conceal whatever learning she attains, with as much solicitude as she would hide crookedness or lameness' since revealing her knowledge would engender envy and hatred. Certainly, Lady Mary Wortley Montagu suffered her fair share of contempt, for all her literary accomplishments and her vital legacy to health. Other well-educated women, such as Elizabeth Carter and Catharine Macaulay, who defied convention by producing scholarly work, did achieve some recognition for their skills. Yet even one of the most strident founding members of the intellectual blue-stocking movement, Hannah More, concurred with the popular view that women had inferior intellects and were incapable of serious study.[26]

George Bowes believed otherwise. Having felt the lack of education in his own youth, and admired the precocious talents of his first wife, he had read widely on the subject. As well as novels and plays by the feminist writer Aphra Behn, his library contained several books on education including *Instructions for the Education of a Daughter*, by François Fénelon, Archbishop of Cambray, published in English in 1713. More famous for his scathing condemnation of the French monarchy in his novel *Telemachus*, Fénelon adhered to the view that women had weaker minds but nonetheless urged that their education should not be neglected, nor left to 'ignorant' mothers. While there was no point in teaching girls language, law or science, since 'it's not their business to govern, make wars, sit in courts of justice, or read philosophical lectures', he advocated that girls should learn reading, writing, grammar, arithmetic and bible studies from a 'tender age'.[27]

Having launched his daughter on her programme of learning at the requisite tender age, Bowes proceeded to engage the best tutors in French, writing and dancing before she turned six, and in music by the age of eight. As she bent her head, with its thick chestnut curls, over her French verbs and English compositions, Mary Eleanor revelled in her father's praise. Enjoying her studies, she became an expert linguist and soon aspired to literary talent in her own right. Her schoolbooks, which still survive, are crammed with neatly copied extracts of poetry and prose in English, French, Spanish and Italian.[28] When she was eight, shortly after the family moved to a rented house at London's most desirable address, Grosvenor Square, her French tutor was dismissed and his place taken by a Swiss pastor, the Reverend Andreas Planta. A brilliant linguist and scholar who had immigrated to London with his young family five years earlier, Planta would shortly take up a post as assistant librarian at the fledgling British Museum. He would later be engaged to teach Italian, his native language, to Queen Charlotte when she arrived in Britain in 1761 as George III's bride, while two of his daughters, Frederica and Margaret, would become teachers of English to the future royal princesses. A third daughter, Elizabeth Planta, was taken into the Bowes household as a governess to eight-year-old Mary Eleanor in 1757.[29] Elizabeth Planta would become her constant companion – not only supervising her lessons but also accompanying the family on outings to the opera and theatre – as well as her chaperone and confidante. The loyalty and ultimate betrayal of the Planta family would be crucial in Mary Eleanor's future fortunes.

Just as he sought to improve his daughter's mind, George Bowes laid as much emphasis on strengthening her body, endeavouring to 'harden' her constitution through field sports such as riding and hunting. It was an intense and rigorous exercise regime, producing a physical strength and resilience which would prove vital in later life. Unfortunately, George Bowes's own health was failing as fast as he sought to improve his daughter's. Now in his late fifties, Bowes suffered a serious illness in the winter of 1758, necessitating almost daily visits from his surgeon and physician. He survived their attentions sufficiently to recuperate at his father-in-law's Hertfordshire estate the following spring, but as Mary Eleanor continued with her lessons, practised her dance steps and learned to play the harpsichord, her father declined.

Well aware the end was in sight, in the winter of 1759 Bowes ordered his workmen to begin quarrying stone to build his final great project: an imposing Palladian-style chapel incorporating a mausoleum which would contain his tomb. Designed by James Paine, by now a highly successful architect, the chapel was to stand at the opposite end of the Grand Walk, a sombre and mature counterbalance to the thrusting exuberance of the column. Workmen had only just begun digging the foundations when George Bowes died on 17 September 1760, aged 59.[30] His chapel being far from ready, nine days later Bowes's body was transported from Gibside Hall in a hearse pulled by six horses at the head of a long funeral procession which snaked along the drive past the chapel building site, the stables, the column and the banqueting house, and through the Gibside gates to halt outside Whickham Church just beyond the estate boundaries. The coffin was borne into church by eight of the most prominent dignitaries of the region, several of them Bowes's coal-owning allies, and placed in the vault, where it would remain until his chapel was finally finished in the following century.[31] At a stroke, eleven-year-old Mary Eleanor had been deprived of the single most influential force in her life.

No sooner had the mourners' coaches clattered away, leaving the house and gardens eerily quiet, than word began to spread. As the only heir to her father's vast estate, conservatively estimated at £600,000 (more than £80m today) and possibly as high as £1,040,000 (around £150m), Mary Eleanor had become the richest heiress in Britain, perhaps even in Europe. Reporting her father's death, the *Annual Register* informed its readers that: 'His immense fortune, 600,000 l. devolves on his only daughter, about 13 years of age.' Given that the newspaper added two years to Mary's age, the figure may have been inaccurate, although it was reported with similar authority in the *London Magazine*. A few years later, the *Complete English Peerage* would put her fortune at more than £1m.[32] Whatever the true value of the collieries, lead mines, ironworks, farms, houses, fine art, jewels, stocks and racehorses that George Bowes had assiduously accumulated and maintained throughout his life, there was no doubt that Mary Eleanor was now the wealthiest eleven-year-old in the country. Well aware that this anticipated fortune would attract keen interest from far and wide, her father had shrewdly placed his estate in trust. His will named his wife, his father-in-law and two of his sisters, Jane and Elizabeth, as trustees to ensure that while Mary Eleanor could enjoy her fortune during her lifetime, it would then be handed down intact to his grandchildren.[33] In this wise precaution, Bowes was following the example of many landowners, anxious to prevent profligate heirs – or in the case of daughters, their spouses – from squandering the family's ancient possessions in the space of one short lifetime. Since Mary Eleanor was to receive a £1,000 yearly allowance until the age of fourteen, and £1,300 from then until she was twenty-one, she was unlikely to feel impoverished.

Approaching her teens, precociously intelligent and with the largest fortune in Britain held waiting for her, Mary Eleanor needed more than ever the firm, loving guidance that her father had so ably provided. Yet with her mother inconsolable in her grief, her grandfather ageing and infirm, and her elderly aunts unused to shouldering responsibility for minors, she was suddenly devoid both of sensible supervision and emotional support. Shutting herself away at Gibside for the next two years, unable to face the giddy entertainments of London or the social round of Durham, Mary Bowes virtually abandoned any interest in her daughter's education and welfare. Her immaculately kept account books stopped abruptly with her husband's funeral expenses; her social life ended just as suddenly with his death. After two years, still incapacitated by grief, Mrs Bowes packed the Gibside valuables, left the estate in the capable hands of an agent and took out a lease on a new house, a few yards from their previous London home, at 40 Grosvenor Square.[34] But London's diversions did no more to console her than Gibside's tranquillity and she remained, in her daughter's words, 'in such affliction, as to be incapable of attending either to my education or morals'. So at a time when the thirteen-year-old daughter probably needed her mother's support most of all, Mary Eleanor was left in London in the charge of ageing Aunt Jane, her governess Elizabeth Planta and an assortment of tutors. Her mother meanwhile retreated to her childhood home of St Paul's Walden Bury, where her own father had recently died.

Having been dominated all her childhood by her formidable father, Mary Eleanor's adolescence was now guided almost solely by women. Living in the sumptuous mansion in the south-west corner of Grosvenor Square, surrounded on all sides by the richest members of the aristocracy, she was introduced into London society by her aunt. A 'celebrated beauty' in her youth, Jane Bowes, now nearly sixty, had since become 'extremely vain', Mary Eleanor would write, although chiefly through 'having a niece who was one of the greatest fortunes in England'. Although the Bowes family could not boast aristocratic roots, the teenage Mary's opulent lifestyle afforded her easy entry into an elite circle of rich, privileged and pampered youngsters who devoted themselves to a life of hedonistic leisure. So while her mother eschewed city life, Mary threw herself into the Georgian social, intellectual and scientific scene with a passion.

Persevering with her lessons, Mary's scholarly accomplishments brought her to the notice of Elizabeth Montagu, whose literary parties at her house in Hill Street, a few minutes' sedan-chair ride from Grosvenor Square, had become highly celebrated. Modelled on the French conversational salons, Mrs Montagu's large mixed-sex assemblies were known as the Blue-Stocking Club, apparently on account of the legwear sported by her flamboyant friend, the botanist Benjamin Stillingfleet. Famed as much for their lavish catering as their sparkling conversation, the literary evenings attracted the brightest intellectuals of the day, including Samuel Johnson, his friend Hester Thrale, the writer Elizabeth Carter and the gossip Horace Walpole. But for all the competition to coin the wittiest quips, the parties could be staid affairs. Guests were seated in formal circles or semi-circles of twenty to twenty-five people, according to Lady Louisa Stuart, the granddaughter of Lady Mary Wortley Montagu. Having taken a chair 'between two grave faces unknown to me' Lady Louisa had stifled a yawn and wondered at the apparent exclusion of any male guests. At that point a door opened from the dining room and the male contingent walked in. 'They looked wistfully over our shoulders at a good fire, which the barrier we presented left them no means of approaching; then drawing chairs from the wall, seated themselves around us in an outer crescent, silent and solemn as our own.'[35]

Having become acquainted with the Bowes family in the north-east, where her husband had inherited a colliery near Newcastle, Mrs Montagu became a friend and patron to the young Mary Eleanor. 'Mrs Montague honoured me with her friendship, approbation and correspondence,' Mary later wrote, recalling Sunday gatherings at Mrs Montagu's house.[36] Although Mary insisted that she kept 'several of her letters' only one example of their correspondence has survived. In a letter written by eleven-year-old Mary from her Grosvenor Square home in March 1760, she thanks Mrs Montagu for sending her a book and in the adulatory tone of the period professes that even a moment in Mrs Montagu's thoughts must 'make her the envy of many'.[37] For her part, Mrs Montagu expressed high esteem for the young Mary Eleanor, telling a friend in 1763 that 'she is realy [sic] a fine girl, lively, sensible, and very civil and good natured'.[38]

Surrounded by the exquisite gardens her father had carved out of the Derwent Valley, and encouraged in her childhood to take an interest in plants and animals by her mother, Mary Eleanor had also developed an early fascination for natural history. She already had her own small garden at Gibside, which had been laid out at some point before she reached the age of twelve. In May 1761, estate accounts record one of the workmen 'Palissading Miss Bowes's Garden in the Green-Close'. Her mother had frequently purchased plants and seeds, as well as exotic wild birds – including a parrot when her daughter was eight, and two swans, two guinea fowl and four wild turkeys the following year – before her withdrawal from society. Mrs Bowes's account books record the purchase of '2 Chelsea Lemons' and 'two Auriculas in China potts for the Child' in February 1760. In her mother's absence, Mary's growing interest in plants may well have been encouraged by her governess, Elizabeth Planta, and her father, Mary's French tutor, Andreas Planta, who had now taken up his post as assistant librarian at the British Museum. Certainly she began to turn her childhood fondness for gardening into a serious study of botany. It was to become a lifelong passion.

At the same time, under the lax attentions of Aunt Jane, Mary was free to embark on more playful diversions. At thirteen years old, the age at which her father's first wife had been engaged, Mary Eleanor was fast becoming a magnet for eligible young men. Intelligent, accomplished and self-confident, and engagingly pretty with her curling brown hair and blue-grey eyes, she quickly attracted a swarm of suitors. But while the unparalleled scale of her inheritance made her an equally attractive prospect to their parents, not all of them regarded her intellectual talents as an asset. Lord Lyttelton, who considered himself something of a scholar, remarked on George Bowes's death that, 'as his vanity descends with his estate to his daughter, I don't wish to see her my daughter-in-law, though she would make my son one of the richest and consequently, in our present ideas of greatness, one of the great peers of the Realm.' Saving Mary Eleanor from a match with his libertine son, who would acquire the sobriquet 'the wicked Lord Lyttelton', he added presciently: 'But she will probably be the prize of some needy Duke, who will want her estate to repair the disasters of Newmarket and Arthur's, or if she marries for love, of some ensign of the Guards, or smart Militia captain.'[39] He could scarcely have expected that both predictions might almost exactly come true.

Living mainly with her aunt in leafy Grosvenor Square, apart from occasional trips to Hertfordshire or Gibside, Mary Eleanor launched herself into London society with gusto. Dressed in the tightly corseted, heavily pleated gowns and silk stockings worn by young and adolescent girls in imitation of their mothers, she would set forth in the family's stylish coach, accompanied by inattentive Aunt Jane. The carriage would rumble slowly along the loose-cobbled streets, impeded by the sheer press of other coaches, carts, sedan chairs, pedestrians and livestock that choked the city's thoroughfares. Visiting in the 1760s, the French tourist Pierre

Jean Grosley was shocked at the congestion both on the roads and the river, which was as crammed with boats as the streets were with traffic.[40] While Grosley gaped at the luxurious display of goods in the brightly lit shop windows of the Strand and Fleet Street, which were 'greatly superior' to anything Paris could offer, he complained that the foul mud littering the streets and the thick smog cloaking the sky meant that 'New London is as much buried in dirt as the old'. So dense was this smog that at times walkers in St James's Park could scarcely see four steps in front of them. That the thick pungent smog which obscured the sun was caused by the coal from her own collieries being burned in the capital's homes and small industries made little impression on Mary Eleanor.

Heading west to parade around Hyde Park in a jam of similar coaches, or trundling south to visit the exclusive shops of The Strand, the chief purpose of these daytime 'airings' was to see and be seen. While the ambling progress rarely exceeded walking pace, the carriages at least afforded their privileged occupants a barrier against the stench, clamour and bustle of London's streets. By night, when the city became even more boisterous and dangerous, the pampered members of the landed classes stuck all the more closely to their protective coaches and exclusive venues. Clothed in rich satins and silks, adorned in the jewels her father had bequeathed her, and accompanied by the ever-present Aunt Jane, Mary Eleanor turned heads at the balls, assemblies and levees which took place nightly throughout the hectic winter season. One socialite, complaining of the incessant treadmill of the social calendar in the 1760s, exclaimed: 'The hurry of this town is inconceivable, for I declare I have been only once to the Play, Opera, & Orotorio, to very few assemblies, & yet I can't find a moment's time to myself'.[41] Mary Eleanor had no such objections. Demonstrating the dance steps she had mastered in her lessons and practising the clever repartee for which she would become well-known, she flirted and laughed with a crush of admirers, noting rather archly that Aunt Jane was so indulgent a chaperone that, 'I must say, if I had not been more prudent than most young girls of my age, I might have been less so.'[42] Her object was plain: to capture the ideal future husband.

As Lord Lyttelton had observed so succinctly, the question of whether to marry for money or for love had become one of the chief dilemmas of the age. The eighteenth century saw an unprecedented shift in society's attitude towards marriage.[43] While people in working-class and agricultural communities had always been more or less at liberty to choose their partners for life, albeit from within the same narrow economic stratum and geographical area, the vast majority of marriages in aristocratic and landed families were arranged by parents, with the prospective bride and bridegroom having little or no say until at least the early 1700s.

Marriage was regarded essentially as a means to cement powerful partnerships between important families, to continue ancestral lines and to transfer or acquire land and property. Children were often betrothed in infancy to be married in their teens, while adolescent girls with generous dowries, or 'portions', were matched with elderly, diseased and often impoverished members of the aristocracy. One seventeenth-century heiress, Mary Davies, was betrothed at the age of seven to marry the 23-year-old Honourable Charles Berkeley as soon as she reached her twelfth birthday; that wedding never took place but a few months after she reached the age of twelve she was married to the 21-year-old baronet Sir Thomas Grosvenor. It was perhaps not surprising that she later suffered mental instability.[44] Sir William Temple, whose family thwarted his marriage plans for many years, lamented in 1680 that marriages were dictated by 'men's avarice and greediness of portions' which had increased to such a degree that 'our marriages are made just like other common bargains and sales by the mere consideration of interest or gain, without any of love or esteem, of birth or of beauty itself.'[45] Since marriage truly was a partnership for life – and almost impossible to dissolve – many relationships were marked by misery, infidelity and even violence. Lord Halifax made the prospects grimly plain when considering marriage in his *Advice to a Daughter* in 1688: 'It is one of the Disadvantages belonging to your Sex, that young Women are seldom permitted to make their own Choice'.[46] The only remedy, he suggested, was to endure whatever faults a husband might possess, lest dislike turn to aversion.

It was little wonder that Mary Astell, herself the daughter of a Newcastle coal merchant, advocated spinsterhood in her *Reflections upon Marriage* published in 1700. 'If Marriage be such a blessed State, how comes it, may you say, that there are so few happy marriages?' she lamented, although she had no more optimism about partnerships based on love rather than money.[47] For Lady Mary Wortley Montagu, betrothed by her father at the age of twenty-three to the improbably named Clotworthy Skeffington, arrangements for the impending wedding day in 1712 were seen as 'daily preparations for my journey to Hell'.[48] Rather than descend into eternal torment, she eloped and married Edward Wortley Montagu just days before her planned wedding. Living to regret her hasty decision, like so many impetuous lovers who fled one potentially disastrous partnership only to embark on another, she took a dim view when her niece and then her daughter followed her example.

As increasing numbers of young couples expressed their

objections to parental control by voting with their feet, disillusion with forced marriages spread. William Hogarth depicted the growing unease in his popular series of prints *Marriage A-la-Mode*, published in 1745. The six scenes portray the tragic story of an arranged marriage between the daughter of a rich city merchant and a foppish earl desperate to refurbish his estate. As both descend into debauchery, the wife drinks laudanum to commit suicide when she hears her lover is to be executed for killing her husband in a duel. George Bowes was among many who bought the series; he hung the pictures in the entrance hall at Gibside in 1746, though he could have had little idea how prophetic the scenes would prove for his daughter.

Increasing criticism of arranged marriages combined with a rising interest in the notion of romantic love – sometimes blamed on the early eighteenth-century development of the novel – fuelled a slow but steady shift from the idea of marriage as a financial agreement to the modern ideal of a companionate partnership. Pressure for change built up gradually, so that while at the beginning of the eighteenth century well-heeled parents almost always retained a veto over their children's choice of partner, by the middle and later 1700s it was generally their children who had the final say. Some landowning parents gave up their control with extreme reluctance, however, perhaps mindful of their own sacrifices and efforts to make an arranged marriage work. It was chiefly concern over thwarted young lovers absconding to marry secretly that prompted the 1753 Marriage Act.

Regulating marriage by the state for the first time, the act laid down that weddings were only valid if performed by a priest in orders within a church. Banns were normally required to be read three times beforehand unless a special licence was obtained. And the act also stipulated that parental consent was required for couples wishing to marry under the age of twenty-one. Overnight the scandal of unscrupulous parsons marrying reckless, and sometimes drunk, runaways in taverns and brothels was brought to an end. Often called 'Fleet marriages', after the London debtors' prison, the environs of which were notorious for quickie ceremonies, such matches were blamed for entrapping numerous feckless sailors, intemperate soldiers and – on occasion – unwilling heiresses. The Welsh naturalist Thomas Pennant recalled walking along Fleet Street in his youth when he had 'often been tempted by the question, "Sir, will you be pleased to walk in and be married?"'[49] Once the 1753 Act took effect, crossed young lovers were forced to trek to Scotland, where its regulations did not apply, if they wanted to evade their parents' commands. The little village of Gretna Green, just over the border on the main road into Scotland, quickly acquired a reputation as the nearest wedding venue.

Not surprisingly, by the 1760s the whole subject of marriage had become more confusing than ever. Relatively few parents now attempted to force their sons or daughters into marriages they patently did not want. When nineteen-year-old Lady Harriet Spencer was married in 1780 at her parents' behest to Lord Duncannon, a man she had barely met, her lack of involvement was highly unusual. 'I wish I could have known him a little better first,' she protested meekly, living to regret her compliance.[50] Most parents were now sensitive at least to the ideal of marital bliss, even if a financially astute match still remained their chief consideration.

For the young hopefuls themselves, aspirations to romantic love and concerns for a comfortable future had become inextricably entangled in the notion of what made a successful marriage. Whereas marriage negotiations had previously been conducted mainly via letters and lawyers with little cause for couples or families to meet, now teenage aristocrats and their pushy parents thronged London ballrooms and assemblies on the prowl for a suitable match. Competition could be fierce. Without the benefit of parental guidance or adult aid, and highly influenced by the romantic novels and poetry she adored, thirteen-year-old Mary Eleanor believed she was more than capable of arranging her own perfect match.

Her first conquest happened to be one of the most eligible bachelors in town. Nineteen-year-old Prince Ernst of Mecklenburg-Strelitz had become a familiar figure in London since the marriage of his younger sister Charlotte to George III in 1761. While seventeen-year-old Charlotte was summarily dismissed as 'certainly not a beauty', her tall, slim-shouldered brother was described as 'a very pretty sort of man, with an agreeable person', by the novelist Sarah Scott, sister of Elizabeth Montagu. By March 1762, Mrs Scott informed her sister, the prince had 'fallen desperately in love with Miss Bowes'. Describing the prince's interest as a 'prudent passion', Mrs Scott believed that, 'the girl has no ambition if she does not choose to be a princess' and added, 'I fancy, should she become such, he would be richer than the duke, his elder brother'. But therein partly lay the problem. George III vetoed the match, apparently on the grounds of the Prince 'being united to a subject' – an objection Mary's great-great-great-granddaughter, Elizabeth Bowes Lyon, would later overcome in marrying Prince Albert, the future George VI – but also because it would have made Prince Ernst wealthier than his brother, the Duke, back home. Charlotte Papendiek, wardrobe keeper to Queen Charlotte, explained in her journal some years later that, 'Prince Ernest [sic] had wished to marry the great heiress of the North, Miss Bowes, whose fortune exceeded that of the heiress of the South, Miss Tilney Long'. She added: 'Most certainly such a fortune in Germany would have made him a Prince indeed; but as he was a younger brother, it might have disturbed the harmony of the house of Mecklenburgh-Strelitz, of which the reigning Duke was not married.'[51]

It is unlikely that Mary Eleanor seriously considered the prince since she never mentioned him in her writings. Certainly, that same year she was far more interested in another beau who was closer to home, and closer in years. Campbell Scott, younger brother of the third Duke of Buccleuch, was fourteen or fifteen years old when they first met. Mary was attracted to him at a 'children's ball' organised by the Duchess of Northumberland. Whether the dance took place at the duchess's palatial London mansion, Northumberland House, which had recently been refurbished by George Bowes's favourite architects Garrett and Paine, or her riverside retreat at Syon Park, only just redecorated by Robert Adam, or indeed at her Northumberland pile of Alnwick Castle, in the throes of being restored by both Adam and Paine, Mary Eleanor did not record. Evidently, she took little interest in the architecture as she danced with the quick-witted and self-assured young Scott who had a distinct flair for flattery. 'He liked my conversation, and as he was smart and clever, I liked his,' Mary later wrote.[52] The innocent banter would have gone no further, she insisted, had not her cousin Thomas Liddell, who was a schoolmate of Scott's at Eton, 'teazed us into a belief that we were in love with each other'. The young sweethearts exchanged rings, and tender words, until Scott joined the army and left for mainland Europe twelve months later. Although Mary kept Scott's ring, the thrill of her first romance did not deter her from embarking on further flirtations, but when Scott died of smallpox in Paris in October 1766, Mary was gravely upset. Her grief was only exacerbated by Scott's mother, Lady Dalkeith, who had already lost three of her six children but seemed scarcely perturbed to have lost a fourth. According to Mary, Lady Dalkeith 'hurt me much by her unfeelingness', a view supported by Lady Sarah Lennox, who recorded that while the Duke, Scott's brother, suffered 'in vast affliction', his 'odious mother I supose don't care, for she never loved her children'.[53]

Playing the field while Scott was still away with his regiment in 1763, Mary dallied half-heartedly with a young Venetian marquis who wooed her for almost a year. Since he spoke little English they exchanged small talk in Italian, one of several languages in which Mary was already proficient. When he finally abandoned his courtship to continue his travels, the marquis sent Mary a present from Paris of two small dogs. The pets fared significantly better in Mary's affections than their donor. Less forthright was the young Charles James Fox, future leader of the Whig party, who was Mary's exact contemporary. Another of the Eton set Mary favoured, Fox had been spoiled by his doting father to such a degree that as a toddler he was allowed to sit astride a joint of meat during a dinner party. Now old enough to enjoy dinner parties from a more conventional position, he cast longing glances at the teenage Mary but had 'too much pride', she later wrote, to divulge his passion. Presumably this shy crush, if true, took hold of Fox before his father had dragged him out of school on a rabble-rousing trip to Paris, where he arranged for his son to lose his virginity with a prostitute, as well as a substantial amount of money at the gaming tables.[54] Certainly, Fox showed little reticence with women in later years.

Abandoning London's giddy lifestyle for a rare visit north that winter, fourteen-year-old Mary found the attentions of her next suitor decidedly less welcome. Staying with her mother at Gibside in October 1763, she narrowly escaped a plot to kidnap her and force her into marriage with an MP. The unknown politician had offered £20,000 via a shifty go-between to a footman in the family, who was the lover of Mary's former nurse. The plan was to lure her to a remote part of the grounds where she would be captured and then whisked abroad to marry the unscrupulous MP, according to Elizabeth Montagu who reported the scam with horror to her friend Lord Bath.[55] Luckily, the two servants got cold feet and divulged the plan to Mrs Bowes who quickly put a stop to the scheme and had the go-between arrested. Convinced that Mary would have resisted all efforts to force her into such a marriage, as she 'is a girl of sense and spirit', Mrs Montagu was certain that the MP, if discovered, would have been 'hanged for his pains'.

More traditional if equally unsuccessful was John Stuart, the eldest son of Lord Bute, who had recently resigned as prime minister. Five years older than Mary, Stuart had attended Harrow and Winchester schools before setting off on an extensive grand tour, during which he met Voltaire and travelled in Italy with James Boswell. Returning bronzed and good-looking, the self-styled Lord Mountstuart created something of a flutter among the excitable young debutantes when he hit London's party scene in the winter season of 1765–66. Announcing him as the 'new importation' of the year, Lady Sarah Lennox gushed: 'Ld Mount [sic] is tall, well made, & very handsome'. It had become the fashion to 'cry him up' and although he was 'very proud & vain', she thought he 'does vastly well for a beau'.[56] Preening himself at Almack's assembly rooms, which had rapidly become the match-making venue of choice since its opening the previous year, Lord Mountstuart fixed his sights on sixteen-year-old

Mary Eleanor. He was not alone. Among a growing band of hopefuls, Stuart had to battle for Mary's attentions with William Chaloner, another of her cousins who belonged to the Eton crowd. Gleefully playing one off against the other, Mary partnered them both until one evening rival passions spilled over into a furious quarrel over who should sit beside her at supper. Tempers inflamed, the two youths stormed outside where they were at the point of fighting a duel before one of them grudgingly backed down.

Plainly enjoying the excitement of finding herself at the centre of such intense competition, Mary deliberately encouraged Stuart's mother, Lady Bute, to believe that her son was in favour by extending 'great civility' towards her and her daughters on an ensuing Almack's evening. Taking the bait, Lady Bute rushed round confidently the following morning to press her son's suit, only for Mary glibly to refuse the offer she had never contemplated accepting. With hindsight, she would later admit, this was 'downright girlishness, mischievousness, and vanity'.[57] Poor Lady Bute was mortified by the rebuff while her son was so distraught he took to bed for a week before pursuing another heiress, described by Walpole as the 'rich ugly' Charlotte Windsor, whom he married later the same year.[58]

There was no shortage of suitors waiting to take his place in the scrum for the hand of Britain's wealthiest heiress. Mary referred each of the many offers she received to her mother, who by now had sufficiently recovered her composure at least to reject her daughter's marriage proposals. Gleefully totting up the score, Mary revelled in the satisfaction of refusing 'a great many people of rank'. In truth, she knew that none of the young rakes she partnered on Almack's dance floor or flirted with at Vauxhall's concerts could measure up to the dynamic father she had lost. Looking back in later years she would admit quite candidly: 'I had no partiality for any man in the world.' And yet at the age of sixteen, even while she encouraged Lord Mountstuart, cousin Chaloner and a host of other unfortunate hopefuls, Mary had already decided on her future husband.

Beside the scrapping and jostling young bucks who were vying for Mary's attention at Almack's assemblies, John Lyon, the 28-year-old ninth Earl of Strathmore, presented a mature and sophisticated contrast. Reserved and taciturn, Lord Strathmore had little patience for the flattery and witticisms which peppered conversation in the salons of Georgian London. More comfortable with his hard-drinking, hard-gambling male chums at the club he had helped to set up in the original Almack's than among the giggling dance-floor debutantes, he cut an aloof and proud figure. Having grown up as neighbours, since the Strathmore clan preferred their hospitable Durham estate to their dilapidated Glamis Castle near Dundee, Mary and John had rubbed shoulders at social engagements since her childhood. Her father, significantly, had high regard for the personable young earl, who succeeded to his title at sixteen, before distinguishing himself at Cambridge, where he became a favourite of his tutor, the poet Thomas Gray. Now that the tall, elegant and good-looking peer – who would become known as 'the beautiful Lord Strathmore' – had returned from the customary grand tour of Europe, he graced London's entertainment venues with a dignified disdain.[59] Mary was intrigued. Renewing their youthful acquaintance, she subtly encouraged the earl's interest to the point where at last he sent her a proposal of marriage, conveyed by a mutual family friend. Insisting, as with all her suitors, that he approach her mother first, sixteen-year-old Mary waited patiently.

When Mrs Bowes instantly dismissed the earl's declaration, pointing to his large family's sizeable financial problems, their meddlesome reputation and – not least – the fact that they were Scottish, Mary's keenness was only heightened. She would always, she later confessed, have a soft spot for Celtic men. Knowing that she needed her mother's consent for marriage until the age of twenty-one, Mary declared that she would make Lord Strathmore her husband or nobody. Already captivated by 'Lord Strathmore's beauty, which was then very great', she was further convinced he was her destined life partner by a dream or 'vision' in which he appeared to her. Her mother, never a forceful influence or a reliable guide, relented and in autumn 1765 the engagement was agreed.

It took a full eighteen months of legal negotiations to finalise the marriage contract, partly due to the complexity of transferring Mary's vast fortune into the Strathmore family's waiting hands, partly to guarantee some future financial security for herself and any children, and partly to confirm the stipulation that her prospective husband, and their children, must adopt the Bowes name. For all the protestations of the Lyons, forced to surrender a name they had honoured since at least the Norman conquest, the Bowes dynasty would continue. As the lawyers haggled, the forthcoming wedding became the topic of the season. The ever-vigilant Sarah Osborn observed the lean Lord Strathmore towering over his petite fiancée at Almack's, along with two more betrothed couples, in March 1766. 'These three Weddings are to be celebrated as soon as the Lawyers can finish,' she wrote. But two months later the lawyers were still wrangling and Thomas Gray informed his friend James Brown: 'The great match will not be till after Christmas.'[60] Throughout the wet summer of 1766, as the lawyers scratched the draft settlement, crowds were thronging to the latest comedy by David Garrick and George Colman, *The Clandestine Marriage*, with its well-timed swipe at mercenary matches and their legal machinations. 'Here we are – hard at it – paving the road to matrimony,' declares the wealthy patriarch Sterling, whose daughter was to bring a handsome dowry to her debt-ridden aristocratic bridegroom, before adding, 'First the lawyers, then comes the doctor.'[61] At last, in September, the ink was dry on the twenty massive pages of parchment and the wedding preparations could begin.

Dressmakers set to work on the gowns, nightgowns, petticoats and cloaks which would make up Mary Eleanor's extravagant trousseau. As well as six dresses, in assorted combinations of silver, white and gold decorated with silver or blond lace, which were designed to be worn over hoops according to the latest fashion, there were six satin petticoats and eight quilted calico petticoats. In all, her wardrobe was valued at £3,000. In addition, Mary's mother gave her a diamond-studded stomacher – a stiffened bodice to fit over the front of a dress – worth £10,000, along with further diamonds to the tune of £7,000. Finally, to complete the ensemble for the wedding of the year, Mrs Bowes donated three carriages – a green landau, a blue post coach and a stone-coloured post chaise – which were brought down from Gibside to London.

It should have proved a memorable occasion, summoning up reminiscences of the royal wedding just six years earlier. Yet by the time that Mary walked down the aisle of St George's Church in Hanover Square, splendidly robed in her silver and white wedding dress glinting with diamonds, on her eighteenth birthday on 24 February 1767, her teenage infatuation was over.[62] She knew she was marrying the wrong man.

3
A Worthy Little Woman

Newcastle, 1767

Living in her late father's house in Westgate Street, one of Newcastle's most affluent addresses, Hannah Newton could not help but be aware of the society wedding of the year between two of her close neighbours. Just eighteen months older than Mary Eleanor, nineteen-year-old Hannah would have brushed skirts with Mary at the concerts, plays and assemblies which entertained the city's polite society. Having grown up in the same region, Hannah and Mary Eleanor would have moved in the same elite social circles for Hannah's father, William Newton, had also accumulated a fortune from coal in the mineral-rich lands of County Durham. The owner of two collieries near the Derwent, Newton had acquired large estates at Burnopfield, less than two miles from Gibside, and Cole Pike Hill, eight miles to the south near Lanchester. Although not in the league of the Grand Allies, Newton had been presented by the city with the 'great seal' in 1749 for inventing a new method to extract coal from deeper pits.[1] When William Newton died in 1762, about the time of Hannah's fifteenth birthday, he left his daughter and sole heiress with a sizeable fortune in collieries and farmland valued at between £20,000 and £30,000 – more than £3m in modern terms.[2] It was little wonder, therefore, that just like Mary Eleanor, Hannah had attracted the attentions of a number of suitors.

Baptised on 11 November 1747 – her date of birth went unrecorded but was probably a few days or weeks beforehand – Hannah was not considered a great beauty by eighteenth-century standards.[3] 'She was not at all handsome; short, and very dark', one acquaintance later recalled.[4] Yet the size of her fortune more than made up for her lack of physical attributes in the eyes of certain suitors. Indeed, it was perfectly possible for the only daughter of a middle-ranking or nouveau riche family to marry well above her perceived station in life and even into the aristocracy – as had Mary Eleanor – given sufficient capital to her name. So Hannah, for all her plain appearance, might easily expect to walk up the aisle with the eldest son of one of the powerful local coal-owning families or at least with an up-and-coming professional man. Why she had therefore set her heart on a young Irish soldier, who marched into Newcastle the most junior and poorly paid officer in his regiment, remains something of a mystery.

Andrew Robinson Stoney had enlisted with the Fourth or King's Own Regiment of Foot as an ensign – the lowliest rank of officer – in November 1764 at the age of seventeen and first met up with his regiment the following spring.[5] It was a good time to join the army – for anyone keen to avoid the perils of battle. Although William Makepeace Thackeray would place the anti-hero of his novel, *The Luck of Barry Lyndon*, who was modelled on Stoney, in the brutal pandemonium of the Seven Years' War, the real Stoney never once faced enemy fire. In fact, the global conflict which had raged across Europe, India, North America and the Caribbean since 1756 had ended a full year before Stoney signed the commission book. And since Britain had lost its appetite for further bloodshed or military expense, there was little immediate risk in wearing the scarlet coat. At the same time, with the King's Own freshly returned from a string of conquests in the West Indies, the new recruit would be sure to share in some of his fellow officers' reflected glory. So as the regiment marched across the medieval stone Tyne Bridge into the walled city of Newcastle in early 1767, the young ensign who carried the regimental colours could be assured of a hero's welcome. Certainly, there would be no shortage of admiring women eager to partner the regiment's officers at the various entertainments to which the city had invited its visiting troops. An army officer with a good family background was considered a fairly desirable beau for a younger daughter in a middling family of the gentry. But for a humble ensign to pitch his interest at one of the city's richest heiresses would have required a great deal of charm, imagination and bravado. Unluckily for Hannah, these were attributes Stoney possessed in large measure.

Born on 19 June 1747 in County Tipperary, Stoney was the eldest son of a well-to-do Protestant family which had prospered since emigrating from Yorkshire at the end of the seventeenth century. His great-grandfather, George Stoney, had moved his young family to Ireland under the handsome inducements offered to emigrating Protestant families at some point after 1692 and had established a family estate named Greyfort near the little village of Borrisokane. Eldest son Thomas, Stoney's grandfather, married Sarah Robinson – at nineteen nearly half his age – the daughter of a prominent Protestant family whose ancestors, the Robinsons and the Armstrongs, had fought on opposite sides in the English Civil War. Still a powerfully ambitious military family, Sarah's numerous male relatives were highly placed in the British army. An uncle, General John Armstrong, who was more than six feet tall, was a skilled engineer who had fought at Blenheim and helped found the Royal Military Academy at Woolwich in 1741.[6] Sarah's brother, Captain Andrew Robinson, would ultimately rise to the rank of Major-General, while her cousin, Bigoe Armstrong, and nephew, Robert Robinson, would both become regimental colonels who would take a kindly interest in their nephew. Fiercely independent and staunchly religious – her family bible still survives – Sarah was only thirty-three when her husband died leaving her with three young sons and the family farms to manage in a hostile country. Aged thirteen at the time of his father's death, eldest son George, Stoney's father, studied hard and laboured long under his mother's watchful eye.

Assuming control of the family estate once he came of age, George Stoney worked industriously to nurture the farm before feeling sufficiently comfortable to marry at the age of thirty-three. When he did, in 1746, it was scarcely surprising that he married into another local Protestant military family. Elizabeth Johnston's father, James Johnston, had been one of the defenders of Derry against Catholic forces in 1689, while her brother Robert was even now rising up army ranks. It was, as one of George's relatives commented in the most complimentary terms of the age, a 'prudent choice'.[7] When the couple's first child was born a year later he was named Andrew Robinson after his great-uncle, grandmother Sarah's brother, who would be promoted six years later to the role of equerry to Princess Augusta, mother of the future George III. The family bible, in which Sarah inscribed significant domestic events, records that baby Andrew was immediately sent to a wet-nurse – it even gives her name, Honory MacGilton – in keeping with upper- and middle-class custom. When Sarah died, still only fifty-five, a year after the birth of her first grandchild, she went to her rest in Ballingarry churchyard in the happy confidence that the family's proud army traditions would continue in the infant who bore her surname.

Growing tall amid the fertile countryside which nourished the family's livestock and crops, Robinson – as he was known within the family – took little interest in the daily tedium of farming. Ambitious but lazy, intelligent but scheming, young Stoney could barely wait to escape the familiar Tipperary landscape, with its mountain borders to the south and west and its snaking Lough Derg to the north, or his father's restraining authority. Robinson lorded it over his brothers and sisters, who arrived in swift succession almost year on year, and probably bullied his siblings and his cousins; certainly they deferred to him meekly in later life. As future acquaintances would discover, their strapping elder brother could swiftly change from being friendly and charming one minute to vindictive and sadistic the next, and they quickly realised it was better to be on his side than against him. Leaving the farmyard chores to his brother Thomas, a year his junior, Robinson ran rings around his indulgent, adoring mother and his overworked father.

A well-educated man with simple tastes, who enjoyed country pursuits like hunting, fishing and the typically Irish sport of hurling, George Stoney could never get the measure of his eldest son. His natural hopes that his heir, the future head of the household, would develop into a relentless worker and dedicated family man like himself were abruptly disappointed. Instead he found Robinson conniving and manipulative when he wanted something, arrogant and defiant when he was spurned. George Stoney's surviving letters and two diaries record his incomprehension, despair and ultimate helplessness at his eldest son's increasingly wayward behaviour.

George Stoney's earliest diary in 1765 – none survive from his son's childhood – reveals a careful, parsimonious businessman, who recorded the farming accounts in diligent detail and noted debts from friends for as little as sixpence. With his farm and large labour force to run, as well as managing lands for his relatives serving in the army overseas, it was an arduous, time-consuming business. Up one morning at five, for example, it took him six hours to herd livestock to a county fair, which he left for the six-hour return journey at nine that night. With cattle to tend, sheep to fleece, hops to pole and corn to thresh, there was little time for leisure. As the family grew – ultimately there would be five sons and six daughters – the farm and domestic labour increased and profits were stretched increasingly thin. Among other necessities, all six daughters would require generous portions if they were to secure advantageous marriages. So while his wife and daughters mixed in genteel county circles, Farmer Stoney worked long hours and worried over the price of bullocks, his own indifferent health and his implacably unruly eldest son.

Although George Stoney evidently cared deeply about his family, employing a tutor for the younger children and fretting when they caught the inevitable childhood diseases, he was a distant, sometimes cold, father who showed little affection to his offspring, much in the manner of most Georgian parents. As the head of the family, he demanded unconditional respect and compliance from his wife and children, yet frequently showed himself ineffectual at engendering such authority. One of his brothers-in-law on one occasion remarked pointedly that Thomas, the second eldest, was 'a very promising boy' who took a keen interest in farming, but added, 'his Father does not encourage him as he ought'.[8] Although he may have been stern when the children were little – it was commonplace for Georgian fathers to beat their sons – any discipline on his part seems to have been frequently reversed by Mrs Stoney who spoiled the children and countermanded her husband's orders. Certainly in later life he would become bitter and resentful over what he regarded as his wife's indulgence and children's indolence. Such inconsistency between parents may perhaps have been one of the explanations – though not sufficient excuse – for their eldest son's later conduct.

As the putative heir of his father's successful farming business and the family seat of Greyfort, young Robinson could have counted himself lucky in expectation of a comfortable, if dull, future as a country gentleman. Yet although he enjoyed a privileged, if not pampered, upbringing, Robinson soon became aware that he would never achieve the opulent lifestyle he so obviously desired if he remained in rural Ireland. His best chances of the money, power and influence he craved lay, he knew, across St George's Channel. Since it was plain to both his parents that their eldest son displayed neither the inclination nor the application to run the family estate, his father grudgingly groomed young Thomas, a keen and able worker, to take over the farming duties. No doubt his parents were optimistic that by enlisting in the army, Robinson would distinguish himself and rise through the military ranks just like his illustrious ancestors. Secretly, his father probably also hoped that some military discipline would knock his quick-tempered son into line.

It was Uncle Robert, by now a regimental colonel, who secured his nephew a commission as an ensign in the King's Own in November 1764, initially without pay.[9] After kicking his heels on the farm over the winter, Stoney said goodbye to his then eight siblings the following spring and set sail to join his regiment in England. At first the military life appeared to suit him. Relating news of his enrolment that July, one of his uncles reported that 'General Armstrong and Col. Robn give very good accounts of him'. With two such powerfully placed great-uncles keeping a paternalistic eye over his progress, Stoney was set for a medal-encrusted military career. The first signs of tension surfaced just two months later. Colonel Robinson, stationed in Southampton, wrote to tell George Stoney that he planned to buy his great-nephew a promotion to lieutenant as soon as an opportunity arose but added ominously, 'I mean to tell him that it will be done only on condition of his *making good progress at the Academy*.'[10] Evidently, Stoney's record so far left room for improvement.

By June the following year, serious concerns had erupted over the behaviour of the young ensign, who appeared resistant both to army discipline and to common etiquette. Now billeted in Plymouth, Stoney had been reprimanded by several senior officers for his insolence, bad temper and debauched lifestyle, in addition to running up debts amounting to £40. Precisely what this dissipation comprised, and where the £40 had been expended, were not revealed although later events would suggest that the money had been squandered on drinking, gambling and women. So seriously was his conduct viewed that Lieutenant Colonel George Maddison, commanding officer of the regiment, felt moved to complain to the regiment's formal colonel – essentially an honorary figure – the MP Robert Brudenell. 'He's very averse to taking advice,' wrote Maddison, 'and I assure you both [Captains] Boarder & Henderson have taken great pains with him, with such little effect that they have given him up.' Although Maddison had 'taken him in hand once or twice myself pretty strongly', he concluded: 'He does his duty, but not with seeming pleasure a boy of his age ought to do, and he's a very Indifferent Temper.'[11] While army discipline in the eighteenth century was notoriously lax, with soldiers who had been lured into enlisting with cash or alcohol frequently deserting or defying orders, these were stern words with which to describe a commissioned officer. They had little effect on Stoney, however, who would always baulk at authority and prefer to command his own actions.

By the following month, July 1766, Stoney was back in Ireland, sent home in disgrace in the vain hope that his father might tackle his recalcitrant behaviour. Seemingly his great-uncles had intervened with the regiment to save him from a worse fate. Writing from Dublin, General Armstrong – Uncle Bigoe – informed George Stoney gamely: 'No doubt you will be surprised at your son's arrival in Ireland. It is an expedient thought of by Col. Robinson (& approved of by his Colonel) to get him away from his Regt for a few months, that he may be under your eye, and they hope that you will be able to break him of that idle extravagant turn he has taken.'[12] His poor father's heart must have sunk; he knew only too well that he had long since lost any gainsay over his arrogant nineteen-year-old son.

Yet for all his misbehaviour, when occasion demanded the young ensign possessed a magnetic charm and disarming amiability that could win him friends and patrons who were often older and more senior – and should have been wiser – than he was. Despite conduct apparently so disruptive that even the army had failed to whip any sense into him, he had somehow ingratiated himself with his superior officers, as Uncle Bigoe made plain. 'He is very sensible and smart,' he pleaded in his favour, 'and I make doubt but that he will in a little turn out a clever fellow.' Indeed, young Stoney was already a clever fellow. For, as the general reported, Colonel Brudenell himself had taken 'a very great liking' to the junior officer who presented such an apparently poor role model to the platoon under his command. Like Stoney's easygoing uncles, no doubt Brudenell regarded the ensign as a spirited but generally loveable rogue and excused his behaviour as youthful exuberance. After lending his great-nephew ten guineas, which Uncle Bigoe fully expected to see again, he added: 'He desires you will send Horses for him as soon as you can.'

How George Stoney greeted his prodigal son went unrecorded but one thing is certain: any harsh words or discipline that he may have meted out had utterly no effect. When Stoney returned to England to rejoin his regiment in time to begin a long march northwards in February 1767, his extravagant tastes and bullish self-confidence remained intact. And as he marched through the arched gate into the bustling city of Newcastle at the head of his platoon on 8 May, the nineteen-year-old ensign held his head high.

Most visitors assailed for the first time by the overcrowded tenements, heaving quayside and noisome street markets wrestling for space within the medieval walls of mid-eighteenth-century Newcastle recoiled in disgust. 'The town of Newcastle is horrible, like the ways of thrift it is narrow, dark and dirty,' complained Elizabeth Montagu on her first trip to the city that had helped make her husband's fortune. The streets were so narrow that her carriage scraped the walls as it passed while the goods from the shops swung so far outwards that she could only marvel that 'I have not yet caught a coach full of red herrings'. For another visitor, newly wed Sophia Curzon, first impressions of the town exceeded 'all the horrible discreptions' she had already heard. 'I really thought when we enter'd the Town that we was going into the deepest & darkest Pit ever heard off, as it was hardly possible to breathe for want of air & the horrid stink of the Tan Yards,' Sophia informed her aunt.[13] With its large and predominantly poor population densely packed between the tanneries, tenements and the fish and flesh markets near the quayside, there is no doubt that Georgian Newcastle exuded a pungent stench. But as he marched past the slum housing, the rowdy taverns and overflowing street stalls, Ensign Stoney could detect a sweeter smell. It was the smell of money.

Billeted in a tavern or private house within the town walls, for the army had no barracks to call its own, Stoney no doubt enjoyed the seamier pleasures that the city had to offer. Cock-fighting and even bull-baiting were popular in the warren of streets leading up from the 'Keyside' and stakes could be heavy now that the warmer weather marked the revival of the coal trading season. With almost the entire town's economy dependent on the fluctuating fortunes of the coal business, the winters – when no ships could sail – were frequently long, bleak and hungry, while the summers – when hundreds of colliers shuttled the coal from the Tyne to the Thames each week – brought ready money for all. Having lived most of the winter on credit, the pitmen, sailors and keelmen, who navigated the coal-bearing boats downriver to the estuary, were impatient to spend their long-awaited wages and the shopkeepers were eager to serve them. So as Stoney made his first forays into the town that spring, the ale-houses would be crammed, as would the brothels, clustered in the steep, stepped alleys or 'chares' which climbed up from the quay. Judging from his conduct so far, both kinds of establishment would find a willing customer in the young officer. But Stoney soon set his sights higher – literally – for the source of the money now rapidly changing hands at the teeming riverside all flowed from the grand houses up the hill. It was here, in the wide and pleasant streets such as Westgate, where Hannah lived, that those who had made their fortunes from the coal business resided. And with the hectic summer social season about to begin, Stoney lifted up his eyes in anticipation.

He did not have long to wait. From the traditional Ascension Day festival at the end of May to the anniversary of the King's accession to the throne in October, the Newcastle populace celebrated every conceivable religious, royal and civic occasion. The troops of the King's Own were only too eager to help, providing regimental music, drinking their royal patron's health and firing volleys into the sky at every opportunity.[14] And while the regiment's rank and file caroused merrily with the townsfolk, its officers became acquainted with the civic worthies and dignitaries at a packed calendar of balls, assemblies and musical soirees. According to Mrs Montagu, feeling rather better disposed to the city by 1760, the social life was relentless. 'I was at a municipal entertainment yesterday morning, at a concert last night, at a musical entertainment this morning,' she boasted to her friend Lord Lyttelton. 'I have bespoken a play for to-morrow night, and shall go to a ball for choosing a Mayor on Monday night.' Although the northern diversions were admittedly 'less elegant' and the conversations 'less polite' than their southern equivalents, she had to confess that the 'desire for pleasure and love of dissipation rages here as much as in London'.[15]

It was at just such an event that Hannah Newton first set eyes on the swarthy, good-looking junior officer with the penetrating stare.[16] Tall, lean and with a soldier's upright bearing, Stoney exuded the kind of confident, easygoing manner that made him popular with men and fatally attractive to women. Although later caricatures would show him as hook-nosed, double-chinned and bug-eyed, these were plainly crude exaggerations, for women would always be drawn to Stoney, some of them desperately so. Certainly Jessé Foot, his surgeon, friend and biographer, would insist that Stoney presented a handsome face with a 'captivating' manner. 'His speech was soft, his height was more than five feet ten, his eyes were bright and small, he had a perfect command over them, his eye brows were low, large and sandy, his hair light, and his complexion muddy, his smile was agreeable, his wit ready.'[17] Only one flaw marred the young Stoney's good looks, described by Foot as 'something uncommon in the connexion of his nose with his upper lip' which meant that whenever he talked his nose 'moved ridiculously'. In order to avoid this comical trait Stoney was forced to lisp when he spoke. Lisping or not, in his imposing officer's uniform with its white breeches, knee-length red coat and black boots, his sword swinging from his belt and his tawny hair pulled tightly back in the regulation braid or 'queue', Stoney cut a dash at the city's assembly hall. Hannah soon fell under his spell.

If Stoney's fiery temper and reputation for debauchery were well known within his regiment, in polite company he took pains to present himself as well-mannered, attentive and generous – in short, the perfect officer and gentleman. Escorting Hannah to social occasions throughout the autumn and winter, Stoney flattered her incessantly, showered her with gifts and gave ostentatiously large tips to servants in a determined effort to inflate his family's perceived wealth and his own expectations of fortune. Running up even higher debts than usual, which he had no means of paying on his scant ensign's pay, Stoney had to beg his father for handouts which were forwarded from Ireland with reluctance. By the beginning of 1768, Hannah was besotted with her passionatc and well-connected Irish gentleman whom she was determined to marry at the earliest opportunity. But the course of true love – as it certainly seemed to be for Hannah if not for her intended bridegroom – did not run smooth and the couple had to cool their ardour as their desired union encountered a series of obstacles.

Both aged twenty in early 1768, Hannah and Stoney still required parental consent in order to marry. This was no problem for Stoney, whose father was understandably keen to see his errant son settled. Hannah's mother, Catherine Newton, proved equally easy to handle. Convinced by Stoney's conveniently distant claims to fortune, the widow had no suspicions about the charismatic officer her plain daughter introduced as her suitor. More troublesome, Hannah's inheritance was overseen by guardians who were bound by a clause in her father's will which stipulated that her future husband must own property providing an income of at least £50 a year to inherit the Newton fortune.[18] Just like George Bowes, William Newton had been determined to manipulate his only daughter's future from beyond the grave. Although Stoney pressed Hannah to elope with him to Gretna Green – only a tantalising day's journey from Newcastle – he was soon deterred from this plan by the realisation that she would thereby forfeit her inheritance. Further difficulties arose in the shape of Hannah's uncle, Samuel Newton, who held a half-share in parts of the Burnopfield estate, and who was not so easy to convince. Angling to marry Hannah to his own son, Matthew, and thereby keep his brother's fortune entirely within the family, he vowed to do all in his power to prevent the match to 'that damned Irishman'.[19]

Exhibiting the typical anti-Irish prejudice of the day, Uncle Sam was not alone in branding Irishmen as fortune hunters. A satirical pamphlet published in Dublin in the 1740s went so far as to list the various landed heiresses available for pursuit in England, under the title *The Irish Register: or a list of the Duchess Dowagers, Countesses, Widow Ladies, Maiden Ladies, Widows, and Misses of large fortunes in England.*[20] And the stereotype was not without some foundation, since several Irish landowners and their heirs did cross to Britain in a bid to secure an English heiress as a route to money, power and influence on the mainland. What Uncle Sam could not have predicted was that Andrew Robinson Stoney, fictionalised as *Barry Lyndon*, would come to epitomise the type.

By March, Stoney was desperate to capture his quarry. Knowing his regiment was shortly due to march northwards to Scotland, he was horrified at the prospect of the Newton riches slipping through his hands. In a series of alternately wheedling and vituperative letters to Tipperary, Stoney begged his father to settle sufficient of the family property on him to satisfy the terms of William Newton's will.[21] When his father declined – well aware of his son's aversion to maintaining an Irish estate – Stoney staged a revealing piece of play-acting which he gleefully related in his next letter home. Brandishing his father's refusal to a distressed Hannah and her mother, he made a show of resigning himself to his sorry fate like a true gentleman, releasing Hannah from all obligations to him, then 'took my Hatt, & wished her a good Morning'. It was all a cunning performance, for as Stoney explained: 'You may be assured I had no intention of going, for I well knew I would not be permitted. However, with the help of a few Tears, I was prevailed on to remain with her.' Now he piled the pressure on his father to comply with his request, pleading that only the transfer of the desired property stood between him and 'a woman I love & regard' who would, furthermore, 'be a credit to our family, as well for her accomplishments as, without doubt, a fortune as large – above twenty thousand pounds – as I cou'd ever expect to get.' Warning that, rather like a livestock investment, 'so good an opportunity may never happen to any of our family again', Stoney appealed simultaneously to his father's romantic instincts and his avarice, arguing that, 'I love the lady sufficiently well (was I independant) to marry her without any fortune; therefore how much more happy must I be when I can get her with so good a one'.

Further letters followed in rapid succession, as the regiment prepared to march and Stoney grew increasingly fraught. By May George Stoney had relented and was drawing up title deeds for his son, although Hannah's guardians still needed to be satisfied that the promised property would provide the requisite £50 annual income. As he celebrated his twenty-first birthday in June, being now able to marry as he wished, Stoney secured three months' leave to stay behind in Newcastle and clinch the deal. Urging his father to hurry with the necessary legal requirements, he pointedly reminded him that 'a woman a man loves with a fortune of at least Twenty Thousand Pounds should not be trifled with'. If any doubt remained, the capital letters made plain his true interest. On tenterhooks, Stoney continued the expensive business of wooing Hannah and was livid in July when his father's bankers in Edinburgh refused to honour a bill he had submitted. Protesting to his father, he insisted that his expenses were 'absolutely necessary for a young man paying his addresses to a Lady with Twenty Thousand Pounds fortune'. Itemising costs which must have horrified the penny-pinching farmer, Stoney explained: 'I have attended with this lady at all Publick divertions within fifty miles of Newcastle, I have had two Horses, it has cost about Fifty Pounds for different presents, besides at first Fees to servants, & many other expenses attending such a scheme.' With an agent now despatched to Ireland by Hannah's guardians to check out her suitor's supposed means, Stoney was more anxious than ever to secure his father's compliance, assuring him that once married his only wish was 'to be settled near my parents'.

By now Stoney's mask was beginning to fall. Having written what even he admitted was an 'extremely rude' letter to the bank, he was forced to eat humble pie and write them an apology in September. The pain this afforded him says much about his uncompromising self-belief. 'I do assure you it hurts my spirit not a little,' he told his father, 'as I believe it to be the first acknowledgement I ever made in my life, except to a Parent; which, perhaps, you will say I am nothing the better for.' But he could not contain his fury at such indignity since, as he complained to his father, if news that he had had a bill refused had become known in Newcastle 'many people here would have been happy at the account' which would have lent credence to their 'unjust Reports'. Evidently Stoney's high-handed conduct and transparent aims had generated unsavoury rumours and spawned enemies in the city which had so recently welcomed him. He dealt with them in the manner which would become customary to him: brutally. 'I think they are now at an end,' he informed his father, 'though I believe it to be more owing to fear than regard to me, as I have brought every person that I could find out that mentioned my name to a severe account, & obliged them to beg my Pardon in the most penitent manner.'

Hints were emerging that even Hannah herself now harboured doubts about her impetuous beau for she had expressed a desire to settle near Greyfort after the marriage, Stoney wrote, 'in order to have my Father to govern me'. There was little danger that George Stoney would ever govern his eldest son, but then neither did Stoney have any intention of moving back to Ireland. However, as Hannah's guardians had finally declared themselves satisfied with the young ensign's credentials, there was no going back. Indeed, as Stoney had skilfully made certain, the young lovers had been so much in each other's company that – according to Georgian society's strict codes of conduct – their marriage was 'looked upon as impossible to be avoided with propriety on either side'. Ordered to rejoin his regiment by mid-October, Stoney begged his obliging uncle, Colonel Robinson, to secure him a few more crucial weeks' leave, 'for it is impossible I can think of going before I am marry'd'. With his paralysed prey just within his grasp, Stoney was even prepared to resign from the regiment rather than leave Newcastle a bachelor.

At last, on 5 November 1768, Stoney hurried Hannah down the aisle of St Andrew's Church in Newcastle to sign the marriage register and seal her destiny. Just eighteen months after he had breached the city walls, the young soldier had captured one of the town's richest heiresses and claimed his fortune – for under Georgian law, as Stoney well knew, every last item of Hannah's property now belonged entirely to him, at least during her lifetime. The local newspapers reported the match, with full details of the prize, almost with incredulity. 'Saturday was married in this town, Mr And. Robison [sic] Stoney, an ensign in the fourth regiment of foot, to Miss Newton, daughter of the late Mr Will. Newton; a young lady possessed of a very large fortune,' announced the *Newcastle Journal*, while the *Newcastle Chronicle* referred to the bridegroom as 'Capt. Stoney', a title which the ensign found he rather liked.[22] Writing to his father on his wedding day, Stoney announced: 'I have the pleasure to inform my dear Father that my long-wished-for Happiness was this morning compleated by adding to our Family a woman whom I have reason to think will in every particular be agreeable.'[23] Obsequiously respectful for the most part – for he was still drawing bills on his father's account – Stoney let his guard drop momentarily in declaring that the estate his father had dutifully bought for the newly weds was 'not worth sixpence'. Confident that his father would 'find some more advantageous Purchase for us', Stoney enclosed a promissory note for £500, to cover the large amounts he owed his father, which he hoped to be in a position to honour shortly. It was never drawn.

There was scarcely time to move his few belongings into his new family seat at Cole Pike Hill in County Durham, and survey the surrounding farms and valuable woodland he now owned, before Stoney had to kiss his bride goodbye and dash north to rejoin his regiment in Scotland.[24] At just twenty-one, the ensign had become a wealthy landowner and a member of the gentry with farms and mines guaranteed to provide a handsome quarterly income. By Christmas he was celebrating his newfound riches and status with his army fellows in Edinburgh.

Money opened many doors. Marching across the Scottish lowlands, quartered in taverns during the harsh winter, under canvas in summer, Stoney could afford to employ a valet, one John Smith, to assume the laborious tasks of looking after his uniform and tending to his horses. But riches did nothing to smooth his temper. Setting out from Perth to Stirling at one point in 1769, Stoney horsewhipped Smith because – Stoney claimed – he was too drunk to continue the march.

When the valet threatened to bring the law on him, Stoney was so incensed that he gave him a 'few more lashes with his whip' for insolence. Smith's complaint – it is not clear to which court or what the outcome was – did nothing to hinder his master's advancement. At the end of the year, Stoney was promoted to lieutenant and shortly afterwards transferred to the 30th Regiment of Foot.[25]

For all his preferment, Stoney saw little of military life during his army career. By dint of his fortune and his influence with his high-ranking military relatives, he was frequently granted leave from his regiment to tend to his business matters in England and Ireland. So while the regiment built roads and aided civil forces in Scotland in 1769 and 1770, Stoney visited Ireland, presumably to introduce his 'agreeable' wife to the Stoney clan, although needless to say, the newly weds did not settle near Greyfort.[26] Dividing the remainder of his time between Newcastle and Bath – where Hannah frequently repaired for her health – he left his Durham estates in the hands of agents. The first agent, who managed the farms and mines from the manor hall at Cole Pike Hill – commonly described as Cold Pig Hill – happened to be Rowland Stephenson, whose two brothers both worked at Gibside only eight miles away.

Squandering the income collected from his farms and mines, Stoney dealt meanly with his agents and dodged demands from his creditors. While Stoney enjoyed elegant lodgings and fine food in Bath, Rowland Stephenson grumbled into his accounts over the £5 – a huge sum to a poor family – his master had refused to pay him for accommodation.[27] Stephenson did not live to grumble much longer; he died in 1770 and was succeeded by another unfortunate agent, Robert Morrow. When storms prevented the coal-carrying ships from leaving the Tyne for longer than normal one bleak winter – spreading destitution throughout the region – Stoney pressed his agent to harass the starving tenants for their rents. Morrow, who was faring little better than the desperate tenants, pledged to try his best but warned that 'a general poverty reigns amongst us'.[28] And while Stoney ran up hefty bills for new items of uniform and other luxuries he led his creditors a merry chase for payment. One poor trader pursued him for a bill of £100 over several years.[29] While running up large amounts of credit was commonplace and widely accepted in the eighteenth century, especially among the land-rich, cash-poor aristocracy, Stoney saw it as a matter of principle never to settle a debt until creditors either gave up or threatened him with imprisonment. Often, it was later said, he would jingle loose change in his pockets when making a purchase to hoodwink traders into believing he was flush with cash.[30] But if Stoney's tenants, servants and creditors suffered under his severe regime, they would count themselves lucky compared to his wife.

How soon Hannah Newton discovered the true nature of the adoring officer she believed she was marrying is unknown. None of her correspondence has survived; her voice is unheard. But certainly she was unwell within three years of her marriage and when not accompanying her husband to Ireland or sharing lodgings in Newcastle, she spent much of her time at Bath, presumably to take the health-giving waters. The nature of her illness, mentioned in letters between Stoney and his family, was never revealed. Young as she was, there were any number of lingering infectious diseases or chronic conditions to which she may have fallen victim, tuberculosis being among the most common, although equally she may have suffered complications from pregnancy and miscarriage. Without a doubt her husband exacerbated, if not physically caused, her long-running sickness.

Rumours about Stoney's mistreatment of his wife abounded. One anonymous pamphlet entitled *The Stoniad*, which would be published in Newcastle in 1777, accused him of ruthlessly beating and abusing Hannah while squandering her fortune. Having hoodwinked her into marriage by feigned declarations of love and false claims to wealth and ancestry, Stoney had made Hannah's life wretched, the poem declared. Rhetorically, it enquired: 'What had she done such violence to cause?/Was she not *faithful* as REBECCA was?/Did she not give thee all that mortal cou'd,/Bear thee to *bruise her head* and shed her blood.' While *The Stoniad* was doubtless motivated by political ends – published as it was when Stoney was seeking electoral support – Jessé Foot, writing some years later, cited two letters from correspondents living in Newcastle in the 1770s who testified to Stoney's brutality towards Hannah.[31] One of them recorded that he 'treated her in a most cruel manner' to the extent that he 'shortened her days'. 'She bore the character of being a very good woman,' said Foot's informant, 'which in all probability increased her sensibility, upon feeling her melancholy lot from the choice she had made.' Foot's second letter writer remembered that Stoney 'behaved like a brute and a savage to his wife, and in a short time, broke her heart'. On one occasion he locked Hannah in a cupboard in just her underwear and kept her there for three days, allowing her only an egg a day for sustenance. Another time, attending a public meeting together in Newcastle, he threw Hannah down a flight of stairs 'in a violent fit of rage'. Generally more discreet in company, Stoney usually made a show of treating his wife with studied kindness but 'knew secret ways of provoking her' so that when she complained he would appeal to his guests as if to say she was impossible to please. His second wife would become well accustomed to such tricks.

'He made a very bad husband,' said Foot's informant, 'and she was a most wretched wife, and brought no children alive into the world; which he much desired for his own sake.'

Providing Stoney with an heir was of crucial importance. During Hannah's lifetime, the law gave him complete control over his wife and all her belongings but should she die, all her property would pass to her nearest male heir – currently her Uncle Samuel or his descendants. Since the terms of her father's will gave Hannah only a life interest in the estate, supervised by trustees, Stoney was unable to sell any of the property and realise his capital in that way. The only route by which Stoney could be certain of retaining future control over the Newton fortune was by fathering an heir to inherit the estate; this would entitle him to maintain his right to the property throughout his own lifetime. So for all his apparent distaste for his sensitive young wife, Stoney made sure to exact his conjugal rights.

It seems Hannah became pregnant at least once, and possibly several times, during their marriage but no child was born alive. On one occasion, according to the second of Foot's correspondents, Stoney paid the bellringers of St Nicholas's Church in Newcastle in an effort to proclaim that a stillborn baby had initially survived. Quite possibly Hannah's frequent visits to Bath were to seek treatment for her failed pregnancies or even to boost her fertility; Georgiana, the Duchess of Devonshire, would stay there in 1782 in the hope that the waters would help her to fall pregnant.[32] Quite probably Stoney's brutality contributed to Hannah's difficulties; it is common for abusive men to mistreat their partners more severely than usual during pregnancy.

When Stoney finally retired from the army in 1771, gaining himself half-pay for life while ensuring he would miss out on the next military conflict – the American War of Independence – the violence at home continued unabated. That summer his decadent lifestyle and unbridled temper caused even his normally indulgent relatives some alarm. Writing from his regimental quarters in Scotland, Captain Robert Johnston, his mother's brother, meekly encouraged Stoney: 'If you should alter your way of life, it will require all your resolution, as nothing is so difficult as to get the better of any habit.'[33] Good-naturedly confessing to his own less than spotless past, Uncle Robert added: 'I have gone through many scenes of debauchery and yet I always had the greatest faith and trust in the Almighty God at intervals.' Evidently, Hannah was at that point recovering from either another bout of illness or a failed pregnancy, for Uncle Robert was 'very happy to hear Mrs Stoney is better'. Chillingly, he added, 'be assured its your interest she should continue to get so'. But Uncle Robert was equally conscious of the desire for an heir, pointing out that if Stoney decided to live alone at Cole Pike Hill – as he had seemingly suggested – he would need to bear the expense of 'going backwards and forwards continually at Bath until that event happens'. The following spring, in March 1772, Stoney was with Hannah in Bath – perhaps on one of his conjugal visits – for Uncle Robert had heard that his expenses there were 'great'. A year later, in May 1773, Uncle Robert tentatively enquired: 'Let me know how you and Mrs Stoney are, and particularly what state of health the worthy little woman is in'. Stoney was only too well aware of his wife's worth. Having now settled at Cole Pike Hill, as debts mounted and the Newton fortune drained away, Stoney was casting around for a new way to raise funds. He did not need to look far for inspiration.

Only a few months earlier, in December 1772, Hannah had made a will which bequeathed land worth £5,000 to her husband if no children were born of their marriage before her death. Evidently Stoney had thought it prudent to make contingency measures in case Hannah died without providing the requisite heir.[34] But with the sickly Hannah confounding fate by lingering on in the spring of 1773, Stoney desperately needed an alternative source of income. Striding about his estate at Cole Pike Hill his eyes fell on the surrounding ancient woodlands. Sold for timber, the splendid oak trees could fetch a handsome sum. Stoney lost no time in advertising this prize asset, placing a notice on the front page of the *Newcastle Chronicle* seeking offers for 'about fifteen Hundred Old OAK TREES, now standing and growing at Coldpighill'. There was just one problem: Uncle Sam. Furious at the interloper who had not only seduced his niece but now planned to lay waste the lands which he still hoped might descend to his son, Samuel Newton leapt into action. The following week – and for the week after that – Stoney's advertisement appeared again but this time with a notice underneath it in which Newton warned that he would prosecute any bidder. Determined to safeguard the cherished property of his ancestors, Newton sought an injunction from the Court of Chancery in London to prevent Stoney selling any timber.[35] The bill of complaint affords a revealing insight into Stoney's bag of tricks, for Newton complained that both Stoney and Hannah had by turns claimed that her father had died without leaving a will or had owned his property 'in fee simple', meaning without restriction, allowing it be sold. The outcome of the case went unrecorded – as did many Chancery suits – although the fact that Samuel and Matthew Newton were declared bankrupt later that year doubtless invalidated their claim. It was the first, but by no means the last, of Stoney's brushes with the lumbering Chancery system.

In debt once more and increasingly desperate for both

immediate money and long-term security, in 1775 Stoney demanded his father buy back the Irish land George Stoney had been inveigled to give the couple before their marriage. In a demonically abusive letter, which may well have been written when drunk, Stoney thanked his father for his 'flattering epistle' which 'contained more Blasphemy under the cloak of enthusiastick Religion than I ever before observe in the compass of one sheet of paper' and which Stoney could only attribute to the 'Idea that Reason and you are for ever parted'.[36] Rambling incoherently in places, he speculated that his father might live ten more years then added: 'I had like to forget that I myself am mortal. Apropros, pray how old am I?' Branding his father 'an Object of Pity' and one of his uncles 'the Lordling', he urged that the desired purchase be quickly concluded as he was never 'happy when in Debt'. Writing from Bath, he concluded with the ominous news that Hannah had been sent to Bristol – presumably on doctors' orders to try the Hotwell waters there – 'and is now there – I fear for ever.'

Stoney had been prematurely pessimistic, however, for a month later he was back in Newcastle sporting a brand new regimental coat sent up from one of the best tailors in London in time for the Durham Races.[37] He was in celebratory mood, for whether the waters of Bristol or Bath had taken effect, Hannah was pregnant again. Finally the prospect of handing down an English country estate to generations of little Stoneys – and in the meantime taking full control of those assets himself – seemed within his grasp. It was not to be. On 11 March 1776, giving birth at Cole Pike Hill, Hannah died. Anxiously awaiting the cry of a baby, his heir and passport to fortune, Stoney heard only silence – the baby had died alongside her. There were few mourners as Hannah was buried three days later in the graveyard of the little parish church where she had been baptised only twenty-eight years earlier. Her grieving mother, still surviving on a widow's pension, would follow her to the grave less than a year later. Two days after the burial, the *Newcastle Journal* published Stoney's notice announcing that his 'lady' had died 'in child bed'.[38] That much the newspaper's readers, perusing the columns in the city's taverns and coffee-houses, might believe. But they knew it was stretching credulity when he went on to claim that she was 'much lamented'. For the rumours which had already swirled around the town's narrow streets and market stalls, accusing Stoney of making Hannah's life a misery, now blamed him squarely for her death. Before long *The Stoniad* would even allege he should have been tried for her murder. 'Did she not die and leave thee UNARRAIGN'D?' the satirical verse accused before adding: 'Behold poor N*wt** stretch'd upon her Bier!'

It mattered little to her widower. He stayed in the north-east only long enough to prove Hannah's will, by which he lawfully received a lump sum of £5,000 and unlawfully claimed possession of Cole Pike Hill. Handsomely sporting a brand new suit of scarlet regimentals, his sword swinging by his side, 'Captain' Stoney – as he now described himself – was gaily heading south, on the lookout for a suitable second wife.

4
My Imprudencies
Newcastle, 1767

The honeymoon was over. After the lavish wedding ceremony in London in February, followed by two weeks of celebrations at her mother's home in Hertfordshire, Mary Eleanor set off north beside her new husband for the three-day journey to Gibside. The couple made their first public appearance in County Durham on 29 March at the Sunday service in the parish church of Whickham, where Mary's father had been buried seven years earlier. As they descended from their coach at the church gates, accompanied by a 'grand retinue' of relatives and local worthies, the pair were surrounded by villagers eager to catch a first glimpse of their new master and mistress. 'The people thronged from the adjacent places on the occasion, so that the church is not remembered to have been so crowded, by the oldest person living,' reported the *Newcastle Chronicle*.[1] After a busy round of socialising with the neighbourhood gentry over the following two months, Mary took a last look at the figure of Lady Liberty still presiding over her childhood home, before continuing north. Rumbling over the Tyne Bridge on 7 June, less than a month after the King's Own Regiment had marched across, Mary began the arduous two-hundred-mile journey to Glamis Castle to assume her new role as the Countess of Strathmore.

Nobody set out for Scotland without apprehension. Taking the same route northwards just a year later, the agricultural writer Arthur Young would warn: 'I would advise all travellers to consider this country as sea, and as soon think of driving into the ocean as venturing into such detestable roads.'[2] For Mary, the rigours of the road were the least of her troubles. She had been ill at least twice since her wedding – initially during the honeymoon festivities at St Paul's Walden Bury when several guests had suffered upsets that were blamed on her mother's wine, and a second time shortly after when she was thought – wrongly or temporarily – to be pregnant.[3] More frustratingly, she had already grown weary of the assorted members of the Strathmore clan who clamoured around the newly married couple wherever they went. Her husband's younger brother, Thomas, even now accompanied them north, while the brothers' mother, the dowager countess, was following in hot pursuit. But most worrying of all, she deeply regretted ever marrying Lord Strathmore.

Mary could hardly claim she had not been warned. Her mother had advised against the match – not least on account of the large and needy Strathmore family – while her governess, Elizabeth Planta, had similarly pressed her not to go ahead. During the protracted marriage negotiations, Mary had gradually realised that she and the earl, twelve years her senior, had little in common. She found, she would later say, 'our tempers, dispositions, and turns different'.[4] The earl's cool, reserved demeanour, which had at first seemed so alluring, had soon spread a chill over Mary's flirtatious, capricious ways, while his scholarly interest in literary works did not extend to encouraging his young fiancée's talents in the same direction. But although she had desperately wished to call off the engagement, her pride had prevented her either from voicing her doubts to her intended spouse or from confiding in her mother. Keeping her anxieties to herself, she had therefore gone ahead with vows from which she knew there was probably no escape. Since divorce was both unattainable and unconscionable for the vast majority of married couples in the eighteenth century, matrimony truly was for better or worse, till death do us part. In her own home, free to pursue her literary interests and her botanical studies, she could perhaps have convinced herself that the marriage might work. Certainly many couples brought together in arranged marriages later found mutual affection and even love. But now that she was leaving her familiar surroundings, her social calendar and leisure pursuits dictated by her husband, encircled by his tight-knit family, the prospects for a happy, harmonious partnership seemed remote. Finally she had to concede: 'I was imprudent in marrying Lord Strathmore, against my mother's advice.'[5] For although John Lyon had been forced to change his name to Bowes by a private bill through the House of Lords, in compliance with George Bowes's will, he had no intention of letting Bowes's daughter change him.[6]

Born and brought up in County Durham, educated by tutors at his mother's Durham estate before entering Cambridge, John Lyon had seen little of Scotland or his crumbling Scottish seat of Glamis for most of his youth. He probably even spoke with an English accent. Yet with his family's fortunes long entwined with the turbulent history of Scotland, his ancestors as bound to the Scottish throne as the Bowes forefathers had been to the English, there was little doubt that – in the words of his guardian and relative Lord Chesterfield – he had been 'born a Jacobite'.[7]

Descended from Celtic or Norman origins, the Lyon family had first gained prominence in Scotland in the fourteenth century when an earlier John Lyon was created Thane of Glamis by Robert II and soon after married the king's daughter Joanna.[8] The stronghold at Glamis, or Glammis as it was often called, in the marshy land north of Dundee, had originally been built as a royal hunting lodge. King Malcolm II had died there, after being fatally wounded in battle nearby in 1034; six years later his grandson Duncan had been slain by his cousin Macbeth, who seized the crown only to be killed himself some years later by Duncan's son Malcolm. Although Duncan's death most probably happened in combat rather than in cold blood, egged on by a majority of Scottish lords rather than committed in self-serving treachery, and took place at Elgin, nearly seventy miles from Glamis, the name of Macbeth would forever be associated with Glamis Castle through Shakespeare's flight of imagination. Indeed, so ingrained would the myth become that an eighteenth-century architect indicated 'The Room where King Duncan was murdered by McBeath' on his plans for the castle, while another room is still named 'Duncan's Hall' as the legendary site of the regicide.

If the tale of Macbeth was fanciful, there was every bit as much tragedy in the bloodshed that dogged the Lyon family in the ensuing centuries. Caught up in the factional struggles that split the Scottish nobility in the sixteenth century, the seventh Lord Glamis was sentenced as a small boy by James V to be executed as soon as he attained his majority, while his mother, Janet Douglas, was burnt at the stake on trumped-up charges of witchcraft. Finally released five years later, the young lord reclaimed his forfeited castle, where his son, the eighth lord, later entertained Mary Queen of Scots. Judiciously switching allegiances, the ninth Lord Glamis accompanied James VI to England when he succeeded to the crown in 1603, and was created First Earl of Kinghorne for his troubles. The family's influence and affluence were reflected at the time in the extensive rebuilding of Glamis with its imposing fairy-tale towers and tapering turrets. In another deft transfer of loyalty, the third earl – who formally took the title of the Earl of Strathmore and Kinghorne by royal charter in 1677 – belatedly pledged allegiance to William of Orange.

With the family's political clout firmly on the wane as the eighteenth century dawned, its support for the doomed Stuart cause would continue – along with the bloodshed. The fourth earl, John Lyon's grandfather, managed to father the next four holders of the title, who followed him in swift succession. John Lyon's uncles, the fifth, sixth and seventh earls respectively, all died young – before he was even born – and the first two in particularly gory circumstances. Uncle John, the fifth earl, was killed supporting the first Jacobite rebellion at the Battle of Sheriffmuir in 1715, while Uncle Charles, the sixth earl, died an innocent bystander in a street brawl at the age of twenty-eight. Uncle James, the seventh earl, likewise died young, so that Thomas Lyon, actually the sixth son, unexpectedly found himself installed as the eighth earl in 1735. Shrewdly marrying a County Durham heiress, Jean Nicholson, to shore up the family's ever-depleted funds, the eighth earl spent much of his married life quietly avoiding trouble on his wife's estate, leaving Glamis to descend once more into neglect. It was at Hetton-le-Hole, the Nicholson family seat north-east of Durham and just eleven miles south of Gibside, therefore, that their first son, John Lyon, was 'born a Jacobite' on 17 July 1737.

Eager to avoid another of the violent ends which his forefathers had met, the eighth earl established his young family at Hetton-le-Hole, with rare forays to Glamis, and fraternised chiefly with the coal-owning gentry of the north-east, including George Bowes. When Newcastle defended its medieval walls against the second Jacobite uprising in 1745, the eighth earl kept his head down and his family out of harm's way in their County Durham home. As the local supporters of the rebel army were rounded up and hanged the following winter, his fiercely capable wife spent Christmas in Bath where she sent for nine-year-old John, the little Lord Glamis, to join her. And when the earl died in January 1753, before John had reached his sixteenth birthday, the formidable dowager countess was determined to keep her eldest son firmly within her orbit and her influence.

Although she now had to compete for dominance against fourteen other guardians or 'curators' named by the late earl – including the Earls of Chesterfield, Panmure and Aboyne – the dowager countess was a fair match. Travelling to Glamis with her son in tow to discuss the young earl's future education in 1754, she listened politely as 'all the Curators declared in the strongest terms, that it was their opinion, that my Lord should go to an university in Scotland'.[9] Apart from the desire to keep the ninth earl close to his Scottish seat – and, of course, to his Scottish guardians – the curators voiced their concerns at the steep costs an English university would impose on the family's limited resources. Indeed, not only were tuition fees higher at Oxford or Cambridge, the curators persisted, but since the earl was likely to mix there with English aristocrats possessing considerably larger riches 'he might thereby acquire a habit of living at an expense which his fortune was not able to bear'. But Lady Strathmore plainly did not wish to send her son out of her dominion, no matter that the Scottish universities far outperformed their English counterparts academically. Squared up against the united ranks at Glamis, she insisted that as the young earl had expressed his preference for an English university –

which concurred happily with her own opinion – 'she could not think of not giving him his own choice'.

After borrowing an impressive stack of books from the castle library – in English, French, Latin and Greek – Lord Strathmore enrolled on 3 March 1755, at the relatively advanced age of seventeen, at Pembroke College, Cambridge.[10] His brothers James, a year his junior, and Thomas, four years younger, would follow. But if the dowager countess seriously believed that she could keep a close check on her son's activities and expenditure once he left her side, she was sadly mistaken. For no sooner had the earl escaped his mother's iron rule than he began to flex his muscles, quickly acquiring the extravagant English tastes his guardians had feared.

With Pembroke having languished moribund for years, unable to attract students or funds and riven by discord, the fellows eagerly looked forward to the arrival of the 'beautiful Lord Strathmore' and his admission fees. Entered as a 'nobleman', these were almost double the usual rates. 'Pray is the Thane of Glamis come?' enquired William Mason, the former don, of his friend the poet Thomas Gray, at the beginning of March. Gray, who was on the point of moving from Peterhouse to Pembroke, having earned acclaim for works such as his 'Elegy Written in a Country Churchyard', announced the earl's arrival with a flourish a few days later. Writing to his close friend, and former Pembroke fellow, Thomas Wharton, he declared: 'Ld S: is come, & makes a tall genteel figure in our eyes. His Tutors & He appear to like one another mighty well.'[11]

Indeed, the earl and his tutors got along famously – maybe even a little too well. Lord Strathmore forged strong bonds with his personal tutors Henry Tuthill and the Reverend James Brown, later Master of Pembroke, as well as with the affable Gray. His cosy college connections almost embroiled the earl in scandal, however. In early 1757, college authorities abruptly dismissed Tuthill and stripped him of his fellowship amid sensational but mysterious charges of misconduct. Originally a friend of Gray's from Eton, and possibly Gray's lover at some point, Tuthill is thought to have been sacked over allegations of homosexuality, perhaps with Gray, but conceivably with Lord Strathmore or his brother James, who had been admitted to Pembroke the previous year.[12] The college register for February records enigmatically that: 'Since Mr Tuthill's absence fame has laid him under violent suspicion of having been guilty of great enormities, to clear himself of which he has not made his appearance and there is good reason to believe he never will.' Letters between Gray and his friends at the time are thought to have been destroyed or censored to hush up details of the incident. Lord Strathmore's bills include fees to Tuthill for private tuition until December 1756 but the earl and his brother James left Pembroke at the beginning of January – about the time Tuthill made himself absent – and only returned on 10 February. Gray expressed obvious relief at their return, which had plainly been in doubt, writing to Wharton: 'Ld S: & his brother are come back, & in some measure rid me of my apprehensions for the College.'[13] Whatever happened that January in Cambridge was taken to a watery grave: Tuthill drowned himself shortly after.

No whiff of the scandal appeared to reach Durham, however, where the dowager countess continued to worry about her three sons' hefty college expenses as well as her eldest son's health, prone as he was to recurrent chest complaints. While Lord Strathmore dismissed her concerns with characteristic disdain, it was Gray who overcame the countess's objections and persuaded her to allow the earl to visit

Europe as part of a diplomatic mission to Portugal with Thomas Pitt, a fellow Cambridge student and nephew of the former prime minister, William Pitt the Elder. Relating news of the young pair's plans to his friend Wharton in early 1760, Gray urged that the details should remain secret 'for fear my Lady should be frighted at so much Sea'.[14]

A grand tour of Europe was an obligatory requirement in the curriculum vitae of all self-respecting aristocrats and gentlemen in the eighteenth century. Embarking by sea at the height of the Seven Years War may not have seemed the most sensible plan, especially to an anxious mother, but Lord Strathmore assured her that the Mediterranean climate would prove 'a sovereign Remedy' for 'any lurking Complaint in my Breast from Colds'. Before leaving he also wrote to George Bowes, expressing concern for Bowes's declining health and sending respects to ten-year-old 'Miss Bowes'.[15] Having peremptorily discharged his guardians immediately he had come of age in 1758, the 22-year-old earl was now firmly in charge of his own finances. Making up for lost time under his mother's parsimonious regime, over the next three years he would leave a trail of bills across southern Europe, drawn on the Scottish peer Lord Gray's account with Coutts in London, in a frantic spending spree of epic proportions. Faithfully recording their impressions in a travel journal, 'Observations in a Tour to Portugal & Spain 1760', the two friends meandered across the Iberian Peninsula denigrating the food, transport, fashions and women in the manner of typical British tourists.[16]

Buffeted across the Bay of Biscay, the pair arrived in Lisbon in March. First impressions set the tenor for the expedition. Very few of the Portuguese women had 'any pretensions to Beauty' the earl wrote to younger brother Tom, now nineteen and at Cambridge, so that 'you may assure my Country women I shall bring home my Heart safe & sound'.[17] Embarking on a sightseeing tour by mule-drawn cart, the travellers were disappointed in the food – 'garlic, saffron & bad oil'; the transport – 'a miserable calash'; the roads – 'very poor and barren'; and the accommodation – 'full of fleas and vermin'; although the architecture passed muster. Spain offered little reprieve. Only Barcelona won grudging approval and then chiefly for its bullfighting, which drew the praise: 'The spectacle is certainly one of the finest in the world.'

Things looked up considerably once they had arrived in Italy, however. By far the most fashionable destination of any grand tourist, Italy – actually an assortment of kingdoms, duchies and republics – played host to travellers including James Boswell, Adam Smith and Robert Adam who came to sample the opera, art and architecture. Having parted company with Pitt in Spain, where Lord Strathmore had fallen ill, the paperchase of bills reveals the earl to have arrived at Genoa by October 1760.[18] Evidently the warm winter – as well as the uplifting art and architecture – provided a boost to the earl's health and vigour. Touring the cities on the customary itinerary he reported that the women of Milan were 'greatly inferior' to those in Turin, although what the former lacked in beauty they 'make up in Good Will towards Men'.[19] But it was Parma, where he arrived in March 1761, that held the greatest fascination, for there he embarked on a passionate affair with the Countess Sanvitale, 25-year-old Costanza Scotti, which would detain him in Italy long beyond his planned return. When the earl briefly escaped to Florence in August, Horace Mann, who looked after British interests in the city, reported that Lord Strathmore had 'broken the chain that held him so long at Parma'.[20] It was a durable chain, however. For although the earl spent much of the winter in Rome, he was back in the arms of the contessa the following year. His portrait, painted in Rome by the English artist Nathaniel Dance in February 1762, shows a self-assured, elegantly handsome young man with delicate long fingers, a knowing look and a hint of a smile. Although the earl had obtained a passport to travel through France by April, Mann doubted that he would be leaving Parma any time soon. He was right. After escorting the contessa to Florence and Lucca, it would be another year before the earl finally severed the chains that bound him. Mann wrote to his friend Horace Walpole, who was impatiently awaiting letters entrusted to Lord Strathmore a year previously, in May 1763 with the arch comment: 'I have often told you that your letters were in the hands of Lord Strathmore, and he in the hands of the Countess San Vital.' Finally, by the end of June, the earl returned to England.

Aristocratic and attractive, cultured and bronzed, at nearly twenty-six the earl was immediately counted among the eligible bachelors on the vibrant London scene. Although Horace Walpole took an instant dislike to the young man who had detained his mail, branding him insipid and rustic – 'too doucereux and Celadonian' – Lord Strathmore proved popular enough among the *bon ton* frequenting the clubs and assemblies of the West End.[21] 'A sincere friend, a hearty Scotchman, and a good bottle companion, were parts of his character,' declared Jessé Foot, even if the earl's pursuits 'were not those of science'.[22] Continuing the hedonistic lifestyle he had tasted on the continent, the earl's costly hobbies included horse-racing, cock-fighting and collecting fine wines – large quantities of which had been shipped back from France and Portugal during his absence – as well as reckless gambling. The club, Almack's, which he co-founded as a meeting point for fellow travellers to Italy, became notorious for its eccentric dress code and high betting stakes.

With his debts mounting and Glamis falling into disrepair, the earl was belatedly forced to face up to his family responsibilities when news arrived from India that his brother James had been murdered in a massacre at Patna in October 1763. Having joined the East India Company as an officer in 1760, James was among sixty or so prisoners who were slaughtered on the orders of the Nawab Mir Kasim in retaliation for defeats at the hands of the British. The loss of James in such brutal circumstances brought the earl closer to Thomas, who had just left Cambridge, aged twenty-two, while understandably heightening the anxiety of their mother. The brothers developed an intense, protective relationship in which neither could do any wrong. In one letter, the earl confessed that his worries over Thomas's health and prospects 'render me little capable of knowing what I write'.[23] Quite opposite in character, the financially astute Thomas indulged his elder brother's flamboyant lifestyle, while the earl defended his younger brother's stern, stiff demeanour. Finally appraising his draughty castle and its marshy estate in 1763, Lord Strathmore drew up elaborate plans for improvements and renovations. All he needed now was the money to fund them.

Just as Irish fortune hunters sought a 'worthy little woman' to provide financial security, so English and Scottish aristocrats would cast about for a wealthy heiress to help finance their expensive estates and further the bloodline. The only difference was that the latter pursuit was deemed entirely respectable. John Lyon did not have to look far before alighting on the obvious candidate, although it is possible that his mother, the shrewd dowager countess, helped direct his gaze. Since the earl had last seen Mary Eleanor, daughter of his old friend George Bowes, she had been transformed from a precocious ten-year-old, reciting poetry at evening soirées, into an accomplished, vivacious and witty sixteen-year-old. Although she had not grown much taller, reaching only five feet two inches, she had certainly grown more curvaceous. With her abundant brown hair and buxom figure she was considered charmingly pretty by some – according to Foot she possessed a 'very pleasing embonpoint' – even if the earl's erstwhile guardian, Lord Chesterfield, thought her 'the greatest heiress, perhaps, in Europe, and ugly in proportion'.[24] Although she plainly displayed a lively streak of independence, the earl seemed sure that she was young and malleable enough to be tamed, while he also hoped to cure her of her naive literary and scientific ambitions. He lost no time in conveying his interest through a mutual family friend.

By late 1765, the engagement had been agreed. The following summer Lord Strathmore was sufficiently confident of the expected boost to his income to place a colossal order for furniture and furnishings with upholsterers in Edinburgh in a bid to render Glamis habitable again. The eventual bill, for four-poster beds, flock wallpaper, Wilton carpets, mahogany furniture, vast quantities of fabric for curtains and assorted materials for bedding – including feathers weighing thirty-nine stones – would amount to more than £1,000.[25] But there was no longer any concern about payment, since on 24 February 1767, when he placed the ring on Mary Eleanor's finger, Lord Strathmore took possession of one of the largest fortunes in Europe.

If impressionable young Mary was inspired by romantic notions of beauty and a vision, there is little doubt that her 29-year-old beau was spurred to marry by the age-old imperative of hard cash. Certainly Lord Chesterfield had no illusions when he related news of the impending wedding: 'The men marry for money, and I believe you guess what the women marry for.'[26] The marriage settlement guaranteed Mary an independent annual income of £500 up to the age of twenty-one and £1,000 thereafter for her 'sole and separate use and benefit'; if she were widowed it ensured a generous 'jointure' and there was provision for future children too.[27] But beyond this, all the property, land, collieries and other riches Mary had inherited from her father now belonged exclusively to her husband. Except where specified in a legal contract, married women in Georgian England were barred by law from owning land and property or enjoying a private source of income. Indeed, upon marriage a woman effectively lost her legal status entirely since in law her entity was merged with that of her spouse. William Blackstone, the pre-eminent eighteenth-century law writer, put it succinctly: 'By marriage, the husband and wife are one person in law: that is, the very being or legal existence of the woman is suspended during the marriage.'[28] It followed, therefore, that 'whatever personal property belonged to the wife, before marriage, is by marriage absolutely vested in the husband'. Even more pithily, in her unfinished novel *Maria*, Mary Wollstonecraft would lament: 'But a wife being as much a man's property as his horse, or his ass, she has nothing she can call her own.' Indeed, it was in response to this very principle that Dickens's corrupt beadle Mr Bumble infamously quipped: 'If the law supposes that . . . the law is an ass.' Thus stripped of her legal status, deprived of her fortune and disappointed in her spouse, the new Countess of Strathmore headed towards Glamis with understandable trepidation.

Travelling the same route just two years earlier with the earl, Thomas Gray had described the journey with characteristic exuberance. After two days travelling by coach to Edinburgh, Gray had crossed the Firth of Forth in a 'four-oar'd yawl without a sail' and confessed that he had been 'toss'd about rather more than I should wish to hazard again'.[29] Staying overnight at Perth, the party had been ferried next morning across the Tay to reach Glamis by dinner. Gray was enthralled with the scene, lyrically describing the broad Strathmore valley swathed with broom and heather, the extensive farm lands dotted with labourers' huts and the majestic castle 'rising proudly out of what seems a great & thick wood of tall trees with a cluster of hanging towers on the top'. Approaching the castle along its mile-long avenue, Gray admired the walled gardens planted by the third earl before entering the courtyard with its statues of the four Stuart kings of the United Kingdom. As enamoured of Glamis as he seemed to be of its thane, Gray enthused, 'the house from the height of it, the greatness of its mass, the many towers atop, & the spread of its wings, has really a very singular and striking appearance, like nothing I ever saw.' Although he spent six weeks at the castle, where the Scottish poet James Beattie came to meet him, Gray said nothing of the internal accommodation. Another guest, Thomas Lyttelton – the future 'wicked Lord Lyttelton' – took a rather less romantic view when he visited declaring that Glamis was 'a very old castle, but has not a tolerable apartment, and can never be altered for the better'.[30]

Rattling down the tree-lined drive as the forbidding hulk of the pink sandstone castle loomed before her, dwarfed by the effigies of the Jacobite kings as she dismounted in the courtyard, the differences between Mary and her Scottish husband were more apparent than ever. While the earl had gone to commendable lengths to furnish the castle, insulating floors, walls and windows with the best carpets, papers and fabrics, the rooms were still draughty, the paint peeling, the plaster crumbling and the kitchens ill-equipped. Rather like her vision of the beautiful earl, the fairy-tale castle proved cold and inhospitable at closer quarters. With the ghost of Janet Douglas said to haunt the corridors, the spectre of Lady Macbeth wringing her hands in the chambers, and the legend of a secret room known only to the presiding earl, Mary must have found her newly decorated bedroom an eerie refuge. Her in-laws – the over-protective dowager countess, humourless brother Thomas and elderly Aunt Mary who lived at Glamis – did little to make her feel at home. Happy to take advantage of her funds – Thomas had won an expensive election to become MP of Aberdeen Burghs in 1766 in anticipation of his brother's marital windfall – they were unfriendly and vindictive to her face. Mary described their behaviour as 'disagreeable'.[31]

The earl, meanwhile, provided little in the way of compensation. Much of his time was spent supervising the seemingly endless renovations to the castle and improvements to the surrounding land. That summer, the castle teemed with workmen all generating the inevitable mess, noise and upheaval. While carpenters fitted windows, erected library shelves and hung doors, masons were building new hearths and laying stone floors. As painters whitewashed walls and varnished woodwork, upholsterers laid carpets, pasted wallpaper and fitted curtains. So chaotic was the renovation programme that Thomas's room had to be painted a fourth time because the 'work folks spold it'.[32] Beyond the castle walls, the activity was just as intense as labourers built an icehouse, laid roads, dug ditches and drained the swampy grounds. It was only the start of the extensive improvements required, which would eventually include demolition of the west wing and draining of Loch Forfar. When not overseeing the workmen, dealing with estate business or enjoying his brother's company, the earl was distant and aloof with his wife. For all his concern with his grounds, he disparaged

Mary's passion for gardening; despite his scholarly bent for literature, he derided her writing ambitions. Nevertheless, amid the dust, rubble and grime, Mary performed her expected duty in the earl's new mahogany four-poster bed. By July, as the family prepared to return south of the border, she was pregnant.

Back at Gibside by August, as the King's Own regiment was enjoying Newcastle's summer revels, Mary could almost have seen the path of her marriage foretold in the scenes from Hogarth's *Marriage A-la-Mode* still hanging in the hall of her childhood home. Locked in a loveless marriage of convenience, just like Hogarth's ill-matched couple, she and the earl shared neither romantic commitment nor common interests to prevent them from sliding into acrimony and contempt. Just like Hogarth's Earl Squander, Lord Strathmore would run up ruinous debts through gambling and carousing; and while no evidence points to him being unfaithful, it is likely that he had syphilis too – perhaps contracted in Italy – since medical bills included copious doses of mercury, the traditional remedy.[33] Similarly, like Hogarth's countess, Mary would pursue a life of leisure, drifting into half-hearted dalliances and ultimately embarking on an affair. Like many couples marrying in hope, they had simply found themselves to be incompatible.

Preferring the expensive temptations of Durham and London to the simpler life in Scotland, the couple divided their time between Gibside and their London house at 40 Grosvenor Square, whose lease had been passed to Lord Strathmore by Mary's mother, with occasional excursions to Glamis. Frequently, brother Thomas tagged along; he had his own room at Gibside as well as at Glamis. There would always be three people in this marriage. With the earl incapable of managing his financial affairs, it was Thomas who took charge of the vital mining and farming businesses, approving pocket money for his brother and sister-in-law as he saw fit. Lord Strathmore's old college chums remained frequent visitors too. Gray came to stay at Gibside in August, informing his old friend William Mason, 'tomorrow I go *vizzing* to Gibside to see the new-married Countess, whom (bless my eyes!) I have seen here already'.[34] With him he took the Reverend Brown, who had officiated at the wedding and now accompanied the couple to Scotland when they returned in September, crossing the turbulent rivers in the early months of Mary's pregnancy. The visit was most probably timed to coincide with Lord Strathmore's election as one of Scotland's representative peers that October. They were back in Durham before long, since in February 1768 Lord Strathmore had settled sufficiently into his role as master of Gibside to continue George Bowes's passion for foxhunting. His hounds chased a fox which took refuge – sensibly enough – in a pit shaft within the Gibside grounds. He would continue to run the stud that George Bowes had established at Streatlam as well as pursuing his love of gambling on the horses.

When Mary went into labour towards the end of April, probably at Grosvenor Square, her mother was at her side. It was an agonising, long and, consequently, dangerous labour lasting almost twenty-four hours. Finally, on the evening of 21 April, a weary Mrs Bowes scrawled a note to staff at Streatlam Castle: 'I have the happiness to inform you that this Evening, at half an hour after six, my dear child was deliver'd of a Daughter, after a most painful, & tedious Labour. She & the child are as well as can be expected. I can say no more having been up all last night, & my spirits quite exhausted.'[35] The baby was named Maria Jane and baptised in St George's in Hanover Square, where her parents had married and Mary herself had been christened.

Pregnant again within three months, Mary sought diversion in a trip to Paris that winter with Lord Strathmore's sister, Lady Susan Lambton. Just a year after her daughter's birth, on 13 April 1769, she gave birth in London to her first son, heir to both his parents' estates, after a considerably easier delivery. Named John, after his father – his surname Bowes according to his late grandfather's will – the new Lord Glamis was pronounced 'a strong, healthy child' by his relieved grandmother, who informed staff at Streatlam that her daughter was 'Thank God, perfectly recover'd'.[36] According to the housekeeper at Grosvenor Square, relaying the news to Gibside, the little boy was 'a most delightful sweet Babe' who had 'made all our hearts over flow with joy'. Both the heir and his sister were inoculated for smallpox later that year when Lady Maria, who was also teething, 'had the worst of it'. She was happy enough the following spring, when Gray called on the family in London. 'I saw my Ld & Tom the other day at breakfast in good health,' he told Brown, '& Lady Maria did not beat me, but giggled a little.'[37]

Mary Eleanor would pride herself on the fact that all five of her children during her marriage to Lord Strathmore were his.[38] A second daughter, named Anna Maria, was born on 3 June 1770, followed by two more boys, George on 17 November 1771, and Thomas on 3 May 1773. The legitimacy of her children was no modest claim. It was not uncommon for aristocratic couples in Georgian times to condone infidelity rather than suffer the unspeakable scandal of a divorce, usually after a legitimate heir – and preferably one or two spares – had been produced. Some husbands, and many more wives, allowed their partners freedom to take lovers as long as any illegitimate children were delivered discreetly and kept out of sight. Lord and Lady Melbourne, who married in

1769, were a typical example. After their son was born a year after the marriage, Lord Melbourne took a well-known courtesan as his lover while his ambitious wife began affairs with several powerful figures, including the Prince of Wales.[39] At least three of her five children were believed to have been fathered by her lovers. Other husbands were less forgiving. While Georgiana, Duchess of Devonshire, welcomed her husband's illegitimate offspring into the nursery, when she became pregnant by her lover she was forced to give birth abroad and have her daughter adopted. Lady Sarah Bunbury was notable for bucking the trend. Childless by her husband after many years, she became pregnant by her lover and in 1769 eloped with him rather than pass the child off as the legitimate heir, prompting Princess Amelia, George III's aunt, to remark that the idea of not imposing an illegitimate son on a husband was 'quite new'.[40]

Yet despite Mary's unfashionable fidelity early in the marriage, the swift arrival of her young family failed to cement her relationship with the earl or to inspire maternal fulfilment. Of their five children, she took an inexplicable dislike to her three sons – especially the eldest – giving obvious preference to her daughters. Lord Strathmore would later condemn her for 'that most unnatural prejudice you have against your eldest innocent son' while accusing her of 'foolish partiality for your daughters'. Reasonably enough he would argue: 'All children should rank equally in a parent's mind, at least untill they have forfeited that regard which was due to them from their Birth, favour is commonly more hurtful to the child than the contrary, but either without reason, is an infallible mark of the badness of the Parents heart.'[41] Far from denying any bias, Mary would admit that she harboured an 'unnatural dislike to my eldest son, for faults which, at most, he could only be the innocent cause and not the author of'.[42] Enemies would later suggest she preferred her pet cats and dogs – on which she lavished attention – to her children and claim she had described her eldest son as 'that odious & detested little Lord'.

In fact, in line with typical parenting practices among the landed classes in eighteenth-century Britain, Mary probably spent more time and enjoyed a more physical relationship with her pets than with her children, especially her sons. From birth, her children would have been nursed, petted, dressed and groomed by all manner of different hands except those of their parents. Like Mary herself, her babies were undoubtedly handed to a wet-nurse to be breastfed from the moment they were born. Although wet-nursing had been criticised by a few enlightened voices, it was still routine among upper- and middle-class families in the 1770s. A decade later, when Georgiana, Duchess of Devonshire, would defiantly breastfeed her daughter, the decision was still so remarkable that the *Rambler's Magazine* commented: 'Her grace deserves commendation for this, but it is rather a reflection on the sex, that females in high life, should generally be such strangers to the duty of a mother, as to render one instance to the contrary so singular a phenomenon.'[43] Having lost the opportunity to bond with her babies during feeding, there would be little chance for Mary to grow close to them later on. As they grew up, the children would be cared for by nursemaids and a battalion of other servants – little Maria had her own footman by the age of three – and taught by governesses and private tutors. The children had their own nurseries at Gibside, Grosvenor Square and – after further renovations began in 1773 – at Glamis, where the wet-nurses and nursery maids slept alongside their charges. From the age of seven the boys would be sent to private boarding school and the girls would follow soon after. It was little wonder, therefore, that many parents felt remote from their children and that some actively disliked their offspring. Indeed, both George II and George III, along with Queen Charlotte, expressed extreme distaste for their eldest sons.

Yet despite such obstacles, many Georgian parents still enjoyed fond relationships with their children. Indeed Mary would later sincerely repent her aversion to her son John, describing it as the first of her 'crimes'.[44] And there may well have been other reasons for her difficulties. It is possible that, in favouring her daughters, Mary was attempting to compensate for their second-class status in Georgian society just as her own father had done. For all that Lord Strathmore had urged that children should 'rank equally' with their parents, there is no doubt that his sons – the natural heirs – were held in higher esteem than his daughters. When Georgiana gave birth to her first daughter, the *Morning Herald* reflected contemporary reactions by reporting that the 'happy occasion' was 'perhaps a little impaired by the sex of the infant'.[45] Celebrations to mark the birth of Lord Glamis, the heir, included extravagant revels at Glamis – when nineteen bottles of port, eight bottles of rum and copious other beverages were consumed and several 'Brocken Glasses' ensued – as well as a poem commissioned by Uncle Thomas.[46] Nothing comparable had marked the birth of the first-born Maria. To make matters worse, Mary was ill soon after her second or third pregnancy – later she could not remember which – with what she described as 'convulsions'. These attacks, which she would suffer all her life, may have been epileptic fits although – given the inexact science of contemporary medical diagnosis – they could equally have been any number of complaints. It is quite conceivable too that she suffered from postnatal depression. She was, after all, just twenty-four by the time she had had five children, having been pregnant almost continually since she was eighteen.

Spending little time with her infants, Mary threw herself into her twin passions of writing and botany, despite her husband's disparagement. Lord Strathmore would later criticise her 'extreme rage for litrary fame' in the hope of convincing her of the 'futility of the pursuit'.[47] Soon after her marriage, the scholarly earl forbade her from attending Elizabeth Montagu's blue-stocking gatherings, making her break with her friend in what Mary described as 'a very rude and abrupt manner'.[48] Although Mrs Montagu's company was plainly good enough for Samuel Johnson, Horace Walpole and David Garrick, the earl branded her 'a wild, light, silly woman, of bad character' who was 'not fit' for his wife's acquaintance. 'Sadly against my inclination,' she said, 'I was forced to comply, and give her up, with many others.'

Compelled to abandon her literary mentor, Mary refused to abandon her literary ambitions and in 1771, while pregnant with George, she put the finishing touches to a five-act poetical drama entitled *The Siege of Jerusalem*.[49] Having been started in 1769, only two years after her wedding, its subject was unlikely to have proved popular with her husband. A tragedy in blank verse, it laments its heroine's unrequited love and arranged marriage. The drama is set at the time of the actual siege of Jerusalem in 1187 when the Muslim warrior Saladin captured the city and triggered the third Crusade. Mary's poem tells the fictional story of a Muslim princess, Erminia, who is betrothed to Saladin but loves the Crusader Tancred, who in turn is in love with an Amazon-like warrior princess called Clorinda. Disguised as a soldier in armour Clorinda is killed by Tancred, who then dies in a duel with Erminia's brother, Argantes, whereupon Erminia converts to Christianity and consigns herself to a nunnery. At one point bemoaning her noble birth and the 'detested nuptials' set to go ahead, the heroine longs for a simple pastoral life where true love is allowed free rein.

Would we have been some neighbouring shepherd's babes,
Together bred in equal humble state:-
We then had frequent met at rural sports,
In sweeter converse oft beguil'd the day,
'Till love insensibly had crept into our hearts,
And our glad parents had with rustic joy
Join'd willing hands and heard our nuptial vows.

Although not a literary masterpiece, the narrative is moving and the poetry accomplished. It certainly drew enthusiasm from friends who later persuaded her to publish it privately. Hearing that Mary had completed the work in May 1771, her former governess Elizabeth Planta, now living with Mrs Bowes in Hertfordshire, wrote to congratulate her. The following month, having read the drama, she wrote to praise her efforts and suggest a few amendments, declaring the first speech by Saladin 'very fine' but the words of Argantes to his sister 'too warm for a brother'. Locked in her own loveless marriage, Mary would continue to write poetry – in tragic, comic and satirical veins – throughout her life, although no more would be published.

If Lord Strathmore took no interest in his wife's literary talents, Elizabeth Planta and her clever family continued to encourage Mary's intellectual pursuits. Andreas Planta, Elizabeth's father, still corresponded with his former pupil in French and Italian. Having been elected to the Royal Society in 1770, he wrote the following year asking Mary to use her influence to help further his prospects at the British Museum, where he had been assistant librarian since 1758. Elizabeth, who also wrote to Mary in Italian and French – not least to conceal their gossip from Mrs Bowes's prying eyes – was approached in 1771 to become English teacher to the royal princesses. Well aware that her financial interests were better served by remaining with Mary, for whom she hoped to become the children's governess, Elizabeth diplomatically declined. The royal family had to settle for her sister Frederica, reportedly fluent in seven languages, who was recruited to teach the little princesses at a salary – scornfully dismissed by Elizabeth as 'mediocre' – of £100 a year (£13,000 today). Meanwhile Elizabeth and Mary exchanged news about Joseph Banks and Daniel Solander, who had just returned from their three-year expedition to the southern hemisphere with James Cook laden with new flora and fauna.

Inspired by the exquisite surroundings of Gibside where she had cultivated her own garden since the age of twelve, and encouraged by Elizabeth Planta, who tended her plants at St Paul's Walden Bury, Mary had become a serious student of botany. Naturally, Lord Strathmore had nothing but disdain for this enlightened spirit of enquiry. Yet since he was increasingly absorbed by his own consuming interests of drinking, gambling, cock-fighting and horse-racing, the earl appeared willing to tolerate his wife's botanical fascination.

Botany had developed a wide and enthusiastic following in Britain in the mid-1700s, especially among intelligent, educated and wealthy women. George III's mother, Princess Augusta, had established Kew Gardens in 1759 and his wife, Queen Charlotte, had continued her patronage. Several aristocratic women devoted their spare time and riches to amassing impressive stocks of plants – most notably the Duchess of Portland who established a collection to rival Kew at her seat of Bulstrode Park. The introduction into Britain in the 1760s of the binomial classification of species, created by the

Swedish naturalist Carl Linnaeus, helped popularise botanical studies. Consequently, increasing numbers of women collected and studied, cultivated and painted domestic and exotic flora – despite concerns in some quarters over the sexual connotations of the Linnaean system based, as it was, on the male and female reproductive organs. Charles Alston, professor of medicine and botany in Edinburgh, for example, thought Linnaean classifications 'too smutty for *British* ears' while even towards the end of the century the Cornish poet, Richard Polwhele, would voice alarm at the prospect of 'girls and boys botanizing together'. But although women were excluded from formal scientific study – banned from universities and all-male organisations such as the Royal Society – botany became regarded as a socially acceptable and largely harmless female pastime.

Like the Duchess of Portland, Mary plunged her surplus funds into buying rare seeds and plants to be cultivated at Gibside and St Paul's Walden Bury. In 1772, she commissioned workmen to begin building a magnificent greenhouse in the grounds of Gibside, with seven spectacular arched windows divided by stone columns, to provide a suitable habitat for the exotic specimens she was accumulating. Carefully positioned and designed to provide optimum light and warmth for the collection, the greenhouse may have been the work of James Paine who had completed so many of her father's architectural projects. As with her father's works, materials for the building were obtained from within or near the estate and the craftsmanship was provided by local labour. Work quarrying stone began in July 1772, slates were laid on the roof that winter and the great tall windows glazed the following summer. In 1774, eight ornamental urns were carved to top the façade and at the end of the year seven tubs for orange trees were placed in front of each window. Two lobbies at either end kept draughts out, a furnace beneath the floor provided a steady temperature and a wooden 'stage' elevated the plants to maximise the light. A hothouse, to nurture seeds and seedlings, was built nearby. Mary stocked her greenhouse with botanical rarities from specialist nurseries, like the world-famous Vineyard Nursery run by James Lee in Hammersmith, and employed a gardener to tend her specimens. The greenhouse would provide her with some of her most fulfilling moments – as well as furnishing the setting for one of her infamous court-case scenes.

Unlike other female botanists, content to cultivate and catalogue their growing collections, Mary wanted to go further. As explorers and adventurers penetrated previously unknown parts of the globe, they brought back to Europe botanical discoveries to the delight of amateur naturalists. Banks and Solander had returned from Australasia in 1771 with more than a thousand new plant species. Calling briefly at Cape Town on the way home, Banks had found to his wonder and frustration a veritable botanical paradise waiting to be explored. The following year he persuaded George III to finance an expedition to the Cape expressly to harvest new plants for Kew. Francis Masson, a Scottish gardener at Kew, arrived in Cape Town in October 1772 and promptly began sending home a bounty of exotic flora, including the vibrant bird of paradise, named *Strelitzia regina* after Kew's royal patron, Queen Charlotte.

Mixing in predominantly male scientific circles, who were attracted to her London home by the abundance of her knowledge and her wealth, Mary aspired to become a scientific patron in her own right and perhaps even to have her own name ascribed to a new botanical marvel. Probably through her links to the British Museum, she became friendly with the affable and portly Solander, a favourite pupil of

Linnaeus, who had settled in London and was busy cataloguing the museum's natural history specimens. She was friendly too with James Lee, the Vineyard Nursery owner, who had first translated the Linnaean system into English in 1760. Once, admiring some of the 'scarce and valuable plants' at his nursery, Mary said, 'Mr Lee told me, if I would allow him the honour to salute a Countess, he would give me the most curious; which I did, and had the plant.'[50] Although now in his fifties, Lee could obviously still be persuaded to part with a rare flower in return for a kiss from an attractive and wealthy customer. And in 1774 or 1775, when he treated her for another of her unexplained fits, Mary came to know John Hunter, the maverick surgeon and anatomist who was busy accumulating one of the biggest natural history collections in the country.[51] Fraternising with these glittering stars of the Royal Society, all central figures in the Enlightenment, the seeds were sown for Mary to contemplate funding an ambitious expedition of her own.

There were other male admirers too, interested in more than a chaste peck on the cheek in a hothouse. For in 1772, five years after her wedding and not long after the birth of George, Mary met James Graham, the younger brother of David and Robert Graham, twelfth Laird of Fintry. The Grahams stemmed from an ancient Scottish family with a history as chequered as that of the Strathmores and owned a house and lands just fourteen miles south of Glamis.[52] Like Lord Strathmore, the twelfth Laird had lost his father when young – at the age of seven – and had had to assume responsibility for his large family, of two brothers and five sisters, early on and under straitened circumstances. Unlike the earl, Robert Graham had remained close to his Scottish roots, going to school in Edinburgh then enrolling at St Andrew's

University, where he had studied the classics and – it being St Andrew's – learned golf. He would later become a patron and friend of Robert Burns. Exactly the same age as Mary Eleanor, the laird had been appointed 'gamekeeper' or factor to Lord Strathmore's hunting grounds in 1771 and the two families had forged close ties. All three Graham brothers developed an infatuation for the lively, young countess who occasionally graced Glamis with a visit but it was the youngest, James, who inflamed an enduring passion in Mary. She would describe their relationship as the first of 'my imprudencies'.[53]

From the moment she saw James, visiting his mother in 1772, Mary was captivated by the youth – who was as many as seven years her junior – saying 'he was quite a boy, but a very extraordinary one, and I must confess, much too forward for his years'. Two more years passed before she saw him again, in which time the laird himself had pressed his attentions on Mary. All too easily flattered by male attention, Mary had flirted freely with Robert so that when she finally rebuffed his obvious intentions, he was so furious – according to Mary – that he immediately proposed to a cousin, Margaret Mylne. Whether Robert was quite as mortified as Mary suggested is open to conjecture; after marrying in 1773 he and Margaret went on to have sixteen children.

James, however, was a different matter. Having frequently begged his elder brother to take him to Glamis for a second glimpse of its mistress, he finally persuaded one of his sisters to let him escort her there in 1774, where he contrived to stay for a fortnight. It was probably late summer, when the family stayed through August and September, with Thomas Lyon – just married – in tow as usual. What began as childish horseplay and innocent friendship between Mary and James quickly developed into an intense and heady mutual desire.

While Lord Strathmore and his brother were occupied in planning the continuing renovations to the castle and its grounds, 25-year-old Mary wandered the rooms and gardens with 18-year-old James – and his sister – constantly at her side. One morning, with nothing better to do, the three walked round and round the perimeter of the Great Hall marking each turn with a pencil. When they stopped, James pocketed the pencil and pledged to guard it with his life. Whispering in the gloomy corridors, giggling in the lofty rooms, James and Mary exchanged deeper and deeper expressions of affection – despite their supposedly watchful chaperone. Looking back, Mary would admit that she gave James 'very improper encouragement' and won from him 'many improper declarations, not only without anger, but even with satisfaction'. By the end of the fortnight, when he pressed her for a response she admitted he had won her heart.

With her marriage increasingly rocky, Mary was a willing victim. Although she was still, she insisted, scrupulously faithful to her husband, relations with the earl and his family had soured significantly. Staying in Edinburgh for two weeks that August, along with Thomas and his new wife, Mary claimed that Thomas insulted her in public, although she failed to specify precisely how. Perhaps aware of Mary's flirtation, Thomas 'behaved in such a manner, as scandalized the whole town of Edinburgh; who, at that time, hated him as much as they liked and pitied me'.[54] Although she complained of his conduct to the earl, Lord Strathmore refused to concede any fault since 'it was an unfortunate and most prejudiced rule with him, that Mr Lyon could not err'. With antipathy between Mary and her brother-in-law an open secret, and her husband unsympathetic or indifferent, Mary fell back on the tenacious interest of her young admirer. Once Mary returned to London, the pair exchanged letters which were apparently so incriminating that Mary not only burnt them but drank the diluted ashes. Anxious to keep their love a secret – not only from the earl but also from the jealous laird – they proceeded by swapping coded messages in letters sent between Mary and James's obliging sister. In the goldfish bowl of aristocratic Georgian life – never allowed a private moment without servants watching every move – Mary confided her passion to Elizabeth Planta, now governess to the children, and a footman who conveyed the letters. When James enlisted as an ensign with the army, Mary met him one last time in London before he sailed for Minorca in early 1775. Although Mary was bereft at his departure, she found her lover suddenly 'much altered towards me' and so forced herself to 'treat him with the indifference I ought, though it almost broke my heart'. Although James, still only nineteen, had evidently decided to forget his boyish fantasies and direct his attentions elsewhere, Mary continued to beg his sister for news. For the next year she pined for him, despite receiving only two messages from the young soldier, until finally she wrote a fuming letter to his sister with the message that James could 'go hang himself'.

For all her apparent fury, and although the relationship never evolved beyond smuggled letters and fervent declarations, he would always remain the true love of Mary's life. She would later concede that had he persevered, James might have seduced her but insisted that 'violent as my passion was for him, I do still sincerely think it was pure'. Secret passions notwithstanding, she could not resist noting that the middle brother, David, who was 'still handsomer' than his brothers, was likewise 'a great admirer of mine' and that even the go-between sister professed such a 'violent' friendship that 'had she been a man . . . I should have called it love'.

By the summer of 1775, with her love for James Graham spurned, her eight-year marriage nothing but a façade and her husband showing signs of serious illness, Mary was growing emotionally vulnerable and increasingly reckless. Lord Strathmore had already suffered a repeat of the chest complaint of his youth – now undeniably tuberculosis – at the end of 1774 when he was so ill that Horace Walpole had prematurely reported his death.[55] After visiting Bath in the vain hope that the waters might cure his condition, the earl joined Mary and his young family at St Paul's Walden Bury in August 1775. While his mother-in-law confidently hoped that the wholesome country air would restore him 'to perfect health', there was little doubt that the illness was terminal. Certainly the earl was continuing to run up debts – for horses, fighting cocks, new coaches, building works and the inevitable shipments of wine from abroad – as if there was no tomorrow. Even as builders demolished the west wing of Glamis that summer, the earl's financial agent in London was attempting to keep his creditors at bay.[56] Sufficiently recovered to visit William Palgrave, a former university chum, at his rectory in Suffolk, the earl left Mary in London to follow her own pursuits. With time on her hands for her literary and botanic interests, Mary was attracting an ever larger circle of visitors to her Grosvenor Square home. While some were honest and straightforward fellow enthusiasts, keen to direct Mary's patronage to worthy ends, others had more self-interested reasons for their constant attention and flattery. In the latter group was George Gray, an unscrupulous entrepreneur who had returned from India with an enviable fortune, largely accrued through bribes.[57]

A friend of James Boswell and the playwright Samuel Foote, whose 1772 comedy *The Nabob* is thought to have been informed by their friendship, Gray shared Mary's literary zeal. Born in Calcutta in 1737, where his Scottish father worked as a surgeon for the East India Company, Gray had been sent at the age of seven to boarding school in Edinburgh where he had met Boswell. At seventeen, he had returned to India as a clerk for the rapidly expanding trading company, stationed in Bengal, while his father retired to Scotland, where he spent much of his time lamenting his son's neglect. Clever and well-read, Gray ingratiated himself with his fellow officers and the local nawabs or nabobs, the puppet rulers of the region, and prospered in the lax regime. 'I can now converse familiarly with a parcel of ragged squalid weavers,' he proudly informed a friend soon after arriving, 'who tho' they make clothes to be worn by the Kings of the earth, have scarce a rag to cover their own nakedness'.[58] Keen to exploit his chances further, he almost succeeded in marrying a wealthy widow before he was beaten to the altar by an army captain. Undeterred, Gray secured a seat on the company's Bengal Council in 1765 and soon after pocketed a 'gift' from the new nawab sufficient, he assured his father, to provide him with an 'independent fortune'. When Lord Clive arrived from England a few months later in a belated effort to clean up the mounting disorder and corruption, Gray resigned in apparent – or contrived – protest at Clive's autocratic manner. Gathering up his ill-gotten rupees, and leaving behind some mischievous verses about Clive, he departed briskly for London where he arrived in 1766.

At what point 'Nabob Gray' – as Boswell dubbed him – met Mary is unknown. It is possible that they became acquainted in the early 1770s through Gray's Scottish relatives – his mother was related to the Grahams of Fintry and his niece was the Margaret Mylne who married Robert Graham. Certainly he had become a feature of her life, and a regular visitor to Grosvenor Square, by 1775. Gray smuggled some verses declaring his ardour to Mary just before she left for Hertfordshire that summer and they exchanged letters until her return. Never a good judge of character, or indeed of her own true feelings, Mary encouraged Gray's attentions despite feeling 'nothing for Mr G, that exceeded friendship'.[59] When Lord Strathmore set off for Suffolk, Gray made his move, propositioning Mary in a letter delivered to Grosvenor Square one evening. Fortuitously, for Gray if not for Mary, the proposal arrived at the same time as a letter from James Graham's sister, bringing news of his interest in a woman in Minorca, and a brusque refusal from Thomas Lyon to send her a small sum of money which she had requested on the orders of the earl. Believing she was revenging herself on others – though she later conceded she only hurt herself – she began meeting Gray in secret using her footman, George Walker, as go-between.

Initially the pair had to be satisfied with snatched conversations at 'chance' meetings in Hyde Park and Kensington Gardens, with all the eyes of the promenading *bon ton* alert for any hint of scandal. But as they became more daring – and Gray more insistent – the couple met surreptitiously at her house when her faithful footman let Gray in by a back door. When the earl returned to London in November, Mary persuaded Gray to repair to Bath – out of harm's way – but agreed to meet him before he left early one frosty morning in St James's Park. Slipping on the ice in the freezing conditions, Mary returned home with her shoes and skirts soaked but being unable to change them immediately without causing suspicion she caught a fever. Indeed, most of the household, including the footman George Walker and Elizabeth Planta, succumbed to fever that December.[60] As the New Year began there were few celebrations in Grosvenor Square since the house had become a sick ward, with physicians and apothecaries arriving daily with their meddling advice and ineffectual potions. Mary's indeterminate fever had turned into the same complaint she had suffered after her wedding, which she described as 'an ague, in my face' – perhaps migraine – complaining that 'my head swelled so, yet without easing my pain that I was blind'. For Mary, the laudanum prescribed may at least have provided some relief. For Lord Strathmore, in the final stages of tuberculosis, there was no hope. At the end of January 1776, accompanied by his physician, the earl set sail for Lisbon in one last desperate effort to overcome his illness – and perhaps one last attempt to recall his carefree youth.

As Mary languished in her darkened chamber, Gray saw his chance. Scurrying back from Bath, he visited her daily, wrote her long, flattering letters and sat at her bedside every evening. Candidly, Mary told him that she had been 'so unhappy in matrimony' that she was determined never to marry again and that her heart belonged to another but that Gray had won her 'friendship and esteem' and if Lord Strathmore should die she promised to give herself fully to him. Seizing his opportunity, the moment Mary was recovered, he seduced her one evening in mid-February and from that point on they lived as lovers. She would later count this infidelity as her second 'crime'.

Lord Strathmore never reached Lisbon. On 7 March, within sight of the Portuguese coast, he died, aged thirty-eight, in the arms of his physician.[61] It would be another month before news of his death reached Mary in London. By that time she was pregnant with Gray's child.

5
A Black Inky Kind of Medicine

London, April 1776

Reading her late husband's last letter, dressed in her widow's mourning gown, Mary knew that the tell-tale signs of her latest 'imprudency' would soon be all too apparent. Lord Strathmore's savage words, written on his deathbed beneath the rocking deck, were coolly calculated to prompt remorse in all but the most unfeeling of widows. 'As this is not intended for your perusal till I am dead,' he began, 'I hope you will pay a little more attention to it than you ever did to any thing I said to you while alive.'[1] In the stern tone of a disappointed father rather than the emotional farewell of a husband and lover, the earl declared, 'I freely forgive you, all your liberties and follies (however fatal they have been to me) as being thoroughly persuaded they were not the produce of your own mind, but the suggestions of some vile interested monster.' Continuing in the same cold paternalistic manner, he requested Mary to lay aside her 'prejudices' against his family, convinced that these were 'entirely without foundation'. Urging her to treat their five children fairly, he warned her to avoid indulging in malicious gossip and – perhaps having suffered himself at the expense of her sharp wit – not to be 'tempted to say an ill natured thing for the sake of sporting a Bon Mot'. Even as he dismissed the 'futility' of her literary ambitions, the earl insisted that, 'no one ever studied with more attention to promote the Happiness of an other, than I have constantly done to promote yours'. Yet his concluding advice – to safeguard her fortune by vesting control of her estate in the hands of a trustworthy agent – was eminently sensible and well-meaning, if chiefly prompted by concern for the future welfare of his young heir rather than for his wife. The earl's parting words – 'a dead man can have no interest to mislead, a living man may' – would surely haunt his widow in years to come.

Finally released from a passionless marriage after nine years of discontent, Mary Eleanor shed few tears over the loss of Lord Strathmore. As soon as she received news of the earl's death on 6 April, Mary acted with due decorum, immediately ordering mourning suits for the servants in Grosvenor Square and at Glamis with the instruction that 'all possible respect should be paid to the memory of her deceas'd Lord', and exchanging her richly adorned gowns and elaborate hairstyles for sombre black dresses and plain accessories.[2] A portrait, which is thought to be of Mary, painted by an unknown artist at about this time, depicts her with an appropriately sorrowful expression and downcast eyes in a pale face under grey powdered hair, wearing the traditional black ruff and cap of the later stage of mourning.[3] The children likewise, Maria and Anna, aged seven and five, their brothers John, George and Thomas, aged six, four and two, would have been made to wear black clothes. Young John, who was now formally the tenth Earl of Strathmore, reached his seventh birthday just a week after hearing news of his father's death. Having been sent to boarding school in Neasden – then a small village a few miles north of the capital – shortly before his father had set sail, he had little cause for celebration. While the three youngest children were despatched to their grandmother's at St Paul's Walden Bury in the capable care of their governess, Elizabeth Planta, Maria, who turned eight a week after her brother's birthday, remained with her mother at Grosvenor Square, ostensibly to provide support in her bereavement. Yet while Mary outwardly adopted the sober demeanour and costume of grief, inwardly she was jubilant. Free at last from her husband's restrictive demands and her brother-in-law's penny-pinching controls, Mary was finally in command of the immense fortune her father had left her and – more importantly – in charge of her own life.

At a time when divorce was both rare and difficult, and separation spelled social exile, the death of a spouse was frequently the only means of escape from an unhappy marriage. Denied any legal status or ownership of property in marriage, in widowhood many women found a comfortable and rewarding existence. Most eighteenth-century marriage settlements for the wealthy and middle classes made provision for a guaranteed pension or 'jointure' – generally between a fifth and a quarter of the husband's wealth – should the wife survive her husband. Since widows were also legally entitled to own property, even working-class women could earn a decent living – and respect within the community – by taking over a late husband's business. Furthermore, for most women, under the supervision of a father from birth and a husband during marriage, becoming a widow provided a first taste of independence. The playwright John Gay underlined the attractions of widowhood in his comedy, *The Beggar's Opera*, first staged in 1728. 'The comfortable Estate of Widow-hood, is the only Hope that keeps up a Wife's Spirits,' exclaims the villain Peachum, adding: 'Where is the Woman who would scruple to be a Wife, if she had it in her Power to be a Widow, whenever she pleas'd?'[4] And while audiences guffawed at Gay's drama throughout the century, many women truly did enjoy the last laugh. Lady Mary Coke suffered two years of brutality and humiliation at the hands of her husband, Edward, Viscount Coke, before he died suddenly in 1753 leaving her, at twenty-six, a merry widow with a handsome jointure of £2,500 a year.

Widowed at twenty-seven, Mary Eleanor was even more comfortable and decidedly more merry. On her husband's death, she not only became entitled to the independent jointure stipulated in her marriage settlement but also regained her life interest in her father's estate, including Gibside, Streatlam and the coalmines, farms and other properties attached. Although the Bowes fortune remained in trust, supervised by named trustees who were charged with keeping it intact for her eldest son, during her lifetime at least the profits of the farms and mines now accrued to Mary. Precisely how much this fortune was worth is unclear, although one estimate put Mary's income after Lord Strathmore's death at up to £20,000 a year – easily one of the top twenty annual incomes in the country.[5] Certainly, she was one of the richest widows in Britain. And in the year that America would sign its declaration of independence, Mary could look up to the statue of Liberty her father had erected as a free woman for the first time in her life. Wealthy and attractive, intelligent and accomplished, she was finally able to pursue her literary and botanical interests without constraint, associate with her intellectual friends at will and spend time with her children. She lost no time in exerting this newfound independence.

Within days of receiving news of the earl's death, Mary dismissed all his former servants in Grosvenor Square and turned away friends of the Strathmore family when they called.[6] There was good sense in this seemingly vindictive move beyond a pent-up desire for liberation. Secretly entertaining her lover by night, she was anxious to conceal his visits – and the growing evidence of their liaison – from the prying eyes of the Strathmores and their allies. In coming months she would dispense with the Strathmore livery and send away the silver plate to have the initial 'S' replaced with a 'B'.[7] Having regained the Bowes fortune and retained the Bowes name, she plainly wanted to erase all trace of the Strathmores from her life. Cosseted by her eldest daughter, surrounded by her beloved cats and dogs, surreptitiously visited by her lover, Mary could not help exulting in the Lyon family's misfortunes. For the tables certainly had turned.

Ensconced at Streatlam Castle, which he knew he would soon have to vacate, Thomas Lyon viewed Mary's actions as open declarations of war. 'We need expect nothing from my Lady but all the opposition in her power & every thing that can distress us,' he warned James Menzies, the steward at Glamis, and added: 'She has thus soon declared herself as inveterate against every Person that was kind by my Brother.'[8] Devastated by his brother's death, Thomas frantically attempted to put the earl's papers in order and make the funeral arrangements. As the earl's body was conveyed slowly by sea from Lisbon to London, where it was loaded on to another ship headed for Dundee, Thomas sent instructions to Glamis for a sober and austere funeral. Urging strict limits on numbers and on alcohol he ordered 'for Gods sake take care that not a mortal is in liquor for at such a time I should detest the very thoughts of it'.

As the earl's body was interred in the family vault at Glamis, Thomas searched desperately for the will he assumed his brother must have made before embarking on what was almost certain to be his final voyage. When nothing was found in the earl's belongings in London, Thomas wrote to Glamis with mounting alarm, demanding: 'Do you know of no papers he had left, have you the key of his draw in the

Library or his glass bureau in his dressing room.' But no will surfaced at Glamis, Gibside or Grosvenor Square making Mary, as his widow, the lawful executor of the earl's estate. Relishing the confusion this would inevitably cause, Mary could not resist pointing out that 'the difficulties will be endless'. She had no intention of making them any easier. Only after several meetings with her lawyer, Joshua Peele, and under sustained pressure from Thomas Lyon, did Mary agree to renounce her role as executor in favour of Thomas.[9] In truth this was no sacrifice, since she was scarcely more adept at managing money than had been the late earl. Untangling his brother's financial affairs, Thomas had worse shocks in store.

For all the vast wealth generated by the Bowes coal and despite Thomas's parsimonious management of the proceeds, the earl had chalked up a colossal backlog of bills as well as numerous bonds for cash borrowed from friends, bankers and money-lenders. Sorting through the jumble of papers, Thomas discovered the debts totalled a staggering £145,000. Even by the standards of the debt-ridden eighteenth century, when aristocrats routinely lived on credit and fortunes were lost or won at the gambling tables in a single night, this was an exorbitant sum – equivalent to roughly £17m in today's terms. Hardened gamblers had shot themselves for significantly less. Added to this a further £50,000 had to be raised for the children's maintenance and education, according to a legal deed drawn up by the earl, meaning nearly £200,000 – roughly £24m – had to be found. As lawyers representing Mary and the Strathmores met to assess the damage, it was plain that drastic action was required.

Prevented from selling any of the Bowes properties or heirlooms, since these now belonged to Mary, Thomas was determined at least to save the castle which had been his family's home for four centuries. All renovation work at Glamis was abruptly halted, leaving the demolished west wing only half rebuilt, the gardens neglected and poor Aunt Mary, now frail and aged, alone in her apartment with only occasional visits from a cleaning woman. The fine furniture and plush furnishings bought with the Bowes fortune just nine years earlier, along with livestock, farm implements and the contents of the late earl's wine cellar, were all put up for sale. As local gentry flocked to the auction that June, Robert Graham, the Laird of Fintry who had been rejected by the Lady of Glamis, drew some small pleasure in buying the four-poster beds which had once belonged to her lord. Determined to offer the Strathmores no respite, Mary insisted that her personal breakfast table and basin stand be removed from the sale. She could do nothing, however, to prevent Thomas from selling livestock, racehorses, furniture, wine and even greenhouse plants, bought for Gibside since her marriage and therefore legally the late earl's estate, in another sale later that year. Yet even while she gloried in Thomas Lyon's downfall, Mary could not remove the Strathmores from her life as easily as she had changed the initials on her silver. Resolved to safeguard the Strathmore legacy for future generations, Thomas devoted his energies to protecting the rights of his young nephew – at the expense of the boy's mother if necessary. For if Mary was now in command of her own life and income, she was not in charge of her children.

In keeping with eighteenth-century legal attitudes towards women, mothers enjoyed no right of custody over their offspring. When parents separated the courts invariably awarded custody of the children – including breastfeeding infants – to their fathers. The Duchess of Grafton, for example, had to say goodbye to her three children on her divorce from the Duke in 1769 and would not be permitted to see them again until she was on her deathbed thirty years later.[10] In a farewell letter to her eight-year-old daughter, enclosing a lock of hair, she described herself as your 'unhappy mother who dotes on you'. Lady Elizabeth Foster, who married in the year Mary was widowed, would likewise have to give up her sons, aged four and eighteen months, on separation a few years later and would not see them again for fourteen years. Indeed, one resourceful mother, eloping with her lover in 1796, would go so far as to fake the death and funeral of her youngest daughter in a desperate attempt to keep her; after three years she gave the child up and did not see her again until the girl was an adult. Only when specified by prior legal contracts would mothers be granted guardianship – and sometimes not even then. Fortunately for Mary, Lord Strathmore had signed a deed in 1774 naming Mary as one of four guardians to his children on his death.[11] Unfortunately for Mary, the other three guardians were Thomas Lyon and his Scottish allies, the agent James Menzies and the lawyer David Erskine. Acting in unison, these three would always be able to outvote Mary on any issue. For the moment, Thomas was willing to leave the children in the care of their mother; maintaining a close scrutiny on her conduct he knew he wielded a potentially powerful weapon.

Blithely oblivious to the future threats Mary entrusted the care of her three youngest children and Maria to the talented Miss Planta; they spent most of their time at their grandmother's Hertfordshire home, where Mary sometimes visited. Maria, who had changed from the cheerful toddler who giggled with Thomas Gray into a mature and sensible child with a keen sense of decorum, wrote from there to her great aunt Mary at Glamis in May. Plainly identifying with her aunt's isolation in the empty castle, she confessed herself 'quite uneasy lest you should have forgotten that there are two such little girls in the world as my Sister, and me, who love you dearly'.[12] But if Maria, with her three siblings, her grandmother and her governess for company, felt abandoned this was nothing to the experience of her brother John, now boarding at the little school run by the puritanical Richard Raikes in Neasden. According to Maria, citing a letter from John to Miss Planta, he was 'in perfect health, and says Mr Raikes commends him'. A thoughtful and diligent boy, who studied hard at his French, writing and music, he would remember the importance of strong family bonds.

Keeping out of the public eye, as mourning etiquette conveniently dictated, his mother had more pressing problems on her mind. Mary thought she had been scrupulously careful to avoid becoming pregnant. She had begun having a sexual relationship with George Gray in mid-February, just before Lord Strathmore had left for Portugal, having succumbed to the 38-year-old Scot's advances 'one unfortunate evening' when she was 'off my guard'.[13] Once the earl had left the country, she had welcomed her lover with increasing regularity to her bedchamber in Grosvenor Square. Let in discreetly late at night by her faithful footman George Walker, Gray crept up one of the back staircases unseen by the other servants and usually stayed until four or five the next morning, stealing out before the maids awoke. Naturally anxious to avoid a mishap, Mary asserted that, 'All the time of my connection with Mr Gray, precautions were taken'. But since eighteenth-century contraception was rudimentary at best, this was far from foolproof.

Although condoms had been invented a century earlier, apocryphally attributed to a physician to Charles II called Dr Condom, these were normally used only as prophylactics against venereal disease rather than as contraceptives. The fact that they were fashioned from sheep's or pig's gut and secured with a silk ribbon, and were designed to be washed and reused, did not recommend them for regular encounters. James Boswell, an inveterate brothel visitor, described donning 'armour' in a rare effort to prevent another bout of gonorrhoea when engaging with a seventeen-year-old prostitute in 1763. He found the experience, he confided in his diary, 'a dull satisfaction'.[14] Although condoms were on open sale in at least one London shop in 1776, they were advertised as 'implements of safety which secure the health of my customers'. In common with most couples of the period endeavouring to avoid an unwanted pregnancy rather than an unwanted rash, therefore, Mary and Gray probably adopted the withdrawal method. Certainly her remark that 'an instant's neglect always destroyed' their precautions makes this most likely. It was scarcely surprising, then, that in less than two months Mary had found herself pregnant.

Acutely aware that Thomas Lyon, and his ever-watchful sisters, would welcome any opportunity to discredit her, Mary knew that she needed to avoid all hint of a scandal. For any woman giving birth to a child out of wedlock in Georgian Britain the prospects were bleak; the large numbers of children abandoned on the streets and surrendered to the Foundling Hospital were tragic evidence of this. For a titled, recently widowed heiress to give birth to an illegitimate child in a society obsessed with celebrity gossip would be disastrous. Not only would the newspapers report each detail with glee, she would also be shunned by polite society and almost certainly deprived of her children.

Her options were therefore limited. She could give birth in secret and arrange for the child to be quietly adopted in the manner of several women who found themselves in similar straits. Yet such clandestine births were highly risky and for Mary to disappear for any length of time soon after her husband's death would surely have raised the Strathmores' suspicions. Alternatively, she could marry Gray and – given general eighteenth-century ignorance about pregnancy – pretend the ensuing child was born prematurely. Yet there were several overriding objections to the marriage. To wed so soon after becoming widowed would not only offend etiquette but would also inevitably provoke unseemly gossip about her suitor. At the same time Mary knew that Thomas Lyon would do his utmost to protect the Bowes fortune – and its young heir – from the grasping hands of any prospective husband, especially one with such a colourful reputation for getting rich quick. Moreover, Mary had already warned Gray that her miserable experience of matrimony had convinced her 'never to engage myself indissolubly' again. The only course left was to attempt an abortion.

There is no doubt that women have known and used a variety of methods to end unwanted pregnancies since earliest times, often with the sanction of Church and State. In early China and Egypt, ancient Greece and Rome, various herbs and plants deemed capable of bringing about a miscarriage were well-known and widely used. Aristotle actually recommended abortion for families that had reached an optimum size; Roman law allowed for abortion as long as it was authorised by the woman's husband. Although rarely written down, folklore knowledge of natural abortifacients was discreetly passed by women from generation to generation. Plants such as rue and savin, which were known for their ability to procure abortions, were often grown by midwives and herbalists, while the fungus ergot was popularly known as 'Kindesmord' – child's death – in Germany. Male medical practitioners, whose faith in the ancient doctrine of balancing bodily 'humours' dictated that it was harmful for women to miss menstruation, often prescribed potions to the same purpose and quite probably with the same ingredients. Although early Christians condemned attempts to end pregnancy, English common law permitted the abortion of a foetus as long as it had not been felt to move – up to about four months – and this may well have been interpreted loosely by the female midwives charged with the test. Even when later abortions were suspected, these were exceedingly difficult to distinguish from a natural miscarriage or stillborn delivery and prosecutions were few. Only in 1803 would Parliament pass a law that specifically outlawed abortion and even then only after the baby's movements could be felt.

Throughout the eighteenth century, therefore, when contraception was little used and unplanned pregnancies could spell disaster, methods of abortion were widely available. One woman seeking a divorce from her adulterous husband in 1774, for example, described to the ecclesiastical courts how he had made her sister pregnant then persuaded her to take some pills which he had obtained from a midwife in Fleet Street.[15] Precisely because such practices were legally constrained and took place mostly within women's circles, very few personal accounts have survived. Lady Caroline Fox, believing herself pregnant for the third time in three years in the 1750s, informed her husband, 'I took a great deal of physic yesterday in hopes to send it away' and later added jubilantly: 'I am not breeding (is that not clever!)'[16] Mary Eleanor Bowes's candid description of attempting an abortion – not just once but four times – is therefore quite unique, although her frank words were never intended for public consumption.

Immediately Mary discovered she was pregnant she asked Gray 'to bring me a quack medicine he had heard of for miscarriage'. Gray duly obtained the potion which Mary described as a 'black inky kind of medicine' that looked and tasted as if it contained copper. Although Gray was reluctant to let Mary drink the substance, rightly fearing that it may have been poisonous, she insisted on knocking it back since she was 'so frightened and unhappy' at the prospect of being pregnant. The potion worked, or at least a miscarriage ensued; in early pregnancy it was, of course, difficult to discern which. Yet despite her scare, and the potentially devastating consequences, Mary soon found herself pregnant again – not once but three more times in rapid succession during the summer and autumn of 1776. The second time, probably in May or June, the inky medicine once more did its work but the third time, possibly in July or August, it failed. In desperation, Mary downed an emetic to make her vomit, along with a large glass of brandy and liberal quantities of pepper, which seemingly induced her third abortion or miscarriage. She would number these three abortions among her 'crimes' in the 'Confessions' which she was later forced to write. Her most damning attempt was still to come.

The fact that Mary fell pregnant with such regularity was little wonder given that Gray had inveigled himself sufficiently to visit her bedchamber every other night. The purpose of this pattern, Mary revealed, was 'that by the intervention of one night, we might meet the next with more pleasure, and have the less chance of being tired of each other'.[17] Moreover, since Gray commonly stayed until nearly dawn and their 'conversation' was lasting, she found that 'a night of sleep was absolutely necessary'. Whenever Mary visited St Paul's Walden Bury to see the children and her mother – and presumably to enjoy a well-earned rest – she relayed messages via George Walker, or occasionally her housekeeper, arranging future rendezvous.

Having endured her late husband's inattention for nine

years, there can be little doubt that George Gray's interest and apparent devotion were both flattering and welcome. Whether Gray tendered any genuine affection for Mary, or simply viewed her as his latest route to easy riches, is hard to determine. In all Mary's relationships – with lovers and friends, servants and acquaintances – money would always cloud a person's true motives. Certainly, judging by Gray's previous attempt to marry a wealthy widow in India, his eagerness to pocket an indecently large bribe in Bengal and his indifference to his ailing father in Scotland, he nursed few scruples about making his way in entrepreneurial Georgian Britain.

Having made London his home since returning from Bengal, Gray had seemingly failed to endear himself either to his family or to society. The satirical ballad *The Stoniad* would employ typical colonial prejudice by suggesting, wrongly, that 'half-wake orient G*y' had not only been born in India but was actually a Hindu or '*tout á fait* GENTOO'. But his friends were no more complimentary. It was after dining with Gray and Boswell at the house of Samuel Foote in 1772 that the playwright had been inspired to pen his savage attack on imperialism, *The Nabob*. The satire, published in 1778, would help establish the contemporary view of East India Company employees like Gray as jumped-up, greedy, arrogant villains. 'These new gentlemen,' explains one character, 'who from the caprice of Fortune, and a strange chain of events, have acquired immoderate wealth and rose to uncontroled power abroad, find it difficult to descend from their dignity, and admit of any equal at home.'[18] On the other hand, Gray's behaviour in India had been no more disreputable than that of Lord Clive who committed suicide in 1774 following sustained censure over his own approbation of significantly larger 'presents'.

Living in Portman Square, a popular address with overseas entrepreneurs, Nabob Gray could reach Mary's house on the other side of Oxford Street in a few minutes. Since luxurious Grosvenor Square was as famous for its aristocratic residents as it was notorious for their scandalous lives, it was not long before his visits were noticed. Among the first to tender suspicions was Elizabeth Planta, who initially dismissed Gray's interest as a harmless flirtation but soon realised his intentions were less than honourable. Fearful that Elizabeth would convey her information to Mrs Bowes, or worse to the Strathmore family, Mary affected a sudden and violent dislike for her former governess, who had effectively lived as a member of the Bowes family for nearly twenty years. Keeping her actions a secret from her mother, Mary borrowed money from her lawyer, Joshua Peele, when he visited St Paul's Walden Bury soon after the late earl's death, and offered Miss Planta an irresistible payoff totalling £2,000.[19] Furnished with sufficient funds to keep her comfortable for life, that July Miss Planta, or Mrs Parish as she would become on her marriage not long after, left the children she had looked after since they were babies.

Carefully covering her tracks, Mary was at pains to denounce the governess's behaviour as 'the most vile, ungrateful, and pernicious that ever was heard of', insisting that she exhibited an 'uninterrupted series of ill-temper, deceit, self-interestedness, and ingratitude; with obstinacy, and in many respects a bad method with my children' and that 'in short, she was too insufferable, else I would have retained her'. It was plain that the lady did protest too much. There is little doubt that the goodbye gift was hush money to buy the governess's silence over Mary's adulterous relationship with Gray, and quite probably her first pregnancy and abortion too. There were generous presents too, in the shape of a watch and some old furniture, for George Walker, the discreet footman. But no amount of skulking up backstairs or offering backhanders could prevent the affair becoming public in the claustrophobic world of London society.

It was Walker who first related the gossip circulating in the capital's coffee-houses and taverns. Initially the couple encouraged him and laughed together at 'all the ridiculous stories' during their nightly encounters. 'I was always extremely silly, in not minding reports,' Mary wrote, 'on the contrary, rather encouraged them; partly, that I might laugh at other people's absurdities and credulity, and partly, because I left it to time and reason, to shew they were false.'[20] Openly displaying their disdain for public opinion, the pair now ventured out together, parading in the public parks and city streets in Mary's open carriage even though she was still in mourning. The blue-stockings Frances Boscawen and Mary Delany excitedly exchanged news of their sightings that summer: 'Yesterday I was told by a lady that she had met Lady Strathmore with servts still in mourning, *but wearing white favours in their hats* (as at a wedding),' revealed Mrs Boscawen, 'also that in the chaise with her, sat an ill-looking man, from whence inference was made that she was marry'd to some Italian.'[21] According to Jessé Foot, the surgeon, Gray's 'visits were constant, and their airings open'.

It was inevitable then that reports of Mary's excursions flaunting her new lover would reach the ears of Thomas Lyon in Streatlam. Still discovering his brother's unpaid debts and grimly selling off land and chattels to balance the books, he knew that a second marriage by his brother's widow could compromise the future fortunes of Lord Strathmore's children. A new heir, for example, could certainly confuse the inheritance. For the moment he scrutinised the reports and kept his powder dry. The gossip piqued the interest of others with a pecuniary interest too. Coquettishly playing the field, Mary exchanged locks of hair with a suitor she enigmatically called 'Mr C. W.' and sent a short but flirtatious refusal to a certain 'Mr MacCallaster'.[22]

Less easy to dismiss with a keepsake or a brusque rebuff was James Graham, who arrived unexpectedly on her doorstep in London that summer, having heard of her husband's demise. Now a lieutenant, although at twenty still only just out of boyhood, Graham hoped to revive their carefree youthful passion. Still stung by his neglect, Mary refused to see him, even when he attempted to throw himself in her way on further occasions. For all his youth, he was the only man she would ever truly care for, yet her pride and a justifiable fear of further heartache prevented her from admitting her feelings. She would later say that 'having, at the risk of my life, conquered my headstrong passion, I was determined not to expose myself to another conflict, with one whom I had so much reason to be afraid of.'[23] She did indeed preserve herself from the pain of future loss. Less than three years later, in January 1779, James Graham would die, of unknown causes, in Naples.

By July 1776, even as the American colonies declared their independence from the British Crown, Mary had resigned herself to wedlock once again. While she would never feel more for Gray than lust and friendship, she had convinced herself that he would make a dependable husband, a dutiful stepfather and – since she was probably pregnant again – a loving natural father. Certainly they shared common interests in poetry and drama while Gray slotted in well with the ever-expanding social circle that congregated in the drawing room of 40 Grosvenor Square. For regardless of the fact that she was still officially in mourning, Mary's gatherings in the splendid four-storey house in the south-west corner of the square had become popular and animated events within London's tight-knit scientific fraternity.

Conversation at Mary's salons in the summer of 1776 would almost certainly have focused on the treasure trove of botanical delights which had recently been shipped back from the Cape by Francis Masson; the Kew gardener had submitted an account of his explorations to the Royal Society which had been read during three meetings in February. Having linked up with the Swedish naturalist, Carl Peter Thunberg, for one of his expeditions, Masson informed the society that they 'like true lovers of science thought themselves richly overpaid, by the ample collection of curious & new plants, as well as animals which they found in their way'.[24] Since Masson had just set sail again, this time headed for the Canary Islands, the prospect of further discoveries waiting to be plucked in the enticing Cape region naturally enthralled those he left behind. Among the Royal Society fellows who enlivened Mary's scientific discussions, Daniel Solander, the Swedish botanist, was impatient for further plant specimens while his friend, John Hunter, was always in the market for exotic new animal species, like the long-necked, spotted 'camelopard' which was fabled to live in southern Africa.

The fact that Mary was denied entrance to the exclusively male Royal Society, despite her extensive knowledge and devotion to botany, did nothing to quell her interest in reports from Africa nor her desire to further scientific enlightenment as a patron. Inspired by tales of Masson's voyage, and probably encouraged by Hunter and Solander, she now laid plans to finance an ambitious mission to send an explorer into uncharted parts of the Cape in search of new flora for her own burgeoning collection. It may well have been Solander who introduced her to William Paterson, a genial twenty-year-old Scottish gardener with little formal education but a huge sense of adventure who agreed to undertake her expedition the following spring. Certainly Solander had escorted Paterson to a Royal Society meeting in May that year and the pair would remain friends.[25] Other scientific enthusiasts within Mary's orbit included Richard Penneck, superintendent of the British Museum's reading room, and Joseph Planta, younger brother to Mrs Parish, who had taken over as librarian at the museum upon his father's death in 1773. Having just been appointed one of the two secretaries to the Royal Society, the ambitious 32-year-old Planta was rather more immune to Mary's attractions than many of his fellow guests – and had no doubt been kept abreast of her nocturnal activities by the ousted Mrs Parish.

Alongside Mary's earnest discussions on botany there were jovial breakfasts, languid dinners and musical suppers, frequent opera and theatre trips, and frivolous excursions about town on any number of pretexts with a host of less illustrious guests. These included James Mario Matra, a 30-year-old naval officer who had sailed around the world with Banks and Solander in the cramped cabins of the *Endeavour*. Born Magra – he later changed his name – and originally from New York, he was suspected by Captain Cook of slicing off parts of the ears of a drunken shipmate. Despite the fact that Matra was subsequently cleared of the brutal deed, the affable Cook nevertheless described his midshipman as 'one of those gentlemen, frequently found on board Kings Ships, that can very well be spared, or to speak more planer good for nothing'.[26] The bespectacled Matra had been introduced into Mary's set by his fellow voyager Solander and his own brother, a decidedly more shadowy character, Captain Perkins Magra. Having enlisted with the army as an ensign in 1761, Magra had fought for British forces in America but was on leave in London in the summer of 1776. One more constant companion who could not be left out of any social outing was the children's new governess, Eliza Planta. No sooner had Elizabeth Planta packed her bags and bade the children farewell than Mary had employed her younger sister – for the Planta family had a seemingly endless supply of talented daughters – in her stead.[27] Wily, flighty and promiscuous, in stark contrast to her prim elder sister, nineteen-year-old Eliza – baptised Ann Eliza – quickly established herself as an indispensable ally and eager confidante of her mistress.

Intoxicated by her liberty, whether it was to debate the finer points of science with fellows of the Royal Society, practise her skill for languages with her intellectual equals or flirt outrageously with the stream of sycophants who clamoured to her door, Mary was living life to the full. It was her year of behaving badly. Carelessly courting scandal, she flaunted her lover, abused her body, spent extravagantly and jeopardised her relationship with her children, especially the neglected young earl. She would be judged forever on the reckless excesses of this one year – in reality little more than nine months – and come to regret bitterly her waywardness. According to Foot, who would become one of Mary's harshest critics: 'Her judgement was weak, her prudence almost none, and her prejudice unbounded.'[28] In a view that would stand as a lasting image of the Countess of Strathmore, the surgeon described Mary's house as a 'temple of folly' and declared that her undoubted talents and intellect were 'that sort which required to be under the controul of some other'. That Foot regarded the control Mary apparently needed to be male went without saying; that he also, as an avowed enemy of his professional rival John Hunter, was never likely to gain access to Mary's 'temple' was equally left unsaid. Later, mostly male, writers would dispense similarly severe criticism and suggest that Mary's future trials were simply just desserts for her licentious behaviour. Even Mary would subscribe to the view that the miseries in store were all divine punishment for her adulterous affair with Gray. For even as she appeared to be in charge of her life for the first time, in reality she was edging closer to an ever-tightening trap. 'God blinded my judgement,' she later explained, 'that I could not discern, in any case, what was for my children's and my own advantage; but in every thing where there were two expedients, I chose the worst.'[29] The worst, however, was still to come.

Living with Gray effectively 'as his wife', scandalising strait-laced society as a merry widow and a neglectful mother, her home had become an open house to a growing band of unwholesome characters bent on selfish ends. Whenever a trip to the opera or a supper party was planned, the attentive Captain Magra would always be on hand as a ready escort. Whenever she desired a friendly ear for whispered confidences, Eliza Planta was at her side. And when the debonair Irish soldier arrived in London that July, Mary welcomed him into the fold with open arms.

Since Hannah Newton's death on 11 March, conveniently just four days after that of the Earl of Strathmore, Andrew Robinson Stoney had wasted little time grieving. Pocketing the £5,000 which he had inherited through his wife's will, while attempting to hang on to Cole Pike Hill in the face of furious protests from the rightful heir, Sam Newton, the merry widower headed south for the top entertainment spots of Georgian England. As the busy summer season approached, Stoney squandered his money and his idle hours at the gaming tables, race courses and cockpits with disreputable hard-drinking friends from his army past. With his bounty slipping rapidly through his fingers, supplemented only by his paltry army half-pay of about £40 a year, the former lieutenant was becoming anxious to secure a more reliable source of income to maintain his indulgent lifestyle.[30] Accompanied by his valet, Thomas Mahon, the self-promoted 'Captain' Stoney made for Scarborough, the fashionable Yorkshire seaside and spa town to which wealthy and well-bred families repaired during the summer months. Eyeing up the gentry enjoying the sea-bathing and the horse-racing along the sandy beach, Stoney hunted for another gullible heiress to lure down the aisle. It was not long before he chanced upon Anne Massingberd, the 28-year-old daughter of William Burrell Massingberd, a cultured and respected gentleman who lived in South Ormsby in Lincolnshire where he fulfilled the post of sheriff.[31]

Having lost her mother when she was young, Anne had helped to bring up her five younger sisters and two brothers in the family home of Ormsby Hall. Her industrious but sheltered life had scarcely prepared her to withstand the dazzling charms of the tall and genial army officer who now plied her with gifts and flattery at every opportunity. Convinced that Anne's father would offer a substantial portion to speed his eldest daughter to the altar, Stoney worked his customary magic. Swayed by his promises of marriage, Anne was quickly infatuated, and almost certainly bedded – judging by her later remorse – by her impatient suitor in the early summer months. Anne's poignant letters to Stoney, which have survived despite her appeals for him to return them, provide a highly revelatory picture of the irresistible allure which the Irish soldier exerted on women. In one typically desperate letter Anne proclaims, 'to describe the feelings of my heart is impossible, & I should think the attempt unnecessary, for you have known me too long not to be assured that my Love & Regard for you is beyond any thing to me'.[32] Yet even as he fuelled countryside chatter by appearing as Anne's constant escort – and by the rigid rules of eighteenth-century courtship ruining her chances of forming an alternative match – Stoney realised his expectations of her fortune had been overly optimistic. With two sons and six daughters to provide for, Anne's father was in no position to offer Stoney anything but the most meagre of marital enhancements. So as the sheriff and his eldest son, Charles, grew increasingly alarmed at reports of the Irish officer's predilections for bad company, Stoney shrewdly gauged that it was time to move on. Employing the well-worn delaying tactic, that his father was reluctant to settle sufficient fortune on him, Captain Stoney cooled his ardour. By July he was heading for London with an altogether more promising prey in his sights.

Stoney would have heard of Lord Strathmore's death – and the availability of his wealthy young widow – soon after the news had reached England. A death notice in the *Newcastle Chronicle* on 13 April helpfully pointed out that the deceased earl had married into 'one of the most opulent fortunes in this Country'. Having already snared one Durham heiress, the prospect of capturing another endowed with even greater riches was too tempting to resist. Yet since coffee-house gossip asserted that the countess was already being pursued by an ardent nabob and was carefully watched by the vigilant Strathmores, Stoney knew that capturing this prize would demand all the guile and wit in his power. Courting Anne Massingberd was a useful fallback plan – and he continued to maintain her interest through wheedling letters and the occasional visit – but by early July, the gains from his first marriage were fast disappearing. Although he would later maintain that he possessed £7,500 in ready cash on top of £4,000 annual income in 1776, a more reliable source would suggest that the 'half-pay lieutenant' was 'great distressed in his Circumstances, and possessed of little or no Property'.[33] Other reports would even claim that he was bankrupt although this was almost certainly untrue. Straitened but ebullient as ever, Stoney now set out for London purely – Foot would later attest – with the aim of seducing the Countess of Strathmore. Plainly he was not the first, nor would he be the last, to make this attempt. Yet the sheer intricacy of Stoney's scheming would mark him out as quite extraordinary.

Moving into lodgings in St James's Coffee House, a short stroll from Mary's home in Grosvenor Square, Stoney established himself as a well-heeled, up-and-coming man about town, charming everyone he met with his good-humoured repartee and gambling for impressive stakes at the Cocoa Tree Club. Tall, lean and impeccably presented – his valet would say he owned ninety shirts at the time – Stoney was fully conscious of his magnetic appeal to women.[34] Aware that time was short, he quickly engineered an introduction into Mary's circle, most probably through Captain Magra, who happened to be an old army friend. It was Magra, in fact, who had picked out the scarlet uniform and a frocksuit from a tailors in the Strand and had them sent up to his friend in Newcastle the previous year.[35] Having gained entry into the Grosvenor Square sanctum, Stoney skilfully laid siege to its mistress. With Captain Magra already working as his undercover ally, Stoney recruited Eliza Planta, the new governess, as his spy within the household. There is little doubt that Stoney achieved this conquest with his usual oleaginous flattery, and it is likely that she became his lover too, although he could always fall back on simple bribery when required. It was Eliza's job to report on her mistress's activities, divulge Mary's weaknesses and her interests, praise her secret master's attributes and help deploy his plans. So as Stoney dined and supped with the guests in Mary's set that July, he was well primed to fawn over her beloved cats and speak kindly of her children, especially her favoured daughters.

With her self-confessed partiality for Celtic men, her weakness for flattery and her perpetually disastrous judgement of character, Mary was intrigued by the urbane Irish officer who was only two years her senior. Although rumours alleging that Stoney had cruelly mistreated his late wife had percolated down to Grosvenor Square, Mary briskly dismissed these as 'only county of Durham malice' and encouraged – or at least did not discourage – the officer's advances.[36] By the end of July, Stoney was sufficiently emboldened to send Mary a daring declaration of his interest – the first surviving correspondence between the pair – which entirely dispensed with the usual formal address and obsequious homage due to a countess. Bluntly labelled 'It is for you', and evidently hand-delivered, the note was a masterpiece of Stoney's art:

> *I have taken some liberties for which your Ladyship can find no excuse unless you apply to the powerful pleading of Inclination – for such freedom I wish to make every apology, but I cannot get the better of a passion which has taken the intense possession of my Heart.*
>
> *I presume to flatter myself that I am deserving your confidence & my future conduct shall be directed [to] you, for whatever my suffering may be your pleasure only shall direct the conduct of him who can be nothing less than*
> *Your devoted*
> *Andrew*[37]

Whatever Mary's reply it is likely to have been equally indiscreet, for soon afterwards Stoney was heard bragging about his conquest and sharing Mary's letters with a gaggle of friends in a coffee-house in Bath.[38]

Nevertheless, Stoney's brash confidence was premature. Although she was obviously attracted to the hot-headed 'captain', by the late summer – pregnant by Gray for the third time – Mary had resigned herself to marrying her Scottish suitor. Despite having previously declared that she would never again 'engage myself indissolubly', in August or September she became formally betrothed to Gray in St Paul's Cathedral with Eliza Planta and Richard Penneck as witnesses.[39] Although an impromptu ceremony, this was no casual undertaking since such an engagement – actually referred to by Mary as 'marriage' – was regarded as legally binding. Indeed, one jilted fiancée in 1747 successfully sued a vicar for 'breach of promise' after he reneged on his pledge to marry her, winning £7,000 damages for her pains. Now wearing Gray's ring, Mary hastily set off for Hertfordshire to break the news to her mother. Meanwhile, she laid plans to marry Gray the following spring before leaving for the Continent – or even to marry abroad – so that she could give birth in secret if necessary and stay in Europe until all hint of a scandal had faded. She even tendered ambitions to visit France, Italy, Spain, Portugal, Hungary and Bohemia – in a Bohemian version of the grand tour – before returning with her new husband and child.

While most rivals would have gamely abandoned the chase at news of such an engagement, and perhaps moved on to an easier subject, this was not in the nature of Andrew Robinson Stoney. Obstacles and opposition merely sharpened his determination to succeed. As Foot shrewdly commented: 'There was no antiquated, dissipated, impudent, and profligate nabob a match for him.'[40] Briskly severing all ties with Anne Massingberd, who enjoyed her last liaison with her errant lover at the beginning of September, Stoney now focused all his energies, intelligence and remaining funds on ensnaring his prize quarry in a breathtakingly convoluted series of schemes. As the anti-hero of Thackeray's *Barry Lyndon* would argue: 'Who can say that I had not a right to use *any* stratagem in this matter of love? Or, why say love? I wanted the wealth of the lady.'[41]

That October, when Eliza Planta proposed a trip to visit a fortune-teller in one of the seamier parts of town, Mary responded with delight. Well-known for her love of romance as well as her susceptibility to the occult – she had visited gipsies when they encamped near St Paul's Walden Bury – Mary formed a party of friends. After breakfast with Eliza, Penneck and Matra, the group met up with the ubiquitous Captain Magra and proceeded to walk towards the Old Bailey, close by the notorious Newgate Prison. As they neared the court, a young boy approached and offered to escort the group to see the man 'so many people came after'. Mary eagerly agreed, following the lad through the 'blind allies' to a house in Pear Street. Here the little troupe waited for almost seven hours in a cold, bare room crowded with people from all walks of life seemingly intent on discovering their fortunes. Sustained only by bread and water, and warmed by a feeble fire they had kindled from a few green logs, the party passed the hours by composing poems which they inscribed on the walls with a lead pencil. While Penneck amused the group with his ditty on their adventure, Mary – despite her engagement – wrote some lines denouncing matrimony. Conversing with the assortment of characters who emerged from the cellar below, she passed herself off as a grocer's widow with ten children, unimaginatively named

Mrs Smith, who had come to divine 'whether I should marry a Brewer, or Sugar-boiler, who proposed to me amongst others'.

When finally the party was vouchsafed an audience with the mysterious soothsayer, Captain Magra descended the stairs first, declaring himself a perfect sceptic, and returned convinced, of course, of the mystic's astonishing skills. Plainly Mary enjoyed a similar epiphany. Although she did not record her consultation, there can be little doubt that she sought enlightenment over her future spouse and that the many merits of a tall Irish soldier featured prominently in the divinations. Needless to say, as Foot would later confirm, the entire escapade had been orchestrated by Stoney, the conjuror tutored by him and the witnesses instructed by him. Yet although he would later flourish copies of the very verses she had written on the bare walls, Mary never suspected him of involvement in the 'silly affair'.

Now that the hand of fate had advanced his cause, the next logical step was for Stoney to discredit his rival. This he achieved with a characteristic degree of insight and subtlety. Shortly after the fortune-telling expedition, Mary received a curious letter purporting to be a copy of one sent to Stoney from a jilted lover in Durham. Distraught at news that her 'captain' had abandoned her for a countess, the forsaken woman urged Mary to reject Stoney and marry Gray. Cleverly, the letter recommended Gray on the basis that he had secretly reached an accommodation with the Strathmore family, thereby healing the family rift. It is quite possible that Gray had indeed negotiated a deal with Thomas Lyon, probably with financial inducements, smoothing the way for his impending marriage in return for guarantees about the future of the Bowes fortune and its young heirs. But with the Strathmore family still firmly banished from her home, nothing could have been judged more likely to set Mary against her fiancé. Of course no Durham lover existed; the letter – followed by another in a similar vein – had been forged by Stoney.

By November, Stoney was feeling cautiously confident. That month Charles Massingberd, in London with two of his sisters, warned the wretched Anne not to expect any further word from her former lover since, Anne wrote to Stoney, 'he believ'd you wd. marry Lady S'. Although Charles assured his sister that she had had a 'lucky escape' from 'a man of such abandon'd character', this did nothing to console poor Anne who pledged that she would never appear in public again unless Stoney returned to her.[42] Her threats and pleadings were to no avail, for by the onset of winter, Stoney was ready to spring his trap.

It was a more than usually hectic time in the Grosvenor Square household. Anticipating the departure the following spring of her botanical expedition to the Cape, in November or December Mary purchased a villa, with substantial grounds, in what was known as Little Chelsea.[43] Fronting the King's Road, and therefore convenient for Kew Gardens, Chelsea Physic Garden and James Lee's renowned nursery, Stanley House had been built at the end of the seventeenth century on an estate originally laid out in Elizabethan times. A symmetrical two-storey house with three dormer windows in a hipped roof, it was 'a fine old mansion with large grounds, walled in', according to Foot. Appointing George Walker's wife as housekeeper, Mary set about constructing hothouses and greenhouses in the grounds in readiness for the exotic plants she hoped to nurture there.

Blithely running up debts through her scientific pursuits as well as her unflagging social life, that November Mary engaged a chaplain to help tutor the younger children. A widower in his late twenties who was down on his luck and in debt, the Reverend Henry Stephens was introduced through the Magra brothers, almost certainly at Stoney's behest. Ambitious, grasping and unprincipled, in the manner of innumerable eighteenth-century clergy, Stephens rapidly established himself as a regular participant in the giddy round of theatre parties and musical suppers. Flirting with Eliza Planta, he also took a number of familiarities with his mistress, winning kisses and inducing her to sit on his knee. The chaplain's brother, Captain George Stephens, who had formerly worked for the East India Company, likewise inveigled himself into the merry band at Grosvenor Square. Even less inhibited by rules of piety than his brother, the captain was 'free in his way of thinking and acting' even by Mary's lax standards.

When the penniless chaplain eloped to Gretna Green with the young governess just ten days after their first meeting, the Planta family was understandably outraged – not least with Eliza's mistress.[44] Mary freely admitted she had actively encouraged the pair to abscond, partly in an act of revenge against Mrs Parish, partly in the knowledge that Eliza was pregnant at the time – although Mary little suspected the probable identity of the father.[45] An enigmatic letter written jointly by Mary and Eliza to Reverend Stephens in Winchester, probably just before the elopement, reveals that Mary even encouraged Eliza to follow her own example and attempt an abortion. 'Dear Eliza is thank God greatly better, & if she will follow my advice & quack herself (without hurting) she will be still better,' hints Mary, while Eliza adds a note urging her fiancé not to be 'alarm'd at my indisposition T'is the first experiment'. Mary would later admit that she had advised Eliza 'to take a vomit, thinking she was with child; as I had taken a ridiculous notion into my head, that having children, made a man like his wife less'.[46] Sensibly Mary herself now fled London to escape the wrath of the Planta family, although she could not resist instructing George Walker to report every detail of their rage.

By November Mary knew that she too was pregnant once again – the fourth time – by Gray. This time, however, neither the black inky medicine, nor prodigious amounts of pepper, brandy or emetics would induce the desired miscarriage. In desperation, she even resorted to the services of her surgeon and friend, John Hunter. An oblique reference in the letter to Stephens declares: 'I am not able to assure you that either my Soul or Body are at your Service, for to confess the truth I have at present neither in my Possession – J. Hunter having torn to pieces my Body & the D–l having taken a Lease on my Soul.'[47] Asked later about the reference, Hunter would confirm that he had supplied Mary with medicines but when pressed refused to say if he knew she was pregnant or wanted an abortion. Admitting to procuring an abortion would have meant almost certain prosecution for the eminent surgeon as well as his patient. In any event, Hunter's best efforts were in vain and Mary now resigned herself to giving birth to her sixth child in the coming summer.

As the eventful year drew to its close, Mary's future seemed mapped out. Betrothed to George Gray, pregnant with his child, she finalised her plans to marry and spend the next few years abroad putting her linguistic talents to good use. Her sour feud with the Strathmore family seemed finally to have been resolved and she could now look forward to a secure future for herself, her fiancé and her children. With her gardener poised to set sail for the Cape and her hothouses rising steadily at Stanley House, she had been granted a unique opportunity to pursue her ambitions and perhaps make a name for herself in international scientific circles. With the indulgent and educated Gray at her side, she would even have the chance to fulfil her literary aims. It seemed she could not fail. Yet fatally, at the last moment, she wavered. Then Stoney made his move.

Away from the city's prying eyes in the tranquil countryside surrounding St Paul's Walden Bury, in late November Mary received a letter with its familiar spidery handwriting. Ostensibly writing to express surprise at Eliza's elopement and her choice of spouse – although plainly he had been involved in, if not masterminded, both – Stoney pressed home his advantage. Cleverly praising Eliza for not being swayed by the opinions of 'guardians, relations or pretended friends', he reminded Mary that a 'free choice is happiness'.[48] Feigning interest in her 'good mother' and her beloved cats, Stoney silkily professed that he wished he could adopt feline form so that he could be 'stroked and caressed, like them, by you'. And under the pretence that he could no longer contain his passion, he declared: 'I am all impatience to see your ladyship; I really cannot wait till Saturday; I must have five minutes chat with you before that time.' Proposing an assignation, beside a 'leaden statue' in her mother's formal gardens, it was patently not a 'chat' that Stoney had in mind. The statue, a classical figure of a Greek discus thrower known as the 'running footman', survives still beside an ornamental pond within an enclosed garden, close to the woods where Mary's great-great-great-granddaughter, Elizabeth Bowes Lyon, would consent to marry the Duke of York, the future George VI, in 1923.[49] Whether Mary accepted Stoney's proposal and met him covertly behind the tall hedges, shielded from the view of the house in that unseasonably warm

December, is unknown. But certainly by Christmas they had become lovers.

At last Stoney could set in motion the final stages of his elaborate plot.

6

Bowes and Freedom

London, December 1776

When the salacious articles first began to appear in the *Morning Post* in December 1776, Mary could hardly have been surprised. Reporting various sightings of her about town with her rival lovers in tow, such gossip was generally dismissed as an occupational hazard by the celebrities of the day. Revelling in the press fascination with her libertine lifestyle, Mary laughed as she read the articles. But when the first of the letters appeared on 12 December, coldly levelling pernicious accusations at her, Mary felt decidedly uncomfortable. Signed 'A Conscience-Stinger', it charged her with insulting her late husband's memory by prostituting herself and abandoning her children. Also accusing her of infidelity to the earl, the letter bore all the hallmarks of the Strathmore family or the disgruntled Plantas – as was no doubt the intention. Plainly hinting at revelations to come, with a chill blast from beyond the grave, the writer warned her to mend her ways or he would 'harrow up your soul!'[1] Well aware of the need to keep the latest turn in her love-life and her current condition a secret – not least from her two lovers – Mary had good cause to worry.

Two weeks later, on Christmas Eve, an anonymous champion leapt to her defence. Signed by 'Monitus', or warning voice, this letter insinuated that the previous attack had emanated from the Planta family, with a veiled reference to Eliza's hasty elopement with a 'good-natured clergyman'. But if Mary hoped that the response would put an end to the correspondence she was sadly mistaken. On 3 January 1777, her mysterious critic redoubled the assault. Making its literary allusions more explicit with the moniker 'Hamlet', the letter cast the former Lady of Glamis as another of Shakespeare's scheming women, Queen Gertrude. Ludicrously describing her late husband as 'fond and doting', the writer accused her of greeting the earl's illness with 'cold indifference' and of forsaking her eldest son. Inevitably Monitus retaliated, four days later, with a verbose and flowery defence that rather brought Mary into ridicule by its risible exaggeration than vindicating her. The reply insisted that she had been devastated at the late earl's illness and suffered 'agonizing, and heart-felt sorrow' at his death. Knowingly drawing attention to her obvious disregard for widowhood, the writer lamented: 'She no sooner goes to the *Play*, or walks in the *Park*, than there are a thousand eyes upon her, and every step taken to attract her attention!' With leaden sarcasm – and a revealing insight into the trap closing around her – Monitus continued, 'how charming, and profitable would it be, were it possible to prey upon her weakness, or delude her into those snares her sex are most subject to!'

Now two months pregnant, and secretly planning her flight abroad with Nabob Gray even as she entertained 'Captain' Stoney, Mary plainly hoped for a swift end to the intrusive scrutiny of her affairs. Whether she went so far as to promise to marry the man who would avenge her cause on the editor of the *Morning Post* – as the newly wed Eliza Planta, now Mrs Stephens, would claim – is uncertain. But when her suave Irish lover announced that he would defend her honour by challenging the turbulent priest to a duel, it was a gesture guaranteed to appeal to her romantic nature.

Swaggering about her Grosvenor Square house in his scarlet jacket, brandishing his steel sword and melodramatically swearing to fight unto death on her behalf, the athletic Stoney cut an imposing figure. With her trusted friend Captain Magra kindly volunteering to act as Stoney's second, Mary entered into the spirit of the adventure with gusto. Nevertheless, even as Stoney provoked the seemingly reluctant Bate with escalating threats, she continued with her wedding plans to Gray and met her lawyer, Joshua Peele, to sign important legal papers on 9 and 10 January. As the badinage between Stoney and Bate intensified at their coffee-house encounters over the weekend of 11 and 12 January, Mary no doubt relished reports of the unfolding drama. Whether she believed the play-acting would ever come to genuine blows, or that her hero would exact his rashly promised prize, is unknown. But when romance turned to tragedy and she heard that Stoney had been mortally wounded in the engagement at the Adelphi Tavern on Monday 13 January, Mary was understandably distraught.

It was her fiancé, Gray, who was first on the scene, visiting the stricken Stoney in his apartment above the St James's Coffee House the following day to shake his hand in gratitude for rescuing the honour of his future bride. Later that day Mary despatched her footman, George Walker, to enquire as to Stoney's condition. And when Walker reported that the ailing soldier was 'deadly white' Mary herself dashed to his bedside that evening. The surgeon Jessé Foot, whom Mary met for the first time, assured her that Stoney now lay on the verge of death, and she had no reason to doubt his medical opinion. Even so, when Stoney insisted that he could not die happy unless he married the woman for whom he had sacrificed his life, Mary consented from a 'misapplied sense of Gratitude and Honour' and warned him she would go ahead only 'with Reluctance'.[2] Since it was the opinion of no less than three medical men that Stoney was unlikely to live beyond a few days, there seemed no need to inform him that she was already pregnant with his rival's baby, nor that she had taken a vital legal precaution preparatory to her marriage with Gray. And as Stoney solemnly protested complete lack of interest in her fortune, insisting that he would 'never consider himself in any other light than as my steward', she had no reason to doubt that he had any motive for marriage other than the genuine desire of a dying man to marry his true love.

So on Thursday 16 January, as Stoney roused himself sufficiently to apply to the Bishop of London for a marriage licence, circumventing the usual need to read banns in church for the next three weeks, Mary enjoyed a convivial last supper with the unsuspecting Gray. That evening, the eve of her anticipated wedding with Stoney, she apparently spent the night with Gray, 'in one and the same bed, naked and alone', as court spectators – used to marital fumblings among night-clothes – would later be astounded to hear.[3] The following morning, after despatching Gray in the early hours as usual, Mary dressed for her wedding then walked with Eliza to Stoney's lodgings in nearby St James's Street. From here the couple took a chair for the short trip around the corner to St James's Church in Piccadilly. When the gaunt Stoney clung stubbornly to life as he was carried down the aisle in his makeshift bed, Mary may have tendered misgivings. As Stoney murmured the marriage vows, supported at the altar by his friend and financial advisor William Davis, perhaps she experienced the first cold feelings of foreboding. And when her new husband rallied adequately enough to celebrate the nuptial ceremony with the little gathering that returned to his apartment, she may well have regretted her eagerness to enter wedlock for the second time.

It was not long before her doubts were confirmed. Stoney's rapid recovery as he welcomed guests to a jubilant levee at his lodgings the following morning was certainly impressive. Dressed in a new scarlet uniform, pampered by his fond great-uncles Generals Armstrong and Robinson, Stoney reclined on a couch – claiming he was still too ill to stand – as visitors flocked by coach and on foot to pay their respects. That evening the bridegroom had revived sufficiently to move his belongings into his luxurious new home in Grosvenor Square. And as the revels continued into the night, with Stoney's relatives and Irish friends staying to dinner in the sumptuous dining room, Mary was about to discover the true extent of the trap into which she had been lured.

Questions about the veracity of the duel began to circulate within days of the encounter in the Adelphi Tavern as George Gray, furiously discovering that he had been tricked out of both bride and fortune, and the Strathmore family, horrified to hear of the surprise match, raised understandable doubts. As suspicions mounted, Foot and his fellow medic John Scott, and the supposed eyewitness John Hull, had to insert statements in the press attesting to the wounds that they had seen.[4] Foot would insist all his life that the duel had been genuine and the injuries he treated life-threatening. Yet the pompous young surgeon, who was ambitious to make his mark on the London medical scene, would later recount numerous deceptions which he had helped Stoney to perpetrate. Ultimately the cringing Foot would describe his lifelong friend and benefactor as 'an accomplished villain' possessed of 'the most savage, contemptable and low mind' – but only after he was safely dead.[5] Scott, the physician who put his name to the testimony describing his patient's injuries, would likewise prove himself an adept liar on Stoney's behalf, at one point informing Mrs Bowes that her daughter was dangerously ill in order to lure her into town.[6] The so-called 'fighting parson' Henry Bate would later maintain under oath that the duel had been genuine, insisting that Stoney had 'bled like a pig' – although his graphic description might equally be taken to imply that the pair had faked their wounds with pig's blood.

In fact Bate and Stoney were already well acquainted before their skirmish in the Adelphi Tavern, having met the previous summer in Bath. It was probably there that the two army veterans had hatched the elaborate scheme to publish the sparring letters in Bate's journal and stage the sham duel. Certainly the flamboyant journalist was not above a bribe: he was already in the pay of the government to the tune of £200 a year in return for publishing reports in his newspaper favourable to George III.[7] A satirical cartoon published two years after the duel, *A Baite for the Devil*, would describe the preacher as 'A Canonical Buck, Vociferous Bully/ A Duellist, Boxer, Gambler' and, significantly, a 'Cully' or, in plain words, a dupe.[8]

As news of Stoney's seemingly miraculous recovery and surprisingly advantageous marriage gathered pace, so rumours of his skulduggery spread like a nasty rash. The satirical ballad, *The Stoniad*, published just two months after events in the Adelphi, would make plain its scepticism about the reported details. Employing the customary brand of heavy irony to infer that Bate had helped Stoney stage a mock fight, and that Hull had been bamboozled by the darkness, the anonymous author concluded that the only casualty had been a broken mirror. 'Furious and wild, as savage beasts for gore, They fight – as HEROES *never fought before*! Fight and make many a FEINT and many a PASS! Now *wound themselves*, now *kill* – A LOOKING GLASS!' Not long afterwards, doubts about the so-called 'affair of honour' in the Adelphi were aired in a quintessentially Georgian arena: on the stage.

When the curtains opened at the Theatre Royal on 8 May, audiences excitedly anticipated the new comedy by Irish theatrical entrepreneur Richard Brinsley Sheridan.[9] Having taken over management of the theatre in Drury Lane from David Garrick the previous year, Sheridan had written his play, *The School for Scandal*, expressly for the new venue. Ironically following hard on the heels of *A Trip to Scarborough*, which told the tale of a penniless adventurer's seduction of a wealthy heiress, Sheridan's latest satire mocked the contemporary obsession with celebrity and gossip. The comedy opens with the journalist Snake assuring his aristocratic patron Lady Sneerwell that her 'paragraphs' relating malicious gossip about leading members of London society had been 'all inserted' into his newspaper. Lady Sneerwell is thought to have been based on Sheridan's friend, Georgiana, Duchess of Devonshire. But dressed in clerical black and described as the 'editor of a morning paper', Snake was readily identified as the preaching journalist Henry Bate, reinforced by later references to 'bate' – meaning to slacken – and 'be baited' – or harassed – and, most pointedly, the invocation: 'May your love for each other never know abatement'. Tellingly, Bate had met with Garrick, Sheridan's mentor, only a day or two after his encounter with Stoney and may well have been the unwitting source for the laughter later directed against him. Trampling the familiar territory of a loveless marriage, the drama unfolds to describe a duel which is rumoured to have been fought between two love rivals. Himself the combatant in two duels in 1772 over a popular singer whom he later married, Sheridan was well supplied with knowledge of such events. But the confused details which the characters relate – the duellists first said to have fought with pistols then with swords, a stray bullet striking the bust of Pliny on the mantelpiece and, especially, the remark: 'You seem to differ strangely in your accounts', would have been well understood in 1777 as lightly veiled references to the recent duel between Bate and Stoney.

Naturally enough Stoney would always profess his innocence of all subterfuge, in public at least. Yet evidence of the fabricated letters and faked fight would accumulate to the point that it was incontrovertible. Stoney's valet, Thomas Mahon, who had been sent on the fateful day to purchase duelling pistols from Wogdon's renowned gun shop, would later testify twice, under oath, that the whole escapade had been contrived.[10] Having returned from a fruitless quest to fetch Stoney's second, Captain Magra, to find his master being tended by Scott and Foot, Mahon was adamant that he saw no blood except where the surgeon was bleeding his patient. Later he noticed several tears in Bate's breeches which appeared to have been made with a hot poker, and two or three holes in Stoney's waistcoat but he swore there were neither holes nor bloodstains on his master's shirt. Plainly Mahon was in a good position to testify since not only was he responsible as Stoney's valet for his wardrobe but the shirt Stoney wore that day had actually belonged to Mahon and the waistcoat was later given to him. Other witnesses would later reveal that Stoney had painted his face white to provoke a deathly pallor and had been bled by Foot to hoodwink the elderly surgeon Hawkins into believing him faint from his injuries.[11] Certainly successive judges in ensuing court contests would have no difficulty in dismissing the Adelphi duel as yet another of Stoney's twisted stratagems.

Weighing up all the evidence, the most likely sequence of events was that Stoney had concocted his plot with Bate in Bath, and that together they had faked the letters published in the *Morning Post* then bribed Foot and Scott, and possibly Hull, to play supporting roles in their drama. While some manner of skirmish almost certainly took place in the parlour of the Adelphi, the supposed injuries were either superficial cuts which the duellists inflicted on each other or entirely fictitious. But if the truth about the sham duel emerged only slowly to public view, it was only days before Mary herself suspected that she had been the victim of an intricately plotted hoax.

While her doubts must certainly have been aroused by the rapidity of her champion's return to health, it was not long before Mary uncovered solid evidence of the conspiracy in overheard conversations and glimpsed correspondence. Eventually a letter which Stoney had carelessly left open on a table convinced her that the daring duel that had won her heart and her hand had been nothing more than 'an amicable transaction between the soi-disant Heroes'.[12] Sent by Bate, within a month or so of the Adelphi encounter, the letter threatened Stoney with 'a real Duel' or with exposure unless he stumped up a promised annuity, which had plainly been Bate's reward for his part in the plot. And as the quarrel between the so-called heroes now intensified in earnest, one of Stoney's friends reported him to be exercising with pistols every morning. 'I expect almost certainly to hear of a Duel that will be serious,' the friend wrote while shrewdly adding, 'the former, I suspect, was not so.'[13] Indeed, as Stoney grew increasingly belligerent, Bate warned him not to attack the man 'to whom you owe every thing you now possess'. In the event, Stoney deputed another in his legion of willing clerics, the Reverend William Maxwell, to fight Bate – there was no chance that he would seriously put his own life at risk for as Foot astutely noted, 'he was by nature a coward'. The dispute was finally settled that spring in arbitration arranged by friends, with Stoney being forced to make an apology.

That Mary, highly intelligent and well educated, should have been so easily fooled by the charade has in itself raised eyebrows. Indeed, one writer has postulated that smitten by Stoney she was a willing accomplice in a scheme designed to extricate her from marriage to Gray.[14] If true – and there is no direct evidence to support this, but much to contradict it – then she was as much a victim of Stoney's cunning and manipulation as she would have been if she had known nothing in advance. In her own testament she would answer such suggestions with the apt observation that Stoney was 'master of the most consummate arts that can be displayed'. She added: 'I am not therefore, ashamed to confess myself amongst the large number of those whom his Cunning, and unparalleled Villanies have deceived. How should an unsuspicious young Woman, accustomed to study Books more than the World; whose knowledge of it was partially collected from living with the most Worthy, and whose sex did not permit her those opportunities for experience, which are beyond all Theory; expect to escape the snares of a Wretch, who suffered neither truth, nor even common Honesty, to interfere with his Interest, and whose consummate art has deceived Men long conversant with public life and of acknowledged abilities?'[15] And in that she was, of course, only one in a long line of people – men and women, of all ages, ranks and stations in life – who had been and would be duped by Stoney's unparalleled talent for invention and subterfuge. From army generals to journalists, barristers to maidservants, aristocrats to prostitutes, few would be immune to the compelling charms of this master of deception. But long before her realisation about the duel, on the very day that she brought her new spouse back to her home in Grosvenor Square and heard the front door shut behind them, Mary discovered that her husband was anything but the charming, gallant and mortally wounded champion she had supposed.

Inviting his great-uncles to his splendid new abode to dine that evening, Stoney no doubt hoped to impress. When he called for champagne and discovered there was none in the house, he flew into a rage and angrily despatched servants to a nearby tavern.[16] It was only the beginning. No sooner had the wedding guests disappeared than the fond, attentive and generous lover Mary had known for the past six months changed before her eyes into a sneering, rude, aggressive bully who 'began to treat me with the utmost indignity'.[17] Just three days after the wedding, when some trimming Mary had ordered for a dress arrived, Stoney erupted in fury. Without offering any explanation, he immediately countermanded her order and sent the adornment back. Later that week, when an Irish friend joined them for dinner and Mary indulged in the chance to converse in French and Italian, Stoney sent Walker to the other end of the table with a terse note ordering her to speak only English. A short while later Stoney took a dislike to a bonnet Mary had donned in readiness for going out. With his strength now obviously restored, he ripped it from her head, cut off the ribbons and forbade her from leaving the house.

After these initial outbursts, which Mary tried to dismiss as uncharacteristic lapses, Stoney began to set rigid curbs on her activities and her freedom. At first he ordered his valet, Mahon, to follow Mary's carriage whenever she went out and report back on her outings but before long he told the servants that her coach could only be used with his express consent. Having initially instructed Mary's footman, Walker, to bring him all the letters that his mistress sent or received, after a short while Stoney himself dictated all her correspondence to family and friends, forcing Mary to sound cold and high-handed. In one typical letter, sent to her new father-in-law George Stoney a few days after the wedding, Mary was made to adopt a hectoring tone. Writing at Stoney's command, ostensibly because his arm was still wounded from his fracas, she added a secret postscript: 'Tho' I am conscious of the ill-usage Mr Stoney has received, I must confess I should have wish'd to address you in a different stile. I am writing by Mr Stoney's Bedside, and add this without his Knowledge.'[18] There was very little Mary could now accomplish without her husband's knowledge and consent.

Watching her every movement, Stoney exerted control over the clothes Mary wore, the visitors she received, the conversations she held, the food that she ate, the journeys she undertook and every aspect of her daily life from morning until night with a pathological eye for detail. Planned outings were cancelled at the last minute if Stoney disliked Mary's costume; visitors to the house were turned away unless he approved. She was forbidden from visiting her gardens and hothouses in Chelsea except on rare occasions when accompanied by Stoney and was prevented from enjoying the company of her scientific friends. For all the feigned interest he had professed in Mary's literary and botanical pursuits, she now discovered: 'He had an invincible aversion to every species of rational, scientific, or elegant conversation by which knowledge is mutually communicated and acquired.'[19]

If Mary had strained at the strictures on her favourite pastimes and her friendships imposed by Lord Strathmore, they now seemed like an indulgence. Although her three youngest children and Maria were staying with the newly weds in Grosvenor Square, while the young earl remained at boarding school in Neasden, Mary was forbidden from visiting her mother and was forced to refuse her mother's anxious appeal for a private conversation. Angered by Mary's last-minute switch of suitor and hurt by her subsequent refusals to visit, an aggrieved Mrs Bowes wrote, 'it is rather extraordinary that in such early days, you have not influence enough to prevail, nor power sufficient to put that desire in execution, & at the same time comply with a mother's request.'[20] Deterred by pride from confiding in her mother over her disappointment in her first marriage, Mary was now prevented by force from revealing her misery in the second. According to Foot, who only a few days earlier had helped coax Mary into his friend's trap, her house had now undergone a transformation from 'folly to tyranny' and Mary herself, the surgeon blithely declared, 'may truly be pronounced to be DEAD ALIVE'.[21]

The violence began almost immediately. If Mary said or did anything to annoy him, Stoney would respond by pinching, kicking or slapping her while warning her not to reveal the abuse to friends or servants. 'He very soon began to beat and pinch me,' wrote Mary, 'threatening me at the same time to kill me if I did not tell my Maid, or any person who observed my bruises, that I had fallen down, or run my head against something.'[22] Like so many victims of domestic violence before and since, Mary was reduced to blaming her cuts and bruises on walking into doors and falling down stairs. Since it was virtually impossible for masters and mistresses in wealthy Georgian households to say or do anything without the knowledge of the army of maids, footmen, butlers and valets who did their bidding, inevitably the servants witnessed the tell-tale signs of Mary's mistreatment. But as they were all answerable to Stoney, and in his pay, there was little any of them dared do. Mary's maid Ann was the first to spot the signs of abuse. Having helped her mistress dress to go out, she saw Mary enter Stoney's dressing room – presumably for his perusal – but return minutes later 'very much dejected, and biting her lips' with her hat torn, the ribbons cut and Mary's eye 'swelled and red'.[23] Powerless to help, Ann observed and bided her time.

Not long afterwards it was Stoney's valet, Thomas Mahon, who witnessed his master's conduct. Enraged because he could not find his cane for an outing, Stoney followed Mary into his dressing room from which Mahon soon heard a scream. Running to help, he was ordered away by an enraged Stoney who stood with his sword drawn. The erstwhile duelling hero who had apparently fenced so courageously in defence of his lover, now chased her around the room with his sword. Driving her into a corner, Stoney imprisoned Mary for half an hour 'beating me incessantly all the time with the hilt of his sword, and an heavy silver candlestick over the head, arms and shoulders'.[24] Although Mary was forced to keep to her bed the following day, to hide the swellings and bruises on her face and body, Mahon was quick to spot the black eye when she next appeared in company. It was not long before Mahon left, fed up with his master's increasingly belligerent behaviour, and eloped with Mary's maid Ann. They were the first of many to leave Stoney's employ in disgust at his autocratic manner.

Their mistress, of course, had no choice but to stay. Yet whatever excesses of misery, cruelty and humiliation Mary might now be enduring she could expect no sympathy from her contemporaries. Her free-living lifestyle of the past year had made her fair game for every gossip, satirist and opinion-former and, without exception, they took the moral position that she had brought all her woes on herself. So the MP George Selwyn referred his friend Lord Carlisle to 'This match of that lunatic's, Lady Strathmore, with Mr Stoney'.[25] Satirical ballads followed the same line. Addressed to her friend, the surgeon John Hunter, in a limp homage to his anatomical interest in electric eels and torpedo fish, 'The Torpedo, a poem to the electrical eel', ranged over the latest scandals to beset the nobility and inevitably one verse homed in on Mary's love life:

> *Though oft electrified before,*
> *Still pants the* Countess *of ST--THM--E*
> *For one more stout and boney:*
> *Long has she tasted, some folks say,*
> *Each different sort from Black to GRAY*
> *But fixt on that of ST-N-Y.*[26]

In a similar vein, a bawdy ballad entitled 'The Diabo-Lady' imagined the devil's quest for a suitable mate amongst the most notorious women of the day. Accusing Mary of breaking a 'too fond husband's heart' by embarking on affairs with two suitors before his death, it lampooned her for jilting her first lover as 'too tame' in favour of 'the Bully of her ticklish fame'.[27]

If the true character of Andrew Robinson Stoney was a revelation, however, Mary had kept back a few surprises for her new husband too. Firstly, there was the small matter of the debts she had accumulated. Stoney would later claim that these amounted to a startling £32,000.[28] Given her recent purchase of Stanley House, the impending expedition to the Cape – William Paterson set sail as planned on 9 February

1777 – and her weakness for rich gowns, elaborate hats and other finery, this was not impossible. Secondly, there was the fact that she was at least two months pregnant. Stoney would later protest his 'great astonishment and grief' when he discovered soon after the wedding night that his new wife was 'five months' pregnant, exaggerating her condition in order to eliminate any suggestion that Stoney himself might have been the father. In reality, it is highly likely Stoney already knew or suspected Mary was pregnant and even possible that the baby was indeed his own. Whether two months or five months, there was no denying that Mary's swelling belly would soon be evident to servants, visitors and the entire gossip machine of London's high society. Keen to avoid further scandal, Stoney scouted around for a suitable hideaway for a secret birth while telling his friends the couple were going abroad for his health. This sacrifice, he no doubt reasoned, was a small price to pay for the spectacular fortune he now possessed. The third surprise was infinitely more shocking.

Strutting about as the new lord and master at 40 Grosvenor Square, Stoney was eager to lay claim to the vast wealth he had greedily anticipated during his campaign of seduction. To his horror, within one week of his triumphant marriage, he now discovered that all the property and profit he had schemed so cleverly to obtain were entirely beyond his reach. A week before the wedding, on 9 and 10 January, even as Stoney stoked his fake argument with Bate, Mary had signed a prenuptial deed which vested all the estates, assets and income in which she enjoyed a life interest under her father's will, into the hands of two trustees: her solicitor Joshua Peele and the brother of her chaplain, Captain George Stephens. All proceeds from the Bowes fortune, the deed specified, could only be paid to Mary 'for her separate and peculiar use and disposal, exclusive of any husband she should thereafter marry'.[29]

Signing such a deed was an unusual but not unprecedented step at the time. Ordinarily, of course, Georgian law stipulated that upon marriage the husband gained possession of all his wife's property, income and belongings, as Stoney well knew. Prenuptial deeds were occasionally drawn up, however, usually at the behest of a bride's parents keen to safeguard the family fortune from a potentially profligate or untrustworthy husband. In Mary's case, she had asked her solicitor to prepare the deed in anticipation of her marriage to Gray, with her fiancé's agreement and probably at the urging of the Strathmores determined to protect the children's future inheritance. After making her last-minute switch of grooms, Mary had seen no reason to alter the document. This was not through any mistrust of Stoney, she would later insist, but that 'it struck me, that having taken <u>such precautions on my children's account</u>, (for whom I was answerable, though not for myself) with a man who I knew I could trust; I ought not to be less cautious with one whom I could not be so strongly assured of.'[30] Even so, she had kept the deed a secret from Stoney until several days after their wedding for fear, she later claimed, that the document suggested a distrust of him – although fear of her new spouse may very well have contributed. When she confessed the truth he was apoplectic. Not only was he personally penniless and faced with a baying horde of his own creditors, but as her husband he was now accountable for Mary's debts too. All along, he now felt, it was he who had been the victim of a hoax.

Stoney responded with characteristic resolve. As the creditors circled, and Gray threatened to sue Mary for breach of contract for jilting him at the altar, Stoney knew he had to raise a substantial amount of money quickly. Immediately he ordered Mary to write to Peele demanding he surrender the deed and despatched Walker to deliver the letter.[31] When Walker returned empty-handed, as Peele refused to comply with the request, Stoney was furious but undefeated. Little did he know that Mary retained one further secret which would ultimately prove vital. Just before her marriage she had entrusted her own copy of the deed to Walker, asking him to keep it safe. Cowed as she now was by Stoney's bullying behaviour, she kept her head sufficiently to beg Walker to keep the deed hidden with the insightful comment that 'I did not know whether I should be able to lead my life with Mr Stoney.'

Despite this temporary hitch to his well-laid scheme and his spending plans, Stoney entertained lavishly at Grosvenor Square and now turned his attention to promoting his own rise in public life. Less than one month after the wedding, Stoney saw the chance for advancement that he had been waiting for. After changing his name to Bowes at the beginning of February, in accordance with George Bowes's will, he now sought to use the respected family name to change his fortunes. The death of the Newcastle MP Sir Walter Blackett on 14 February provided the opportunity.[32] After representing the city unopposed as one of its two MPs for nearly half a century, Blackett had been shaken but survived when radical campaigners had opposed him at the general election in 1774. The by-election now triggered by the 69-year-old Tory MP's demise presented the radicals with their second chance to mount a challenge. Having first marched through the city gates just ten years earlier as a lowly ensign, Andrew Robinson Bowes – as he would in future be known – now aspired to represent the people of Newcastle in Parliament by hitching his fortunes to the populist platform.

Dashing off a letter to the mayor three days later, Bowes

formally presented himself as a candidate while pleading that 'the present state of my indisposition' sadly prevented him arriving in person.[33] Although his injuries, if they ever existed, had certainly healed by this stage – a letter from his cousin Isaac to Bowes's brother Thomas a week earlier reported that 'Robinson is quite well of his wounds' – the delay gave Bowes time to plot his assault and borrow the cash he needed to finance it.

George Greive, the son of a local lawyer and friend of the popular radical John Wilkes, stepped forward to spearhead Bowes's campaign against Blackett's nephew and heir, the Somerset country gentleman Sir John Trevelyan, who fully expected an easy ride. But while Greive mobilised support from the tradesmen and up and coming professionals who were entitled, as freemen of the city, to vote, Bowes idled in London. Although the prospective candidate was 'hourly expected' on 18 February, Greive assured the voters, it was eight more days before Bowes finally crossed the Tyne Bridge with Mary at his side on the day before the polls opened on 27 February.[34] Having left four of the children in the dubious care of the Reverend Henry Stephens in Grosvenor Square, while the young earl remained in Neasden, the couple's thirty-two-hour dash north was a grim counterpoint to the stately northern progress which had followed Mary's first marriage. Charming and manipulative by turns Bowes fully expected that Mary would play a central role in his audacious campaign.

Although votes for women were not to happen for nearly 150 years, several aristocratic women helped muster votes for their menfolk during election campaigns in the latter half of the eighteenth century. In a society which placed a high value on female modesty and passivity, this was rarely without public opprobrium. Lady Spencer had decorously lent her support in Nottingham in 1774, but when her daughter, Georgiana, Duchess of Devonshire, canvassed zealously for Fox in the controversial Westminster election ten years later, she would be roundly lambasted, with lewd caricatures in the press and snobbish retorts from society. 'What a pity that any of our sex should ever forget what is due to female delicacy,' lamented the blue-stocking Mary Hamilton while female solidarity similarly went out of the window with Elizabeth Montagu's observation that the duchess had been 'canvassing in a most masculine manner'.[35]

Despite standing on a populist ticket exhorting free elections and parliamentary reform for honest tradesmen and aspiring professionals in the face of the property-owning gentry, Bowes knew that Mary's esteemed family name would give him the gravitas he needed to stand a chance in the Newcastle by-election. During the two weeks in which the polls were open daily, Mary was therefore called upon to dispense charity and woo the electors as the perfect political consort smiling benignly at her husband's side. Accordingly, on 6 March she gave orders for an ox to be slaughtered and distributed among the poor of the city while the following day she hosted her own belated birthday party with open house at Gibside.[36] On other days Elizabeth Montagu's husband Edward, a Trevelyan supporter, was aghast to see the daughter of his old friend and partner George Bowes blatantly distributing cash handouts to passers-by in the city centre. 'Her Ladyship sits all day in the window of a public house,' he wrote, 'from whence she sometimes lets fall some jewels or trinkets, which voters pick up, and then she gives them money for returning them – a new kind of offering bribes.'[37]

Staying at Gibside, where she was forbidden from visiting the gardens or greenhouse without her husband's consent, and only allowed a glass of wine at dinner with his permission, Mary was now totally subject to Bowes's commands.[38] Passing the Column to Liberty her father had erected on her way to the hustings each day, it must have been with supreme irony that Mary plied voters with handbills headed 'Bowes and Freedom!' and poems which hailed her as the 'Queen of Liberty!' Meanwhile, the jibes of her husband's opponents as they drew attention to his humble background as an 'Irish ensign', the allegations of cruelty to his first wife and his predilection for the gaming houses and brothels near the Keyside must have given her pause for thought.

When Bowes lost to Trevelyan in the final count by a slim ninety-five votes, he bullishly appealed to Parliament against the result with the somewhat rich charge of bribery levelled against the opposing camp. John Scott, the 25-year-old son of a Newcastle coal agent, cut his teeth as a lawyer attempting to argue Bowes's cause. A future Lord Chancellor, he would gain a peerage as Lord Eldon, while his elder brother William, another vocal supporter of Bowes, would go on to become Lord Stowell and a prominent divorce lawyer. Eight-year-old Maria, taking a precocious interest in current affairs back in London, relayed details of her new 'papa's' parliamentary challenge to great aunt Mary at Glamis with more than a touch of her mother's naivety. 'It is believed Sir John Trevylian got the Election by bribery, and Papa has petioned [sic] the House of Commons,' she wrote.[39] Although the appeal was in vain, Bowes had hoodwinked Newcastle's radicals sufficiently to promise a return match. But if Bowes's smooth political wiles had attracted both personal and political slurs, Mary's apparently compliant devotion brought her equal condemnation. The anonymous author of *The Stoniad*, published during the by-election campaign, not only accused Bowes of sending his first wife to her grave but presciently predicted that he would beat his second wife '*black and blue*'. Yet the satirist expressed no sympathy for her plight, instead proclaiming that the pair were well-matched as 'the greatest R**** [rogue] and W**** [whore]'. Likewise Edward Montagu would grimly predict: 'I believe this gentleman will revenge the wrongs Lord Strathmore suffered from her Ladyship.'[40]

Having expended colossal amounts fighting the by-election – he would later put the total at more than £15,000 – and with his creditors pressing in, Bowes set off with Mary on the return journey to London at the end of March with renewed determination to seize the fortune so long in his sights. 'The very large sums I have been obliged to pay here, on Act. of the Election etc etc has destroyed me for the present not a little,' he told one friend.[41]

Before leaving Gibside he sacked George Walker, telling servants and friends that the footman had 'taken familiarities' with his mistress and had boasted that he was 'too well acquainted with her secrets ever to be dismissed'.[42] Bowes would later allege that Walker had slept with Mary both before and after her second marriage, a claim backed by Eliza Stephens née Planta, who had accompanied the couple to Newcastle ostensibly as Mary's companion but in reality as Bowes's spy and probably his mistress; Bowes was spotted leaving Eliza's room at five o'clock one morning while at Gibside after the election.[43] Testifying that Mary had had sex with Walker even as Bowes lay wounded after the duel and that they had resumed their affair soon after the wedding, Eliza's only evidence was having heard the pair laughing together in Mary's locked bedchamber. In reality Bowes had obviously dismissed the footman after learning that he had been given a copy of the trust deed, as a letter which Bowes sent to the Reverend Stephens indicated. 'I have discharged trusty George this morning in great disgrace,' he cryptically informed Stephens, while instructing him to allow Walker to collect from Grosvenor Square 'anything that is really his Property'.[44] An accompanying letter from Mary, almost certainly dictated by Bowes, urged Stephens to search the footman's boxes and drawers, remove any papers bearing her handwriting and fasten the locks as if nothing had been disturbed. Packing his trunk, which naturally Bowes had searched, Walker left the family – with the deed safely concealed in a false bottom.

Back in London at the beginning of April, Mary – now truly five months pregnant – was reunited with her eldest daughter who turned nine that month. While the three youngest children had been despatched for the Easter holidays to their grandmother's, where eight-year-old John was to join them as a rare treat, Mary kept Maria close. 'She is now so far advanced & so much improved as to be a most pleasant & entertaining companion to her mother, who could not possibly spare her,' Bowes informed a friend.[45] Dictating when Mary was allowed to see her children, Bowes was careful to portray himself the doting stepfather.

When the departure of her faithful footman was followed by that of the Reverend Stephens and his wife Eliza a few days later, Mary felt more alone than ever. Having given the couple £1,000 on the night of her wedding, most probably in the spirit of a bribe to conceal her pregnancy, Mary little suspected that Eliza's own expected confinement was not all it seemed. After staying in France for ten days the couple headed north to Cole Pike Hill, the estate Bowes had wrested from the heirs of his first wife Hannah, whose mother had only just died there. Here Eliza gave birth to the child she had been expecting when she married her compliant chaplain. Whether Stephens initially believed the child was his is unclear; he would later admit he had married Eliza only ten days after their first meeting although she would deny having placed an advertisement seeking a husband.[46] Plainly Bowes had masterminded the match – the £1,000 gift a thoughtful honeymoon present – and doubtless the child was his, judging from the later reaction of the Reverend Stephens. George Walker, who visited the couple at their hideaway that spring when Eliza was 'big with child', later recalled that 'the Parson damn'd Stoney very much to me'.[47] Unaware of their complicity in Bowes's deceits, Mary grieved at losing the couple she thought were her 'sincere and faithful friends'. Yet within a year, her views poisoned by Bowes, Mary would fume, 'had I known her as I do now, I should not only have intreated you to turn her out of the house directly [but] have confessed, that such a wretch was not fit to live on the earth' while of Eliza's husband she stormed, 'I should have thought only with horror of his ever being near my sons, or in my house.'[48] How the couple had offended Bowes at that point was unclear but after a reconciliation some years later they would prove vital to his cause.

By now desperate to lay his hands on Mary's tantalising riches, on 1 May Bowes threw a dinner party in Grosvenor Square to which he invited a few trusted friends, including Mary's surgeon John Hunter, a cleric named the Reverend Dr John Scott, and a pliable lawyer from Newcastle called William Gibson. Retiring to the drawing room after a generous dinner, where he continued to ply his guests with copious quantities of alcohol, the genial host casually asked his fellow diners to witness himself and Mary signing a legal document. Hunter, quite probably chosen for his acknowledged distaste for reading – he was dyslexic – would later admit that he never read the document. Mary herself would swear that she had no recollection of signing her name but admitted that she frequently signed papers at Bowes's command and often when befuddled by beatings. Signed in the dim light of candles, the five-page parchment revoked Mary's prenuptial deed and gave Bowes control, during his lifetime at least, over all income and profits from his wife's entire estate.[49] Once again Mary found herself devoid of all possessions, income and rights. Nearly a year after Bowes had first devised his tortuous moneymaking scheme he had finally got his hands on the Bowes family fortune.

There was much call on the funds. Forcing Mary to lace her corsets tightly to conceal her blooming figure as they visited moneylenders in the City, Bowes raised £24,000 by selling annuities – a popular way for cash-poor life tenants to obtain capital – which assigned future rents from the Gibside estate to various brokers.[50] With the proceeds he appeased the most urgent of his own and Mary's creditors – Bowes always detested settling debts unless it was absolutely unavoidable – then paid a hefty £12,000 in compensation to George Gray. Seemingly satisfied with his windfall, the once ardent suitor embarked for Bengal the following year only to die there two years later.[51] Having despatched Mary's erstwhile lover, Bowes now faced the delicate problem of his illegitimate child.

Even the most constricting of corsets and generous of gowns could no longer disguise Mary's condition to the ever-vigilant scrutiny of servants and acquaintances. So as the *bon ton* fled the hot and pungent capital in their annual exodus for the countryside that May, Bowes and Mary packed their belongings and rattled out of Grosvenor Square on the pretext of a holiday on the Continent. Informing one of his political allies in Newcastle that he was embarking on 'a Journey to the South of France' on the advice of his physicians to treat a 'cough & pain in my side', Bowes promised he would soon be returning to 'my friends in the north'.[52] But instead of heading east towards Dover, the couple's carriage turned west along the King's Road towards the quiet pastoral retreat of Hammersmith.

With contraception unreliable and unpopular, and attempts at abortion both precarious and taboo, many women had no alternative but to go ahead with unexpected pregnancies. Just as Eliza had scurried into the wilds of County Durham to give birth to her illegitimate child, so women of all classes, from prostitutes to duchesses, were forced to arrange clandestine deliveries for their unplanned babies. Among the medical fraternity, several 'man-midwives' were well-known for their circumspection in attending secret births. William Hunter, the physician brother of the surgeon John Hunter, was as infamous for his discretion in delivering the offspring of illicit aristocratic liaisons as he was famous for supervising the births of the fifteen royal princes and princesses. So William had helped Lady Diana Spencer give birth secretly in 1767 to the daughter of her affair with Topham Beauclerk and with the couple's collusion the following year he gave evidence of the event to enable her husband, Viscount Bolingbroke, to secure a divorce.[53] A year later William similarly attended Anne, Duchess of Grafton, the daughter of Bowes's coal-owning partner Henry Liddell, when she gave birth to the child of her affair with John Fitzpatrick, the Earl of Upper Ossory. And although he was generally the soul of discretion, at dinner parties William would boast of having once delivered twins to the daughter of a well-known peer in the basement of her family home while her parents maintained complete ignorance upstairs. He even arranged for the unwanted babes to be deposited in the Foundling Hospital. Yet such clandestine births were highly risky – not least for the medical men involved. One man-midwife who was called to a birth in Bristol in 1755, was escorted blindfolded to a luxurious mansion where he was asked to deliver a woman whose face was kept covered throughout. Three weeks later the hapless practitioner was found dead.

Laden with their scant belongings, accompanied by a few, if any, servants, Bowes and Mary drew up outside a remote cottage on the north bank of the Thames beyond Chelsea. Bowes would later describe this simply as 'a house in Hammersmith' which he had rented as a secret hideaway for Mary's expected delivery. His surgeon Jessé Foot, in his usual grandiloquent style, referred to it as 'a house the Margravine of Ansbach had left, quite secluded from the busy prying eye of curiosity'. Here, Foot added, in a snide allusion to husbands being cuckolded, 'Bowes might hear the cuckoo ... without its being unwelcome to the married ear'.[54] The most probable candidate for the isolated riverside abode was Craven Cottage, a simple two-storey thatched villa which had recently been built as a pastoral retreat by Lady Elizabeth Craven, the future Margravine of Brandenburg-Ansbach-Bayreuth.[55] Just a year younger than Mary, Lady Craven had already established a reputation that was at least as scandalous. The daughter of the Earl of Berkeley, she had married William Craven in 1767 whereupon both indulged in flagrant extra-marital liaisons. After winning the lottery in 1776 or 1777, Lady Craven had bought or built her secluded villa with the proceeds and invited friends such as Boswell and Walpole to visit. With its six bedrooms plus servants' quarters, and 'fine view of the river', it would be described by another visitor, Lady Mary Coke in 1781, as 'pretty as everything upon the Thames must be'.

Bounded by the river to the south, meadows to the east

and high walls on the remaining two sides, the riverside retreat provided the perfect location for Mary's clandestine delivery. Concealed from inquisitive city eyes, Mary spent the summer days in her arcadian isolation awaiting her first contractions while Bowes tormented her with his petty restrictions and violent outbursts. When she went into labour in August, it was not William Hunter but his brother John who was called upon to assist the birth, along with Dr James Ford, a physician with a lucrative West End obstetrics practice.[56] Both were sworn to secrecy. Unplanned and unwanted, kept hidden from society and from her siblings, the baby, Mary's third daughter, was also named Mary and took the Bowes surname. Her only child conceived out of wedlock, this bubbly, mischievous, cheeky infant would become Mary's most precious child as well as a favourite with her siblings.

The following month, with the newborn baby probably despatched to a well-bribed wet-nurse, the couple travelled north to Gibside where Mary pretended she was a respectable seven months pregnant. The pair attended church at Whickham two Sundays running in October, doubtless to create the impression that the birth was imminent and very likely with Mary's gown padded to suggest a bulge, for there was nothing Bowes enjoyed better than play-acting. In a characteristically abusive letter to his father on 14 November, Bowes claimed that his physician friend John Scott was close at hand since Mary was 'so very near her time'.[57] When the supposed time arrived, Bowes despatched an urgent request to two physicians who arrived breathless at Gibside Hall – just a little too late. Assured that the baby had been born healthy and that the mother was now asleep, the medics accepted their fees and left.[58] The bouncing baby, now almost three months old, was duly baptised in a private ceremony in

Whickham Church on 25 November, her birthday given as 16 November 1777, and her arrival announced in the London magazines the same month.[59]

Mary would always vehemently deny any suggestion that her beloved third daughter was illegitimate for to make such an admission would almost certainly condemn the child to a lifetime of social stigma and tarnish her prospects of a decent marriage. With its characteristically unenlightened approach, eighteenth-century law regarded illegitimate children as nonentities, so that they were unable either to inherit or to bequeath property.[60] Straitened parishes, which were obliged to support illegitimate offspring, might force their parents to marry and the father to provide maintenance, sometimes after whipping the errant couple through the village streets. Mothers, who were inevitably regarded as the chief bearers of guilt, could be sent to houses of correction to atone for their crime. Usually dismissed from their employment and unable to find further work – even when their employer was the father of the expected child – many working-class mothers were unable to support their illegitimate children and were therefore forced to surrender them to the Foundling Hospital or workhouse. Children born out of wedlock to the aristocracy and gentry fared considerably better. Following the example of successive monarchs, many wealthy parents acknowledged their 'natural' children; some of them rose to positions of significant power. Yet as social attitudes to marital infidelity hardened towards the end of the eighteenth century, even high-born illegitimate children found themselves struggling against a tide of prejudice.

Little Mary's birthday would therefore always be celebrated within the Bowes family in November. At one point her mother anxiously begged the Gibside agent to check the parish register and was relieved to hear that 'Miss Bowes his

Maria, nine and Anna, seven, the children themselves were
ffectively asking the court to remove them from their
other's care. With rights for children an alien concept in
ghteenth-century legal circles, they were almost certainly
t consulted. Tenuously arguing that Mary's right to guard-
ship of the children had been rendered void by her second
riage, Lyon – as the children's 'next friend' in customary
language – insisted that the children be delivered into
re of the three remaining guardians. Giving full vent
s of resentment, Lyon blustered that Mary had now
l 'improvidently and much below her dignity and
a man who possessed 'very small and Inconsiderable
fortune in his own Right'. By reason of her second
among 'many other accounts' Mary had therefore
rself 'improper and not fit to have the Care and
nt of the persons and fortunes' of her five children.
's principal concern was the children's future
nd the £50,000 now due for their education and
was plain from his repeated references to their
the Gibside estate.

ely left four of the children in the care of their
nd the dubious Stephenses for most of the
ken little interest in her eldest son, it was
ary began to realise how much she valued
Perhaps softened by her recent experience
aps frightened at her enforced loneliness,
the maturity she had previously lacked,
n a desperate battle to keep them. Bowes,
n reasons for valuing the children, well
produced his own heir to the Gibside
f maintaining control over its profits
esent heirs. But it was already too late.
iate demand to deliver the youngsters

[sic] properly registerd in Whickham Church B
there was really no doubt that the baby had b
delivered that summer, as rumours were quic
The following year a typically vindictive sati
latest society intrigues would accuse Mary c
months pregnancy at least' before giving
Midwife's vulgar aid'. A year later a pc
allege that Bowes 'contrives also to hav
into the world with *teeth*, after the m
Bowes himself would have none
about the child's welfare. For all
baby as his daughter he would
been born six months into th
delivery had been a concocti
tantly admit under oath tha
six or seven months after h
late on whether the fathe
Walker. Her maid Isab
that the child had b
'common conversati
was Gray or Walke

Yet as she dot
Gibside, Mary
her other five
seized the fa
over its you
begun co
care of
of Cha
that
fell
th
earl,

into his care and relinquish all rights to them, Mary and Bowes stalled the repeated requests of Lyon's lawyers for a response to the Chancery bill. Playing for time, which was always a generous commodity in Chancery suits, Mary could have had little doubt that ultimately the courts would tender no sympathy for a mother's rights.

Of course, as Lyon so pertinently alleged, and Mary was acutely aware, in reality Bowes was neither a responsible steward of Gibside nor a respectable stepfather to its heirs. Virtually a captive in her own home, with only her baby daughter and watchful servants for company, she was powerless to prevent Bowes neglecting the magnificent gardens and woodland. Equally, as the rumours over the likely father of her baby swirled around the Durham countryside, Mary knew that it was Bowes who had already been unfaithful on at least two occasions – and probably more – in their first year of marriage.

Bowes's reputation as a Lothario was already well established in the north-east, as the snide asides about his familiarity with Newcastle's brothels demonstrated. How much Mary had gleaned of her husband's previous dalliances is unsure. Certainly she had learned of his involvement with Anne Massingberd – if not the full extent of their relationship – soon after her marriage, since which time Mary had exchanged letters with Bowes's former mistress. Distraught to hear of her ex-lover's reported injuries, and even more so of his subsequent marriage, Anne had continued to bombard Bowes, and later Mary, with her pitifully tragic letters. Guilelessly revealing her infatuation, as well as her credulity, she assured Mary: 'You are my dear Madam possess'd of a Treasure, the heart of the most amiable of Men, which may you ever retain unmolested.'[65] By the summer, however, even the gullible Anne had begun to doubt Bowes's honesty, wretchedly telling him that 'my Eyes now begin to be opened, the dream is almost over & wth. it my sad life must end, for to outlive the idea that you have some truth & sincerity in you is impossible.' It was not long before Anne was fully woken from her dream – or nightmare – for a friend who met her in Scarborough in August reported with satisfaction that, 'Miss Massingberd is here, & seems to have pretty well recovered the loss of Captain Stoney.' A few months later 30-year-old Anne was married – to the 46-year-old Reverend William Maxwell, the Irish friend that Bowes had deputed to duel on his behalf that summer – and soon after she left her family home to begin married life in Ireland. If Mary's suspicions had not been aroused by Anne's gushing correspondence, clear evidence of her husband's voracious sexual appetite arrived by letter that same summer.

As she had awaited the first birth pangs beside the river in Hammersmith that July, Mary had been asked by Bowes to read his post while he was temporarily absent. Eight months pregnant, Mary had accordingly opened a letter to Bowes from a young woman begging to see him. Obviously a kept mistress who had recently been abandoned by Bowes, the poorly educated woman complained that, 'none but the Almighty can tell of my secret sufrings of hart and calamity of mind'.[66] Describing Bowes as a 'man of honour', the writer signed herself Elizabeth Dock, with an address near the Haymarket, a short stroll from their Grosvenor Square house. Most probably desperate for money, if not for her errant lover, Elizabeth added the postscript: 'I have been very often in the Gardens But was not so fortunate as to see the much desired object of my Desire.' When Mary angrily confronted Bowes with the letter he fervently denied all knowledge of the writer and insisted there had been a terrible mistake.

Finally alive to her husband's trail of deceit, Mary feigned belief out of 'delicacy and humanity'. It was the first and only time, she later said, that she ever saw contrition from him.

There was no mistake about his next indiscretion. That August Bowes had shown Mary a letter from a young woman, a certain 'Mrs G', whom he had entertained alone at Grosvenor Square. Now he insisted that Mary return the favour by visiting the woman who, he candidly told her, had previously been his mistress and given birth to his stillborn child. It was only the beginning of a succession of young women, most of them poor servants, destitute working girls or prostitutes, whom Mary was expected to entertain and befriend as her equals. As a respectable, wealthy married woman in the highest ranks of Georgian society, this was demeaning and distasteful. Yet in reality these vulnerable women, many just teenage girls, were her equals in misfortune. From now on, Mary decided there was no need to pretend ignorance of her husband's philandering.

It was a cold and gloomy winter in the north. As the year drew to a close, and Bowes caroused on his bawdy nights on the town while Mary cradled her little daughter alone in Gibside Hall, she came to realise that her husband was nothing but a cheat, a fraud and a serial adulterer. Gazing from the windows at the forbidden walks and mocking column, Mary waited in fear for the crunch of gravel which signalled the return of her husband's carriage. If Bowes had been disappointed at the betting table, thwarted in a sexual conquest or enraged by any obstacle to his schemes, Mary knew she would bear the brunt of his temper. Frequently, she later wrote, he was 'out of humour with his Mistresses or money matters; and always on those occasions came home and beat, pinched, kicked or pulled me by the ears and nose, often thrusting his nails into my ears, which he made stream with blood; spitting also in my face, and telling me, that he only married to torment me'.[67]

The New Year brought no resolutions for change. On the first anniversary of their wedding, 17 January 1778, Bowes coldly informed Mary that he intended to make every day of her life more miserable than the last – a pledge which, unlike his marriage vows, he intended to keep. Yet even as Mary looked back on her first year with the man who had become her jailor, tormentor and abuser, she managed to convince herself that he might still change for the better.

7
Loathsome Weeds

Cape Town, January 1778

Returning to his lodgings in Cape Town at the end of his first expedition into the inhospitable interior of southern Africa, William Paterson was exhausted but inspired. As he unpacked the bounty of seeds, bulbs and dried plants that he had collected, along with his bulging notebook and exquisite paintings, the 22-year-old gardener could hardly wait to set off exploring again. Having arrived in Cape Town in May the previous year after a testing three-month voyage, Paterson had spent the intervening months acquainting himself with the exotic landscape.[1] It was a far cry from his homeland in Scotland.

Born in August 1755, in the little village of Kinnettles near Forfar, just four miles from Glamis, William Paterson was the son of a gardener who worked on a nearby estate. Nothing about his early life is known beyond the fact that he followed in his father's footsteps, taking a keen interest in plants, and that, judging from his later writings, he enjoyed little formal education. He may have trained as an apprentice gardener at Syon Park, home of the Duke and Duchess of Northumberland on the opposite side of the Thames from Kew, for he had certainly become friendly with William Forsyth, a fellow Scot who was head gardener there from 1763 to 1771. A letter to Forsyth written a week after his arrival in Cape

Town sent compliments to 'Mrs Forsyth and all the family and my old fellow servants'.[2] Equally, he may have been apprenticed to Forsyth after the latter took charge of Chelsea Physic Garden, the Society of Apothecaries' medicinal garden beside the Thames, in 1771.

How Paterson, a poorly educated but bright young gardener with dark hair and deep brown eyes, had come to the attention of Mary Eleanor Bowes in 1776 is a mystery. Conceivably she had met him as a youth when he lived near Glamis, or alternatively through her northern neighbour, the Duchess of Northumberland, whose balls she had enjoyed as a child. Most probably, however, Paterson had been recommended as a suitable candidate for her botanical mission by one of Mary's friends within her scientific network. He had, of course, attended a Royal Society meeting with Solander in May 1776; no doubt he had read Francis Masson's account of his Cape travels published in the society's *Philosophical Transactions* later that year; and in all likelihood he would have studied Masson's African spoils transplanted into the new hothouse at Kew. One visitor in May 1776, the Reverend Michael Tyson, had marvelled: 'Mr Masson showed me the New World in his amazing Cape hothouse, erica 140 species, many protea, geranium and cliffortias more than 50.'[3] Certainly, by the time he set sail from Plymouth on 9 February 1777, less than a month after Mary's second marriage, young Paterson felt confident in the knowledge that his entire trip was being bankrolled by his generous patron. 'In this undertaking, I account myself particularly fortunate in having been patronized by the Honourable Lady Strathmore,' he would later write, 'whose zeal for botanical researches induced her readily to accede to the proposal of exploring an unknown country in search of new plants, and to honour me with her protection and support.'[4]

Having disembarked in Cape Town at the start of the southern African winter, Paterson had delayed any serious exploration until travelling conditions improved. In the meantime, for all his lack of education, he had successfully insinuated himself into the elite social circle of the settlement's white colonialists and undertook some minor excursions to accustom himself to the habitat. One of these entailed an arduous climb up Table Mountain in the company of Captain Robert Gordon, a highly intelligent and urbane army officer who had been born in Holland to a family of Scottish descent. Having previously visited the Cape in 1773, Gordon had returned in 1777 as second-in-command of the Dutch garrison that controlled the region. Immediately forming a strong bond with the Scottish gardener, with whom he shared a passion for natural history, Gordon would later say that Paterson's 'pleasant personality gave me very much companionship'.[5] Also joining the merry climbing party was William Hickey, the rakish lawyer who had arrived at the Cape en route for Calcutta. In Hickey's naive estimation, Paterson was 'a great botanist' who had been employed to collect rare plants and natural curiosities 'by that strange and eccentric woman, Lady Strathmore'.[6]

Recounting the little expedition with pleasure, Hickey wrote that Gordon and Paterson had called on him at 4 a.m. to begin the ascent. Although Hickey would describe the climb as 'dreadfully steep and rugged', in truth it was far more onerous for the servants burdened with the travellers' baggage and refreshments. After a few hours' climb, the party stopped for breakfast in a large cave where Hickey discovered 'a table spread with tea, coffee, cold ham, fowls, with other articles of food, all of the best kind'. While the party ate and enjoyed the stunning view of Cape Town, they were serenaded by two servants on flutes. It was, Hickey concluded, the 'pleasantest breakfast I ever made'. It took two more hours to reach the summit, where further nourishment awaited the climbers in a previously erected tent, along with chilled wine and two French horn players. When Hickey said goodbye to Paterson a few weeks later to continue his journey to India, he declared his newfound friend 'an ingenious young man'. It would be under quite different circumstances that they would meet again.

After his easy introduction to the region, Paterson had embarked on his first lengthy expedition as soon as weather conditions improved in October, heading due east from Cape Town in pursuit of the promised plants and seeds for his patron. He had not been disappointed. Although pioneer botanists had first explored the immediate vicinity of the Cape in the seventeenth century, the wider region had remained largely untouched by Europeans – and its floral treasures undiscovered – until the 1770s. In 1772, not one but three professional plant collectors had landed at the Cape in search of botanical enlightenment: Carl Peter Thunberg and Anders Sparrman, both Swedes, followed six months later by Masson on his royal quest. Companionably, Masson and Thunberg had teamed up for two expeditions, joined briefly by the capable Captain Gordon on his first Cape visit. Gordon's linguistic skills – he spoke Dutch, English, French, German and Gaelic and quickly mastered several native languages – no doubt aided communications. Although Sparrman had left just as Masson arrived, taking Masson's berth on Cook's *Resolution*, he had returned to the Cape in 1775 for a further two years' botanical study. Beginning his explorations just five years after these pioneers, in October 1777, young Paterson was still one of the first Europeans – and only the second British traveller – to penetrate the enticing Cape interior.

Travelling on horseback with his good friend Gordon, their baggage and provisions sent ahead in carts pulled by oxen, Paterson had followed the coastline before striking out over mountain terrain and grasslands as far as Beervlei at the confluence of the Kariega and Sout Rivers. On the way he discovered an abundance of strange and wonderful flora of varieties he had never seen before. 'Here I found a species of Erica, which was quite new,' he recorded excitedly, 'with a spike of long tubelar yellow flowers, the most beautiful I had ever seen.'[7] Meticulously collecting and describing the specimens he found, Paterson produced exquisite pictures – or had an accompanying draughtsman execute them for him; the identity of the artist remains uncertain.[8] Dogged and resourceful, Paterson spared no pains in his mission, at one time almost drowning when attempting to swim across a swollen river at night, and on another occasion nearly plunging to his death when his horse stumbled on a steep precipice. Braving lions and hippopotami, foraging for food and water, the two explorers enjoyed the hospitality of the 'Hottentot' or Khoikhoi people and excitedly gave their names to natural features including Gordon's and Paterson's Bays.[9] Reluctantly bidding the captain to continue without him when he fell ill, Paterson turned back in December. In poor health, but 'with my collection much increased' he arrived back in Cape Town on 13 January 1778.[10] It was the first of four expeditions Paterson would undertake over the next two years. Eagerly planning his next trip, he was blissfully unaware that the financial patronage that he relied on to foot the bill had abruptly come to an end.

Seated at her desk in her dressing room at Gibside, filling page after page with her neat script, Mary could only dream of the convivial feasts, thrilling adventures and heady freedom being enjoyed by her roving gardener. Barred from walking her gardens and denied the company of her friends, 28-year-old Mary had become subdued and submissive. After a full year of Bowes's beatings she had come to believe – like so many women in the same situation – that her own faults and failings were somehow responsible for the miseries she now endured. Accordingly, she had agreed to write for Bowes's eyes alone a full and frank catalogue of her past 'crimes' and 'imprudencies' in an effort to make amends and start anew. Later she would claim that the account which Bowes would maliciously publish as *The Confessions of the Countess of Strathmore* was completely false, composed at his dictation and extracted under the threat that she would never see her children again; on occasions she would even deny that she had written it at all.[11] Yet there is no doubt that the hundred-page tract was written by Mary and that much of it is accurate and corroborated by other sources. Foot would agree that the text was 'evidently extorted from her, under the tyranny of BOWES' and that it contained 'many falsehoods' but also, he averred, 'some truths'. While its verisimilitude would remain in question, Mary's candid description of her flirtations, love affairs and abortions would make it one of the most explosive documents to be published in the eighteenth century.

'I have been guilty', she began, 'of five crimes.'[12] First among these she numbered her 'unnatural dislike' of her eldest son, of which she had already long repented, followed by her affair with George Gray while Lord Strathmore was alive, her one attempted and three successful abortions, her broken pledge to marry Gray and – lastly and most poignantly – her subsequent marriage to Bowes, 'which together with my previous connection with you, I reckon amongst my crimes'. Her 'imprudencies' took a good deal longer to relate, beginning with her innocent teenage romances, her extra-marital dalliance with James Graham, her encouragement of a string of male admirers after Lord Strathmore's death, her gullibility in visiting fortune-tellers, and a series of ill-judged but essentially harmless social errors in trusting too freely or acting too familiarly with servants and acquaintances. Her folly, she now decided, in trusting Eliza Planta, the Stephens brothers, Captain Magra and Mr Matra, had been 'unpardonable'. 'I was more than imprudent in encouraging and keeping company with people of such execrable and infamous principles,' she submitted, 'though, indeed, I did not think them such then; but that is no excuse for me, as I ought not to have trusted or allowed any body to have frequented my house, without a previous long acquaintance.' Her greater folly in trusting the person with the most execrable and infamous principles of all, of equally short acquaintance, naturally passed unremarked. Above all she regretted entrusting her secrets to her disgraced footman George Walker, although whether she truly believed that he had since burnt his copy of her prenuptial deed, as she claimed, remained to be seen.

Looking back on her carefree childhood, to the tender upbringing and diligent education, she now blamed her father for a failure to instil 'a proper sense of religion' that might have prevented her later faults. Yet for all the snatched kisses and frothy letters she had exchanged with forward boys and rakish men since her father's death, and despite her media-generated reputation for licentiousness, in reality her love-life had been relatively chaste – certainly in comparison to many of Georgian society's more notorious characters. 'I do assure you,' she pleaded, 'that no man ever took the smallest liberty with me (Lord S. yourself, and Mr G. excepted) except three or four times that Mr Stephens kissed me, under one pretence or other; and once or twice that Mr G. S. as we were standing by the fire-side, put his arm around my waist.'

But if the description of Mary's indiscretions showed her in a poor light, the document which Bowes would later have no qualms about publishing revealed him in a far blacker guise. Laying before her husband a 'full account of every thing I ever did, said, or thought, that was wrong', Mary revealed that in return he had made her a promise never to 'repeat past grievances'; whether this referred to his brutality or his philandering was unspecified. That she had already suffered repeatedly from his violent outbursts was evident from her comment, 'I fear you are of an unforgiving, and in this respect, unforgetting temper; else you could not, for so many months together, have behaved so uniformly cruel to one whose wish and study was to please you.' With her spirit almost broken by her twelve months under Bowes's autocratic rule, she declared: 'I am already so loaded with misery that there is only one curse which is not mine already.' That one curse – to die – she now called upon herself should her confessions prove untrue. Seemingly bewildered at her husband's 'more than usual share of dislike to me', she plaintively promised 'if it please God to give me strength and resolution to trail out my existence till even you are convinced, by my example, that a person who has once been vicious, may repent and become good'.

Well aware that by her candid admissions she had provided Bowes with a fresh crop of excuses to ill-treat her, she submitted, 'but you are my husband – I obey you, and if you continue to distrust, abuse, and think of me as you have hitherto done, Providence must and will decide which of us two is most to blame'. Begging her husband to burn her confessions, or otherwise destroy them, when she died, 'that

I may not stand condemned and disgraced, under my own hand, to posterity', she pleaded with him to forgive 'all my sins and faults'. Yet even as Mary wrote the final words to her own denunciation on 2 February, Bowes was far from satisfied. Bursting into her dressing room that evening, he snatched up the sheets of writing and berated her for including trivial events in minute detail. At the same time he demanded that she admit to faking the 'fits' that she had suffered since childhood. A master of pretended illness and injury himself, Bowes refused to accept that the mysterious attacks which had occurred several times in their first year of marriage – quite possibly brought on by anxiety – were genuine; naturally, his physician friend, Dr Scott, had readily concurred. Keeping a tiny flicker of her old independence alive, Mary refused to submit to this diagnosis, insisting that her fits were authentic. Finally, swearing the truth of her testament on the Bible, Mary added the date, 3 February 1778, to the last page and hoped that her months of torture were at an end.

Far from honouring his side of the bargain, Bowes was emboldened by Mary's surrender to his will, pocketing her 'confessions' with unconcealed pleasure. Furnished with this unremitting account of dissipation, sexual precocity and unnatural maternal feelings, he knew that she was more in his power than ever. It was only upon reading this testament, he would later claim, that his eyes had been opened to his wife's true nature. From this point on, he would argue, he was forced to watch her conduct closely and control her actions accordingly. Indeed, just as Mary had feared, her self-confessed 'sins' would provide not only Bowes, but his apologists down the years, with justification for the most outrageous extremes of brutality.

True to his word, Bowes redoubled his campaign of

repression. Squandering Mary's fortune on gambling, presents for his mistresses and lavish entertainments for his Newcastle cronies, Bowes kept Mary impoverished and virtually imprisoned at Gibside. Deprived of money, prevented from buying new clothes and frequently half starved – the cook and kitchen maids were instructed only to take orders from Bowes – Mary's once plump face now looked gaunt, her formerly opulent gowns shabby. Skilfully disguising his neglect and abuse, Bowes hoodwinked the servants and guests into believing the Gibside mistress was eccentric, slovenly and accident-prone. Mary's genuine shortsightedness was conveniently blamed for the numerous occasions on which she supposedly bumped into doors, fell down stairs or singed her hair in the fire; her dishevelled appearance was ascribed to her lack of interest in clothes; her apparent loss of appetite on her faddy tastes. Schooled by Bowes, Mary frequently appeared impolite or deranged in company. On occasions he would warn her only to reply yes or no to any question, at other times only to say that the weather was hot or cold, and sometimes to refuse to speak at all, so that guests presumed her to be mad, rude or stupid. If she deviated at all from this prearranged behaviour, Bowes would briskly administer 'a threatening frown, a sly pinch, or a kick with his foot' out of sight of his guests.[13]

Just as he had done with his first wife, Bowes cleverly sculpted a public image of Mary as truculent, difficult and disordered. Meanwhile, he presented himself as the aggrieved husband, tenderly attempting to guide his awkward wife. Feigning concern for her wellbeing whenever he was away from home, he would frequently despatch messages enquiring after her health and her appetite. As contrived as his sham duel, the performance was a meticulously planned fiction which Mary would find difficult to shake.

Behind closed doors, his brutality intensified. 'In 1778 he beat me several times,' wrote Mary, 'particularly once with a thick stick, the head of which was heavy with lead; and with the handle of a horsewhip, which he had then in his hand, being just come in from hunting.'[14] Now drinking heavily, Bowes would return from his nights on the town inebriated and enraged. One Newcastle friend, who found it hard to keep pace, complained that Bowes's carousing often lasted into the early hours, after which 'one is sure to be in a Condition in which no Man would wish to be in the Streets'.[15] Inevitably Mary bore the brunt of his drunken rages, submitting to his violence in private just as she colluded with his charade in public. By now the servants had learned to turn a blind eye to their mistress's cuts and bruises, accepting the tales of her clumsiness without question rather than risking their master's wrath themselves. Nevertheless they observed the change in Mary's demeanour. One maid who worked for Mary before and after her marriage to Bowes noted the 'great alteration in her deportment' and remarked: 'Her Ladyship appeared dejected, and to have no will of her own.' Another, who had stayed on after the marriage, overheard Bowes order Mary to tell the servants she had received a black eye by accident and stated: 'His whole behaviour was cruel and ill-natured in general, and not confined to particular instances.'[16]

Living in fear of the violence her husband meted out, Mary knew that there was little she could do in her defence. Marital violence is as old as marriage itself; during the eighteenth century wife-beating was not only common and widely tolerated but even supported by law. One legal manual, first published in 1736, explained that husbands could lawfully beat their wives to keep them to their duties, although it cautioned that such chastisement should not be 'violent or cruel'. Another popular legal writer described a husband's right to 'give his wife moderate correction', since by law he was liable for her conduct, but argued that this should be kept 'within reasonable bounds'.[17] One well-known judge, Francis Buller, would even proclaim that a husband could lawfully chastise his wife as long as he used a stick no bigger than his thumb, earning himself the nickname 'Judge Thumb' in the process. Yet even when wives suffered sustained and severe violence, they had little recourse in law. Although a wife could swear 'articles of peace' against her husband if she feared life-threatening injury, the Church courts could still compel her to return to the marital home for 'restitution of conjugal rights'. And while the same Church courts could grant a separation on grounds of cruelty, this was allowed only rarely, in cases of extreme and repeated violence deemed unjustifiable by the all-male judges. Virtually powerless to curb his conduct, Mary simply endured her husband's rages in silence. But content no longer to abuse only his wife, Bowes now endeavoured to lure others into his control.

In May 1778, Bowes recruited a chaplain, the Reverend Samuel Markham, who joined the Gibside household along with his wife Jane. That month – just as William Paterson set out on his second expedition at the Cape – Bowes embarked for Ireland, taking ship from Portpatrick in Scotland, with Mary and the Markhams in tow. Whether he took the infant Mary, now nine months old, to present to his family as his first-born is unknown; a good three months chubbier than her pretended age, she may well have remained with a nursemaid at Gibside.

The purpose of the visit was most probably a desire by Bowes to capitalise on the lands he still owned in Ireland; exacting an advantageous price for them from his relatives had plagued him for several years. It was nevertheless a first opportunity for Mary Eleanor to meet her in-laws and their ever-expanding family in Tipperary. Elizabeth Stoney, her mother-in-law, had given birth to her eleventh child, George Stoney junior, just four years earlier. Despite the haughty letters that Mary had been forced by Bowes to write to his father, she made a favourable impression on the family – an affection which proved mutual, especially between Mary and her namesake, Bowes's 20-year-old sister. When the Bowes retinue returned to England the following month, Mary Stoney accompanied them, encouraged by her ambitious mother in the face of heartfelt objections from her father. The chance to enjoy the English social scene, under the escort of her handsome big brother and his well-connected wife, seemed too tempting an opportunity for a lively young woman of marriageable age. Before leaving Ireland Bowes promised his father that he would send his sister home within six months. He had no such intention.

Back at Gibside in time for the Newcastle races in June, Bowes introduced his sister into polite northern society, taking pains as always to present himself to his potential electorate as the courteous husband, brother and benefactor. One society belle, Judith Milbanke, delightedly reported partnering Bowes at the city's splendid new assembly rooms. 'I . . . had the honour to open the Ball with a double Minuet, Lady Strathmore & Lord Fielding at Top, your humble servant & Mr Bowes at bottom.'[18] Cutting a commanding figure on the dance floor, Bowes never lost his touch with the ladies; a generous subscriber to the new assembly rooms, he knew just as effectively how to charm the city's dignitaries.[19]

Yet the seemingly cosy family scenario belied the bleak truth. Well aware that his play-acting would not pass muster with the shrewd Mrs Bowes, Bowes forbade Mary from any private conversation with her mother and scrutinised their correspondence. Nevertheless, rumours of his ill-treatment and scandalous conduct had already reached Mrs Bowes's ears and she now urged Mary to leave him – despite the inevitable social outcry this would generate – even if she refused to believe the tales of physical violence. Knowing the grief it would cause her mother to hear the truth and hopeful she could still reform her abuser, Mary denied that Bowes mistreated her.[20] But just as Bowes curtailed her connections with her immediate family, so the law now conspired to sever all links with her children.

That June, just after her return from Ireland, Mary was forced to surrender her five children by Lord Strathmore to their three other guardians, as Chancery made them wards of court.[21] Not bothering even to consult their mother, Thomas Lyon immediately removed six-year-old George and five-year-old Thomas from their grandmother's home and sent them to join their brother John, now nine, at his school in Neasden. The two girls, Maria, now ten, and Anna, just turned eight, were summarily packed off to a girls' boarding school in Queen's Square, London. Distraught at being forced to give up all rights to her children, Mary consoled herself with the belief that the other guardians would grant her reasonable access; in reality, she hoped, she would see them scarcely less than she already did. Her optimism was sorely misguided. From the moment that Lyon gained charge of his nephews and nieces – and the funds set aside to maintain them – he enacted a vice-like control over their daily lives. Dictating every aspect of their education and their leisure time, austere Uncle Thomas moulded the children to his demanding ideals, while poisoning their minds against their mother. And not only would they rarely be granted visits to their mother, separated by their schooling they would hardly see each other. When Lyon, at the family home in County Durham he had now inherited from his late mother, was unable to oversee their activities, he dragooned his sister, Lady Anne Simpson, to supervise the youngsters in London. As parsimonious as his brother had been profligate, Lyon maintained meticulous accounts of the children's expenses which survive even now: their bills for shoes, clothes, medicine, haircuts, books and lessons, their accounts for tuition, board and pocket money, all folded and bound in tiny bundles as sad mementoes of their carefully monitored and catalogued young lives.

So the girls' first outings to the opulent West End shops to choose the colourful silks and satins for their first grown-up gowns, to be fitted for their first stays, to buy dancing pumps, gloves and fans for their first balls and theatre trips, were supervised not by their mother but by Aunt Anne with the bills forwarded to Uncle Thomas.[22] When George, always a sickly child, fell ill that autumn, his tutors sent for the apothecary to bring his ineffectual potions to the boy's bedside in Neasden – and forwarded the medical bill to Lyon – rather than let his mother mop his fevered forehead. When Maria visited the dentist four times within twelve months, always an excruciating experience before the advent of anaesthesia, it was without her mother's hand to squeeze. And as all five children progressed at their lessons in reading, writing, French, drawing, music and history, their mother – who placed such importance on her own education – was denied any opportunity to encourage, praise or take pride in their achievements. Each of the children would cope in their own way. Maria, the eldest and most conscious of social correctness, readily conformed to her uncle's exacting regime and grew close to her socially adept aunt, while wayward

Anna remained alert for opportunities to rebel. For the two youngest boys, having scarcely seen their mother since infancy, there would be little lasting memory of her. And John, the quiet and thoughtful head of the little family, simply tried his best to appease both sides.

As appeals and counter-appeals against the Chancery decision lumbered on over the ensuing years, Mary's efforts to see her children would become more and more desperate. In all her attempts to gain access, Bowes would be solidly supportive; naturally it suited his purposes to exert control over the young Gibside heirs. That December, therefore, Bowes wrote to Lyon on Mary's behalf asking that the children be allowed to stay with them over the Christmas holidays.[23] Offering no reason, for he saw no cause to explain his actions to the children's mother, Lyon bluntly replied that he and his fellow guardians 'cannot agree to your Ladyship's request'. Knowing that the children were still allowed visits to their grandmother, who would at least ensure that they remembered their mother, Mary reluctantly accepted the decision.

It was another lonely Christmas at Gibside. As William Paterson set out on his third expedition at the height of the Cape summer that December, Mary watched helplessly from her windows as Bowes destroyed swathes of winter woodland in an effort to raise funds from the valuable timber. Once more beset by debts, Bowes insisted that they stay in the north to avoid his creditors and save money. 'I have given up all idea of going this winter to London,' he told his financial agent, William Davis, 'as I can live here for half the expence; beside I can never be happy TILL I GET OUT OF DEBT, and have money, if possible, to the good'.[24] Besieging Davis with instructions to take out insurance policies on Mary's life, in order to guarantee the numerous annuities he was arranging to raise extra funds, Bowes drove a hard bargain over interest rates.

Perpetually irritated over money matters, Bowes vented his frustrations on the captive little group within the Gibside walls. Markham's religious cloth afforded him no protection from his employer's wrath, for later he would testify that Bowes worked himself into 'the most violent passions upon the most frivolous occasions' and often behaved 'in a very cross savage manner without any Provocations'.[25] On one occasion, towards the end of January 1779, as the elderly chaplain dutifully said grace before dinner, Bowes retorted: 'Damn your Mercies. I want none of mercy.' A few evenings later, Bowes walked into the parlour to find the parson engrossed in conversation – probably with Mary and her sister-in-law – and lunged at the poor man with a barrage of blows for the simple reason that he had remained chatting too long after dinner. The Markhams promptly packed their bags and left. For the two Marys there was no such hope of escape.

No sooner had Mary Stoney passed through the gates of the Gibside estate than she realised her error in leaving her happy Irish home. From the moment that she set foot in Gibside Hall, she became subject to the obsessive rule with which her brother governed the entire household. When her approved six months' leave expired in December, Mary was forbidden from returning home and prevented from writing to her parents, while any letters her parents sent to her were immediately intercepted by her brother.[26] When Mary came of age a few days before Christmas, there had been few celebrations and little prospect of liberty. Indeed, now that Mary no longer required her parents' consent for marriage, it soon became plain that Bowes was concocting a plan to engage her to a wealthy suitor in return for rich pickings for himself. Yet despite her youth and familial allegiance, Mary Stoney's free spirit could not be so easily crushed.

Confined together for hours during the northern winter, effectively prisoners in the Gibside mansion, the two Marys grew close. Mary Eleanor confided in her young sister-in-law, whom she described as 'gentle, compassionate and generous' in complete contrast to her sadistic brother. Appalled by the stories of her brother's abuse as well as by the indubitable evidence in the marks on Mary Eleanor's face, Mary Stoney boldly attempted to stand up to her brother. On one occasion in 1779, when he spotted his wife leaving his sister's bedchamber, Bowes grabbed his horsewhip and lashed Mary Eleanor on the arms and legs on the grounds that she was not permitted to leave her sister-in-law alone. Fearful that his sister might try to escape, he had ordered Mary Eleanor to watch her at all times – a prisoner guarding another prisoner. When she heard about the attack, young Mary declared that she 'wished his hands would rot off'. She was soon to experience her brother's violence for herself.

Preparing for an outing to the theatre in Newcastle, the two women were dressing together when Bowes stormed in, found his sister not yet ready and viciously set about her with his ever-handy whip. When Mary Eleanor shrieked at him to stop, he thrashed her too. The weals that he caused on young Mary's neck were so swollen and painful that the theatre excursion had to be cancelled and she spent the ensuing day in bed. Forced the following evening to get up, under the threat that Bowes would beat her again, she was made to attend the postponed theatre trip with her neck chastely muffled to hide the raw wounds. It was no isolated incident. Now that he had two victims under his command, Bowes abused both his wife and his sister mercilessly; according to Mary Eleanor her sister-in-law was 'beaten & used by him almost as dreadfully as myself'. With no prospect of her brother's ill-treatment relenting and no way of alerting her parents to her plight, 21-year-old Mary was desperate to return home. It would be another eighteen months before she saw her chance.

Financially, at least, circumstances were looking up. In May, Bowes's humour improved when he found a buyer for Mary's beloved Stanley House in Chelsea. Just as William Paterson was preparing to set off on his fourth and final expedition at the Cape, in search of fresh novelties to boost his patron's prized collection, Bowes callously sold the villa complete with its extensive gardens, conservatories and hothouses. Writing to a friend, Bowes announced: 'I HAVE SOLD CHELSEA HOUSE, but have not got the money; which, however, when I do, must go to—, the banker.'[27] Only the conservatory and hothouse at Gibside remained, their exotic blooms and tropical fruits a tantalisingly short stroll away. Even though Bowes frequently sent the produce, including pineapples and melons, to the influential neighbours and city dignitaries he sought to cultivate, the greenhouse had begun to suffer from the neglect that he inflicted on the entire estate. Rather than ploughing his windfall into much-needed maintenance, Bowes paid off his most urgent creditors and in June sank the remainder into a racehorse.

Just like Mary's father and her first husband, Bowes had been bitten by the eighteenth-century obsession for the Turf. Horse racing had long been enjoyed as a popular British entertainment whether on designated race courses or village greens but, as skills in selective breeding advanced, so the competing steeds became bigger, stronger and faster and interest in the sport flourished.[28] Some of the most famous races, including the Epsom Derby and the St Leger at Doncaster, were run for the first time and the Jockey Club was founded, to set rules and govern practices, by a band of aristocratic fanatics in 1752. As the racing calendar expanded and the value of prizes soared, so meetings became magnets for all manner of side-shows, including cock-fights and freak shows as well as their corollaries of ruinous betting and drinking. Naturally, Bowes could not resist the thunder of the horses' hooves nor the attendant charms.

With the race weeks at Durham and Newcastle essential fixtures in the northern social diary, Bowes regarded the meetings as ideal opportunities to flaunt his civic benevolence to the gathered crowds. Shortly after marrying Mary, in July 1777 he had sponsored a £50 prize for one of the events at Durham races in an act of clearly calculated philanthropy.[29] Now he laid out £750 to buy a six-year-old racehorse, named Icelander, so that he could compete on equal terms with the aristocratic owners of the day. Making her first appearance at Hexham races that June she did not disappoint him. 'My mare walked over,' he gloated to a friend, reporting her victory by half a neck over the favourite in 'the finest race I ever saw'.[30] To Bowes's delight, Icelander went on to win major prizes that summer at Durham, Nottingham and Morpeth. Evincing more pride in his mare than he would ever bestow on his wife – and doubtless treating her with greater kindness – Bowes would hang on to Icelander until the end of her days.

Swaggering around the race courses with his rakish friends, Bowes was soon in financial strife again. As he rebuffed one of his weary creditors with a characteristically off-hand response that July, Bowes pleaded temporary poverty while asserting that, 'At this moment, I declare, I am worth, were all effects sold, above £50,000.'[31] It was little wonder that his chief legacy to posterity would be the term 'stoney broke'.

Among the friends who shared his taste for the licentious lifestyle of the Turf was Charles Howard, the Earl of Surrey, who would later succeed as the eleventh Duke of Norfolk but was better known to his contemporaries as 'the Jockey of Norfolk'.[32] An active supporter of Fox's Whigs, Howard championed reforms to end electoral corruption but was more than happy to dispense the boroughs in his patronage for exorbitant sums. A huge, shambling, whiskered oaf who was famed for his vulgar habits and unkempt dress, it was said that his servants waited until he was unconscious after one of his regular drinking bouts to plunge him into a bathtub. His rowdy dinners, at which he consumed quantities of beer and claret sufficient to astound even Georgian imbibers, were legendary and his notorious contempt for hygiene did nothing to deter several mistresses. His first wife having died giving birth to their stillborn child exactly nine months after their marriage, Howard had married a wealthy heiress but quickly had her certified mad and confined for life in a private asylum. Hard-drinking and hypocritical, he was, in short, a perfect companion for Bowes.

For all that Bowes could still charm his high-ranking friends and influential acquaintances on the social scene, his behaviour at home was becoming ever more irrational. One morning that same summer, Bowes sauntered into Mary's dressing room to find her eating breakfast with her long, thick chestnut hair falling over her shoulders. After observing her coldly for a few minutes he flew into a temper then snatched up a pair of scissors yelling, Mary later recorded, that he 'would spoil my locks, and teach me to dress my head lower than I did' before hacking off great chunks with the shears.[33] Such minute attention to Mary's hair, her clothes and her accessories, and the recurrent accusations that she was too familiar with her male servants, suggest that Bowes had a powerful sexual obsession with Mary or at least a compulsion to control her sexually. After all, even though Bowes claimed to despise her, the couple were still sharing a bed and he was eager to father an heir.

Yet for all his slurs on her virtue, and despite the pledges Bowes had made in order to extort her confessions, Mary remained suspicious that her husband was still finding sexual pleasure outside wedlock. Three letters that she discovered by chance, all sent to Bowes from the surgeon John Hunter at some point between 1778 and 1780, confirmed her doubts.[34] Carefully copying their contents before returning them to their place, Mary preserved the texts for future use. Beginning with his customary professional discretion, in the first letter Hunter refers to a 'friend' of Bowes for whom he has apparently been treating a woman in lodgings in Fleet Street, London. Complaining mildly that he has called on Bowes several times without success, Hunter states: 'I am teased & therefore I tease you; I think every Man should know what is going on concerning himself. I therefore apply to you, that you may acquaint your friend how he stands with the Lady in Fleet Street. If something was done in a more frugal way it would be better for all friends.' The second letter is more persistent, as Bowes had evidently evaded his responsibilities, as well as more revealing while maintaining the fiction of the mutual 'friend'. Now despairing that Bowes will return to London, Hunter implores him to decide on the future of the woman in his care and – it transpires – her child. 'My opinion is that she should go to service,' the surgeon suggests, 'for keeping her in the idle life, is doing her more hurt, than all that has been done.' Remembering to send his respects to 'Lady Strathmore and Miss Stoney', Hunter gives the game away with his postscript: 'The small pox was in the house, where the little thing is, should it be innoculated?' Reaching the end of his patience in the third and final letter, Hunter exasperatedly urges Bowes to respond. At last dispensing with the pretence of a 'friend', the surgeon writes: 'I have spent all your money, of which I will give you an account of when I have the pleasure of seeing you, or sooner if you would chuse to have the account.' Having ascertained that the woman in question would be happy to find employment – and save them both running up further bills – Hunter adds: 'There are some Suspicions that the little thing has got the measles. Should he not be inoculated?' Enclosed with one of the letters, Mary found a receipt for £113 'from Mr B' and a bill for a further £45 15s and 4d still owing.

Providing an illuminating insight into the arrangements for illegitimate offspring, the letters clearly indicate that Hunter had delivered the baby born of Bowes's extra-marital affair in an arrangement similar to that involving Mary just two years earlier. The 'Lady in Fleet Street' was obviously one 'M. Armstrong' from whom Mary intercepted a letter to Bowes at about the same time.[35] Written in the poor grammar characteristic of Bowes's impoverished mistresses, the letter pleads: 'I am extremley unhappy that I have not received an answer to my Last letter, you told me that you would leave orders with Mr Hunter wether I was to come to my last place or what I was to do.' Continuing without pause, she adds: 'I am with out Money and Cloase and that makes me very unhappy, I hope you will be kind enuf to send me answer what I am to doo and what sittiuation you would wish to place me.' M. Armstrong may also have been the 'Mary (with Red Hair)' who, George Walker would later declare, had given birth to two illegitimate children by Bowes. Whatever her identity, like all of the poor working girls Bowes would lure into relationships, she would find that the attentions of her generous lover disappeared as quickly as his money once too many inconvenient offspring appeared.

Studiously keeping his vices private, Bowes maintained the image of public virtue. The ostentatious displays of civic generosity and exotic gifts to powerful neighbours proved fruitful. Early in 1780 Bowes succeeded in getting himself elected High Sheriff of Northumberland, one of the most prestigious posts in the country, which brought with it important judicial responsibilities as well as further expenses.[36] Heavily in debt, holding his sister prisoner, regularly abusing his wife and fathering illegitimate children, the new High Sheriff was expected to work with local judges and justices of the peace, organise hue-and-cry chases and attend executions as a pillar of legal rectitude. With his eye firmly on his main goal, a seat in the House of Commons, Bowes threw lavish entertainments at Gibside where Mary was required to act her wifely part. Household accounts reveal the scale of their catering with one bill for the period listing 'Turkeys, Chickens, Butter, Cream, Salmon, Eggs, Pidgeons, Oranges, Apples and Letters [lettuce] for Mr Bowes and the Countess' while another for 1780 records the purchase of turkeys, chickens and seventy eggs.[37] According to Foot, 'his dinners were good, and his table enriched by massive plate' and yet, the surgeon added, 'there was always a smack of mean splendour about him, as he did not purchase one single new carriage, and his coach horses, originally of high value, were never seen in good condition'. Though he pressed his guests with fine wines and rich foods, Bowes's meanness of spirit was apparent too, for he invariably entertained the company by making one of his subordinates the butt of his jokes. To the tenants, villagers and miners who had long enjoyed the philanthropy of the Gibside owners, Bowes was infinitely more miserly. Previously permitted to roam the Gibside woods and lawns at will, now the locals found the walks barred by notices forbidding entry.[38] In truth, the splendour they had previously savoured was already tarnished, for Bowes had not only decimated the woods but had let the lawns become overgrown, the walks neglected and the Gothic architectural projects so proudly created by George Bowes to fall into disrepair. While Lady Liberty still gazed over the verdant valley, the former Eden was now tainted and sullied.

For William Paterson, back in Cape Town in early 1780 after returning from his fourth and final expedition into the south African interior, prospects had taken a severe turn for the worse. His mounting bills for provisions, lodgings, guides, oxen and other necessities having been returned from England unpaid, under Bowes's instructions, he was now seriously in debt, unable even to buy a passage home or pay his daily expenses. Entirely dependent on the 'protection and support' he had trustingly expected from his benefactor he was now destitute and abandoned in a foreign land.

The humble gardener from a remote Scottish hamlet had penetrated further into the Cape interior than any British traveller, collected a treasure trove of botanic marvels and discovered several new species. Still only twenty-four, Paterson had witnessed scenes that fellow Europeans would struggle to believe. Travelling on foot or on horseback, he had crossed mountains and forded rivers, observed zebras, monkeys and elephants in their natural habitats, and made contact with the Khoikhoi and Xhosa peoples, then known as Hottentots and Caffres. While he was not, as he would claim, the first European to visit what was then termed Caffraria – modern-day Eastern Cape – for Thunberg had beaten him to that accolade, he was certainly among the most enlightened. While Thunberg had sworn that a lion would 'much rather eat a Hottentot than a Christian' and had claimed that the 'Caffres' were so greedy for iron they would murder for it, Paterson had admired the Khoikhoi dance rituals and praised the Xhosa tribe's farming skills.[39] Determinedly pursuing his mission to discover new plant life, Paterson had endured all manner of adversity, travelling for days without food or water, and surviving on ostrich eggs, the 'rusty flesh' of hippos and broiled termites – which he pronounced 'far from disagreeable'. Twice he had undertaken expeditions in winter when heavy rainfall and swollen rivers made travelling treacherous, for the simple reason that: 'I was in hopes of discovering many plants which might endure our climate, and be rendered useful.'[40] In all, he had covered a greater distance – some 5,600 miles – than any of his botanical predecessors.

On his last expedition, following the coastline west and north from June to December 1779, he and Captain Gordon had become the first Europeans to locate the mouth of the Great or Orange River, the longest watercourse in southern Africa. Trekking through uninhabited desert where native guides initially refused to venture, their oxen dropping through lack of water, the pair named two hills the 'Two Brothers' in a gush of fraternity, although Paterson wryly noted that 'in this desolate region there was no one who could dispute any denomination by which we chose to distinguish whatever we met with'. When at last they had arrived at the steep sandy bank of the broad delta, Paterson recorded: 'In the evening we launched Colonel Gordon's boat, and hoisted the Dutch colours. Colonel Gordon proposed first to drink the State's health, and then that of the Prince of Orange, and the Company; after which we gave the river the name of the Orange River in honour of that Prince.' Intoxicated as much by their achievements as by their toasts, Paterson never lost sight of his primary goal, rhapsodising on his return journey over 'the most beautiful plant I ever saw of the Pentandria Monogynia class'. Wreathed with long spikes and crowned with spectacular red, yellow and green flowers, the plant towered above him. But before he had regained Cape Town, now travelling with a plantation owner, Sebastiaan van Reenen, Paterson had chanced upon an even more awesome sight: a herd of six giraffes. More commonly termed the *camelopardalis* or 'spotted camel', the giraffe had acquired almost mythical status among eighteenth-century naturalists who had heard reports of the bizarre-sounding creatures but doubted they could truly exist. Pursuing the beasts, before they could disappear into the realms of fantasy once more, van Reenen shot a male and Paterson proudly added its skeleton and skin to the cargo for his homeward journey.

Yet his discoveries and his trophies counted for nothing with his increasingly impatient creditors in Cape Town. Surrounded by his giraffe skin, crates of seeds, bulbs and plants, and some three hundred watercolours of flora and fauna, Paterson was now on the brink of being thrown into prison for his debts. Grudgingly, the garrison's commander, Lieutenant-Colonel Hendrik Prehn, lent him £500 to satisfy his immediate bills so that he could stay out of jail. The scale of his debts, amounting almost to the total £583 expenses Masson had accrued during his three expeditions at the Cape, suggests that Paterson had received little or no financial support from Mary during his entire stay.[41] And it was a much chastened and diminished man who greeted William Hickey when he called at the Cape on his return from India in February 1780. Hickey sadly recorded that, 'Her Ladyship, instead of fulfilling her engagements, suffered his bills to be protested and returned, thereby exposing him to great difficulties'.[42] Still penniless and stranded, Paterson was forced to borrow a further £400 from Hickey's servant, James Adcock, to buy a passage home. Writing Adcock a promissory note, Paterson assured him there was 'a considerable sum due to him from Lady Strathmore', a fact Hickey confirmed while approving Paterson as 'an honest man'. Having stowed his precious cargo of botanical treasures, Paterson sailed from the Cape on 10 March 1780 in a Dutch East Indiaman, the *Held Woltemade*, along with Hickey and his two creditors, Adcock and Prehn.

Arriving at Amsterdam three months later, Paterson's troubles only intensified. First Prehn demanded repayment with interest, threatening Paterson with a Dutch prison if he could not comply, then Adcock grew nervous over losing his loan should Paterson end up in jail. A 'greatly agitated and distressed' Paterson turned to his old friend Hickey for help, lamenting that 'it is as much out of my power to find money here as it was in Africa'. Remembering happier times on Table Mountain, Hickey came to the rescue, underwriting his servant's loan and arranging for an English merchant to pay off Prehn. Once back in England, Hickey felt sure, Paterson's patron would gladly honour her debts.

It was the end of June by the time Paterson arrived back in London to what should have been a triumphant reception. He had brought back several botanical novelties and was bearing the skin of the first giraffe ever to be seen on British shores. He should have been feted by the Royal Society and honoured by fellow naturalists. Instead it was an ignominious homecoming. His bills still unpaid by Bowes, his debt still owing to Adcock and with no income of his own, Paterson was forced to dodge his creditors and live from hand to mouth. At one point, when Adcock bumped into him by chance in the City, Paterson 'prevaricated and shuffled' while mumbling reassurances about his future prospects. In the meantime, Hickey agreed to pursue the money due from Mary Eleanor in order to satisfy the increasingly belligerent Adcock whose loan he had underwritten. Hickey's father called several times at the Grosvenor Square house that summer then wrote a stinging letter to Mary attacking 'the injustice of her behaviour towards Paterson, a young man of merit whom she had sent to a distant and savage clime to gratify her desire of collecting rare natural productions' and whom instead of rewarding 'she had refused to do common justice to'. Hickey's father was now threatening to sue Mary for breach of contract, especially when his son only narrowly avoided being imprisoned for non-payment of Adcock's loan.

Keeping his whereabouts secret, the humiliated Paterson was in no position to laud his discoveries to the illustrious Royal Society or bask in the admiration of fellow botanists. There was, therefore, no report detailing Paterson's achievements or any mention of his travels in the society's records that year. And while Masson's Cape collection had been splendidly housed in a new greenhouse at Kew, Paterson's botanical spoils were casually dispersed in ignoble obscurity. Plainly, Paterson had already sent home a quantity of his discoveries before his return, for in 1779, when the naval physician James Lind called at the Cape on his way to India, he half-heartedly collected only a few plants, 'Masson and Paterson having sent home everything this place produces in the vegetable way'.[43] Probably these specimens had been shipped to Mary, although Paterson was also in touch with Forsyth and Solander while away. Further botanical items were certainly presented to Mary, along with the giraffe skin, soon after Paterson's return in 1780. Whether Paterson met with his erstwhile patron for this exchange is unknown; if he did, he was probably fobbed off over his money by an ever-charming Bowes.

Despite the restraints on her scientific activities, Mary did manage to send some of Paterson's Cape seeds to her mother's home of St Paul's Walden Bury, where they were planted at some point in 1780, while others were despatched to Gibside for cultivation at a later date. A letter from Mary to Thomas Joplin, the Gibside gardener, in January 1781, asked him to send 'all the Cape Seeds which were to have been sown in the spring at Gibside' as she now planned to sow them at St Paul's Walden Bury, because 'all those sown there last year throve so remarkably well'.[44] Despite her instructions, certain seeds obviously remained at Gibside, for a second letter urged Joplin to inform her 'if the Cape Seeds ripen, particularly the White Geranium'.

At the same time, a number of dried plants which Paterson had brought back were preserved in a unique cabinet which Mary had commissioned for the purpose.[45] Crafted in burr elm and decorated with seven cameos of literary figures, in keeping with Mary's interest in literature, the cabinet – preserved in the Bowes Museum – incorporates lead reservoirs for carrying water and a retractable shelf for examining specimens. The fragile African specimens carefully placed in its drawers in 1780 would survive until at least 1854, when Mary Bowes, Mary Eleanor's youngest daughter, sent the cabinet complete with its plants to her nephew, John Bowes. 'It was built by your Grandmother's orders,' she would explain, 'and some of its Cape plants are still in tolerable preservation.'[46]

A number of the Cape exotics brought back by Paterson were duly acclaimed as newly discovered species, although fewer than might be expected given the extent of his four expeditions. The horticultural bible of the day, William

Aiton's *Hortus Kewensis*, would describe three: *Mesembryanthemum compactum* (dotted thick-leav'd Fig Marygold), *Hermannia odorata* (sweet-scented Hermannia), and *Lobelia pubescens* (downy-leaved Lobelia). All, according to Aiton, were discovered by Paterson and 'introduced' in 1780 'by the Countess of Strathmore'.[47] Many more, which Paterson either described inexpertly or introduced obscurely, remained to be claimed by future botanists. Probably sold by Paterson in a desperate effort to survive from day to day, they would end up in other collections. Some found their way to James Lee, the kindly nurseryman in Hammersmith; a full fourteen years later he would report excitedly that one, the unpromisingly named giant cudweed, or *Gnaphalium eximium*, had flowered for the first time 'in great perfection'. The seeds of this 'most magnificent and shewy of all the species hitherto introduced to this country' had been discovered, Lee noted, five hundred miles from the Cape by Paterson. It is likely that other seeds, bulbs and cuttings went to William Forsyth at the Chelsea Physic Garden, to William Aiton at Kew and to Solander and Banks. They would have included many of the geraniums, gladioli, mesembryanthemums, euphorbias and ixias that would bring their exuberant colours to English borders and window boxes from the early nineteenth century onwards.

Meanwhile, Mary donated Paterson's magnificent giraffe skin and bones to her friend John Hunter, quite possibly at the instigation of Bowes in payment for the surgeon's services so recently rendered.[48] Whatever the motive for the gift, Hunter was ecstatic with the addition to his burgeoning anatomical collection. After examining and preserving the bones, and dissecting the ligaments of its neck in an effort to understand its stupendous stature, Hunter had the skin stuffed and placed in the hallway of his Jermyn Street house.

With its legs hacked off so that it would fit the hall, the beast sat on its haunches as an unsettling welcome to patients and guests. Eventually moved to Hunter's purpose-built museum in Leicester Square, which would open to public view eight years later, it caused a sensation in the press. 'Amongst the curiosities of Mr Hunter's Museum is an animal brought from South America,' reported an ill-informed *London Evening Post*, 'called the *Camel Depard*, which, from the report of its size and other circumstances, it was hitherto much doubted by Naturalists whether such an animal did really exist or not.'

It would be many more years before Paterson would achieve the recognition that he deserved. Although on his journey home he had optimistically promised to publish an account of his travels, he was in no position to achieve this goal while living by his wits in a hostile London in 1780. He therefore had little alternative, after Britain declared war on Holland later that year, but to agree to join a British fleet bent on capturing the Cape. Recruited for his extensive knowledge of the south African coastline, most probably on the promise of a commission if he complied, Paterson would guide the British squadron in June 1781 into Saldanha Bay, about eighty miles west of Cape Town, for a surprise attack on the Dutch fleet. With his old friend Gordon, now a colonel in full command of the Cape garrison, caught unawares by the assault, the Dutch lost five merchant ships, including the *Held Woltemade* which had conveyed Paterson homeward the previous year. Hailed as a hero among his army comrades, Paterson's actions were met with less generosity among the international scientific community. The French ornithologist, François le Vaillant, felt 'tears trickle down my cheeks' as he watched his entire natural history collection go up in smoke when one ship was blown up by its captain to protect it from British looters.[49] Five years later, when Masson made his second visit to the Cape, he would be peeved to find his movements severely restricted by the Dutch government which now accused Paterson of spying.[50] Yet Robert Gordon, who had every reason to feel betrayed by his former travelling companion, seemingly bore no grudge. True to his Scottish roots, he remained pro-British all his life and ultimately killed himself in 1795 after being branded a traitor for allowing British troops to take the Cape without resistance. His widow later gave Paterson three merino sheep.[51]

Rewarded with his commission a few months after the Cape assault, Paterson was made an ensign in the 98th Regiment and served in India for the next four years. It was only on his return to Britain as a lieutenant in 1785 that he finally began writing the long-promised account of his Cape adventures. Published as *A Narrative of Four Journeys into the Country of the Hottentots and Caffraria* in 1789, with seventeen exuberantly coloured plates of plants and animals, it became the first book in English to describe the Cape interior.[52] Dedicated to Joseph Banks, by then president of the Royal Society, the first edition pointedly made no mention of Paterson's original patron. Yet only a year later, the second 'corrected' edition included a generous tribute to the 'protection and support' of the 'Honourable Lady Strathmore'. Conceivably in the interim Paterson had been reconciled to his former patron and maybe even received his long-awaited reward.

Vividly conjuring the triumphs and ordeals of his expeditions, the book went into eight editions in French and one in German. Even then Paterson would have to wait nearly another decade before gaining the acclaim he craved. Promoted to captain and newly married, he was despatched with one of the first transport ships to Sydney and served in Norfolk Island and Tasmania before ultimately being appointed lieutenant-governor of New South Wales. Tirelessly shipping specimens of native flora to his friends back home, including Hunter, Forsyth and Banks, he insisted that natural history 'is, and ever will be, my favourite study'.[53] Yet despite his repeated appeals to Banks, his less than zealous new patron, it would be 1798 before he was finally welcomed into the elite fold of the Royal Society. Having introduced several new species from Australia, which were commemorated with his name, he received the ultimate honour in 1810 when the botanist Robert Brown named an entire genus, a member of the iris family, *Patersonia* after his friend.[54] That same year, on his way home to Britain, Paterson died at sea.

Mary Eleanor Bowes, for all her commitment and investment in botany, would never achieve such recognition. Despite having the vision to sponsor one of the most daring overseas explorations of the eighteenth century, and despite her intense study, detailed knowledge and careful nurturing of exotic plant life, Mary's contribution as one of the most accomplished female botanists of the age would never be acknowledged. Her talents effectively nipped in the bud by Andrew Robinson Bowes, who had triumphantly sold her Stanley House gardens and greenhouses during the African journey she had sponsored, she could only seek to protect the few Cape exotics she had salvaged from his neglect. As the *Gentleman's Magazine* would later record: 'The Ladyship had begun to build extensive Hot Houses and Conservatories, brought exotics from the Cape, and was in a way of raising continually an Increase to her Collections, when by Her fatal marriage the cruel Spoiler came, and threw them, like loathsome weeds away.'[55]

There was little hope, of course, that William Hickey would recover his money from Bowes that summer. Skilfully dodging creditors all his life, Bowes was far too intent on his next scheme to let such a trivial claim upset his plans. Having set his heart on obtaining an Irish peerage, either for prestige among his relatives or for pecuniary advantage, he knew that the surest way to achieve his aim was by gaining a parliamentary seat. So as the canvas opened in August for the start of one of the most fiercely fought general elections of the century, Bowes was determined this time to seduce the recalcitrant electors of Newcastle.

8
Improper Liberties
Newcastle, September 1780

After five years of bloodshed, military incompetence and growing insurrection on the battlefields of America, anti-war feeling was running high among the radicals in Newcastle. Linking the American rebels' cause with their own grievances over high taxes, inadequate representation and government corruption, the activists had steadily garnered support among the craftsmen, shopkeepers and middle-class professionals who comprised the city's electorate. Ever since they had narrowly lost their campaign to unseat the ruling oligarchy at the 1777 by-election, the radicals had redoubled their efforts with hard-hitting pamphlets and rousing calls to action in newspapers sympathetic to their cause. So when news reached the city that the Prime Minister, Lord North, had declared a snap general election in September, the popular movement looked forward to the contest with relish.

With elections throughout the eighteenth century being decided almost exclusively on local issues according to local allegiances, the 1780 general election was the first to canvass national opinion on a major political question. Although the beleaguered Lord North had long since lost his appetite for the war in America, as well as for the consequent drain on the national coffers, George III remained resolutely committed to retaining his beloved colonies across the Atlantic.

Convinced that American independence would eventually have to be conceded, particularly since France and Spain had joined forces with the colonists, North had even attempted to broker a coalition with the leader of the opposition, the Marquis of Rockingham. When his conciliatory efforts failed, North had wrongfooted Rockingham by calling an early general election seeking a national mandate to continue the American war. Having already suffered a series of humiliating defeats on allegations of corruption and waste over the summer, North faced the election with some apprehension.

If Lord North lacked enthusiasm for the political fray, Andrew Robinson Bowes had no such qualms when he declared himself a candidate for the Newcastle poll. Although Georgian elections rarely involved a contest – the members usually being agreed in advance at a cordial meeting of civic worthies – Bowes knew that Newcastle promised an intense political skirmish. Having heavily invested his money and his time in wooing the local electorate since his by-election defeat, he now approached the September poll with bullish self-confidence. Of the borough's two sitting MPs, Sir John Trevelyan had staunchly backed the Government's American campaign while Matthew White Ridley had wavered between government and opposition – at one point refusing to present a petition opposing the war to Parliament. Skilfully judging the mood of the moment, Bowes firmly staked his colours to the anti-war platform. Earlier in the year, he had spoken forcefully against the war at a packed meeting in Newcastle's Guildhall.[1] Cleverly appealing to his listeners' pockets as much as their moral values, he had stormed, 'we are taxed to support the luxuries and the corruption which we condemn.' And with no trace of irony, the High Sheriff, who desperately sought an Irish peerage, passionately pledged his backing to the radical demands for an end to government sinecures and pensions. Writing to a sceptical friend at the time he had declared: 'I am glad to find the opinion of people in London against my election; it will give you the opportunity of making some good bets.'[2] So certain was Bowes of victory indeed that he even promised to compensate his friend should he lose the gamble, adding darkly, 'But you must bet upon a proviso, that L—[ady] S—[trathmore] lives.' For all his radicalism, he was well aware that his reputation stood or fell by his connection with the Bowes family name.

With Trevelyan having wisely decided to seek re-election elsewhere and Ridley a certainty for one of the seats, Bowes knew that his biggest challenge was to be adopted as the single radical candidate. As well as avoiding an unpleasant and unnecessary contest, of course, this would save Bowes the immense expense of another election campaign. In May, therefore, Bowes had addressed a meeting in London at the Hole in the Wall, the Fleet Street tavern where Newcastle exiles congregated, insinuating that he and Ridley had agreed to stand on a joint ticket. The cosy compact was upset the following month, however, when a third candidate, Thomas Delaval, put himself forward as the people's choice. As Ridley hurriedly sought to distance himself from both Bowes and Delaval, all three candidates set out their stalls at a lively public debate in August. Delivering what one newspaper described as a 'spirited harangue', Bowes bluntly informed the gathered freemen that since he had already spent a large fortune fighting the previous election they owed him their support for this one.[3] When both Bowes and Delaval vowed to back key radical demands for triennial elections and increased representation – and Ridley stubbornly refused to make any such promises – the contest seemed as open as ever. 'The canvass is begun at Newcastle – three candidates, all upon different interests,' Bowes wrote to his friend in London, adding with a note of desperation, 'for God's sake use your influence with as many people of the WHOLE in the WALL as you possibly can find out, and pray use ANY MEANS to procure them for me.'[4] So as the election campaign began in earnest with the dissolution of Parliament on 1 September, the three Newcastle candidates squared up for battle.

Just as in the 1777 by-election, Bowes was prepared to go to any lengths to win a seat. Inevitably, this would prove an expensive business. Despite his enduring financial difficulties, Bowes threw open Gibside Hall and hosted lavish entertainments in the city in a bid to win over the 2,500 or so freemen eligible to vote. Once again, Bowes demanded that Mary Eleanor turn her literary talents to championing his cause. Taking two meagre rooms above a china shop in the Bigg Market as lodgings for the duration of the campaign, Bowes installed Mary under the scrutiny of loyal servants. Here she was kept busy at her desk from morning to night, churning out stirring messages for handbills, campaign songs and vote-seeking letters while Bowes strutted through the town, she later wrote, 'flirting with his mistresses'.[5]

Just as with the previous contest, Bowes's moral character emerged as a central issue in the campaign. One anonymous correspondent in the government-supporting *Newcastle Courant* branded him 'an abandoned *prodigal*' addicted to 'habitual luxury and extravagance'.[6] Having attained his fortune through the 'fancy of a weak *undiscerning* female', the writer grimly predicted that Lady Strathmore's death would 'soon ... deprive him' of his wealth and status. Lumbering to his defence, one of Bowes's supporters in the radical-leaning *Newcastle Chronicle* feebly countered that his closest friends 'think they observe a real progress of reformation in such parts of his behaviour as seemed to require it'. Having scaled the ladder of rank and fortune, the writer was sure Bowes now felt 'the obligation of becoming more respectable in his personal character'. Falling back on the age-old appeal not to pry into a politician's private life, his defenders hoped to deflect Bowes's failings by pushing Mary into the limelight as: 'A Lady, whose fine natural talents, improved by a most liberal education, have furnished her with a share of good sense, real knowledge, and great proficiency in the politest arts and literature, which are equalled by few men.'

Polling began on 11 September and lasted 11 days, barring Sundays. Each morning Bowes marched confidently from his committee rooms to the hustings with his band of followers to deliver the slick slogans and impassioned promises calculated to win wavering electors to his cause. Each day was dedicated to winkling reluctant voters out of taverns and coffee-houses with inducements of ale, nourishment and other entreaties. Young men fearful of being forced into service with the navy were promised protection from the impress while those Geordies living out of town were tempted with travel expenses, even from London, to return homewards and cast their votes. As Bowes would later put it, an honest freeman of Newcastle could hardly be expected to travel three hundred miles at his own expense to cast his vote in an election. When his attempts to wine and dine the voters failed to secure the desired result, Bowes resorted to his usual dirty tricks. At one point he fooled a group of his opponents' supporters into boarding a ship in expectation of customary hospitality. Once aboard the well-bribed captain weighed anchor and set sail for Ostend blaming unhelpful winds for his inability to return in time for polling.[7] As in most contested elections voting continued, with the accumulated results of the open ballot published daily, until only a trickle of electors remained. Finally, on 21 September, a total of 2,245 freemen having cast their votes, the outcome was announced. As expected, Ridley retained his seat, winning 1,408 votes. His fellow MP, elected with 1,135 votes, a clear 50 ahead of his rival Delaval, was Andrew Robinson Bowes.

As the radicals toasted their hero on his historic victory, the honourable new member for Newcastle broadcast his success by ringing the church bells in Whickham. A week later, Bowes joined with a somewhat reluctant Ridley in hosting a celebratory ball in the assembly rooms, which many of the local gentry pointedly boycotted. As Ridley's brother, Nicholas, wryly remarked: 'Bowes is not the kind of colleague that a man would wish for.'[8] Thomas Delaval, meanwhile, responded angrily to his defeat by launching a legal challenge, levelling accusations of bribery against his rival. When the charge finally came before a House of Commons committee almost two years later, Delaval would withdraw his allegations having failed, rather surprisingly, to gather sufficient evidence of Bowes's trickery.

Certainly, Bowes had expended a colossal sum on his campaign – in excess of £20,000, more than the combined outlay of his fellow opponents, according to one estimate.[9] From his point of view, it had been worth every penny. As a Member of Parliament he was now in a prime position to take advantage of and dispense government patronage and was fully confident that the desired Irish peerage finally lay within his grasp. Just as he had seduced countless women with his false promises and fake flattery over the years, Bowes had cynically duped the Newcastle electorate. And just as he had discarded the women who fell under his spell once they had served their purpose, he now proceeded to treat his constituents and their concerns with barely concealed contempt. Soon abandoning his pretended radical views, Bowes would rarely bother to attend Parliament, vacillate between government and opposition when he did vote, and speak only once – to oppose a bill to reduce election bribery on the grounds that existing laws were already 'too severe'. For all his declared opposition to the American war, he refused to condemn the Government's continued campaign. Indeed it was Ridley, the government loyalist, who would unexpectedly win the freemen's gratitude over the coming parliamentary term for his bold criticism of ministerial policy. Yet while North and his successors would continue to dangle an Irish peerage before Bowes's greedy eyes as a lure to support the Government on crucial votes, the longed-for prize would remain elusive.

Bowes was not the only one with his sights on Ireland as 1780 drew to a close. Now twenty-two, and having been a captive for two-and-a-half years, Mary Stoney had become desperate to escape her brother's tyranny. When Bowes moved the family down to London in order to assume his rightful place in Parliament soon after the election, she finally saw her chance. Having given up the lease on 40 Grosvenor Square earlier in the year, Bowes rented a suite in the Adelphi Tavern, the same building in which he had faked his duel just three years earlier, now making a name for itself as the Adelphi Hotel.[10] But rather than attend to his constituents' interests by immersing himself in parliamentary business, Bowes was busy hatching another of his moneymaking scams, this time plotting to marry his sister to a nineteen-year-old earl with a £12,000 annual income. Plainly intent on securing a sizeable portion of this fortune for himself, in early December Bowes invited the earl and his mother to the Adelphi on the pretext of arranging a match with his eldest stepdaughter, Lady Maria, now twelve. The fact that Maria was rarely allowed even to inhabit the same room as her stepfather let alone become the subject of his marriage schemes was seemingly unknown to the gullible earl and his ambitious mother. It mattered little to Bowes's elaborate plot. Exactly as he had planned, the impressionable aristocrat fell instead for Mary Stoney and – just as Bowes had hoped – begged her to elope with him to tie the nuptial knot in Scotland.

Mary, however, had other ideas. With more than a trace of the family talent for guile, she surreptitiously packed her few belongings and in the middle of the night on 7 December, while her brother and sister-in-law slept soundly, she swapped clothes with a hotel chambermaid, crept down the stairs and fled into the London streets. When Bowes woke to discover his sister's absence the following morning he was incandescent with rage; at the very scene of his most flamboyant deception, his younger sister had outwitted him and escaped his command. Preparing hurriedly to set off in pursuit, on the assumption that his sister would head directly for Ireland, Bowes dictated to Mary Eleanor an even more than usually vituperative letter to his father. Suppressing her grief at losing her one remaining friend and confidante, Mary was forced to upbraid George Stoney over the 'dreadful accident' of his daughter's escape. Warning that the incident had caused Bowes 'the greatest agitation I ever beheld' she declared that she was now severing all links with the family in Ireland on the grounds that, 'I have never met with a greater instance of Impropriety or Ingratitude.' Bowes himself would later renounce his little sister as a 'viper', lamenting that he had raised her from 'obscurity' and polished her 'bad Education' only for her to scupper his plans to advance her through marriage. 'But, base and ungrateful as she has proved herself to be, why do I call her sister?' he raged.

Seemingly he had educated young Mary only too well. For as Bowes raced towards Holyhead in the hope of overtaking his sister, she was savouring her freedom within walking distance of the Adelphi. Knowing that he would expect her to make for the coast, Mary had instead gone into hiding with some friends in London. Assuming a false name and venturing out only under cover of night, she would wait a full three months before risking the voyage to Ireland. It would be March 1781 before Mary Stoney finally arrived home in Tipperary, where her frantic parents and siblings welcomed her with heartfelt relief. 'Had the pleasure of receiving our daughter Mary in good health and spirits,' her father recorded in his diary that month, adding: 'It was a serious, solemn meeting, where tears could not flow and find passage. More serious and violent agitation succeeded; demonstration of the love and affection of a Family to their restored daughter and sister.'[11] All communication between the two families now strictly forbidden by Bowes, it would be five more years before the two Marys could make contact once again. By then happily married, Mary Stoney would confess that the only bar to her pleasure since the day of her escape was the knowledge that she had been forced to leave her sister-in-law behind. 'At the time I left him I would have given the World I could have brought you out of the misery you were in,' she wrote, adding that she had hoped her flight might act as a warning to Bowes to mend his ways.[12] Instead, as she would later realise, 'it only made him worse'.

Indeed, having allowed one victim to escape from under his very nose, Bowes was now doubly intent on keeping Mary Eleanor under his despotic control. With her fellow captive gone, she felt the full force of Bowes's violent temper and draconian restrictions. And when her mother died in January 1781, at the age of sixty, Mary was more alone than ever. Having always detested his shrewd mother-in-law, who had done her best to protect her grandchildren and their inheritance from his grasping fingers, Bowes now gloated over her death and exulted in Mary's grief. She wrote that he 'insulted and triumphed in agonies I felt', while his 'cruelties and infidelities increased to an incredible degree'.[13] From now on, Mary wrote, 'scarce a day passed, in which I did not receive undeserved abuse, or blows and very often the latter during every day in a week'. Despite the fact that Mrs Bowes had cannily altered her will soon after Mary's marriage, to replace her daughter as trustee of her estate with the sensible Joseph Planta, now joint secretary of the Royal Society, and John Ord, a lawyer and MP friendly with the Strathmore family, her annual widow's jointure of £1,600 now descended to Bowes as legal recipient of his wife's property.[14] And even though Mrs Bowes had tied up her estate at St Paul's Walde Bury in trust for her grandson George until he reached t age of twenty-one, it was Bowes who assumed possession taking advantage of the will's proviso that Mary could move there within three months of her mother's death if she so desired.

Only thirty miles from London, the elegant Adam-style house provided a convenient base for Bowes's occasional parliamentary business. Hastily bundling the family and servants into coaches, Bowes rattled up the snaking driveway almost the moment Mrs Bowes's coffin departed in the opposite direction, bound for interment beside her beloved late husband at Gibside.[15] Strutting from room to room as he inspected his latest acquisition, Bowes forbade Mary from walking in the beautiful formal gardens – where Bowes had seduced her only four years earlier – or from visiting the hothouses where her Cape seeds were now flourishing.

Reduced to gazing on the formal walks and hedges from the French windows, her every movement monitored by maids and footmen reporting to Bowes, Mary had only her youngest daughter, now three years old, for company. Despite, or perhaps because of, her uncertain paternity, they enjoyed a strong and loving bond; Mary Stoney would later ask about the 'little Darling' whom her mother took 'so much Pleasure in'.[16] No doubt Mary's delight in her infant daughter was intensified by the fact that contact with her five older children was being increasingly rationed by Thomas Lyon. While later writers would suggest that she continued to neglect her sons after their father's death, never paying them a visit at their boarding school in Neasden, the truth was that she was actively prevented from doing so. Having last seen her three boys in November 1780, she had since been refused permission for them to visit. A letter sent by John, now eleven, at the end of November had reported that he and his brothers, George, nine, and Thomas, seven, were 'very well' at Neasden but were not allowed leave to see their mother.[17]

As she grieved for her own mother at St Paul's Walden Bury, Mary now begged Lyon to let her see her sons. 'The severe affliction I have lately experienced by the loss of an affectionate and beloved parent naturally leads me to claim with more than usual earnestness the satisfaction of my Childrens Company as the greatest Consolation I can receive.' Pointing out that the boys' school was less than thirty miles from her new home, where previously the children had stayed with their grandmother during the holidays, she could not resist adding that the ample provision they all enjoyed was almost entirely due to her family's fortune. Lyon was unmoved. Having always detested his sister-in-law and being

Mother's pride. Mary Eleanor Bowes portrayed in maternal mood with one of her daughters (probably Maria), during her first marriage to the 9th Earl of Strathmore, by Daniel Gardner *c.* 1775. Mary points to her daughter's book in a clear signal of her zeal for learning. (National Portrait Gallery, London)

A gaunt and fearful-looking Mary Eleanor, glancing anxiously over her shoulder, during the fourth year of her marriage to Andrew Robinson Bowes, sketched by John Downman in 1781. (Fitzwilliam Museum, Cambridge)

The honourable member. Andrew Robinson Bowes, the newly elected MP for Newcastle, drawn for a family portrait which never materialised, by John Downman in 1781. (Fitzwilliam Museum, Cambridge)

RIGHT: 'The beautiful Lord Strathmore'. Mary's first husband, the 9th earl, painted in Italy in 1762 during his grand tour, by Nathaniel Dance. The earl's Mediterranean sojourn was extended by a passionate affair with an Italian contessa. (Strathmore Estates)

BELOW LEFT: Glamis Castle, the Strathmore family's imposing fairytale home in Scotland, from the main approach. (Strathmore Estates)

BELOW RIGHT: Finally free. Mary Eleanor pictured with a favourite dog, in front of St Paul's Walden Bury, in her last portrait, by an unknown artist in 1791. (Country Life)

TOP: Mary Eleanor depicted suckling her cats in a scurrilous cartoon by James Gillray entitled 'The Injured Count..s', probably commissioned by Bowes, in 1786. (© The Trustees of the British Museum)

ABOVE: In an equally scandalous pose, also probably at Bowes's behest, Mary was portrayed in Gillray's 'Lady Termagant Flaybum going to give her step son a taste of her desert after dinner' in the same year. (© The Trustees of the British Museum)

ABOVE: Gibside Hall. Mary's childhood home and the scene of her marital ordeal, the mansion was built in the seventeenth century and the third storey was replaced by a parapet in the early 1800s, but today only a shell remains. (National Trust Gibside)

LEFT: George Bowes, painted by Enoch Seeman in 1744, about a year after his second marriage and five years before the birth of Mary Eleanor. Mary's doting father was one of the period's most successful entrepreneurs. His wealth brought her fabulous privilege but was also the source of her later misery. (Strathmore Estates)

Relaxed and cheerful after her escape, Mary Eleanor is depicted in characteristically elaborate hairstyle in a miniature by J. C. Dillman Engleheart, copied in 1800 from an original portrait, now lost, by George Engleheart. (The Bowes Museum, Barnard Castle, County Durham)

In disgrace. A hook-nosed and bug-eyed Bowes after his sensational King's Bench court appearance, caricatured by an unknown artist in 1799, in an unflattering engraving based on an earlier cartoon. (National Portrait Gallery, London)

TOP: Lawyers haggling over an arranged match in scene one, 'The Marriage Contract', of William Hogarth's 'Marriage A-la-Mode', published in 1745. The series hung in Gibside Hall. (© The Trustees of the British Museum)

ABOVE: Bowes at bay. Play-acting as ever, Bowes is shown being brought to justice before the Court of the King's Bench, by Gillray in 1786. (© The Trustees of the British Museum)

Fashionable artist John Downman captured Mary Eleanor's children in 1781 in nine sketches intended for a family portrait.

CLOCKWISE FROM TOP LEFT: A sophisticated 13-year-old Maria; coquettish Anna, aged 11; thoughtful 12-year-old John, the 10th earl; and a giggling three-year-old Mary. (Fitzwilliam Museum, Cambridge) understandably suspicious of Bowes, he issued strict instructions to the boys' schoolmaster, Richard Raikes, to deny all visits to their mother. So when Mary wrote to Raikes in May 1781 requesting that her sons come to stay for the ensuing holidays she was distraught to learn that they had already set out for Uncle Thomas's house in County Durham, passing on their journey within five miles of St Paul's Walden.

Worse news was to come, for shortly afterwards Mary discovered by chance that John had been sent onwards from Durham to continue his education at Edinburgh High School. Denied any consultation on the decision, or even an opportunity to say goodbye to her eldest son, Mary complained bitterly that the move was 'extraordinary and unjust', especially since the late Lord Strathmore had declared that Scotland was 'the last place in the world' where he would educate his sons. Plainly Uncle Thomas had decided he could keep a closer watch on the Bowes heir in the north than if he remained a tantalisingly short drive from his stepfather. Alone in his new school, in a country he barely knew, a full three days' journey from his mother and his siblings, the little Lord Strathmore poured his attentions into creating a garden and tending a pet tortoise, the bills meticulously sent as usual to Lyon. It would be more than two years before Mary heard from him at all, a full six before she would see him again. Her son's silence, doubtless dictated by Uncle Thomas, wounded her deeply. Having always prided herself on the respect she had tendered her own parents, Mary was both hurt and offended that her eldest son failed to demonstrate the 'duty' that Georgian children were expected to show towards their parents. Yet while she would scold him for his 'extremely unusual' conduct, she plaintively assured him that she was 'more warmly interested in your welfare than any other person can possibly be'.

Hoping at least to see Maria and Anna, who turned thirteen and eleven respectively in 1781, Mary was desolate when she discovered that they too had been despatched to County Durham for the spring holidays. Although she had so far been permitted more frequent visits from her daughters, who had often spent Sundays with her in London, once they returned from their little sojourn with Uncle Thomas these meetings were sharply curtailed, possibly on the basis of the girls' depictions of life in the Bowes household. From May onwards her requests to spend time with the girls were repeatedly refused by their schoolmistresses in Queen's Square and on the few occasions they were granted the girls were not permitted to stay overnight. Now months would go by without any contact from her girls and when they could not spend holidays in Durham they had to stay behind at school – even during Christmas – rather then be permitted to visit their mother. Growing increasingly estranged from their mother, the girls were nevertheless encouraged to visit other relatives and see playmates approved by their vigilant guardian. Progressively deprived of contact with her children and even denied news of their health, Mary became anxious and dejected. Yet her continual appeals to Lyon, by turns poignant, terse and despairing, were coolly rebuffed with the insistence that he sought only to 'promote their happiness and welfare'.

At the very moment that the family was being splintered ever further apart, Bowes chose to commission a family portrait from one of the era's most fashionable artists, John Downman.[18] As popular as he was prolific, Welsh-born Downman was heavily in demand with the aristocracy and the gentry for his delicate portraits which were mostly executed in black and white chalk with smudges of red sometimes applied to the reverse to lend a subtle blush to lips and cheeks. Particularly noted for his charming portraits of children, Downman often scribbled unguarded comments about his sitters on his preliminary sketches. His nine portraits of Bowes, Mary and the six children (Anna being drawn twice) were made at some point in 1781, according to Downman's inscription, in preparation for a group family picture. Since at no point that year were all eight members together in one place, Downman must have made the Strathmore children's portraits separately, possibly at their schools before John was banished to Edinburgh.

Probably commissioned to mark Bowes's elevation to the House of Commons to furnish the customary image of the respected politician surrounded by his cheerful family, the sketches show the 34-year-old MP dressed smartly with a white cravat wound tightly around his throat and his hair neatly curled and tied in a fashionable queue at the back. Haughty and confident, his profile displays the handsome visage which had allured so many women with its full lips and large, striking eyes framed by long lashes. By comparison, Mary's portrait depicts a gaunt, anxious face and although her hair is powdered and piled high in contemporary fashionable style, her wide, sunken eyes look to one side in apparent fear. Of the children, the young Earl of Strathmore looks mournful and solemn, despite inheriting his father's good looks and his mother's curls, as if bearing the entire family's misfortunes on his narrow shoulders. While his brother George wears an equally serious expression, young Thomas is the only one of the boys to sport an impish grin. Slightly plump, in a low-cut dress tied with bows at the back, their elder sister Maria casts her eyes demurely down, although pretty Anna smiles coquettishly at the artist. Of all six children, only three-year-old Mary appears truly childlike and carefree, with her mischievous big eyes and cheeky smile beneath thickly tousled hair, in marked contrast to her mother's frightened face. On the mount, Downman had written: 'Her Ladyship had only this Girl by her present Husband.'

The happy family portrait anticipated by Downman never materialised – just as the politician's model family envisaged by Bowes would never exist – and only the individual portraits remain. But despite Downman's presumption the family was set to expand once more. That summer, at the age of thirty-two, after four wretched years of marriage, Mary found herself pregnant again, for the first time bearing Bowes's child. But her condition did nothing to ameliorate Bowes's behaviour.

After spending the long summer recess in County Durham, Bowes seemed in no particular hurry to return to London to pursue his constituents' interests. That October he organised a shooting party to Wemmergill, the remote grouse moor in the North Pennines which had belonged to the Bowes family since the sixteenth century.[19] Among the party, joining himself and Mary at Wemmergill Hall, were Bowes's long-suffering financial advisor William Davis and his spinster sister Ann, along with another sister Sarah and her husband General Frederick, who had all been spending the greater part of the summer with the family in the north. Experiencing the cravings common to early pregnancy, Mary looked forward to eating the plentiful grouse being shot on her ancestors' moorland. But when the men and dogs returned that evening with their bags full, Bowes laid out the plump birds in front of her then promptly packaged them up to send to a mistress in Durham. Sick with hunger and disappointment Mary spent the next day in bed.

Normally so careful to present himself as the tender and attentive husband, catering to his fickle wife's every need,

Bowes's behaviour had now degenerated to the point that even his guests were struck by it. Ann Davis would later describe his conduct towards his wife as 'very austere and overbearing' while her sister, Mrs Frederick, noted that Mary had been 'exceedingly disappointed' over the anticipated game. A little later, having returned with their hosts to stay at Streatlam Castle, Mrs Frederick was woken in the night by the sound of Mary screaming but when she enquired at breakfast as to the cause of the sudden alarm, Mary insisted that all was well. Despite the denial, the guests were beginning to suspect that their generous host, the esteemed MP for Newcastle, was perhaps not the upstanding member of society he had led them to believe. On another occasion, Bowes forced Mary to go riding with the two sisters on the most uncomfortable mount the Streatlam stables could provide, a 'hard trotting Scotch Galloway' – a pony traditionally renowned for its stamina in the lead mines. After four miles over the potholed country roads, Mary was suffering such violent pains that she had to lie in a ditch while Ann Davis sent ahead to alert Bowes and request a carriage. Returning home, her agony was 'so great', Mary would later write, that she suffered 'convulsively hysterical fits for most of the day'. Undeterred by her protests, Bowes insisted that Mary continue to ride daily along the rough, rutted roads to pay formal visits to their neighbours. At the same time he forced her to drink milk, which she loathed, and banned her from drinking tea, which she loved.

Yet even as he persecuted and beat Mary, Bowes fretted over her health. 'He was tremblingly alive for the fate of the Countess,' his surgeon Foot would recall, 'and watched all her movements like ARGUS.'[20] While he may have been as vigilant as the hundred-eyed giant of Greek myth, Bowes's anxiety had little to do with Mary's own welfare. Terrified that if she died in childbirth or from its after-effects – the common fate of countless Georgian women – and left him without an heir he would lose all rights to the Bowes fortune, he hedged his bets by insuring her life. Plying his agent in London with repeated requests to take out new insurance policies, while instructing him not to mention Mary's pregnancy, Bowes explained, 'for though Lady Strathmore is in Perfect Health, yet as she is with child, I am determined to insure her life deeply'.

Much to Bowes's relief, on 8 March 1782, Mary gave birth in London to a healthy son, and soon recovered from her ordeal.[21] A legitimate heir for Bowes at last, the boy was named William Johnstone Bowes, in honour of Mary's grandfather and Bowes's maternal ancestors. When news reached Newcastle three days later, the city's church bells were rung into the night in celebration of the absent MP's happy event. But far from mending divisions between his parents, the new infant would only provide further opportunities for Bowes to humiliate and torment his wife.

As Mary regained her strength during the traditional lying-in period in the new lodgings Bowes had rented in St James's Place near Green Park, William was handed to a wet-nurse hired for the purpose. His father had taken particular care in choosing the woman for the job – Bowes always handpicked the servants without consulting his wife – but his close attention to the task had little to do with the dietary needs of his son. Although he was no book lover, conceivably Bowes had read contemporary advice on choosing a wet-nurse which described the ideal candidate as between twenty and thirty-five years old, clean and neat, with sound teeth and no signs of 'distemper'.[22] If so, he would no doubt have lingered on the recommendation that her breasts should be large, full and soft and the nipples 'rather long and slender, of a moderate size and firmness' and quite possibly even tested the suggestion that 'by gentle pressure' the milk should easily flow. The woman he duly appointed, Mrs Houghton, was grubby, illiterate and totally unsuited to looking after a young infant – at least in Mary's eyes. 'She hurt my son much by bad milk, dirt, and every species of neglect,' she would complain.[23] Bowes, by contrast, found her highly desirable.

For all his political friends' assurances that he was a reformed character, the public focus on Bowes's private foibles had done nothing to curb his voracious sexual appetite. No longer attempting to maintain the charade of the faithful husband and devoted family man, Bowes now openly cavorted with the female servants, brought his mistresses and prostitutes into the house and exultantly informed Mary of his sexual exploits.

While many Georgian husbands indulged in extramarital affairs and fathered children out of wedlock few were quite as brazen, or quite as prolific, as Bowes. Although Mary had long been aware, through the letters she intercepted and remarks she overheard, that Bowes had frequented brothels, maintained mistresses and spawned illegitimate offspring, until now he had always attempted to deny or conceal his intrigues. Now that he had an heir, he dropped all efforts at subterfuge and flaunted his affairs before Mary, the servants, his friends and even his children. Having already made a point of sending a present of game to one lover in Durham, Bowes fawned in public over a wealthy Newcastle woman, a certain 'Miss W—', for whom he even contemplated that well-worn ruse of fighting a duel. But never content with only one object of sexual desire, he informed Mary in 1782 that he intended to seduce the beautiful daughter of a farmer living near St Paul's Walden and install her in the house as a companion for Mary. In the event, his lustful ambitions went comically awry. Spying on the daughter through the farmhouse window one night as she undressed for bed, Bowes was attacked by her father's dog which savaged his leg. Frustrated by this unfortunate escapade, Bowes now threatened to dismiss Mary's maid, Isabella Fenton, and replace her with another of his mistresses. When Mary insisted that this was 'a dignity not to be endured' he flung wine in her face then emptied a decanter of water over her head. While Mary kept her maid, Bowes was undeterred.

That December he arranged another shooting party, this time inviting some of his male cronies to join the family at Cole Pike Hill. Cramped as it was with the additional guests, Mary and Bowes had to share their bedroom with nine-month-old William and his nurse, Mrs Houghton, put up on camp beds. On the second night Mary woke with a start to find the bed empty beside her. Upon drawing back the bed curtains she saw Bowes suddenly leap from the nurse's bed and pretend to stoke the fire. Asked what he was doing, Bowes claimed he had got up because he had heard the baby cry. When one of the guests departed the following day, Mary instructed Mrs Houghton to move into the vacated room only to receive a severe reprimand from Bowes.

Back at Gibside, Bowes abandoned any last effort to hide his lust for the obliging wet-nurse, insisting that she eat at a side-table in the dining room each evening then sending Mary to her room so that he could entertain Mrs Houghton alone into the early hours. Gossip over the unseemly familiarity between master and servant spread quickly through the household; one maid was shocked to find Bowes and Mrs Houghton deep in private conversation late one evening in the nursery as young William tottered unheeded around them.[24] Poorly educated, ill-groomed and down at heel, Mrs Houghton was typical of the women Bowes preyed upon. Lured by the heady mixture of power, money and good looks, such women were eager to advance their fortunes by tending to the well-connected MP's predilections. For his part Bowes could indulge his prodigious sexual needs without fear of being intellectually outsmarted.

Staying north throughout the winter of 1782 to 1783, Bowes informed the new premier, Lord Shelburne, that 'a severe indisposition' had prevented him from attending to his parliamentary duties.[25] Yet there was nothing wrong with the MP's health as Bowes explained to a friend – 'A want of money, not a want of health, has detained me here so long.' Not long after William turned one that spring it became apparent that his negligent wet-nurse was steadily gaining weight. 'I soon perceived the Nurse's situation,' Mary wrote, 'and when appearances began to be apprehended, the Husband was written to, unknown to me, acquainting him she was ill, and the poor Man was actually so complaisant as to come from London to Gibside, seven miles beyond Newcastle upon Tyne, merely to answer Mr Bowes's purpose'.[26] Having tricked the cuckolded husband into hastening to Gibside with reports that his wife was sick, Bowes ensured he stayed long enough to enjoy his conjugal rights in order to justify her burgeoning figure. A week later, Mrs Houghton had miraculously regained her health and her gullible spouse was packed off back to the capital.

As Mrs Houghton bloomed, rather precipitously after her husband's hurried visit, news of her circumstances spread so that, according to Mary, Bowes's conduct became 'either the scandal or the jest of the Country'. His sexual indiscretions and his political negligence now well known, Bowes's popularity was rapidly waning. At Durham races in July, Bowes was furious to find himself 'pretty unanimously sent to Coventry', in the words of one spectator.[27] 'His friend Lord Darlington was not here, nor would he come tho' Bowes went over Post to Raby to entreat him to appear for one day, but his Lordship had not courage to do it.' Shunned by his aristocratic friends and mocked by his affluent neighbours, Bowes was fast becoming a pariah. And as details of his debauchery, political apathy and tyrannical behaviour percolated upstairs and downstairs within the county's stately homes, the erstwhile people's MP had fallen from grace as the working man's hero too. Treating his servants and estate staff with arrogance and contempt, Bowes refused to pay the workmen at Gibside, raised rents on the farms and sacked loyal workers in his increasingly frequent fits of passion.[28] Having clashed with Bowes the previous year, Thomas Joplin, the Gibside gardener, swore that Nature had been determined to insult mankind when she made 'such a monster wear the Human forme'.

Humiliated by the spiralling rumours and the expanding Mrs Houghton as she staggered around Gibside with little William and six-year-old Mary in tow, Mary decided she had had enough. Finally she confronted Bowes, 'telling him it was high time to part with so useless a servant, who cut so indecent a figure when she brought in the children after Dinner'. But instead of discreetly sending Mrs Houghton away, in August Bowes hired a new maid, a local tenant's daughter called Dorothy Stephenson, to wait upon the wet-nurse.

A simple country girl of seventeen who had grown up on the Bowes family estate, Dorothy was somewhat surprised to discover the state of affairs at Gibside Hall.[29] Taking her orders from the heavily pregnant Mrs Houghton, Dorothy watched in astonishment as the master of the house fussed over the nurse's well-being yet raged at his meek and dutiful wife. While Bowes plied the smug Mrs Houghton with presents, Dorothy heard him refuse his wife's requests for money to buy clothes and shoes for herself or the children. On only her second night in the house, an even more shocking surprise was in store for Dorothy. Sleeping in the nursery with Mrs Houghton and little Mary – William being then elsewhere – Dorothy had locked the door upon retiring to bed. Just after midnight she heard the handle rattle and then, when the door refused to yield, a man's voice calling urgently to Mrs Houghton to open the door. Feigning sleep, Dorothy peeked from under the bedclothes to see the nurse tiptoeing over in her shift and opening the door to the master of the house dressed only in his night cap and dressing gown. Next she saw Bowes climb into the nurse's bed and minutes later heard the unmistakable sound of springs being pounded. Innocent but not naive, Dorothy had no doubt that the noise was due to 'two Persons in the act of carnally knowing each other'. The following day Bowes made a point of handing the nursery door key to Mrs Houghton with instructions to her and Dorothy that it must never be locked again. A fortnight later, Mrs Houghton, now seven months pregnant, left the household. Tenderly escorting her to his carriage, Bowes accompanied her to London where she would begin her lying-in.

If Bowes treated Mrs Houghton with significantly more kindness than he usually reserved for his mistresses, her absence did not cause him to pine for long. Moving the household down to London that autumn, Bowes leased a new house in the West End; only a few doors from the family's former home, in the south-east corner of Grosvenor Square, number 48 was even more spacious and came fully furnished.[30] For young Dorothy, seeing London for the first time, the square's spacious garden, crowned by its statue of George I and surrounded by opulent mansion houses, was a stirring sight. But even more startling than her new home was the role she was now expected to adopt within the household. Sleeping in the nursery with eighteen-month-old William, with the door unlocked as her employer had dictated, Dorothy awoke one night in alarm to discover somebody climbing into her bed.[31] Screaming in terror, she immediately recognised the voice of her master who brusquely warned her to hold her tongue then crammed a handkerchief into her mouth. Gagged and pinned to her bed, Dorothy, a virgin, was powerless to resist as Bowes brutally raped her. Deflowered and degraded, Dorothy knew she could neither denounce Bowes nor rebuff further assaults; as his employee and, moreover, the daughter of his tenants, any defiance would mean disaster both for her and for her family. From now on, whenever she heard Bowes steal into the nursery at night – whether in Grosvenor Square, Gibside or St Paul's Walden Bury – she had no alternative but to submit to his violations while the children slept innocently in their beds. Nevertheless, unlike the willing Mrs Houghton, Dorothy succumbed to Bowes's advances with disgust while carefully storing up details of the abuse she suffered and the scenes she witnessed for future use.

With his political ambitions frustrated – as Shelburne steadfastly resisted Bowes's cringing appeals for an Irish peerage – and his society pretensions thwarted, Bowes's behaviour was becoming even more irrational, and his violence more sadistic. Possessed by a compulsive, quite probably psychotic, urge to control everyone and everything around him, he could never feel at ease. No matter how much wealth or privilege he accrued he would never be content, as his father perceptively remarked: 'Notwithstanding Mr Bowes's great Fortune, I am persuaded there is not one of his family who is not happyer than he is.'[32]

Unable to bear his aspirations being obstructed, Bowes increasingly visited his rage on Mary. Soon after Dorothy's arrival in the household, when the family was staying at St Paul's Walden Bury, she rushed to her mistress's aid when Mary left the dining room saying she felt ill.[33] Upstairs Mary began to have one of the fits to which she was increasingly susceptible and sent Dorothy to seek help from an apothecary who, by chance, was dining with the family that evening. Bowes, however, refused to permit the apothecary to tend to his wife and instead stormed upstairs to her room, slamming the door behind him. Immediately, Dorothy heard Mary scream 'as if beat or pinched violently'. The following day she noticed her mistress's face 'much discoloured' and heard Mary complain that she could barely lift her arms from pain. On other occasions, when Bowes thought he was unobserved, Dorothy witnessed him pinch, punch and kick his wife, raining blows on her face, head and body, for the most trivial of reasons, such as making too much noise when playing with their son. 'The life of the Countess', Dorothy would later attest, 'was, by the cruelty of Mr Bowes, made one continual scene of distress and misery.'

Mary Eleanor would later date Bowes's worst abuses from the birth of their son. From that point on, she would say, 'he used me with more cruelty and indignity than ever, and seized the most frivolous pretences, such as merely walking from one room to another'.[34] At one point, he beat her around her eyes so badly as to make the 'whole room appear in a Blaze'. At other times he would amuse himself by striking her repeatedly on the back of her head in the knowledge that her 'treacherous' thick hair would obscure all signs of injury. 'I was constantly in such terror and confusion', Mary would recall, 'from the Blows, threats, curses and ill language I had recently received (frequently only the very instant before) that I was, for some time rendered incapable of hearing or replying to what people said even in common conversation; and upon these occasions Mr Bowes used to intimidate me still more by saying "are you deaf?"'

While his assaults were calculated and sustained, Bowes maintained constant control over Mary's life with elaborate rules and rigid constraints. Refused money for clothes, shoes and undergarments, Mary's gowns became so ragged that she looked, according to Dorothy, 'worse cloathed than any of the Servants' and 'frequently had scarcely a shift or Pair of Stockings fit to put on'.[35] At times she was forced to borrow underwear or stockings from her maids; on other occasions she borrowed money from them to pay for minor expenses. Permitted only to eat or drink according to Bowes's orders to the kitchen staff, Mary was frequently weak or ill. One kitchen maid, Susanna Church, who cooked and smuggled some chicken to Mary during one of her bouts of sickness, was immediately reported by the cook and promptly sacked by Bowes.[36] And at all times, whether on her rare walks in the gardens or simply walking from one room to another, Mary was accompanied by a servant or companion who reported all her movements to Bowes.

Forbidden sight of her children by Thomas Lyon, Bowes ensured that Mary was denied any consolation in her chief interest: botany. Since Paterson's return from the Cape, Mary had continued to write to Thomas Joplin, the long-suffering gardener at Gibside, with instructions on tending the shrubs and beds, nurturing her plants in the greenhouse and hot-house, and preserving a collection of feathers, skins and other curiosities which she kept in a 'museum' at Gibside Hall.[37] Yet she was rarely allowed sight of any of these treasures.

When Joplin left or was dismissed in late 1782 or early 1783, Bowes issued strict orders to the new gardener, Robert Thompson, to ignore all his mistress's instructions, to bar her entry to the walled garden or greenhouse on pain of being sacked and to refuse her any fruits or flowers that grew within. At one point Bowes ordered Thompson to release hares in the garden deliberately to destroy Mary's flowers. A dedicated gardener and a kindly man, though he suffered poor health, was riddled with lice and was clothed in rags, Thompson obeyed his orders reluctantly and keenly felt his mistress's disappointment. On one occasion he gave in to her plea to visit the garden for a moment in order to see a single flower but instantly regretted his lapse when Bowes suddenly appeared and began abusing her 'in the most ridiculous manner'. Once when Mary walked to the greenhouse without permission, Thompson saw Bowes rush from the house and was shocked when he 'struck and beat her Ladyship's Back-side'. Ordinarily, he would later affirm, Mary was escorted on her brief garden visits by a servant or female companion chosen by Bowes as her guard 'as if she was a prisoner for life'.

Pale from being confined indoors, gaunt from lack of food, dressed in tatters and cowed by perpetual abuse, Mary could easily have been mistaken by guests for the household's lowliest scullery maid. Even Jessé Foot, visiting St Paul's Walden Bury at some point in 1783 to inoculate young William against smallpox, noticed the change. 'The Countess, whom I had not seen for sometime before this visit, was wonderfully ALTERED and DEJECTED,' he recorded. 'She was pale and nervous, and her under jaw constantly moved from side to side. If she said any thing, she looked at him first. If she was asked to drink a glass of wine, she took his intelligence before she answered.' During a brief walk through the sadly overgrown gardens one morning, Mary wanly showed the surgeon the ruined beds, shrubs and lawns. 'She even pointed out the assistance her own hand had lent to individual articles,' added Foot. 'In observing her during her conversation, the agitation of her mind was apparent by this action of her mouth. She would look for some time, hesitate, and then her under jaw would act in that convulsive manner, which absolutely explained her state of melancholy remembrance beyond all other proofs abstracted knowledge could confirm, or technical teachers could demonstrate.'[38]

At heart an intellectual snob – as a young apprentice to his apothecary uncle he had insisted on replying to any criticisms in Latin – Foot had always felt somewhat in awe of Mary's education and intelligence. But fundamentally a money-grasping social climber – he pompously appointed himself 'voluntary watchman' over his older and superior rival John Hunter – he would remain fawningly faithful to Bowes.[39] Ignoring, therefore, any duty to medical ethics, in November 1783 Foot delivered Mrs Houghton of a baby girl at her London lodgings, assured her husband it was not unusual to give birth at six months and was paid generously by Bowes for his troubles.[40]

As the country lurched into constitutional crisis at the end of 1783, when George III summarily deposed the short-lived Fox–North coalition by appointing 24-year-old William Pitt as premier, Bowes's conduct was becoming dangerously volatile. His political intuition had plainly deserted him, for this time Bowes backed the wrong horse, voting with the debauched Fox just as the clean-living Pitt began dispensing peerages to bolster his minority government's chances. All hope of an Irish peerage now evaporated for good. While Pitt soldiered relentlessly on after the Christmas recess, braving his repeated defeats with a cool and calculating head,

Bowes floundered in fits of inebriated rage as he saw his ambitions flouted. Just as the country yearned for an honest, dedicated and incorruptible leader, in contrast to the hard-gambling, extravagant, licentious Fox, so Bowes misjudged the mood of the electorate and the patience of his long-suffering supporters. If Pitt was the man of the moment, so Bowes was fast becoming a figure of the past, unable to hide his greed, his lasciviousness or his brutality even in front of his close friends or his children.

That January, Dorothy was playing with William, nearly two, in the dining room while Mary wrote to Bowes's dictation.[41] Abruptly accusing her of misunderstanding his meaning, Bowes snatched a knife from a side table and threatened to cut her throat. Only the intervention of William Davis, Bowes's financial advisor, who walked into the room at that point, defused the situation. Quickly replacing the knife, Bowes switched his grimace to a smile and purred, 'go up stairs my Dear, & finish your letters'. The following month, Bowes brought Mrs Houghton to Grosvenor Square to show off her baby daughter. When Mary asked to be excused, humiliated by this latest indignity, he kicked her and flung an inkstand at her head, which only just missed its mark. Ushering in Mrs Houghton, Bowes cooed over her infant, while his son William ran in fear from the nurse he had not seen for four months. Sternly Bowes informed him he would have to get used to the nurse since she would shortly be taking charge of him again. He then turned to Mary and brazenly asked her to agree that the baby was 'a very fine Girl', to which she responded with rare spirit, that 'it was the largest I had ever seen, considering it came at seven Months'. For all her sudden defiance, Mary was forced to vacate her bedroom so that Mrs Houghton could spend the remainder of the day there being waited upon by the servants. Ultimately, it was only the objections of the family's latest chaplain, Reverend Henry Reynett, that dissuaded Bowes from moving Mrs Houghton and her baby into the house.

By spring 1784, as a new general election loomed, poor Dorothy was herself pregnant with Bowes's child and knew her working days were numbered. Already Bowes had attempted to recruit a sixteen-year-old prostitute, Elizabeth Jackson, as a replacement for Mary's maid, who was finally leaving. Only the protestations of the wealthy lawyer who normally 'kept' the girl as a mistress and threatened to expose Bowes, forced him to let her go. Now Bowes set about appointing a new nursemaid to replace Dorothy, with his usual close attention to the task. Arriving at Grosvenor Square for an interview in February, eighteen-year-old Elizabeth Waite soon realised the broad remit of the job in question when her prospective employer lunged at her and took, what she later termed, 'improper liberties'.[42] Despite this unorthodox interviewing technique, being out of work, desperately poor and with her father in debtors' prison, Elizabeth returned one evening a few days later on the understanding that she would meet her future mistress. Escorted upstairs to the dining room by Bowes, Elizabeth waited patiently to meet the children's mother while their father pawed and kissed her. When finally she objected to his 'indecent familiarities' in the realisation that the anticipated meeting was not going to happen, Bowes threw her onto a sofa and raped her. The promised job never materialised; a few weeks later the wretched Elizabeth made a pathetic effort to blackmail Bowes in a letter intercepted by Mary which warned, 'you told me that I was bad but I never was bad but to you and i am very sorry to think i was so easily taken by you as i was for you took me in a very undesent manner'.

When the blackmailing attempt proved fruitless, Elizabeth had little alternative but to turn to prostitution. For the moment Dorothy's position was secure. Yet well aware that her condition would soon become obvious, and that her presence in the household would then be an embarrassment to her master, Dorothy was becoming increasingly anxious over her own and her mistress's safety.

When the general election was finally declared at the end of March, Bowes was summoned north to justify his woeful parliamentary record to the disgruntled voters in Newcastle with Mary his stalwart consort as usual. Having expended vast sums securing his parliamentary seat only to have his aspirations to the peerage repeatedly stalled, Bowes was in no mood for a third expensive contest to woo the Newcastle freemen. Having placed their trust in the radical campaigner only to see him flagrantly ignore their interests in Parliament, the city's electors were equally in no mood to squander their vote on Bowes a second time. Not surprisingly, therefore, many of the radicals were eager to switch their support to an alternative candidate, Charles Brandling, an independent thinker from a long-established local coal-owning family. So as the three prospective candidates – Ridley standing on a certainty again – set out their policies in the Guildhall, the gathered freemen anticipated a vigorous meeting. Bowes did not disappoint them. After Ridley gave a 'short, though sensible' speech, Bowes launched into a belligerent, menacing and, quite probably, drunken tirade which lasted nearly two hours. Dismissing well-founded rumours that he had been seeking a seat in Durham, he tersely informed the voters that it was their fault if he had not followed their desires in Parliament as they had not given him adequate instruction. He then levelled a personal attack on Brandling with such ferocity that he would later be forced to quash suggestions that this amounted to a challenge to a duel.[43]

As popular support for Pitt swelled across the country, it was little wonder that the tide of feeling ran strongly against Bowes in the weeks leading to the opening of the poll on 26 April. One anonymous voter summarised the mood in the local newspaper: 'Can the Free Burgesses of Newcastle stoop to support a man who intended to have deserted them? Will they suffer themselves to be made a mere step ladder to Mr Bowes's ambition to be kicked down when he has attained the summit of his views? Have we not seen, whilst he was in Parliament, that his duty to the public, and to his private debts have been discharged with equal punctuality?'[44] Reminding the electors that Bowes's fortune would be entirely lost on Lady Strathmore's death – which those with memories extending back to his first marriage may have thought relatively imminent – the anonymous correspondent asked: 'And is there any one action of his life which an honest man can imitate, or a good man applaud?' As Ridley and Brandling marched eagerly to the hustings at the start of the poll the crowds waited in vain for Bowes to appear. When finally he arrived it was to announce his resignation from the contest. It was a 'handsome farewell speech', Ridley's brother, Nicholas, remarked with some relief, adding: 'Mr B's leave-taking seemed to be *for ever*.'[45] As Ridley and Brandling were chaired through the narrow streets by their jubilant supporters, Bowes walked away from the hustings a defeated and a dangerous man.

Stopping at St Paul's Walden Bury on the family's return to London, Bowes looked for an excuse to vent his fury on Mary. It was not long before an opportunity arose. As the family sat down to dinner that evening, with Dorothy sitting at a side table helping two-year-old William with his food, a male servant slyly informed Bowes that he had seen Mary walking in the gardens earlier in the day without permission.[46]

Immediately spiralling into a rage, Bowes flung a dish of hot potatoes in Mary's face, swiftly followed by a glass of wine then coldly instructed her to eat the spilled potatoes. Humiliated and terrified in front of the watching servants and her young son, Mary swallowed the potatoes while Bowes stood over her until she was physically sick. At that point, Bowes snatched a large knife from the table, grabbed Mary by the hair and threatened to cut her throat. Visibly shaken at what she had witnessed, Dorothy hurried young William from the room. When Mary later appeared upstairs, her face covered in bruises and one of her ears bleeding, Dorothy gently asked how she had attained her injuries. Mary replied that 'she durst not tell'.

Having twice been threatened with a knife in a matter of months and knowing that Bowes had accumulated a stack of insurance policies on her life, Mary now genuinely feared for her own safety. Only her concern for her two youngest children, toddling William and six-year-old Mary, deterred her from fleeing, or worse. 'The only thing that kept me alive was that my younger children's future interest depended on my existence,' she would write.[47] If she tried to leave, she knew she would almost certainly never be allowed to see her children again; equally she could be forced back to her marital home by law only to face even worse retribution. Petrified, distraught and friendless she saw no prospect of escape.

And then into her life walked Mary Morgan.

9
An Artful Intriguing Woman

London, May 1784

Since the moment she was born, servants had played a vital and pervasive role in Mary Eleanor's life. As a baby she had been handed to a wet-nurse to be breastfed, as an infant she had been washed, dressed, fed and entertained by servants. Growing up she had her own maid who tended to her every need and her own footman who stood behind her chair at meals. And when she married at eighteen she had taken command of a taskforce of housekeepers, butlers, footmen, cooks, maids, gardeners and grooms who supplied the family's every whim with military-like efficiency. Omnipresent from first light to lights out, Mary's welfare and happiness had always been dependent on servants. Yet from the moment that she had married Andrew Robinson Stoney, she had learned not to place her trust in any of them. All hired and paid by Bowes, all subject to his orders, they had little alternative but to conform to his totalitarian regime. So the male servants acted as Bowes's pimps and spies, while the women servants had either been coerced into becoming his concubines or were terrified of suffering his wrath. Although they were all well aware of the abuse and deprivations their mistress suffered – they heard her screams from behind locked doors, saw her black eyes and cut lips, served up her meagre portions at mealtimes – they were powerless to help.

While some – like Susanna Church, the maid who smuggled chicken to Mary when she was ill, and Dorothy Stephenson, who comforted Mary when she had been beaten – were sympathetic to her plight, they were simply too young, too poor and too ill-educated to offer any practical aid. Mary Morgan was different.

After the fiasco of his efforts to find a new maid for Mary among London's plentiful prostitute community and his own sizeable coterie of mistresses, Bowes had departed from his usual rigorous control over the appointment of household staff. Distracted by his risible campaign to retain his Newcastle seat, he had instead ordered his chaplain, the Reverend Henry Reynett, to procure a suitable new maid. It was a decision Bowes would deeply regret. With due concern for his master's soul as well as for his own reputation, Reynett had succeeded in locating a mature and experienced maid who came with impeccable references from a string of respectable families. Interviewed in April by the chaplain's wife, Mary Reynett, in a more conventional manner than most previous applicants, Mary Morgan was duly appointed, worked her notice and arrived at 48 Grosvenor Square on 18 May.

Aged thirty-three, just two years younger than Mary, Morgan was an educated, intelligent and conscientious woman who prided herself on the responsible positions she had held within influential families in Georgian high society. A widow with her own small private income, Morgan had entered service four years previously, probably from necessity after her husband's death. No stranger to the political arena, she had initially worked as a lady's maid to one of the five daughters of Sir John Wrottesley, the respected MP for Staffordshire, at his house in Bloomsbury Square. Equally at home in the field of finance, two years later she had obtained work with the eminent banker Henry Hoare, owner of Hoare's Bank in Fleet Street. There she had remained for a year, before lastly obtaining a post with the elderly Frances Sackville, or Lady Sackville as she styled herself, the sister of the Duchess of Bedford, at her home in George Street, just a few minutes' walk from her new position in Grosvenor Square. Calm, practical, devoutly religious and with a strong sense of propriety, Morgan arrived to meet her new mistress for the first time on that May morning as the spring flowers bloomed in the verdant square. Shrewdly weighing up the situation in the Bowes household, she formed an immediate affinity with her nervous and downtrodden namesake. For her part, Mary Eleanor was surprised and relieved to discover that her husband had appointed, albeit inadvertently, 'a proper person' with an 'excellent character'.[1] But Morgan had scarcely time to unpack her bags before she was thrown headlong into the family's latest drama.

Having squandered his chances for political preferment, lost his opportunity for a peerage and bungled his plot to marry off his sister, Bowes was casting around for a fresh scheme in his perpetual quest to augment his fortune and his status. Pestered on the one hand by his numerous creditors, and on the other by his many mistresses who demanded financial aid to maintain his various illegitimate children, Bowes felt besieged on all sides. His gaze soon fell on Mary's teenage daughters, sixteen-year-old Lady Maria Jane and thirteen-year-old Lady Anna Maria. Plump, pretty, accomplished and, most importantly, soon to command generous fortunes, the girls were rapidly approaching marriageable age. Calculating that he might secure a share of this potential wealth by engineering useful matches, Bowes laid plans to lure the girls within his control. But with an uncanny ability to predict the wily workings of Bowes's ever-active mind, Uncle Thomas was already one step ahead.

Having ensured that the Strathmore heir, the fifteen-year-old earl, was safe in Edinburgh, at arm's length from Bowes and Mary both in terms of distance and affections, Thomas Lyon had maintained a close watch over George and Thomas at their school in Neasden. Earlier in May, at Gibside after the election charade, Mary had begged Lyon to let her visit John in Edinburgh and see the younger boys who were staying with their uncle for the coming Whitsun holidays.[2] Airily, Lyon had informed her that since John had already begun his vacation it was 'impossible to say' where he was, while George and Thomas had no free time to see her since they had to be 'in readiness' to return to London any day. Growing increasingly depressed by her isolation from her children, Mary retorted: 'It must seem incredible to the World in General that one who is himself a father and whose own interest should teach him to promote the duty and affection of children towards Parents endeavours on the contrary to estrange their hearts from a Mother after having for years been deprived of the happiness of seeing my Sons.' Quite confident that the Georgian world would see nothing in the least out of the ordinary in denying a mother access to her children, Lyon knew that the safety of his two nieces was rather trickier to guarantee.

Having long insisted that the girls were not permitted to stay with their mother overnight, Lyon had recently added the stipulation that Mary could only see Maria with a trusted third party present. Inhibited from a normal fond relationship with her daughter by the constant surveillance of a hawk-eyed aunt or governess, Mary had protested at 'too severe a restraint upon the affections of a Mother'. In truth, it was already too late; seven years of such restrictions had

had their desired effect. Having spent scant time with her mother since early childhood and with any lingering affections poisoned by the Strathmore clan, Maria already felt a stronger bond with her socially acceptable and morally upright Lyon kin than with her troublesome mother and disreputable stepfather. Nevertheless, Lyon had remained apprehensive over Maria's safety and so as she neared sixteen in December 1783 he had moved her from her boarding school in Queen's Square to live with her aunt, Lady Anne Simpson, in Harley Street. Anxious to find her niche in Georgian society, Maria had immediately felt at ease with her charming and clever aunt whose home was a favourite refuge for the rebellious sons of George III.[3] Meanwhile, Anna Maria – as high-spirited and precocious as her sister was conformist and compliant – had remained under the watchful eyes of her teachers, Mrs Carlile and Mrs Este, at the Queen's Square school where she had recently been joined by her half-sister Mary.

Devoted to her lively youngest daughter, who was now six, Mary Eleanor had endeavoured to provide little Mary with the privileged education she herself had enjoyed. Snatching as much time with her as her husband's demands and restrictions would allow, she had set Mary to work at her lessons from an early age, her unruly curls falling over her books just like the young Mary Eleanor's. In the opinion of the chaplain's wife, Mrs Reynett, which seemingly carried some weight with her employer, this was far too demanding for a child of six and she had accordingly advised Bowes to send his young daughter away to school.[4] Ignoring his wife's tearful protests, Bowes had despatched little Mary to Queen's Square at some point before the April election, quite probably surmising that her presence in the school would also provide him with convenient excuses to visit. A few weeks later, a homesick Mary had written a poignant letter to her mother imploring to be allowed home for the coming Whitsun holidays. 'My Dear Mama,' she began, 'I hope this will find you quite recoverd and my dear Papa and Brother very well and as I wish much to see all my friends I hope my dear Papa and Mama will not disapprove of my spending the Whitsuntide Holidays with them.'[5] Dutifully conveying her sister Anna's respects, Mary entreated: 'We break up the 27 of this month and as almost all the Ladies are to go Home I think Papa and you will not object to my having the same pleasure.' But 'Papa' was entirely indifferent to the child's pleasures for it was not little Mary's holiday arrangements but those of her two sisters that were uppermost in his mind. And so on 21 May, a full six days before the school holidays began and only three days after the arrival of Mary Morgan, Bowes moved to unroll his latest scheme.

Forcing Mary Eleanor to play her allotted role in his intrigue, Bowes demanded that she write two letters – one to Mrs Carlile and Mrs Este in Queen's Square, the other to Lady Anne Simpson in Harley Street – asking to say farewell to her daughters the following day in Grosvenor Square on the pretext that the family was leaving to spend the holiday in Bath.[6] Early the next day, on 22 May, the Reverend and Mrs Reynett set off from the house and returned with Anna, gleeful at an early escape from her lessons while her half-sister Mary was kept hard at her studies. A short while later Maria arrived in the company of Eleanor Ord, Lady Anne's sister-in-law, who had been carefully briefed to maintain a close guard on her charge. Arriving in Grosvenor Square, a cautious Maria spotted her sister at an upstairs window and immediately warned Mrs Ord of her misgivings. Shown into the drawing room, Maria and Mrs Ord were met by Mary Eleanor who, after a few pleasantries, casually invited her daughter into her dressing room to read a letter from the young Lord Strathmore. Patiently waiting for Maria to return, Mrs Ord became agitated when she failed to reappear and the servants declined to find her. As she realised the folly of letting Maria out of her sight – and no doubt fearing the rancour of Thomas Lyon should her precious charge disappear – Mrs Ord insisted on being shown to the dressing room. Finding the door locked, the frantic Mrs Ord became thoroughly alarmed when she was handed a letter, in Mary's handwriting, which coolly explained that she and Bowes had decided to detain Maria until they could put their case for increased access to the children to the Lord Chancellor. Well aware of the plodding pace at which Chancery generally moved, since her husband was a Master, or official, of that court, the doughty Mrs Ord demanded a chair and insisted on sitting outside the dressing-room door until the hostage was returned. And when she heard Maria yell from within, she called back: 'Maria! I shall not quit the house till you come to me.'

Mrs Ord's admirable perseverance paid off, or at least Bowes soon tired of his eldest stepdaughter's truculence. Although he had probably viewed Maria, being the elder and therefore more eligible daughter, as his main quarry he had doubtless already surmised that she would present him with far more trouble than her pliable younger sister, who was evidently more susceptible to his charms. Obviously viewing the whole escapade as a welcome reprieve from the tedium of boarding school, Anna proved a distinctly more willing captive. It was not long, therefore, before the door opened and a fraught Maria emerged in the company of William Davis, the financial go-between who was never far from Bowes's moneymaking scams.

Discovering that their coach had been sent away, Maria

and Mrs Ord fled the house on foot, hurrying through the congested West End streets to take refuge with nearby friends. As Maria revealed that Bowes and her mother had attempted to persuade the two sisters to quit their guardians and live with them instead, Mrs Ord despatched an urgent message to her husband to summon help. Despite Mrs Ord's quick-thinking it was too late for Anna. By the time the guardians gained leave to petition Chancery to return the girl five days later she was already far away.[7] For no sooner had Mrs Ord and Maria departed than Bowes had bundled Anna, Mary and a handful of servants into a hackney carriage and hurtled east out of London on the road towards Dover bound for France.

A perilous 22-mile journey in a wooden boat at the mercy of winds and tides did little to deter innumerable British travellers from crossing the English Channel to France every year, whether embarking on the grand tour, pursuing business on the Continent or simply beginning a family holiday.[8] The voyage from Dover to Calais, usually in the regular 'packet' which transported the mail, could take as little as three hours in a calm sea with benevolent winds or as many as twelve if the boat was becalmed or carried off course. Lady Harriet Spencer, the future Lady Bessborough, betrayed an eleven-year-old's excitement at the anticipation of her family's jaunt to Europe when she made the crossing with her sister and brother in 1772. 'We were all wrap'd up in blankets and put into the little boat which rowed out to sea to the ship at one o'clock in the morning,' she wrote in her diary. 'We got to Calais before nine.' Older but no less enthusiastic, the Devon-based traveller Jane Parminter boasted a 'charming passage' of three hours during which she was 'sick twice but [it] did not spoil my enjoyment' when she made the voyage in 1784. Landing, eventually, in Calais many British tourists were disgruntled at their gruff reception by French customs officials who peremptorily seized and searched their bags for contraband before they were free to seek accommodation at one of the town's two inns. Most, like the novelist Laurence Sterne, arriving in 1762, opted for the *Hôtel d'Angleterre*, run by the obliging Pierre Quillacq, who had gained riches and minor celebrity status since featuring as Monsieur Dessein in Sterne's comical *A Sentimental Journey through France and Italy*, published six years later.[9] After a night's rest and a breakfast of coffee and rolls, the majority of cross-Channel travellers set out early the following morning, either paying for a seat in the stage coach or hiring a chaise from the hotel coach yard, on the long straight road for Paris.

Entering through one of the stately gates into the capital's narrow streets, visitors were universally struck by the density of the crowds impeding the progress of carriages, carts and sedan chairs. Although well-paved in comparison with London's rutted and mired roads, the Parisian thoroughfares provided no pavements as refuge for pedestrians. And while London boasted nearly twice the population of Paris by the late eighteenth century – nearly one million compared to the French capital's five hundred thousand or so residents – the crowds milling through the confined streets under towering apartments could still feel oppressive. 'There are infinite Swarms of inhabitants,' grumbled the poet Thomas Gray, the late Earl of Strathmore's tutor, '& more Coaches than Men.'[10] Accustomed as they were to the extremes of poverty and wealth rubbing shoulders on London streets, British visitors were shocked at the even sharper contrasts in Paris. Gawping at the opulent palaces of the nobility, the elegant townhouses of the bourgeoisie and the luxury goods such as porcelain, glassware and tapestries on show in the new

Parisian factories, newcomers could not fail to notice the hungry faces of the tax-burdened poor. Pronouncing the humdrum city food shops as the 'poorest gloomy Dungeons', the Reverend William Cole noted robins, larks and stinking 'carrion' on sale in the markets.[11] A guidebook of 1784 observed wryly: 'Poverty and narrowness of circumstances soon meet an experienced eye.'

Nevertheless, the glaring iniquities did little to quell the tourists' appetites for the city's sumptuous cuisine, abundance of entertainments and opportunities for sightseeing. No trip to Paris could be complete without taking in a play or opera at the numerous theatres, promenading in the Tuileries, and, of course, visiting Versailles to watch members of the royal family going about their daily lives blithely ignorant of the approaching storm just five years ahead. Indeed, with memories of London's frightening anti-Catholic riots of 1780 still fresh, one French writer could confidently predict: 'Any attempt at sedition here would be nipped in the bud; Paris need never fear an outbreak such as Lord George Gordon recently led in London'.[12]

For Mary Eleanor, fluent in French, a connoisseur of the arts and a patron of science, the prospect of a trip to Paris, unquestionably the cultural and scientific capital of Enlightenment Europe, in the spring of 1784 should have promised a sensory and intellectual delight. Hostilities with France over the American War of Independence had ceased the previous year and the resulting French national debt which would ultimately precipitate state crisis had yet to be fully felt. In the lull between war and revolution, therefore, British visitors could be assured of a warm Gallic welcome. But fleeing England with a thirteen-year-old ward of Chancery stowed away, as fugitives from British justice and her husband's creditors, the journey ahead held little joy for Mary.

In his haste to leave Grosvenor Square, Bowes had left his tangled finances in the hands of William Davis, his loyal agent, and his two-year-old son in the care of Dorothy, his reluctant mistress who was now three months pregnant. Fearful for her future, Dorothy had already confided in her mistress that the expected baby was Bowes's child. Little Mary, pining alone in her Queen's Square boarding school as the holidays approached, had been all but forgotten. Mary Eleanor was in no position to help either of them. Bereft at leaving her two youngest children, befuddled by her enforced role in Bowes's latest ploy, she barely knew her own mind. She had been ill repeatedly since the start of the year, suffering debilitating pains in her legs which Bowes assured the doctors were caused by anxiety at missing her children but were almost certainly due to the violence and distress caused by him. On the day of their departure Bowes had pinched her left arm so severely, as punishment for not playing her part in the deception to his satisfaction, that her upper arm from shoulder to elbow had been left black and blue.[13] As she headed for the coast, in anxiety and pain, she was as much a captive as her teenage daughter, albeit one far less willing.

After spending the night in Dover, the little party crossed the Channel in an open boat hired by Bowes, rather than the busy packet favoured by most travellers, doubtless to avoid being detected by fellow passengers. Safely landed in Calais, where Bowes knew the British legal authorities had no jurisdiction, he could afford to be a little less circumspect. There he took rooms, almost certainly in the popular *Hôtel d'Angleterre*, for Bowes would refer to its famous proprietor by his pseudonym Monsieur Dessein in later correspondence. And it was on that first night in Calais, as she helped Mary prepare for bed, that Mary Morgan first began to uncover the truth behind her new mistress's wretched demeanour. Since the elaborate gowns worn by fashionable eighteenth-century women generally came in several sections held together with pins, it was literally impossible to dress and undress without assistance. As she unpinned and removed the sleeves, bodice and skirt of her mistress's tattered gown, Morgan's eyes fell on a 'large black mark as large as the Palm of [my] hand' between Mary's left elbow and shoulder.[14] When Morgan asked her mistress how the bruise had been caused, Mary swiftly replied that she had bumped herself in the carriage on the way to Dover. Remembering that her mistress had sat on the right side of the carriage for the journey, Morgan kept her suspicions to herself.

As the family sped through the open countryside towards Paris with the carriage blinds fastened to keep out inquisitive stares, Morgan noticed Bowes slyly kicking and pinching Mary whenever he thought nobody was watching. If Mary made a comment, Bowes contradicted her, when she pulled down the blinds to look at the passing farmland he immediately drew them up, and throughout the journey he 'treated her upon all occasions with the greatest indignity possible'.

Once the party arrived in bustling Paris, Bowes took a suite of rooms in the *Hôtel de Luxembourg* in the fashionable Faubourg Saint-Germain – the 'politest part of the Town' according to an earlier visitor.[15] Long popular with British tourists, the hotel had provided hospitality to both Gray and Walpole on their Parisian jaunt in 1739 and to Lord Chesterfield, the late Earl of Strathmore's guardian, two years later. But the opulent surroundings only furnished a new stage for what Morgan would later describe as 'one continued scene of abuse, insult and cruelty'. When Bowes summoned Mary to his bedroom, which adjoined that which Mary Eleanor shared with Anna, Morgan almost invariably heard 'Slaps or Blows' followed by the sounds of Mary crying or screaming. Helping Mary undress for bed each night, Morgan noted that her flesh was 'seldom free from bruises upon her face, neck, or arms'. Yet to all Morgan's inquiries, Mary maintained a steadfast silence. She well knew, as Bowes had warned her on numerous occasions, that he would beat her 'most unmercifully' if he ever found that she had confided in one of the servants. Meanwhile, Bowes assumed his customary pose as the indulgent husband sorely tried by his obstinate wife – a myth which fooled the gullible Anna if not the observant Morgan.

Settling into his comfortable rooms at the *Hôtel de Luxembourg*, Bowes bombarded William Davis in London with instructions on the conducting of his legal battle to retain his grip on Anna. Having committed the grave offence of abducting a ward of Chancery under the noses of her guardians, Bowes knew that not only could Anna be seized the moment they set foot back on British soil but also that he could be arrested and possibly imprisoned for contempt of court. It was imperative, therefore, that he not only develop a plausible case for abducting Anna but also – should his pleadings fail – be able to exonerate himself from all blame. His paper trail of letters to Davis, which crossed the Channel in the trusty packet throughout the summer, would provide a lasting testament to the extraordinary gymnastics of his nimble mind. Dictated by Bowes to Mary, they would faithfully be reproduced by Foot as a powerful example of the 'masterpiece of villainy' of which Bowes was capable.[16] Seemingly concerned only for the happiness of his dear wife, Bowes portrayed himself as an innocent pawn caught up in Mary's obsessive campaign to regain custody of her five eldest children. Declaring himself perfectly willing to comply with whatever the law decreed, and return to England immediately if required, he insisted that it was Mary Eleanor who refused to yield up her daughter.

On the receiving end of this deluge of excuses and procrastinations, the hapless Davis was expected to mastermind Bowes's crusade for justice. Prior to leaving, Bowes had also instructed his lawyer friends, John Scott and John Lee, to champion his case. Both popularly known as 'Jack' and both MPs – albeit now on opposite sides of the floor – the two high-flying barristers had first met during Bowes's 1777 by-election campaign when they had won their spurs contesting the result.[17] Newcastle-born Scott, the youngest son of a coal agent, had attracted local scandal when he eloped with a city beauty, Bessie Surtees, in 1772; after working with Bowes during the by-election, the pair had become regular drinking chums. Now carving out a successful career at the bar in Chancery, Scott had shrewdly switched political allegiances to support William Pitt. He would shortly be appointed Solicitor General within Pitt's administration and would ultimately become Lord Chancellor, as Lord Eldon, the top legal officer in England. Destined to become the longest-serving holder of that post, Scott would preside over some of the court's longest-running cases, mercilessly lampooned in Dickens's *Bleak House*. Lee, the youngest son of a Leeds cloth merchant, was a fiery radical and dissenter who had defended John Wilkes and served as Solicitor General and Attorney General under Fox. Coarse, outspoken and hard-drinking, his liberal tendencies extended only so far: in 1783 'Honest Jack' had unsuccessfully defended the owners of the slave ship *Zong* when they were accused of throwing 133 sick captives overboard in order to claim insurance money. Ambitious, industrious and ruthless as they were, the two Jacks were nevertheless taking on one of their most challenging briefs in defending their fugitive friend.

Having presented their bill to reclaim Anna to Chancery on 27 May, it was nearly two weeks later, on 9 June, that the two guardians, Thomas Lyon and David Erskine, were given leave to argue their case before the Lord Chancellor, Baron Thurlow.[18] The petition, as usual, was presented in the names of the children, including Anna, ranged against their mother and Bowes. Relating the sorry tale of Anna's abduction and the attempted kidnap of Maria, the petition described how an increasingly desperate Mrs Carlile had scoured the West End attempting to discover the whereabouts of her pupil when she had failed to return to school that evening. Refused any information by Bowes's servants and William Davis, who were all bound to secrecy, the guardians had only discovered Anna's fate when Lady Anne Simpson received a letter from her niece posted in Calais several days later. Inured as they were to Bowes's ploys, the family had been so aghast at this latest turn of events that Maria now declared herself willing to attend court in person and to testify against her mother and stepfather. Nicknamed 'Tiger' for his ferocity in court, Lord Thurlow lost no time in ordering that Mary and Bowes should bring back Anna and defend their actions in court, while also demanding that William Davis and Mary Reynett should explain their role in the affair.

Having embroiled his friends as accessories to his misdeeds while he remained at a safe distance in Paris, Bowes pronounced himself 'very satisfied' with the outcome of the preliminary hearing.[19] Studiously maintaining the myth that he was a mere bystander in Mary's bid to regain her children, his next letter assured Davis that he was determined to return to England but issued the proviso that, 'I am equally resolved to permit Lady S— and her daughter to do exactly as their own wishes may happen to dictate.' He added: 'They wish, I believe, to remain in their present asylum.'

For Mary, if not for Anna, remaining in Paris certainly resembled life in an asylum, although not the tranquil sanctuary that Bowes had invoked. Even as Bowes forced her to write letters pleading his concern for her wellbeing, he subjected her to 'unequalled' cruelty.[20] Anxious to avoid being recognised, he beat her several times for failing to pull her bonnet far forward enough to conceal her face and on one occasion he pinched her for not standing behind Anna when watching a public firework display. When visiting their friends, the physician John Scott and his wife, whom Bowes had summoned to keep them company in Paris, Mary unthinkingly removed her cloak, revealing her tattered gown with gaping holes beneath the arms. Marching her to a quiet spot in the Luxembourg gardens, Bowes scolded and pinched her for half an hour before almost tearing one of her diamond earrings out of her ear.

Equally determined that Mary should enjoy none of the cultural or intellectual treats that Paris had to offer, Bowes forbade her from visiting any of the famous sights, conversing in French or studying the native botany. 'Having incautiously mentioned that one of my chief delights in France would be picking up any curious plants which might fall my way, Mr Bowes gave me the strictest orders never to pull them,' she would write. '[B]ut as we were walking through a Vineyard at l'Etoile, near Paris, I perceived so very curious a flower within my reach, that as I thought he was too earnest in discourse to observe me, I snatched at, and slipped it into my pocket, however not unnoticed for Mr Bowes instantly said "What is that you have got, shew me." I did, upon which he flung it away, and whispering some abusive language, gave me a sly pinch on my arm.'

While Mary Morgan quietly observed each fresh assault and noted the marks on her mistress's flesh each night, Mary

Eleanor contrived to suffer Bowes's brutality in silence. But towards the end of June, his abuse reached extremes that would have far-reaching consequences.

Alone in her hotel room, Mary was drawing back the curtains to look down on the coach yard below when Bowes walked in.[21] Enraged that she should expose herself to view, he flew at her with his fists, punching, kicking and pushing her around the bedroom. He then seized her ear and wrung it so hard, with his nails digging into the flesh of her neck, that blood started pouring from the wound. As blood soaked into Mary's neckerchief and gown, Bowes attempted to staunch the flow with his own handkerchief. It took two handkerchiefs and a towel to stop the bleeding. Sick with pain and sobbing, Mary leaned against a chest of drawers as Bowes opened the door and yelled for Morgan. Summoned from the adjoining room, Morgan was horrified as she took in her mistress sobbing uncontrollably, the blood-soaked handkerchiefs and the bloody towel strewn on the floor. But far from suggesting she offer solace to her mistress, Bowes angrily instructed Morgan always to place a chair against the door because 'that woman' – pointing at Mary – 'can take no care of herself'. Mary, he declared, had let the wind slam the door causing her to run a pin through her ear. Well accustomed by now to Bowes's violence and Mary's lame excuses, Morgan was incredulous. Observing the torn flesh behind Mary's ear, which looked 'very unlike any Wound made with a Pin', she was convinced that Bowes had clawed at the skin with his own nails.

This time, when Morgan later pressed her about the incident, Mary Eleanor finally confessed the truth: it was Bowes who had caused all her bruises, black eyes, scratches and cuts with his sustained campaign of violence. Swearing Morgan to secrecy, Mary had taken what was probably the most crucial step of her life. Although the ill-treatment continued, she finally had an ally.

If Mary's maid now fully appreciated her misery, her own daughter was seemingly indifferent. Sharing a room with her mother in the close confines of the hotel suite, Anna frequently heard and on occasions witnessed her stepfather beating her mother. When Bowes abused Mary at length in the Luxembourg gardens, Anna had watched the entire performance; she would later admit that she frequently heard her mother scream and saw her cry during her time in Paris.[22] And yet, having just turned fourteen, a naive and impressionable adolescent, Anna had plainly fallen for the Bowes magic. Relishing her role at the centre of the family drama, flattered by the attentions of the stepfather who had whisked her away from the dullness of boarding school life, she was in thrall to Bowes. Still handsome at thirty-seven, impeccably dressed and as silkily manipulative as ever, Bowes filled the vacuum left by the father she barely remembered and presented a welcome antidote to her severe and puritanical uncle. While in Paris, she would later say, her stepfather bought her expensive gowns, engaged the best tutors for her lessons and in short 'did all in his power' to make her happy. So when Bowes scolded her mother for wearing tattered clothing, complained of her clumsiness or admonished her for being too familiar with the servants, Anna placidly swallowed the charade. Indeed, she would later argue, if her mother had only followed her husband's instructions more carefully 'they might all have lived more happily than they did'. But not only did Anna condone Bowes's cruelty, she was even emboldened to emulate him, treating her mother with contempt and callousness. The friction led to fierce arguments, which Bowes eagerly fanned by supporting Anna and admonishing

Mary for treating her daughter too harshly. Mary herself would later accuse Bowes of prevailing upon Anna to 'treat me almost as ill as you did'.[23]

Precisely how far the alliance between Bowes and Anna extended is unclear. Although Bowes had evidently plotted to marry Anna to a wealthy suitor in France, it is plausible that his thoughts may even have turned to acquiring a second Bowes heiress for himself. After all, his own claim to fortune lasted only for the duration of Mary's lifetime which – under his bullying regime – might not be overlong. Certainly Anna's school teachers would later refer obliquely to her having 'erred' during her time in France, while her mother would express a desire to 'avoid exposing my Daughter' to unwelcome scandal. Most tellingly, Bowes's own sister would write to Mary with the words: 'Your account of your unnatural Daughter (as you justly stile her) indeed strikes us all with horror. Can they be so base? God Almighty reform them.'[24] And while her uncle harried his lawyers to secure her rescue, Anna seemed in no particular hurry to return.

By early August, when Bowes still defied the Lord Chancellor's order to surrender Anna, the guardians had applied to the Foreign Secretary, Lord Carmarthen, to help procure Anna's release through the French courts. Determined to thwart this fresh assault, Bowes tellingly complained that the guardians had 'represented the child as taken off under thirteen years of age, for the purpose of getting her married to some improper person, UNKNOWN TO THEM'.[25] While this was undoubtedly Bowes's plan, he knew he could count on his friends in England loyally fulfilling their roles when the case came up for its full hearing in Chancery. On the day Scott and Lee turned in bravura performances, insisting that Mary Eleanor was the chief instigator of the plot and Bowes merely her assistant, pleading the case with, in Foot's words, 'their eyes brimful of tears'. Their lachrymose appeal was lost on Tiger Thurlow, who summarily rejected their case, censured the spineless Davis and charged him with bringing Anna back from France within six weeks.

Receiving news of the outcome in Paris, Bowes submissively vowed that he was 'ready to attend the wishes of the Chancellor' and even, magnanimously, to 'confess I assisted Lady S— in the execution of this affair'. Promising to meet Davis in Calais, he apologised for having been 'the involuntary cause of the troubles you have lately experienced'. But he continued: 'As to our immediate return, no man ever took greater pains than I have done to convince Lady S— and her daughter of the propriety of that step. But it is not in my power to succeed, without extracting from their minds their dread of what may follow, by the death of my wife, and equally her daughter, their affections are so much interwoven.'

Throughout August and early September Bowes dangled his friend on a string, promising to meet him in Calais, then in Lille and then, after Davis had wearily trekked from one French city to the next, pleading that illness had prevented him leaving Paris after all. While Davis traversed northern France on his friend's wild goose chase, Bowes idled his days away by sampling the pleasures of the French metropolis – in Mary's words he 'satiated all vices (beyond all bounds)'.[26] Doubtless this entailed excursions to Paris's saucy boulevard shows and its numerous brothels although Bowes now set his sights on a more intense relationship with a certain fashionable woman about town. Since Bowes could not speak French, he instructed Mary to translate a letter of seduction he had drafted. When she refused, on the grounds this constituted 'such an indignity as I believe never any wife was exposed to', he not only beat her but threatened to place her youngest daughter Mary 'where I should never see her again'. Grossly humiliated, she copied the letter into French including Bowes's supplication that 'my fortune, which is more than ample, and every thing honourable which I can confer, shall be for ever devoted to your service and happiness'.

With time running out, as Bowes knew he must return to face his accusers and his creditors, in early September he ordered Mary to begin writing a 'Book of Errors'. In the same literary mould as the 'Confessions' which he had wrung out of Mary six years earlier, the Book of Errors was intended as a catalogue of Mary's daily offences. It began:

> *Septr. 2d – not being able to sleep I got up at five O'Clock in the Morning, and was found by Mr Bowes in the powdering closet to my Bedroom, sitting near the window (writing a comparison between a Frenchman and an Englishman) with only my petticoat and Bedgown on.*

For this gross infringement of Bowes's rules, as well as for feeding some bread to a donkey, Mary was 'severely beaten about the head and lower part of the face'. Her litany of supposed misconduct continued in a similar vein. On 5 September, when Bowes entertained guests to dinner in their hotel suite, Mary committed the sin of eating some chicken instead of waiting for the vegetables which Bowes had earlier insisted were all his fickle wife would eat. For this she was beaten and confined to her room for several days.

It was a heartfelt relief for Mary when at last the party packed their bags on 13 September and departed Paris. Downtrodden and oppressed like the ragged paupers that she passed in the Parisian streets, she was as much a victim of absolute rule as they were. Arriving in Lille, Bowes was maddened to find that his friend Davis had given up his vigil and had left for England. Insisting that Davis return to meet them in Calais, Bowes urged him to bring clear legal instructions to persuade Mary to give up Anna, otherwise, he warned sinisterly, 'I may as well put a dagger in their breasts'.[27] But even when Davis scurried back across the Channel to find the family holed up in the *Hôtel d'Angleterre*, Bowes kept Mary confined for two further days while dolefully informing Davis that she refused to see him. Although she was now desperate to return to England, Mary was still forced to act out her part in Bowes's French farce by pretending to faint in terror when Davis was finally granted an interview. At that point, Davis would later recall, Bowes climbed on to the bed beside Mary and wept floods of tears as he attempted to persuade her to relinquish her daughter. The performance so affected Davis that he postponed the home voyage – retrieving the family's baggage from thc boat hired for their return – and even offered to remain in France with them for years if necessary, to allow a resolution to be negotiated with the guardians.[28] Finally on 30 September, more than four months after absconding with Anna, the group embarked for Dover.

If the guardians heaved a sigh of relief at the imminent reunion with their fourteen-year-old ward, they were sadly optimistic. Arriving back in London on 2 October, Bowes installed the party in the Royal Hotel in Pall Mall rather than return to Grosvenor Square where he knew he would be expected. Determined to evade both his legal and financial pursuers, after a single night in London Bowes took the family on the run again, this time heading north. On a fleeting visit to Grosvenor Square the evening before their departure, Mary barely had time to collect a few clothes and embrace her young son, now an energetic two-and-a-half-year-old handful for the weary Dorothy who was eight months pregnant. Having been left without money or credit, and frightened that Bowes might harm her or her child, Dorothy begged Mary to lend her sufficient money to return home to her parents. But as she had been refused so much as a shilling by Bowes since the beginning of the year, Mary sorrowfully confessed that she could offer no help. Dorothy's fears for her own safety were not assuaged when Bowes stormed into the bedroom, shouted at Mary for wasting time, and – unaware that he was being observed – attempted to cram her into a closet while punching, kicking and cursing her. Finally noticing Dorothy, he executed a brisk about-turn and began yelling at Mary: 'God damn you, you bitch! Why don't you come out of the Closet.'[29]

Leaving an anxious Dorothy and the compliant Reynetts in charge of Grosvenor Square, Bowes laid low with Mary and Anna at St Paul's Walden Bury for a few days before continuing north to the fashionable spa town of Buxton where they arrived on 9 October. Although he had no compunction in dragging Mary away from her two youngest children, and was apparently indifferent to seeing them, Bowes remained determined to win the battle for Mary to regain access to her five eldest children. So although he was already in contempt of court for refusing to surrender Anna – and his lawless escapades had effectively estranged Mary from Anna's siblings – he ordered his legal team to continue the custody battle. Meanwhile, he lured the pliable Anna deeper into his web, to the point of encouraging her to collude with his cruelty to her mother.

On their first evening in Buxton, Bowes was dictating another letter to Mary while Anna occupied herself in the same room. Suddenly impatient that Mary was writing too slowly, he snatched a candlestick and – in front of Anna – brought the flame to Mary's face, scorching her twice.[30] Next he picked up Mary's pen and thrust the nib into her tongue before punching her on the cheek with his clenched fist. When Mary undressed for bed that night in the room she shared with Anna, both Mary Morgan and Ann Parkes, a housemaid, remarked on the raw burns on her face. As she was warming the bed, Parkes noticed that her mistress's face was 'black in two or three places and swelled on one side with marks thereon bearing the appearance of her Ladyship's said Face having been burned with a Candle'. At the same time Morgan observed that Mary's face bore two or three 'very sore' burn marks where wax had adhered and that 'one side of her face appeared swelled and greatly bruised'. Before Mary had a chance to explain the injuries, Anna briskly told them to 'observe how her Mama had been burning her face'. It was not the first time that Anna would cover for her stepfather.

Unable to delay surrendering Anna any longer, after a brief detour to Streatlam Castle, Bowes turned the party towards London at the beginning of November. Before returning Anna to school, however, there was more pressing business to attend to. Conscious that his pleadings to Chancery as a responsible stepfather would appear somewhat less plausible should a teenage mistress with a story of rape and an illegitimate child surface, Bowes made arrangements for Dorothy's lying-in. An old hand by now at organising clandestine births, Bowes called on Susannah Sunderland, a widow he knew, at her house – almost certainly a brothel – around the corner from Grosvenor Square.[31] Spinning the familiar yarn that he was helping a married friend who had carelessly made his servant pregnant, Bowes promised to pay Mrs Sunderland handsomely for her discretion. That evening he returned with Dorothy, whose delivery was imminent, and assured the girl that he would provide for her and the child. Bowes then engaged a man-midwife called Richard Thompson to deliver Dorothy's baby. She gave birth on 10 November to a daughter. True to form, Bowes would fail to return, leaving Dorothy destitute and Mrs Sunderland fuming. Informed by Dorothy, as if she had not already guessed, that Bowes himself was the father of the unfortunate infant, the doughty widow promptly strode round to his house and demanded cash. Confronted on his own doorstep, in full view of his nosy aristocratic neighbours, Bowes branded Mrs Sunderland 'a foolish ignorant Woman' then marched her back to her lodgings where he abused and kicked Dorothy for her indiscretion. Having no alternative for now but to remain at the brothel, Dorothy would not forget her ill-treatment.

Obsessively pursuing his cause through Chancery, Bowes had little time to consider the latest addition to his illegitimate brood. After delivering Anna, at last, to her school in Queen's Square on 9 November and returning to visit her the following day Bowes began formulating plans for his next theatrical venture. Determined not to relinquish his hold over Anna, Bowes took Mary to visit her again on 11 November and on their return exclaimed: 'By God she is gone, did you not observe how coldly she behaved to us to day.'[32] Whipping himself up into an apparent frenzy, he rashly declared that he would kidnap Anna again, with an armed gang if need be, and fly to France that very night. After Mary's protestations, and a hasty visit to his ready accomplice Davis, the French plan was abruptly dropped in favour of a new and decidedly more sinister design.

Calling once more upon Mary's acting skills, Bowes coolly instructed her that she must take laudanum in a faked suicide attempt, supposedly in despair at being kept from Anna, in order to persuade the guardians to let her see the children. Widely prescribed by Georgian physicians to dull the pain of innumerable ailments and almost as widely enjoyed by Georgian pleasure-seekers in search of temporary amnesia, laudanum was freely available from apothecary shops. Lord Strathmore had consumed substantial quantities of the drug, essentially opium dissolved in alcohol, in the final stages of his tuberculosis; the writers Thomas de Quincy and Percy Bysshe Shelley would find inspiration in its embrace. But with pharmaceutical measurement in its infancy, overdoses of laudanum – both accidental and intentional – were commonplace and often fatal. The author Mary Wollstonecraft would attempt suicide by downing laudanum in 1795; she later wrote notes describing a similar episode for her unfinished novel, *Maria: or, The Wrongs of Woman*.[33] Mary herself must have gazed many times on the final scene in Hogarth's series *Marriage A-la-Mode*, hanging on the walls at Gibside, in which the heroine consumes laudanum on hearing that her lover is condemned to die following a duel. Not surprisingly, given the general ignorance over dosage and effect, Mary expressed herself reluctant to fall in with Bowes's latest ploy. But after the usual threats of physical injury and separation from her youngest children, she assented.

Having despatched a servant to procure the laudanum, Mary took to her bed. On the following morning, 12 November, Bowes stood at her bedside and poured almost the entire contents of the phial of medicine into a large glass mixed with a tiny amount of water. Given that the maximum recommended dose was two grains – about 120 mg – of opium dissolved in alcohol to produce 40 drops – roughly 2.5 ml or half a teaspoon – of laudanum, Mary felt understandably anxious.[34] 'Perhaps there is a further design in this than you have acquainted me with,' she told him, 'but I fear not to die, for I have long been weary of life, and if you will promise me to take care of Mary, I will drink it off.' Assuring her that the dosage would not be fatal, Bowes lifted the glass to her lips and poured the poison down her throat.

Once Bowes had scuttled away, Mary dutifully acted out the prepared scene by calling for Mrs Reynett and announcing her suicide bid. Running shrieking from the room the clergyman's wife fetched both Mary Morgan, who was distraught to see her mistress sinking into unconsciousness, and Bowes, who immediately affected tears. Only the swift arrival of John Hunter, her trusted surgeon, and Richard Warren, physician to the King, saved Mary from almost certain death. Even though the pair immediately administered an emetic to make her vomit, Mary languished in her drug-induced stupor for the next four days. For once allowed the luxury of drinking tea, on doctors' orders, she was nevertheless warned by Bowes to turn down the delicacies he showily sent her from his own table; when he caught her eating a slice of bread and butter he pulled her ears.

At least the deception achieved its desired – or stated – aim, for Dr Warren now persuaded Thomas Lyon to let Mary see her young sons. Ushered into the darkened sickroom under strict escort, her son Thomas, now eleven, and George, nearly thirteen, were granted half an hour at her bedside. Having not seen their mother for a full four years, the sight of the pale, gaunt face and the frail figure prostrate in the bed must have come as a heavy shock. Their sister Maria, who had recently assumed the surname Bowes Lyon in a clear indication of her loyalties, pointedly stayed away. But on the fourth day of Mary's recovery, Anna, the supposed target of the entire charade, was finally brought to visit by an exceedingly grudging Mrs Carlile. Understandably wary of being fooled again, the schoolteacher accused Mary of feigning her illness and her tears; yet inexplicably leaving Anna alone for a few minutes, she immediately found that her charge had been locked in the bedroom. Impervious to the hysterical Mrs Carlile's protests, Bowes kept Anna captive overnight and swore that she would never return to the school again. Only the arrival the following day of Thomas Lyon, in a rare confrontation with his courtroom adversaries, restored Anna to her tutors – if not to her senses.

Curiously, since she was the least likely to comfort her mother and the most vulnerable to Bowes's malign influence, Anna was now the only one of the Strathmore heirs with whom Mary was allowed contact. Whether Lyon was keen to present himself in a reasonable light to Chancery or had simply decided that the wilful teenager was a lost cause, he apparently sanctioned regular visits, including overnight stays, by Anna to Grosvenor Square. All four other children were effectively lost. A stranger to her two young sons, despised by their elder sister, Mary was heartbroken to discover that John, now fifteen, also refused to see her. Having completed his Scottish schooling, the tenth earl had been admitted to his father's old college of Pembroke at the beginning of November.[35] A tall and good-looking youth in his father's image, he had decked himself out in a new velvet suit with a 'fine Round Hat' embellished with a silver buckle for the start of the autumn term. But when Mary journeyed to Cambridge at the end of November and sent a note asking to meet him, he returned her letter unopened. Since the young earl was not only the titular head of the family but the chief petitioner of the Chancery suit against her, she should scarcely have been surprised.

In reality, while she was forced to support Bowes's mission to obtain custody of the children, Mary had long since concluded that it was in her children's best interests to keep them as far as possible from his clutches. Powerless to exert her own will, however, she dutifully signed a hundred-page affidavit detailing her thwarted efforts to see the children and the distress she suffered from their loss in a poignant testimony for Chancery.[36] When she ended her statement on 16 December with the assertion that unless she could see her children more often, 'a period will soon be put to her Existance', she genuinely believed that her death was imminent.

Having stealthily cultivated the notion that Mary was liable to die of a broken heart or kill herself in grief at being deprived of her children, Bowes had set the stage for the inevitable next act in his drama. His inducement to take laudanum and his unremitting cruelty now convinced Mary that he was bent on murdering her or confining her for life. His first wife, after all, had lasted only eight years. Bowes had threatened before in rages of passion to kill her if she failed to comply with his will but now the oaths became cold and calculating statements of intent. After warning Mary on several occasions that he planned to shut her away in an asylum, in December he handed her a letter explicitly detailing this aim.[37] Mary knew it was no idle threat.

Throughout the eighteenth century husbands had successfully shut away disobedient or inconvenient wives in private asylums or country houses and often won the backing of the Georgian courts.[38] One aristocrat who suspected his wife of having an affair with his brother, locked her up in 1744 in a remote Irish mansion where she died, still a captive, thirty years later. Successive court rulings made plain that husbands were entitled to confine or restrain wives who were deemed to be behaving badly through extravagance or lewdness. The only legal route for challenging such imprisonment was for family or friends to obtain a writ of *habeas corpus* from the King's Bench court. Lady Mary Coke had been kept a prisoner by her lascivious husband for six months in 1749 before her mother secured her release by obtaining such a writ. Eight years later the notorious Earl Ferrers kept his wife, Mary Meredith, a captive in his Leicestershire mansion until her brother rescued her through the same legal process; she had a lucky escape, for three years later Ferrers was hanged for murdering his steward.

For those husbands who eschewed the role of jailor themselves, private madhouses were popular places of confinement. Until regulation in 1774 there was no requirement for potential inmates to show the slightest indication of lunacy before incarceration, possibly for life, and no inspection of the often squalid premises. Three women who had been confined at different times by their husbands in one asylum in Chelsea were all later declared to be perfectly sane. Although the 1774 Act for Regulating Private Madhouses required that inmates could only be confined on a doctor's signature, there was no shortage of corrupt medical practitioners willing to diagnose a wife's insanity for a generous fee. One woman who was released from a madhouse in Newcastle told the court that the asylum's inspectors were her husband's friends. And while the *habeas corpus* route remained the only way for confined women to secure their freedom, husbands would continue to lock away unwanted wives in asylums or country piles until the late-nineteenth century. Well aware that Bowes's written declaration might constitute crucial evidence for the future, Mary entrusted his letter to Anna. She never saw it again.

While Mary would have been the first to point out that confinement in an asylum would make little material difference to her daily life with Bowes – 'not having permission even to walk down stairs without asking his leave' – she genuinely feared that he intended to murder her. Having already demonstrated his ability to achieve that end through assisted suicide if not brute force, he now had a pecuniary motive too. Calmly informing her that he had accumulated so many annuities and insurances on her life that he would be better off if she were dead, he revealed that he had yet another rich heiress in his sights.[39] So when Bowes threatened to strangle Mary towards the end of 1784 she had every reason to believe he would carry out his aim. At the same time he told her that if his own life was ever in doubt, 'he would send for me, and shoot me through the head'. Mary Morgan now became convinced that her mistress's life was in danger. Few days passed, she would later testify, without her apprehension that Bowes would murder his wife.[40]

Growing reckless for her safety, submissive to her torture, as the year drew to a close Mary sank into her most dejected and desperate state yet. In a permanent condition of dread and confusion, she could barely hear from the continual beatings about her ears and scarcely walk from the recurring pains in her legs. Her face bruised, her teeth shaken, her head swollen, she rarely passed a day without pain. As Foot, with his professional if not sympathic eye, would put it: 'Mind and body jointly submitted to receive the pressure which Bowes, like a MANGLE, daily rolled upon them, and both were grievously collapsed.'[41] Yet at the darkest point of the year, when London was cloaked in fog and snow, a tiny flicker of hope kindled into life.

With no friends of her own circle or family members she could rely on, Mary freely confided her sufferings and her fears in Mary Morgan. Appalled at her employer's conduct and grieved by her mistress's misery, the upright and law-abiding maid had become Mary's closest friend. Since returning from France, Mary had also taken the housemaid,

Ann Parkes, into her confidence and when a new maid, Ann Dixon, joined the household that December, she too was quickly initiated into the circle of sympathisers. Blithely unaware of the groundswell of support for Mary below stairs, at the end of December Bowes appointed Susanna Church, the kitchen maid he had dismissed the previous year for smuggling chicken to Mary, back to her old job. These four women, among the least regarded and least influential members of Georgian society, would prove themselves Mary's firmest allies and her truest friends. Offering Mary their comfort in her wretchedness, they even lent her money from their meagre wages to pay for essentials and gave her cast-off underwear and stockings when hers were in tatters. One further addition to the Grosvenor Square household that December would be critical in turning around Mary's fortunes. George Walker, the former footman who had been sacked for 'taking familiarities' with his mistress in 1777, was secreted in the house by Bowes in a typically contrived scheme to prevent him from being subpoenaed to give evidence for Thomas Lyon in Chancery. Snatching a hurried moment with her erstwhile confidant, Mary asked Walker whether he still possessed her copy of the prenuptial deed that she had signed before marrying Bowes.[42] When Walker assured her that he did, Mary begged him to keep it safe.

Emboldened by Walker's revelation, encouraged by her servants' support, as the New Year dawned Mary began to entertain an almost unconscionable idea. When Bowes glibly announced in January that he intended to take both Mary and Anna abroad if the Chancery suit floundered, Mary knew that she had to act quickly. Once abroad she was certain he would kill her while she could only speculate on Anna's likely fate. As Bowes showed signs of growing irritation with Mary Morgan, she feared her friend would be dismissed any day and realised that time was running out. His suspicions aroused by the defiant maid who was seemingly immune to his oily charms, Bowes would later describe Morgan as 'an Artful Intriguing Woman'.[43] At the end of January, when Bowes flew into a fury because Mary had invited Mrs Reynett to visit with her dog, Mary knew there was no more time to lose. 'He told me to kneel and I thought he was going to kill me,' Mary later wrote, 'but he only made me kiss a book and swear not to do the same again or he would strangle me.' On her knees, frantic with terror, Mary made a momentous decision. Once she was alone with her most trusted aide, she implored Mary Morgan to help her escape.[44]

At first Morgan was aghast at Mary's plea and urged her to reconsider. Only too accustomed to her master's vengeance, she knew that helping her mistress could have grave consequences for both of them. But when she realised that Mary was determined on her course, and 'knowing how very unhappy her said Ladyship was while she lived in the same House with Mr Bowes', Morgan consented. Shrewdly, she advised Mary to find out whether the law could offer her any protection before fleeing impetuously. It was crucial advice. But since the only lawyers that Mary knew were deep in Bowes's pocket, Morgan herself offered to consult a barrister, named Charles Shuter, who was the brother-in-law of a woman she knew. Urged on by Mary, and at immense risk to herself, on 30 January Morgan crept out of the house for a secret rendezvous with Shuter. Somewhat perturbed at this rather irregular mode of correspondence with a prospective client, the barrister duly assured Morgan that her mistress should qualify for legal protection provided she could furnish evidence of her ill-treatment. Well aware of Georgian sensibilities, he felt obliged to point out that this legal opinion should in no way be taken as 'encouragement' to

Lady Strathmore to leave her husband. Morgan hurried back to Mary with the news. She made no attempt to persuade her mistress to escape, the maid would later insist, but accepted that 'a great degree of Confidence was placed in her for Honesty and Integrity'.

In the genteel reception rooms above stairs at Grosvenor Square Bowes entertained his drinking companions and dinner guests as usual, happily oblivious to the whispered conversations and mounting tension below stairs.

10
Vile Temptations

London, 3 February 1785

As dark closed in on Grosvenor Square in the early evening of Thursday 3 February, Bowes set out to dine with his uncle, the indulgent General Armstrong, at his house in Percy Street beyond the Oxford Road. Despite having kept his sister a prisoner and severed all links with his father, Bowes retained the talent to charm his high-ranking army relations. Having left his trusted guards, Mary Reynett and Anna, to watch over Mary he anticipated a convivial evening. But no sooner did she hear the carriage clatter away than Mary and her fellow conspirators swung into action. Primed with their prepared roles, Mary Morgan struck up a conversation with Anna and Mrs Reynett about the latest fashions in millinery while the housemaid Ann Parkes picked a quarrel with the footman, Denham Dally. With her warders momentarily distracted, Mary hastened below stairs. Covering her tattered gown with a servant's cloak and concealing her hair beneath a maid's bonnet, she stole out of the basement door accompanied by the new maid Ann Dixon. In her second-hand clothes, with a few guineas borrowed from her maids, Mary took nothing of her own. With the family fortune in Bowes's hands, she possessed neither money nor belongings; once the richest heiress in Britain, Mary walked out of her marital home penniless and destitute. More significantly, she was walking out on her two youngest children, William, nearly three, and Mary, now seven, with no certain hope of ever seeing them again.

Creeping through the fog in the dimly lit streets, Mary and Ann headed north towards Oxford Street where they suffered an agonisingly long wait for a hackney carriage. Shivering in their thin clothes and flimsy shoes in the chilly evening, they knew that Bowes would set off in pursuit the instant he discovered that they had gone. When at last a carriage pulled up, they urged the driver to head eastwards but had only travelled a short distance along Oxford Street when they spotted Bowes in another hackney carriage hurtling straight for them. Having been alerted to the escape in a hurried message despatched by Mrs Reynett the moment she had realised the deception, he was racing back to Grosvenor Square to intercept the fugitives. Bowling towards them with his head straining out of the window as he scoured the pavements for the escapees, his coach passed within feet of theirs but rattled on in the opposite direction. With Mary now almost hysterical with panic, Ann Dixon implored the driver to hurry. Arriving at Charles Shuter's chambers in Cursitor Street, a popular residence for legal professionals off Chancery Lane, Mary met the lawyer for the first time. After a cursory consultation lasting less than fifteen minutes, Mary and Ann Dixon headed for Holborn. Here, at 2 Dyers Buildings, in a modest apartment secretly arranged by Morgan hidden in a narrow alley on the south side of the busy thoroughfare, they were met by Mary Morgan and Ann Parkes. Making her getaway a few days later, Susanna Church came to join them.

Free at last from Bowes's iron grip, though not at liberty, Mary would never forget the courage and kindness of the four women who had rescued her and quite probably saved her life. Having left behind their own few belongings and unpaid wages, her maids now became valued friends who served her for no recompense; indeed she owed money to them all. Not one male servant, she would later stress, had been party to the plan. But through the selfless and audacious actions of these four, she would later say, 'it is not only myself, but innumerable other more worthy objects, who may through them, in future be saved from oppression, seduction, indigence, and a shameful end'.[1] It was the culmination of 'the eight most memorable years of my life', Mary would later write in a narrative describing her marriage to Bowes. At the time, she would add, she was 'fully sensible of the hourly danger I am in from the greatest Monster that ever disgraced the human shape and at the same time, the most artful.'

For Bowes, arriving back at Grosvenor Square to find the household in uproar, with Anna screaming hysterically and Mrs Reynett in a panic, the discovery that Mary had fled with several servants was devastating news. Swearing in fury he dashed into the drawing room where Anna was wailing and seemed to be 'in a great Flutter', according to Mrs Reynett. For her part, Anna would proclaim herself 'extremely hurt' that her mother had left her behind when she quit the house, although the fact that she had been kept in complete ignorance of the plans might have had more to do with her distress. Bowes would later claim that his stepdaughter had been so distraught at her mother's flight that he had to prevent her from throwing herself over the banisters. When his gaze fell on a note in Mary's handwriting addressed 'To Mr Bowes' his worst fears were confirmed.

In the farewell letter that she left her husband, a copy of which survives today, Mary was able to put into words her true feelings about Bowes for the first time in eight years of wedlock.[2] 'I think neither yourself nor the World will be surprised at the step I now take,' she began, 'as it is the only resource left me to secure my own Life & the Honour of my Family, which has long been tarnished by your Conduct, & the Actions you have forced me to.' Insisting, in a feeble attempt to delude him, that she would already be far away by the time he read her words, Mary said she had long hoped that he would reform his behaviour over time or that the restoration of her older children might provide a check on 'your Vices, Follies, & Extravagance'. But as she had learned to her horror since Anna had come to live with them, not only had Bowes's behaviour become 'more openly scandalous, & Indecent than ever' but he had also even encouraged her daughter to treat her with contempt. Having decided that she no longer wished to bring up her five eldest children 'under the Roof of Viciousness & Illnature' she was fleeing 'to save my two youngest from Beggary' as well as to preserve her own life. Vowing to claim 'My Dear Boy & Girl' as soon as she could, she looked forward to guiding their future education as her 'chief Delight & amusement'. Ending with a flourish she declared: 'Farewell – I forgive, but will never see you again. I can add no more, as you have long ceased to treat me, in any respect, as a Wife, or a Friend.'

Mary's touching faith that the Georgian world would express no surprise at her departure was only matched by her misplaced confidence that her troubles with Bowes were at an end. Utterly ignorant of her ordeal, thanks to Bowes's efficient propaganda campaign, those in polite circles were largely mystified by her actions as chief gossipmonger Horace Walpole made plain. 'The news of my coffee-house, since I began my letter, is, that Lady Strathmore eloped last night, taking two maids with her,' he informed his dear friend Lady Ossory, adding 'but no swain is talked of.'[3] As Lady Ossory could have told her, having not seen her own three children from her first marriage since her divorce sixteen years previously, the road ahead was liable to be strewn with obstacles. But as Mary placed her trust in the antiquated, labyrinthine English legal system one fact was certain: she would furnish material for coffee-house gossip for many years to come.

Staying in her Holborn hideaway and assuming a false name – just as Bowes's sister had done after her escape – Mary immediately initiated three separate legal causes through three distinct branches of the legal system: the King's Bench, Chancery and the ecclesiastical courts administered by the Church of England. Pitting herself, her tiny band of supporters and her meagre resources against Bowes's limitless guile and powerful connections, Mary hoped that simple tenets of English justice would keep her safe, restore her fortune and end her miserable marriage. While these may have seemed entirely reasonable aims, within the male-dominated, tradition-bound society of the eighteenth century they were bold ambitions indeed.

Not surprisingly, given her knowledge of Bowes's temper, Mary's first priority was to safeguard her life. So on 7 February, just four days after her escape, she appeared before the King's Bench to exhibit articles of peace against Bowes. One of England's oldest and highest ranking courts, the King's Bench – or Queen's Bench under a female monarch – dealt with those criminal cases that were not punishable by execution. Held in one corner of Westminster Hall, the oldest part of the Palace of Westminster, since the thirteenth century, its crowded and boisterous sessions competed with the proceedings of two other courts – Chancery and the Court of Common Pleas – as well as with the cacophony of spectators, hawkers and shopkeepers that milled around the cavernous building. Appearing before Lord Mansfield, the enlightened and hard-working Lord Chief Justice who had presided over the King's Bench for nearly thirty years, Mary pleaded that she was in fear of death or 'some great bodily hurt' from Bowes and laid six charges of 'great Cruelty and Barbarity' as evidence of his violence.[4] Relating a mere handful of Bowes's most vicious attacks through the course of her married life, these described how he had beaten her with clenched fists, a stick, the hilt of his sword and a silver candlestick, kicked her, burned her face, stabbed her tongue, pulled her ears, threatened to strangle her and ultimately sworn to murder or confine her. Readily granting Mary's petition, Lord Mansfield ordered that Bowes be bound over to keep the peace for the next twelve months, guaranteed by sureties provided by himself and two others. Leaping to his aid, the bail was volunteered by his drinking cronies, the lawyer John 'Honest Jack' Lee and Charles Howard, the future Duke of Norfolk. At Mary's request the court provided a tipstaff, a court constable named for the staff or stave he brandished, to protect her in her temporary home. Returning to her lodgings with her court guard, as the snow which had been threatening for days now blanketed the streets, Mary remained on edge.

Perversely, the legal step which now promised Mary protection drew attention to her activities – and consequently her whereabouts. Court reporters immediately scurried back with details of her proceedings so that the following morning's newspapers carried the news. Unable to resist a moralising tone, the *Morning Chronicle* later added: 'It is said, Lady S—e's exhibits against her husband prove – wedlock's a pill, bitter to swallow.'[5] Having despatched his spies to hunt for Mary immediately she escaped, Bowes now frantically attempted to track her down, bribing servants and correspondents to betray her address. At the same time Bowes forbade London tradesmen and shopkeepers to provide her with food or other essentials in the hope, in Mary's words, 'that the sharp pangs of hunger might force me to return to my old prison house'.[6] Naturally he imposed no such deprivations on himself. Furiously scheming to force Mary back, he stayed awake through the night drinking heavily and, according to Foot, eating spicy food such as peppered biscuits.[7]

Well aware that one of the most powerful lures to compel Mary to return was her anxiety over the two children she had left behind, Bowes took immediate steps to prevent her from seeing either of them. In the past he had threatened to place little Mary where her mother 'should never see her again'; now he proceeded to do just that. The little girl who had begged to come home for the holidays was removed from her London school to a carefully concealed countryside location where she was entrusted to the care of Eliza Stephens, Mary's one-time friend and confidante who had become Bowes's spy and probable mistress. William, meanwhile, he kept by his side. At the same time Bowes suddenly remembered his latest offspring. Turning up on the doorstep of Mrs Sunderland's brothel after three months' absence, he seized Dorothy and her three-month-old daughter and hid them in lodgings in Kensington in order to prevent her testifying against him.[8] In the meantime he set out to coerce or bribe any other servants or acquaintances he suspected might prove favourable to Mary.

Yet even as Bowes scoured the town for Mary, constrained her children and intimidated potential witnesses he still adopted his customary stance as the put-upon husband anxious to appease an eccentric wife who had callously abandoned her infants. In an emollient letter on 11 February to the lawyers who had been instructed by Shuter, Bowes wheedled: 'Gentlemen, It having been intimated to me that Lady Strathmore is uneasy lest I should disturb her quiet I then trouble you to inform her Ladyship that after the step she has taken I never will directly or indirectly molest or in any way interrupt her.' Proposing that their respective lawyers should come up with mutually agreeable terms for separation he pledged that their suggestions would be binding on him. A few days later an even more conciliatory letter arrived in which Bowes repeated his offer for arbitration as 'the most speedy method' to resolve 'the unfortunate Dispute' to their reciprocal benefit as well as that of 'two poor little helpless Children'.[9]

Far from convinced that Bowes would suddenly prove so amenable to reason, Mary pressed on with her legal steps. With no means of supporting herself beyond the paltry savings of her maids, far less finance costly law suits, she now embarked on a mission to retrieve her lost fortune. Since, of course, every woman in eighteenth-century England from dairymaid to duchess surrendered all her possessions to her husband upon marriage, unless explicitly specified in a legal settlement, on the face of it her ambition seemed fanciful if not totally perverse. Certainly Bowes thought so. When Mary sent her attorney, James Seton, to retrieve the family heirlooms – silverware, paintings, jewellery, diamonds and watches worth more than £10,000 – at a time prearranged with Bowes, he found the door shut firmly in his face. Instead Bowes ordered William Davis to deposit the valuables in Child's Bank while he continued to live richly on the rents and profits from the Bowes mines and farms.[10] But Bowes had a nasty shock in store.

Having forced Mary shortly after their marriage to revoke her prenuptial settlement, which had vested all her estate in two trustees to secure it for her own use, Bowes remained convinced that no trace of the original deed existed. He had even sacked her former footman, George Walker, after searching his belongings to ensure no copy survived. Yet 'trusty George', as Bowes had cryptically nicknamed him, now lived up to his moniker. For not only had Walker smuggled a copy of the deed out with him when he left the household, but he also now delivered it to Mary. Furthermore, she had tracked down the one remaining trustee, Captain George Stephens – the lawyer Joshua Peele having died – to his current job as treasurer of the Middlesex Hospital, not a mile from her current lodgings.[11] Now Mary launched an audacious attempt through the court of Chancery to restore the original deed and regain all her land, mansions, mines and income, on the grounds that the revocation had been extracted under duress.

Already the defendant in one suit still pending in Chancery, over her eldest children, Mary applied to Lord Thurlow to reinstate her prenuptial deed of 9 and 10 January 1777. Just like the fictional Jarndyce v Jarndyce case in Dickens's *Bleak House*, Bowes v Bowes would drag on almost interminably, run up immense costs and blight the lives of scores of innocent descendants and dependants. Affecting the farms, homes and livelihoods of the many servants, tenants and miners whose families had been reliant on the Bowes estate for centuries, just as in *Bleak House*, children would be born into the suit, marry into it and die out of it. And although the Chancery caseload had not yet approached the mountainous heights or its deliberations the ponderous lengths of the early nineteenth century as lampooned by Dickens, those affected by the Bowes cause would doubtless have echoed the author's description that, 'it's being ground to bits in a slow mill; it's being roasted at a slow fire; it's being stung to death by single bees; it's being drowned by drops; it's going mad by grains'.[12]

Yet while she sought valiantly to defend her safety and regain her fortune Mary knew that the only way she would ever truly be free of Bowes was by ending their marriage. And so at the end of February, eight years after their wedding, Mary initiated proceedings for divorce. This legal journey would prove the most arduous of all, dragging Mary's reputation through a variety of courts and exposing her to sensational, lewd and outrageous allegations that were gleefully reported in the press and devoured by the public for years to come.

While getting married in eighteenth-century England – then as now – was a disarmingly simple procedure, ending a marriage was a distinctly more difficult challenge.[13] For a woman it was well nigh impossible.

Prior to the establishment of a divorce court in the middle of the nineteenth century, England was the only Protestant country in Europe without a specific divorce law. Ironically, given his success in extricating himself from wedlock, Henry VIII was to blame. Until the Reformation, as Henry famously discovered, a marriage could only be dissolved by the Pope and only in exceptional circumstances, such as evidence that the alliance was incestuous or unconsummated. Contrary to the received wisdom of numerous schoolchildren, when Henry was refused permission by Pope Clement VII to dissolve his marriage with Catherine of Aragon on grounds of incest – her previous marriage to his brother – he did not unilaterally proceed with a divorce. Rather he had the marriage proclaimed null and void and – following his breach with Rome – subsequently had two further marriages annulled, with Anne Boleyn on the grounds of her alleged incest and adultery, and with Anne of Cleves for his supposed inability to consummate the alliance on account of her ugliness. Having invested himself as the head of the Church of England it would have been a simple matter for Henry to introduce a general law allowing for divorce, in common with other Protestant countries across Europe. Laws permitting divorce on grounds including adultery, impotence and desertion had been introduced from the mid-sixteenth century onwards in Germany, Scandinavia, the Netherlands, Scotland and even some English colonies in America. Yet despite encouragement from several clerical advisers, Henry denied his subjects the chance to emulate his marital enthusiasm and this rigid stance would effectively continue for the next three hundred years.

For the vast majority of English couples, therefore, death – of oneself or one's other half – remained the only possible means of release from a violent, adulterous or otherwise miserable marriage. Yet for those who were powerful, wealthy or desperate enough, other alternatives inevitably developed. Desertion – simply walking away – proved a solution for a number of discontented spouses and although a fugitive husband or wife could be compelled to return to the marital bed this was rarely pursued. While desertion did not free either party to marry again, this did not deter some from bigamous marriages. More ingenious and certainly more dramatic was the idea of 'wife sale' which emerged in the sixteenth century and quickly gained popularity, especially – as Thomas Hardy would later illuminate – in south-west England. Frequently such sales took place on market day when a husband might lead his wife to the marketplace with a halter around her neck and offer her to the highest bidder. Barbaric as it might sound, in reality such transactions were commonly prearranged by mutual consent between all parties. One woman, accusing her husband of assault in 1795, produced a receipt to prove that he had sold her, for one guinea, which stipulated 'both parties being willing to part'.[14] Such sales would continue into the nineteenth century although they were not – as the eponymous *Mayor of Casterbridge* would discover – legally recognised as divorce.

Rather more mundane, as well as socially and legally more acceptable, were private separations by deed. Originating in the late seventeenth century, the practice had become relatively standard by the early 1700s and the settlements drawn up by lawyers between a husband and a trustee of his wife – since she, of course, had no status in common law – often provided for custody of the children and financial maintenance for the wife. Such deeds gradually became recognised as legally binding during the eighteenth century – much to the chagrin of some recidivist husbands – and even helped to underline women's separate legal status. The forward-thinking Lord Mansfield consistently ruled during his tenure as Lord Chief Justice that a wife granted an estate under a separation deed should be regarded as a single woman for legal purposes. But by 1800 such progressive notions would be reversed when his successor, Lord Kenyon, reinforced the principle that a married woman was not entitled to own property – with the enthusiastic backing of John Scott, by then Lord Eldon, who described earlier rulings as 'impertinent and scandalous'.[15] Popular as they were, such deeds did not allow for remarriage nor did they deter recalcitrant husbands from attempts to seize their wives or their property. They also required the consent of both parties.

Less subject to the vagaries of judges and errant husbands were legal separations obtained through the ecclesiastical courts. Although the Church of England had inherited the Roman Catholic view that a valid marriage was indissoluble, religious authorities did accept – in common with Rome –

the undesirability of a couple remaining together in extreme circumstances. So the same Church courts which could declare a marriage null and void through incest or impotence – as for Henry VIII – could also decree that a couple should live separately, if it was considered that the physical or spiritual wellbeing of one of them was at risk by the conduct of the other, principally through adultery, cruelty or heresy. Known as divorce *a mensa et thoro* – literally from bed and board – such rulings released the pair from conjugal duties and cohabitation but did not, of course, permit remarriage. To all intents and purposes, however, and certainly in the eyes of polite society, these separations were regarded as permanent divorce and the courts even awarded maintenance to successful wives. Yet winning a Church divorce case was a lengthy, expensive and fraught experience – especially for women.

Granted with exceeding reluctance and only when a marriage was found to be intolerable, applicants had to prove severe cruelty or serial adultery and preferably both. Given society's tolerance of violence and male sexual freedom this was a tall order for any spouse; given the prevailing double standards towards women it was hard work indeed. Aggrieved wives were expected to show not only that their husbands were violent but also that their abuse was unprovoked, repeated and life-threatening; not only had they committed adultery but also that their sexual liaisons were particularly perverted, prolific or profane. Furthermore, the courts required two witnesses to every alleged act – not just one as in common law – and specifically excluded evidence from interested parties, chiefly the wife, husband and assorted lovers. Under such burden of proof where witnesses existed at all they were almost invariably servants who were subpoenaed to relate incriminating details of crumpled couches, stained sheets and clandestine romps spied through keyholes. In one case servants stood on a table the better to hear – and report – the creaking bedsprings in the room above; in another, three servants crammed into a cupboard to ogle their mistress and her lover.[16]

Since the proceedings were fully reported, the Church authorities' efforts to preserve the holy sanctity of marriage ironically supplied Georgian society's most salacious publications with sufficient titillating material to keep the printing presses busy. A veritable industry of magazines, books and pamphlets sprang up in the latter half of the eighteenth century, devoted to reporting these ecclesiastical divorce cases. One such publication, *Trials for Adultery or the History of Divorces*, ran to seven volumes when printed in 1780. Naturally, while they related the sordid details verbatim, such publications adopted a high moral tone. Reminding its readers that adulterers were stoned or thrashed by ancient civilisations, one collection argued that lax contemporary standards meant that reporting such cases 'may, therefore, be found the most effectual Means at present of preserving *Religion* and *Morality*'.[17] All the same, the publisher betrayed his pecuniary motives with the aside that: 'The rapid sale of our former Volumes has induced us to add to the present.' As if public exposure were not sufficient, Church divorce cases were invariably convoluted, drawn out and expensive with exorbitant fees for lawyers and payments to court clerics. Applicants therefore needed both a thick skin and a deep pocket to embark on the ecclesiastical route. Nevertheless, as expectations of marital bliss rose just as perceived standards of marital fidelity declined, so the ecclesiastical courts saw a rise in divorce trials, particularly after 1780.[18] The vast majority of the plaintiffs were wealthy members of the aristocracy or gentry and – not surprisingly – two-thirds were male.

Yet while these various avenues allowed disgruntled husbands, and occasionally wives, to cast off an unwanted partner, none permitted them to do what so many wanted most – and Henry VIII had so flagrantly achieved – to marry someone else. Although it took them more than a century, eventually English nobles did succeed in finding a way to follow the royal lead. In 1670 Lord Roos secured a private act of parliament which both dissolved his marriage to his wife, Anne, and allowed him to remarry. His argument that his wife's adultery and subsequent illegitimate child deprived him of his right to a legitimate heir won support from Charles II – with an eye to his own marital disaffection – who declared the debate 'better than a play'.[19] With the precedent set, an act of parliament became the only route to a full divorce which allowed the partners to remarry, although solely on grounds of adultery, until the mid-nineteenth century.

The procedure usually began with the aggrieved husband suing his wife's lover, or alleged lover, for 'criminal conversation' – essentially seeking damages for trespassing on his property – in the civil courts. He would then obtain a separation through the ecclesiastical courts before finally moving a bill for divorce through the House of Lords. Although used only rarely at first, during the late 1700s private divorce acts increased in popularity both with the landed classes, who could free themselves from unsavoury marriages, and the general public, who could salivate over their sexual exploits as each suit dragged through its three legal stages. Lady Diana Spencer, later Lady Beauclerk, endured public scorn when divorced from her first husband, Viscount Bolingbroke, by act of parliament in 1768, as the steamy details of her adultery were paraded in court while her husband's serial philandering went unmentioned. The following year the Duchess of Grafton, later Lady Ossory, suffered a similar trial by humiliation. Yet while some wives, Lady Ossory and Lady Beauclerk among them, connived with the unseemly procedure in exchange for their freedom and the opportunity to remarry, initiating a parliamentary divorce would remain the preserve of a very rich, well-connected and exclusively male elite. Only 132 such divorces were granted before 1800; none were to women plaintiffs.[20] Indeed, there were several attempts from 1771 onwards to prevent wives implicated in such cases from themselves remarrying. When finally the first parliamentary divorce sought by a woman was granted in 1801, she would have to prove her husband had committed not only adultery but incest – with her sister – and even then it took an impassioned argument by Lord Thurlow to persuade such diehards as Lord Eldon to support her cause.[21]

Ultimately it would require a sustained campaign led by enraged women in the early nineteenth century to end the shambolic system and introduce the 1857 Matrimonial Causes Act, which established the divorce court in which both sexes enjoyed the right to seek a full divorce. Even then the only grounds were adultery and women still had to prove further indignity, such as cruelty, desertion or sodomy. It would be 1923 before women were awarded equal rights in seeking divorce and only as recent as 1969 before the principle of divorce for incompatibility – breakdown of marriage – was at last recognised.

In 1785, therefore, the only way for Mary to sever her chains from Bowes was to seek a separation from bed and board through the ecclesiastical courts. Almost penniless and virtually friendless, she knew that her chances of success were slight while the process would inevitably expose her past indiscretions to public scrutiny. Nevertheless, on 28 February

1785, Mary Eleanor launched her suit for divorce from Andrew Robinson Bowes on grounds of adultery and cruelty with the London Consistory Court, the biggest and busiest of the bishops' courts dealing with marital disputes.

Based at Doctors' Commons, a muddle of seventeenth-century courtyards and quadrangles between St Paul's Cathedral and the Thames, the LCC had become renowned as the country's chief divorce court. Running in parallel to the common law system, the Church courts had a separate hierarchy of lawyers known as proctors and advocates, equivalent to solicitors and barristers, along with their own distinctive procedures and jargon. Accordingly, anyone initiating a suit had first to engage a proctor – 'a kind of monkish attorney' in Dickens's words – to register a citation which effectively launched the suit.[22] Providing a comprehensive litany of Bowes's outrages, Mary's citation accused him of 'beating, scratching, biting, pinching, whipping, kicking, imprisoning, insulting, provoking, tormenting, mortifying, degrading, tyrannizing, cajoling, deceiving, lying, starving, forcing, compelling, and wringing of the heart'.[23] Having instructed her proctor to prepare a 'libel', which outlined Bowes's atrocities in detail, Mary now needed sufficient sworn testimonies, known as 'depositions', to prove her case. With Bowes determined to thwart her suit, she was going to need all the support that she could muster.

While Bowes, of course, had the entire income generated by Mary's family estate at his disposal to fight the various law suits now stacking up against him, Mary had no source of funds to support herself or to finance her litigation. Throughout the drawn-out legal process she would remain reliant on the generosity of friends and sympathisers. While her maids stayed with her without wages, her lawyers pursued her various suits without fee in the hope that they would be paid if she were successful. 'My Lawyers act most zealously for me,' she told one correspondent, 'without Fees, the 4 Maid Servants who attended me in my flight, serve me without Wages, & two of them even left behind a great deal of Money which Mr Bowes owes them.'[24] The majority of her aid came from those at the poorest levels of Georgian society, principally the servants, estate staff and tenants who had served her family for generations. Gardeners on her estates sent her fruit and vegetables at the risk of losing their jobs, while tenants forwarded their rent at the risk of losing their farms. Even so, according to Foot, she was 'reduced very low indeed'.[25]

More significantly, and more dangerously for those involved, Mary needed witnesses who were prepared to testify to Bowes's years of violence and sexual philandering. While Bowes was prepared to bribe, harass or kidnap servants, friends and assorted disreputable characters to lie on his behalf, Mary could only appeal to her witnesses' basic honesty to speak out in her support. Confined in her lodgings she devoted her days to writing scores of letters in her looped neat handwriting, or dictating them to her closest ally – 'my female Secretary Morgan, who takes all the Business of Routine off my Hands'[26] – in a stream of correspondence to relatives, friends and acquaintances from the past. Free to reveal her genuine emotions for the first time in years, often to people she had previously been compelled to treat with rudeness, Mary rapidly regained her old confidence and determination. She now discovered who her true friends were, for in this dispute it was impossible not to take sides. Indeed, for those who were swept up in the Bowes divorce case, this was not a simple break-up between two married people so much as a brutally fought civil war which divided whole communities and even split families.

Among the first people Mary turned to were Bowes's family in Ireland. After hearing nothing from Mary for nearly five years, her sister-in-law rejoiced to learn that she had finally escaped her brother's tyranny. Now happily married, Mary Lawrenson, as she had become, enthused 'it is not in words to express my feelings' and urged Mary to stay safe. Having just lost her first son at only three months old, she wrote that news of Mary's release had helped assuage her grief and added bitterly: 'What a Blessing it would be had Bowes been taken off at that Age.'[27] Her father, George Stoney, declared himself 'deeply afflicted' to learn of his eldest son's conduct. Now seventy-two and increasingly infirm, he wrote an emotional apology to Mary for the 'base unnatural Treatment' she had suffered at the hands of 'the most wretched man I ever knew'. Yet although he told Bowes's uncle, General Armstrong, that it would have been a blessing had his son 'never been Born', the Stoney patriarch adamantly forbade his daughter Mary from testifying to her brother's villainy in court on the grounds that: 'Tho' we abhor Bowes and his proceedings, yet to join in prosecuting him would be unpardonable in a Sister.'

There was scarcely more support from Mary's own family. In a stiff and formal letter sent after two entreaties from Mary, Thomas Lyon icily responded: 'I have the pleasure to acquaint your Ladyship that Lady Maria is perfectly well. She rejoices with me in hearing of your Success & desires her due respects.'[28] And while he maintained a close watch on how the legal disputes might affect his wards' prospects, even a year later he would brush off her appeals for help with the excuse that 'my name could not be of the smallest use'. Meanwhile Lyon took steps to rein in his wilful niece Anna by placing her in the care of Elizabeth Parish, née Planta, the pious governess Mary had dismissed so acrimoniously while in the throes of her affair with George Gray nine years earlier. With memories of her former mistress's past excesses evidently not forgotten, Mrs Parish, elder sister of Eliza Stephens, promised that she would try to curb Anna's newly acquired extravagance but warned: 'It will give me some trouble to conquer the habits of inattention and disorder which she has contracted.'[29] Not long afterwards, reporting a conciliatory letter received from Mary Eleanor, Mrs Parish gleefully informed Lyon: 'I do not perceive in Lady A– M– the least desire either of seeing her or of hearing from her.'

Much to Mary's sorrow, Mrs Parish was right. Although Anna would grudgingly sign a deposition testifying that she had heard her mother scream and seen her cry from the abuse meted out by Bowes, she was still sufficiently under her stepfather's spell to conspire with his pretence that Mary was accident-prone, slovenly and quarrelsome. The only family members who tendered Mary any significant aid were William Lyon, a distant relation of the ninth Earl, who agreed to support her petition to Chancery, and General John Lambton, widower of the late earl's sister Susan, who called once and 'made her a present'.[30] Likewise Mary enjoyed scant support from the former friends and acquaintances with whom she had rubbed shoulders at masked balls and select salons. Anxious to distance themselves from the vulgar stain of divorce, the pillars of respectable society stayed away from her door.

Turning to the various medical men whose casebooks contained ample details of the fruits of Bowes's sexual voracity, Mary encountered sharply divided loyalties. The surgeon Jessé Foot would later proclaim that Bowes 'considered all females as natural game, and hunted them down as so many FERAE NATURAE'.[31] The legions of illegitimate children Bowes had spawned, Foot added, were 'vastly more, perhaps, than the granary of any other man has been found to produce'. But asked by Mary to give evidence to this effect he refused to testify unless subpoenaed 'for my own Reputation as well as for the Honour of my Profession'. Duly summoned, in his subsequent deposition Foot admitted that Bowes had paid him to deliver the wet-nurse Mrs Houghton's baby and then dupe her husband into believing it was not uncommon for babies to be born at six months. With little regard to professional honour, he would remain firm friends with Bowes, pandering to his contrived ailments and enjoying the spoils of his table.

Foot's sworn rival John Hunter, by contrast, congratulated Mary on her escape and pledged his full support to her cause.[32] In a frank depiction of Bowes's austerity towards his wife, his testimony declared that Bowes always exhibited 'a very strict and severe Disposition' and refused to indulge Mary with 'such Trifles' as tea and coffee. Later writing from Bath, where the surgeon was recovering from a heart attack, Hunter assured her: 'I hope to see the Day when Your Ladyship's person will be safe when you can enjoy your Children and your lands again.' Likewise the male midwife Richard Thompson would freely testify to his role in delivering Bowes's illegitimate child with Dorothy Stephenson.

Yet it was those who had most to lose who showed Mary the greatest loyalty. All four maids who had helped Mary escape – Mary Morgan, Ann Dixon, Ann Parkes and Susanna Church – willingly jeopardised their livelihoods and risked their lives by testifying to their former master's violent behaviour and sexual outrages. Their courageous descriptions of the bruises, burns and weals which Mary had suffered at Bowes's hands coupled with his oppressive curtailment of her movements, diet and dress furnished a resounding indictment of his cruelty. Other servants, who had worked in the Bowes household in years past, similarly came forward to describe the despotic regime that they had witnessed stretching back to the days immediately following the couple's marriage. Even one of Bowes's current servants, his footman Robert Crundall, made a statement detailing his master's brutality. He was inevitably sacked for his betrayal and promptly offered his services to Mary with whom he would remain for the rest of her life. Further down the slippery Georgian social ladder, denizens of London's sexual underworld willingly gave evidence on Mary's behalf. Nineteen-year-old Elizabeth Waite, who had been reduced to living in the Magdalen Hospital for 'penitent prostitutes', told how Bowes had raped her when she applied to work as a nursery maid, while the brothel keeper Susannah Sunderland related how Bowes had brought Dorothy to her house for the delivery of her illegitimate baby. Yet there was still one crucial witness whose testimony, Mary knew, could prove vital to the success of her suit.

Nothing had been seen of nineteen-year-old Dorothy or her baby daughter since Bowes had abducted them from Mrs Sunderland's brothel in February. When Mary had sent friends to call on Dorothy shortly after her escape they found no sign either of her or the baby. Knowing Dorothy's dread of Bowes, Mary feared the worst. Meanwhile, her parents, William and Mary Stephenson, who had been loyal tenants of the Bowes family all their lives, were blithely unaware of their daughter's pregnancy and subsequent disappearance. So when they received an urgent message from Bowes announcing that their daughter was dangerously ill, they set off immediately from their farm in Whickham to bring her home. Arriving in Durham, to catch the first stage coach to London, the couple were shocked to hear not only that the mistress of Gibside had left her husband but also that Dorothy had given birth to a child fathered by its master. Fearful for their daughter's safety, the Stephensons managed to contact Mary at her secret hideout in London and at the end of April they joined with her in obtaining a writ of *habeas corpus* demanding that Bowes produce Dorothy. One of the earliest editions of *The Times*, founded at the beginning of 1785 under the title the *Daily Universal Register*, reported Lord Mansfield's order that Dorothy be surrendered.[33]

It would be nearly two more weeks before a terrified Dorothy was brought before the King's Bench. Having been kept captive at a house in Kensington, where her six-month-old daughter was still being held, Dorothy had been forced by Bowes to put her cross to an affidavit swearing that she had suffered no violence or restraint. Unable to read or write she had plainly no understanding of the document's content. Taking a dim view of the abduction of potential court witnesses, Lord Mansfield reunited Dorothy with her relieved parents at which, *The Times* related, her mother 'stretched out her arms to receive her and kissed her with great rapture'. Charging her parents to treat Dorothy 'gently and indulgently', Lord Mansfield told them to accompany her to Kensington to retrieve her child. As Dorothy now joined Mary in Holborn, her parents carried their granddaughter back to County Durham where they gamely hosted a christening party. Reporting the revels to Mary in London, one loyal worker could not resist observing that, 'I think that the Child [is] very much like Mr Bowes.'[34]

Restored to safety, Dorothy lost no time in agreeing a lengthy and incriminating testimony which described how Bowes had repeatedly raped her and made her pregnant, committed adultery with Mrs Houghton who had subseqently given birth to his baby, as well as his catalogue of assaults on Mary with fists, knives and sticks. Declaring Bowes to be 'a Man of a very cruel savage and abandoned Disposition and also of a loose wicked and lustful Disposition',[35] Dorothy's statement would prove critical to the outcome of the Bowes divorce.

As news of Dorothy's ordeal spread among staff and tenants at Gibside, bolstered by many families' own experiences of Bowes's bullying and vindictive behaviour, so support for Mary's cause gathered force. In a groundswell of resistance, estate workers, farmers and their families at last found the courage to oppose Bowes's worst excesses and they reported their little triumphs in regular despatches to London. For Mary, cut off from her childhood home, the letters which shuttled almost daily between London and County Durham were a lifeline.

Plagued by rheumatism and worn down by poverty, the Gibside gardener Robert Thompson had no doubt where his loyalties lay. Expressing 'great joy' at the news of Mary's escape, he wrote to assure her that 'the Hot house and Greanhouse' were in good order although the garden had become overgrown through lack of help. When he was sacked by Bowes in April for refusing to surrender his correspondence with Mary, he continued to tend her plants regardless. Despatching a box of fruit from the hothouse, he described in his semi-literate scrawl how Bowes had ordered his agent 'to settle with me & to begon out of the place' but assured Mary that 'I will not be turnd out of the Garden for none of Mr bowes partey'. Saddened at the neglect the garden was suffering, Thompson dutifully worked without pay to weed the beds and pick insects from the flowers saying it 'greaves me very sor to see them spoild at this time'.[36]

Likewise Francis Bennett, once a footman to the late Lord Strathmore, who had stayed on as gamekeeper at Gibside, assured Mary of his continuing devotion and vowed 'I never intend to serve Mr Bowes any longer'.[37] Sending Mary regular bulletins on the fortunes of her beloved plants he also kept her abreast of Bowes's trail of destruction and terror in the neighbourhood. So the revelation that 'there is 4 Cape plants come up from the seed' in the greenhouse was somewhat outweighed by news of Bowes's relentless felling of ancient trees in the woods and his plans to sell off the livestock. As Bowes and his henchmen stormed about the estate threatening staff with dismissal and tenants with eviction, Bennett told Mary 'I think that Mr B. wants to do all the mischeif he possible can about this place'. He added: 'I can safely say that your Ladyship has more friends in this part of the Whorld than ever you had, there is hardly a person but what takes your part and wishes that your Ladyship may get the better of Mr B.' Sending Mary two pineapples by stagecoach to the Blue Boar at Holborn he warned her to avoid replying to Newcastle since Bowes was intercepting their post. But standing up to the renowned might and guile of the master of the manor was no easy undertaking. As Bennett attempted in vain to collect rents for Mary from the terrified tenants in late spring, he was forced to concede 'at present things goes on very Bad at Gibside all want to be masters'. Finding a hare caught by its neck in the woods, he confided to Mary, 'I could a wist it had been something eals.'

With tenants divided by their instinctive loyalty to Mary and their understandable terror of Bowes, it was a relief when Thomas Colpitts, Mary's agent before her marriage to Bowes when he had summarily been replaced by Henry Bourn, volunteered to collect their rents on Mary's behalf. Thanking him for forwarding a much-needed £100 at the end of May,

Mary wrote: 'I am greatly obliged by the unabated Regard you express for my Family, & by your very friendly attention to my own Interest'.[38]

By early summer of 1785, with avowals of support and money from tenants arriving regularly at her lodgings in Dyers Buildings, while testimonies from her witnesses mounted at her lawyer's office in nearby Cursitor Street, Mary had good cause for optimism. So when Bowes made a formal application to the Lord Chancellor in July proposing arbitration to settle the couple's land dispute if Mary would halt her suit for divorce, and offered the lawyer John Scott as referee, Mary felt she had little to lose by giving conciliation a trial. Assured that all due rents and profits would in the meantime be deposited with Chancery and that Bowes was willing to negotiate an amicable legal separation, she reluctantly suspended her divorce case just as the law courts began their long summer holiday.[39]

Well aware that Mary enjoyed no redress to the courts during their traditional three-month break Bowes, of course, had no intention of seeking an amicable resolution, nor of allowing the tenants to pay their rents into Chancery. Instead he redoubled his efforts to track down her sanctuary, wreaked havoc on her estates and stepped up his campaign of intimidation. Variously informing the staff and tenants that Mary and he were reconciled, or that her case was lost, he offered generous incitements to any who would swear false testimonies against her and threatened them with eviction or dismissal when they refused. Many, like William and Mary Stephenson, valiantly rejected his advances. Offered substantial rewards to deliver up Dorothy or betray Mary's whereabouts, William Stephenson wanted Mary to be informed of 'my unalterable resolution to withstand all his Vile Temptations & that I would rather starve than betray her in any respect'.[40] Others, distressed by poverty and petrified by his threats, were eventually seduced. Ann and George Arthur, the housekeeper and gardener at St Paul's Walden Bury, had sent Mary hampers of garden produce ever since her escape, but by May their fidelity had begun to falter. 'Now my Lady I am at a loss again how to obey with safty,' George Arthur confessed, 'as your Ladyship gives me Orders & likewise Mr Bowes.'[41] In July, when Bowes sent his footman to intercept the weekly food parcel, the Arthurs meekly surrendered the hamper, complete with Mary's address.

It was a close shave. Alerted just in time that Bowes had discovered her lodgings, Mary fled to a country retreat with Morgan and three of her trusted servants. Warning Thomas Colpitts to communicate only through Charles Shuter, she begged him: 'For Godsake don't tell any body that I am in Staffordshire, or that you have the least Idea, or guess as to the place of my Retirement, for it is of the utmost consequence to keep it secret, lest Mr B. shd. pursue me.'[42] When she returned to London in November, for the start of the new law term, it was little surprise to hear that Bowes now adamantly refused to consider any negotiated settlement.

Moving into more salubrious lodgings in Bloomsbury Square in December, at which point she also hired a coach, Mary was now resolved to press ahead with her divorce suit at all costs. Anxious to make public her determination to sever all links with Bowes, on Christmas Eve she issued a handbill which declared, 'my *immutable* resolution to endure persecutions, sufferings, and dangers, still greater, if possible, than those to which I have hitherto been exposed' and 'even to starve in the most miserable manner' rather than endure any further communication with Bowes.[43] Packed into the stagecoach bound for Newcastle, the posters were eagerly seized on by her friends in County Durham where they were distributed to tenants. The following day, Christmas Day, Mary travelled to Neasden to see her sons, George and Thomas, in their boarding school. Although snow enveloped the countryside, the visit marked the beginning of a slow thaw in relations with her children. Two weeks later the boys were permitted to dine at her house. And as the new year of 1786 began, with her resolution firmer than ever, Mary handed supervision of her various legal cases to a new attorney.

Sharing premises with his partner Thomas Lacey in Bread Street Hill, Cheapside, James Farrer dealt principally with criminal cases before the King's Bench.[44] Often confused with his namesake, another James Farrer who worked with his brother Oliver at the law firm Farrer and Co in Lincoln's Inn Fields, relatively little is known about Mary's attorney. Indeed, the two legal families may have been related since both hailed from Yorkshire. Yet while the Lincoln's Inn Fields Farrers were well known for their dealings in celebrated divorce cases of the time, Mary's lawyer had seemingly little experience in this arena. But for all his obscurity, James Farrer was to prove invaluable to Mary. An enthusiastic Mary Morgan was certainly cheered, informing Colpitts that Farrer had 'taken up the Business with so much spirit that every Circumstance weares a so much better Appearance, & rejoices every individual concern'd with this affair'.[45]

Immediately grappling with the thorny issue of money, Farrer paid Mary's current lawyers the several hundred pounds they were owed and insisted on working for no fee. At the same time he succeeded in winning an order that the estate's rents and mining profits should all be paid to receivers in Chancery. With prospects looking brighter by the day,

Mary rejoiced: 'He is indeed a man amongst ten thousand, nor can any words express my obligations to him sufficiently.' Utterly reliable and resolutely practical, James Farrer would more than prove his determination to pursue Mary's case to victory, at one point proclaiming that 'the effectually settling my Lady S's concerns, is the most anxious moment of my Life'.

Meanwhile Bowes was equally adamant that he would win the courtroom battles and was prepared to go to any extremes to succeed. Exacting vengeance on Mary's supporters, he had sacked Francis Bennett in October – ordering three of his hoodlums to kick the loyal retainer out of his sickbed and turf him out of his tied house – then in December he demanded Robert Thompson surrender the keys to the greenhouse, hothouse and banqueting house.[46] When Bowes's dog was killed after falling down a mineshaft, Thompson could not help remarking, 'i wish it had benn him self'. Blaming the severe winter for his inability to leave the north throughout January and February, Bowes delayed the divorce hearing before the ecclesiastical court. In March he finally filed his counter petition in Chancery, urging the court to declare Mary's prenuptial deed 'fraudulent' since it had been drawn up without his knowledge and 'in derogation of his marital rights'.[47]

Ignoring the Chancery order that tenants pay their rents into court, Bowes issued threatening letters to any farmers still withholding their rent 'at the instigation of a Banditti of Villainous Conspirators and Imposters'.[48] Attempting to persuade the tenants to keep their nerve, Colpitts confessed to Farrer: 'I shall rejoice to hear that any thing can be done this Term for the poor injured Lady, and her Tenants. What a being must that be, that seeks for revenge in punishing every individual who has lent the least assistance in time of her Ladys. greatest distress.' Up to his usual tricks, Bowes procrastinated further by feigning illness in April and at the end of the month locals were astonished to hear that he had shot himself.[49] It seemed, to Mary and her tenants, that their problems were at an end when they read in the *English Chronicle*: 'Yesterday advice was received of the death of Andrew Robinson Bowes, Esq. formerly Member for Newcastle.' Inevitably, it transpired that the report was premature, having been placed in the newspaper by Bowes himself to spread further confusion.

At last, on 6 May 1786, when Bowes could prevaricate no longer, the divorce suit came up for its hearing at the London Consistory Court at Doctors' Commons. Described by *The Times* as 'the great cause depending between the Countess of Strathmore and Mr Bowes', its outcome was awaited with trepidation not only by the two combatants but by tenants, servants, estate workers, family and friends throughout the country.[50] After more than a year of lawyers taking depositions from witnesses on both sides, who had subsequently been examined and cross-examined in private by the court's officials, the presiding judge, William Wynne, wasted no time in finding the case in favour of Mary Eleanor Bowes. Declaring the couple 'divorced from bed, board and mutual cohabitation' on the abundant evidence of Bowes's adultery and cruelty, the court ordered him to pay Mary £300 a year in alimony. A staggering triumph, one of only sixteen cases seeking divorce on grounds of both adultery and cruelty in that decade, the result sent a clear signal to abusive husbands and a message of hope to abused wives everywhere.

But the victory was short-lived. Bowes immediately gave notice of his appeal to the next level of the Church courts, the Court of Arches, and readied himself for a ferocious war of propaganda.

11

Say Your Prayers

London, 25 May 1786

Stopping to ogle the pornographic literature in the window of the popular little print shop at 66 Drury Lane, passers-by were drawn to the latest addition to the erotic display. Prominent among the pictures of prostitutes in lewd poses and women wielding instruments of discipline was a new print by the aspiring caricaturist James Gillray. Having so far failed to distinguish himself as a conventional artist and engraver, Gillray had recently decided to devote his talents to the burgeoning cartoon industry in league with William Holland, who sold topical prints from the Drury Lane shop he shared with the pornographer George Peacock. Ultimately, Gillray would produce more than a thousand satirical works lampooning every quarter of Georgian society, from politicians to princes, courtiers to courtesans, in flamboyant and frequently obscene detail.

Unusually large, at 16 by 21 inches, and exquisitely executed in delicate lines and rich colour, the caricature was indecorously entitled, 'LADY TERMAGANT FLAYBUM going to give her STEP SON a taste of her DESERT after Dinner, a Scene performed every day near Grosvenor Square, to the annoyance of the neighbourhood'. Although Lady Termagant Flaybum was a reference to a well-known comic character in a book on flagellation previously published by

Peacock, customers would have been in no doubt that the real target of Gillray's ridicule was Mary Eleanor Bowes. A statuesque figure lounging provocatively with her breasts bared and her plump legs indecently crossed, she holds a bundle of birch twigs with which she is evidently about to beat a protesting boy whose breeches are being unfastened by a maid. The wine bottle and glass on a nearby table suggest a life of debauchery, the character's elaborately piled hairstyle and voluminous clothing evoke vanity and extravagance, while her exposed flesh and the anticipated act of flagellation are a blatant slur on her morality as well as a titillating morsel with which to tempt customers. While no evidence of correspondence survives, it is highly probable that Gillray was commissioned to produce the print by Bowes.

Having just lost his case against divorce in the first level of the ecclesiastical courts, Bowes was making it clear, in commissioning such a brazen and offensive cartoon, that he intended to play dirty in his forthcoming appeal. No matter that Mary had left Grosvenor Square more than a year earlier, nor that the scene was meant to portray her eldest son, rather than a stepson, the message in the print was plain. For all Mary's allegations of savagery and infidelity recently founded against Bowes, it was in fact she who was promiscuous, degenerate, cruel and an unnatural mother to boot. The print was one of two, possibly three, produced by Gillray lampooning Mary in 1786. The second, and even more outrageous picture, entitled 'The Injured COUNT..S', depicts her carousing with servants as she suckles two cats from huge exposed breasts while a small boy at her side cries: 'I wish I was a cat my mama would love me then.' Recalling an anecdote from *The Ton Gazette* in 1777, which attributed the same words to the little Lord Strathmore, the grotesque scene furnished more ammunition for Bowes's campaign. Behind

Mary the print shows her footman, possibly George Walker, inviting her to bed, while on her left sits an emaciated maid, apparently Mary Morgan, with her waist reduced to a slender line and a pock-marked face. The same bizarre figure features in a third Gillray caricature, 'The Miser's Feast', which had been published two months earlier. In this a similarly wasp-waisted character, this time with bare breasts, opens the door for a sumptuously dressed woman on to a scene of bleak poverty. The fashionable woman carries a book entitled 'Woman of Pleasure', better known as the erotic novel *Fanny Hill*, an obvious slight on her virtue. Although the identity of the wealthy female character is unclear, the print was later assumed to refer to Mary.

Expensively priced, at 7s 6d, the Lady Termagant print was aimed at an affluent market, effectively Mary's peers. For the radical politician John Wilkes, writing to his daughter in Paris, it was 'too extravagant' to buy. Yet the high cost apparently did not deter a regular stream of customers, for the cartoon was still on sale three years later. And for those who could not afford to purchase their own copy, there was always the opportunity to press their noses against the window of Holland's shop where best-selling prints were generally displayed.

It was the beginning of a paper war. Dangling the lure of seamy revelations to come, Bowes was ensuring a ready audience eager to follow each twist and turn of the couple's high-profile divorce. As the Gillray caricature signalled, he would be willing to unearth all Mary's past indiscretions as well as peddle monstrous lies in his campaign to sully her reputation and damage her support. The fact that Bowes was plainly projecting his own lasciviousness and debauched lifestyle on to Mary, not to mention his perversity in debasing the wife he avowedly wished to win back, did nothing to deter him. Over the ensuing months he would use every possible medium – from false reports and vexatious advertisements in newspapers to spiteful cartoons and mendacious handbills – in his effort to achieve his goal. The threat to Mary was clear: Bowes would stop at nothing to prevent their divorce.

Determined not to be cowed by media ridicule, Mary steadied her nerve for the next round of legal wrangles as she kept close to her Bloomsbury Square house and her loyal coterie of servants. While letters from the north-east brought almost daily reports of Bowes's antics there, at least she knew that he remained at a safe distance.

Denied the usual punchbag for his temper, Bowes stormed about the Gibside and Streatlam estates with his hired henchmen laying waste the land and venting his fury on the defenceless country folk. Alerted by the tenants who stayed faithful to her, Mary attempted to prevent Bowes hacking down more trees by applying for an injunction in Chancery in June.[1] With Bowes having already felled timber worth more than £20,000, including many young and ornamental trees, Mary complained that he had declared he would 'not leave a single tree standing'. On the very day that she filed her bill, Bowes advertised 908 oak trees for sale in the *Newcastle Courant*. Just as with his previous battle with the Newton heirs over the woods at Cole Pike Hill, the advertisement appeared alongside a counter order from Mary declaring that the sale was unlawful. Gaining her injunction in July, Mary now circulated handbills warning potential buyers not to purchase the felled trees, while Bowes responded with his own handbills claiming the injunction had been dissolved. More damagingly, Bowes also set forth rumours that Mary had been reconciled to him and had dropped her divorce suit, which Mary then had to contradict with a further announcement in the *Courant*.[2] Robert Thompson, the ever-loyal gardener, displayed one of the handbills forbidding the sale of wood prominently in the window of his house. When Bowes threatened him, Thompson promptly rode into Newcastle and handed the bills out in every tavern in town.[3] Yet Thompson was concerned at the rumours that Mary had returned to Bowes, which he told her 'most people here believe true', begging her to deny the reports 'or eals we are broken harted'.

As Bowes persecuted all who supported Mary, the fearful tenants put their faith, as she had, in common justice. 'He says that he will starves us out if possabill & that we shall have no farem under him . . . and he says that all of the old tennents shall quit ther farems,' Thompson informed Mary. True to his word, that summer Bowes served a raft of eviction notices on farms and smallholdings throughout the region regardless of the desperate circumstances of their occupants. 'The poor man who has sent you the notice, which he recd. from Mr Bowes, is in great distress for fear of being turn'd out of his farm on acct. of his large family,' Mary Morgan reported to James Farrer. One woman appealed to Mary for help five days after she had lost her husband – Bowes had seized the family's entire possessions. 'The reason Mr Bowes destraind [distrained] upon us was for my late husband keeping up the name and dignity of the Honble. Countess,' she explained, 'which Mr Bowes got intelligence and being so revengefull as to take the bread from us, and destrain also upon our goods.'

Furious at Robert Thompson's efforts to preserve Mary's plants from neglect, despite having already been sacked, Bowes now ordered the gardener to be thrown off the estate. Aged and infirm, Thompson was forced to flee his home when Bowes threatened to burn it down. Having failed to tempt William and Mary Stephenson to hand over Dorothy, Bowes now rained threats and writs on them and encouraged his annuitants, to whom Bowes had guaranteed Gibside farms in return for ready cash, to order them to quit their farm. Writing to Mary, Mrs Stephenson pleaded, 'We hath nothing left save just our familey which is all gon but onley one that canst work & if my husband be to go to gayle [jail] it will be berri hard.' As Bowes turned his anger on Mrs Stephenson's brother, who had agreed to swear an affidavit against Bowes, the couple wrote in desperation, 'We have Mr bows amongst us like a roring lion threatnin that he will punish my brother aboot the writ.' After months of such intimidation, the brother finally confessed himself too petrified to testify. Reduced to poverty, turned out of their farms and sacked from their jobs, the majority of tenants and workers still pledged their allegiance to Mary and supported each other in their adversity.

The old Bowes charm appeared to be growing tarnished. When Bowes sued poor Robert Thompson for the theft of a saddle at the Durham assizes in July, the grand jury threw the case out of court telling Bowes's witnesses – in Thompson's words – that 'thare was no more such villins to be found in the county as them & thare master'.[4] In another vengeful lawsuit in the same court that month, however, Bowes successfully sued Thomas Colpitts for receiving rents in Mary's name, asserting his right to the profits of the estate on the basis of the questionable revocation deed. Sending her regrets to Colpitts, Mary hoped he would have more success on appeal. But when Chancery overturned Mary's injunction against felling the woods later that summer, having been convinced by Bowes's counsel that the young Lord Strathmore's guardians would have intervened if serious damage had occurred, it seemed that the Gibside master's fortunes had turned. Evidently Thomas Lyon preferred to stand by and watch his ward's fortune be ruined than lend his voice to Mary's cause. Vowing that 'there is no condescension wch I wd. not make even to my worst Enemies, to get the better of that Villain', Mary appealed again to Lyon for help in defeating Bowes.[5]

Remaining steadfast and optimistic despite the setbacks, Mary was slowly attempting to rebuild her life, spending part of the long summer break with friends in the countryside and even embarking on a new romance. Having spent a week with one set of friends at their 'charming & extensive seat' at Bury Hill, in West Sussex, Mary had stayed for ten days with other friends at Leybourne in Kent. In a newsy letter to Colpitts that July, she enthused, 'Their little neat Box is surrounded with fine prospects, beautiful gentlemens seats, & places to see all within a small distance'.[6] With Morgan her constant companion, Mary enjoyed an excursion to fashionable Tunbridge Wells and outings to tea with neighbouring gentry. After years of being forced to appear rude or deranged in company, her conversation schooled by Bowes, she seemed almost surprised to find that those she met were 'extremely civil to me'. And now at liberty to follow her own desires for the first time in a decade, at the age of thirty-seven she had discovered a new admirer who was rather more than civil.

Indebted to the support of James Farrer since he had taken charge of her legal business at the beginning of 1786, Mary had forged a firm friendship with the attorney and his family. Farrer and his wife had been invited to dine in Bloomsbury Square and Mary grew fond of the couple's young daughters, but it was Farrer's brother, a 41-year-old ship's captain named Henry Farrer, who brought spice to her summer days. Having returned from India and China at the helm of the East Indiaman *True Briton* after a two-year round voyage the previous October, Captain Farrer quickly inveigled himself into Mary's affections.[7] By the summer, the dashing captain was rarely away from her side, and seldom absent from her letters, joining Mary and her friends at their Kent retreat and accompanying them on their jaunt to Tunbridge Wells. Still plainly unable to resist a man in uniform, Mary was reassured by the courteous captain's presence, telling Colpitts that 'Captain Farrer ... came down to protect us here'. When Mary returned to London in August, he remained her escort.

The fact that the gallant captain was already married and had previously, if not still, kept a mistress in town, suggested that Mary's judgement of character was as flawed as ever. Having married Mary Goldsmith in 1781, Captain Farrer had kept his wife a secret from his family – possibly because it was not the most advantageous of matches – and on his return from his travels he evidently wished that his wife would remain conveniently out of sight. Mrs Farrer would later claim that her husband had left her destitute, forcing her to wash laundry to make ends meet, though in reality it seems that she had resorted to a rather less salubrious method of earning her keep. Certainly the pair had endured a strained and largely estranged relationship since the captain's return; indeed, it is possible that Mary had no idea that Mrs Farrer existed.

Staying in London, where she felt safer than in the country, Mary tentatively dipped her toe into the city's social life, although always remaining on guard for Bowes's next move. In September, when Captain Farrer departed to spend three weeks at Cheltenham, Mary visited friends in Chelsea and dined with the artist George Engleheart at his home in Kew. Whether it was at this point that Engleheart painted

Mary's portrait is unknown; a prolific artist who portrayed many of the Georgian nobility, Engleheart did not list Mary in his fee-book but a miniature later painted by his nephew, John Cox Dillman Engleheart, which shows Mary at about this time, is said to have been copied from an earlier portrait made by his uncle.[8] There was time too for her sons, George and Thomas, who had recently enrolled – at Uncle Thomas's behest – at Eton. Enjoying the company of her teenage boys, now fourteen and thirteen, Mary promised George a puppy. Relations with her older children remained difficult, while her two youngest, of course, were still in Bowes's custody. That same month she rejoiced with Colpitts at the success in Lancaster of his appeal against Bowes's vexatious lawsuit over Colpitts receiving her rents, and hoped the decision boded well for her ongoing Chancery plea to reinstate her premarital deed. While she confided to Colpitts that James Farrer was far from confident that her deed might be restored, understandably given the prevailing legal climate against women's rights to property, she remained convinced that ultimately she would succeed.

By October, as the metropolis swelled with the return of the usual well-heeled pleasure-seekers for the start of the winter season, Mary had almost regained her zest for society life. 'There has been a vast deal of mirth & elegant entertainment going forwards amongst us for this last fortnight,' Mary reported in a chatty letter to the faithful Colpitts.[9] Relating details of her visits to the theatre, concerts and parties, she confessed, 'I have been an incessant Rake during the time I mention; every Night (except one that I was at the Play) has been spent either at a Rout or a Concert; besides wch. I frequently both dined & supped out; so that I was rarely longer in the House than was necessary to dress myself for going out again.' With Captain Farrer returned from

Cheltenham apparently reinvigorated by its restorative waters, Mary seemed as skittish as a teenage debutante. At least now she had a little more regard to society gossip – fully aware that Bowes would use any scandal to oppose their divorce – and told Colpitts that her devoted captain was 'skipping about the town, & is to be seen in all places, except Bloomsbury Sq. & Bread St'.

For all her newfound liberty and re-entry into society, as the autumn law term neared, Mary remained wary. Even as she enjoyed games of quadrille in elegant salons and attended routs in opulent ballrooms, she told everyone she met that she lived in constant terror of Bowes seizing her. Accustomed to the fabricated image of Mary's eccentricity, most dismissed her anxiety as fanciful. When Mary told friends that strange men claiming to be law officers, or women feigning madness, had attempted to force their way into her home, they assumed she was being over-imaginative. When she claimed that her coach was being followed whenever she ventured out, they put it down to the inevitable congestion of city streets. And when she complained that her post was being intercepted, she was dismissed as overwrought. Only Mary Morgan, and the other servants who had experienced the extent of Bowes's guile and vengeance for themselves, shared her fears.

At the end of October, Morgan informed Colpitts that a chaise with its blinds shut and a hackney carriage had been spotted loitering in the square before following Mary's coach when she went out. Only the quick-thinking of Ann Parkes, who spotted the chaise setting off in pursuit of her mistress's carriage and sent a footman to overtake Mary, had averted possible danger. Seeing the chaise and hackney carriage stop, Morgan was certain she spotted Bowes leaning out of the window. 'The watchers are grown desperate & I am afraid some dreadful disaster will Terminate in this business,' she warned. But three days later, when Bowes was discovered by Colpitts's son, lying in the road near Barnard Castle after apparently falling from his horse, the suspicions were assumed to be groundless. With Bowes reported to be confined to his bed by life-threatening injuries, a condition verified by the lawyer John Lee who circulated the news in London, it appeared that Mary Eleanor had nothing to worry about. Nevertheless, on 2 November, when Morgan noticed two coaches following Mary's, then stopping at either end of a lonely section of the King's Road, she feared the worst. This time Robert Crundall, Bowes's former footman who was now in Mary's service, swore he saw Bowes – despite the reports that he was still lying injured in Streatlam Castle – but the pursuers made no attempt to stop them and Crundall returned home relieved.

Growing increasingly alarmed, Mary now insisted that no strangers be granted entry to her house and declared that she would remain locked inside until the conclusion of the divorce appeal expected imminently. 'Our House is all over Bolts, Bars, Bells, Alarms, Swords, Pistols, Hangers, Guns, & Clubs,' she informed Colpitts, '& we have borrowed a House Dog that wd seize any Man by the Throat, so I trust that through the Blessing & Justice of God we shall escape all dangers. All the Garret windows are barricaded with Iron.'[10] Her house locked and barred, her servants armed and alert, and with her ferocious guard dog by her side, even then Mary did not feel secure. And so when an earnest and bespectacled young constable named Edward Lucas called at the house that same week and offered to provide protection against dubious characters he had spotted lurking near her stables, Mary gratefully engaged him as a bodyguard for the princely sum of 12 shillings a week. Informing Colpitts a few days later that 'we have got a trusty additionall Watchman, a Constable in the House', Mary Morgan put her faith in God and the law to preserve her mistress 'from the murderous hands of this Wretch'.

At midday on Friday 10 November 1786, Mary set off in her carriage from Bloomsbury Square with Captain Farrer and Mary Morgan on a social visit to the owner of an ironmonger's shop, Edward Foster, in nearby Oxford Street.[11] Although still apprehensive, Mary had felt faint from being confined in the house and longed for an 'airing'. Assured by her new bodyguard Lucas that all was quiet in the neighbourhood and secure in the knowledge that her staunch protector, Captain Farrer, was armed with a pistol, she had decided to venture outdoors. Enjoying her first excursion for days, Mary was taking refreshments with Mr Foster when she heard a sudden commotion in the street outside. Rushing upstairs in alarm, Mary and Morgan locked themselves in a garret room. To their relief, moments later, they heard the calm voice of Lucas at the door assuring them that it was safe to descend.

Emerging into Oxford Street, however, Mary realised that her carriage was surrounded by men armed with pistols, blunderbusses and swords and that her own footman and driver had been replaced with strangers. Now Lucas announced that she was his prisoner, informed her that he had a warrant for her arrest and demanded that she accompany him to appear before Lord Mansfield at his home, Kenwood House, near Highgate. Confused and frightened, Mary was bundled into her carriage but managed to drag Captain Farrer with her as Morgan slipped away to raise the alarm. Knowing that James Farrer was away on business in Carlisle, Morgan rushed to alert his partner, Thomas Lacey, to summon help. With a crowd of curious onlookers gathering, the carriage sped off east along Oxford Street towards the Tottenham Court Road turnpike where it was joined by a hackney coach. As Mary alternately screamed for help from the windows and begged Lucas on her knees to save her, the two carriages hared northwards out of town. When the coach pulled up at the Red Lion tavern in Highgate Mary was horrified as, standing in the yard of the inn, she saw Bowes. Now frantic with terror, Mary implored the tavern keepers to help her escape but bribed with a guinea by Bowes they ignored her pleas. Leaping into the carriage beside her, his pistol at the ready, Bowes maintained the notion that they were headed for Kenwood but when the coach continued up the Great North Road beyond Highgate it was clear, as Mary had suspected, that the story was a concoction. When Captain Farrer protested, Bowes simply stopped the coach, shoved the hapless defender into the road and left him to trudge meekly back to town as the carriage disappeared in a flurry of mud.

Alone now with Bowes and his armed ruffians, hurtling north through the rapidly darkening day, Mary faced the horror she had long been dreading. Just as she had feared, it transpired that Bowes had been plotting her abduction for weeks.[12] Anxious that his appeal against the divorce was likely to be lost, but determined to cling on to the Bowes fortune at all cost, he had resolved to coerce Mary into relinquishing her suit or, failing that, force her to cohabit with him again, thereby invalidating her case. Having waited until his bail had expired at the end of July so as not to forfeit his friends' sureties, Bowes had recruited a gang of lawless hoodlums culled from the dregs of the Durham criminal underground. After following Mary's coach on several occasions in London he had scurried back north to fake the fall from his horse and while supposedly fighting for his life at Streatlam Castle had secretly returned to the capital and rented a house in Norfolk Street near the Strand.

Adopting a variety of false names and disguises, masquerading as a sailor, a judge and a crippled old man, Bowes had bribed the constable Edward Lucas to infiltrate Mary's household. Typical of the feckless wastrels appointed by London parishes as constables and watchmen, Lucas had duly reported to Bowes on Mary's daily activities. Acting well beyond the call of duty, on 8 November Lucas had helped obtain warrants for the arrest of Mary's coachman and footman, Daniel Lee and Robert Crundall, on the trumped-up grounds that they had threatened the lives of two of Bowes's hirelings. And when Lucas had relayed word that Mary intended to venture out on 10 November, Bowes had immediately swung into action. As his armed vagabonds seized Mary's coach, despatching Lee and Crundall to swear their innocence before a bewildered magistrate, Bowes waited eagerly in a hired carriage for his reunion with the wife he had not seen for nearly two years. The period of separation, Mary discovered, had not improved his behaviour.

Petrified for her safety but utterly determined never to return to Bowes's violent regime, nothing would now induce Mary to bow to his bullying tactics. So as Bowes urged the coach onwards at reckless speed, stopping only to change horses or snatch refreshments at inns, Mary attempted every possible means of escape.

At the first halt to change horses, at Barnet, Mary smashed the carriage window with her bare hands and yelled, 'Murder for God's sake help me', but she was immediately gagged by Bowes and held fast by Lucas. Halting shortly afterwards at the Brick Wall turnpike, she begged to be allowed out for a call of nature. Trembling so much that she could hardly hold the chamber pot, she persuaded the tollbooth keepers to fetch her a pen and paper. But having been told by Bowes that they were headed for St Paul's Walden Bury, on the pretext that one of her children was seriously ill, she scribbled a note to Morgan urging her to hurry there. Incredibly, the hastily scrawled note found its way back to London; even more incredibly, torn and stained with damp, it still survives. 'My Dear Morgan,' she pleaded, 'Let me beg that you and Mr Lacey will come to me immediately upon the receipt of this to Pauls Walden, & bring any other of our Friends with you, & for Heaven's sake don't lose a Moment.'[13]

Further along the road, when the carriage pulled in that evening at the George Inn, Buckden in Cambridgeshire, Mary succeeded in snatching a few words alone with a sympathetic serving maid whom she entreated to send a message by express carrier – a messenger on horseback – to Lord Mansfield. Later the maid would testify that Mary seemed 'in great fear trouble and distress and wept very much and appeared to be very sick and vomited'. But reassured by Bowes that Mary was merely ill through fasting, the maid never sent the message. Continuing up the dangerously rutted northern road, the dishevelled party arrived at 1 a.m. at the Bell Inn, Stilton. Raising the tavern staff from their beds, Bowes dragged Mary into a parlour, held a pistol to her head and threatened to shoot her unless she signed a paper suspending the divorce. When she adamantly refused, he clenched his fist and punched her in the head. Dragged by his ruffians towards the coach, Mary managed to wrestle free and ran screaming up the high street, but although her cries were heard in several houses nobody came to her assistance. Recaptured by Bowes's hoodlums she was forced back into the carriage where Bowes struck her on the chest with the heavy chain and seals of his watch.

Charging on through the night, Bowes stopped at Stamford, where Mary again screamed for help, and at Grantham, where Bowes kept her locked in the coach while the horses were changed. Arriving in Newark at 7 a.m. on Saturday, Mary was allowed under tight escort to visit the garden privy, where she was recognised from past visits by an ostler who noted that, 'she appeared to be in great agitation and distress of mind and seemed worn out and spent with fatigue' while a chambermaid remarked that Mary seemed 'not in her senses'. Closely guarded as the carriage dashed on through Saturday, Mary was given no further chance to seek help until Bowes stopped for fresh horses at Barnby Moor in Nottinghamshire. Complaining of sickness, probably exacerbated by the swaying motion of the speeding coach, she was allowed upstairs to a parlour. Hurriedly whispering her plight to a chambermaid while Bowes was out of sight, Mary was finally rewarded. Shocked at details of the kidnap, the maid promised to send an urgent message to Lord Mansfield in London. On her knees, Mary kissed her in gratitude.

Convinced by now that Bowes planned to continue on to Scotland and from there set sail for Ireland, where her lawyers would have little hope of retrieving her, Mary was frantic. When they reached the familiar town of Barnard Castle, close to her ancient family seat of Streatlam Castle, she screamed as loudly as she could. 'My whole conduct from Highgate to Streatlam was alternately screaming out, where there were hopes of assistance', she later wrote, 'and remaining quiet where there were few.' Three miles further on, when the carriage rattled up the sweeping drive of Streatlam Castle and pulled up in front of the stone steps at about midnight, Mary shrieked to the postboys who had driven the horses from their last staging post that she had been brought there by force. Always ready with an answer, Bowes assured them that Mary was out of her mind. Bedraggled and exhausted, at the end of a journey lasting thirty-four hours, Mary certainly must have had the appearance of a madwoman. And as Bowes dragged her into the castle, shutting the great wooden doors behind them, she had no idea whether she would ever emerge again.

Originally built to withstand attack from Scottish invaders and powerful northern barons in the fifteenth century, Streatlam Castle provided Bowes with the perfect stronghold in which to keep Mary captive.[14] Sited in a deep valley, surrounded by forested hills and encircled by a broad channel, originally the moat, the castle had kept Mary's ancestors secure for a century before Sir George Bowes had been forced to flee from advancing Catholic forces during the Northern Rebellion of 1569. Promptly captured by the rebels, the castle had been wrecked and plundered before the patriotic Sir George could return lamenting that, 'I am utterly spoiled of all my goodes.' It was Mary's supercilious uncle William who had transformed the Gothic pile into a family mansion at the beginning of the eighteenth century. Never fully completed, the gloomy and forbidding house had been disliked by Mary's father, who preferred his cherished Gibside, and it had never evoked fondness in Mary either. Comfortless and dilapidated, the power base built to protect Mary's ancestors now served as her prison.

Met at the door by Henry Bourn, Bowes's right-hand man, Mary was taken to the oak-panelled dining room where generations of her ancestors had lingered over lavish banquets and toasted family triumphs. Having demanded food after the arduous journey, Bowes grabbed Mary and pointed his pistol at her breast then threatened to fire unless she consented to live with him again as his wife.[15] Once cowed and submissive, terrified of her husband's violent assaults, now

Mary was defiant, refusing to comply with his demands, even at gunpoint. Flinging down his weapon in exasperation Bowes berated her until supper arrived but no sooner had their plates been cleared than he snatched up his pistol again. Holding the gun once more to Mary's breast, Bowes calmly informed her that he was determined to shoot. When he ordered her to 'Say your prayers!' Mary did just that. Closing her eyes, she declaimed, 'I recommend my spirit to God, and my friends to his protection: – fire!' Mary heard the trigger being pulled and waited for the fatal blow but the gunpowder failed to ignite, probably due to the damp conditions of the journey, causing the proverbial 'flash in the pan'. Demented with rage, Bowes punched Mary twice so that she fell to the floor, her head pounding so much that the room seemed 'in a blaze of fire'. Towering over her, Bowes demanded to know whether she had had enough to which Mary retorted, 'Not the thousandth part enough; you may shoot me, or beat me to a mummy: my person is in your power, but my mind is beyond your reach.' At that Bowes threw his ineffectual pistol aside and exclaimed in evident awe, 'By God you are a wonderful woman.'

Undeterred, nonetheless, Bowes now ordered two of his ruffians to carry Mary up the grand oak staircase to bed. Once alone with her in the bedchamber, he told Mary to undress and get into bed with him; when she refused, he began to tear at her clothing then forced her on to the bed. Well aware that if Mary consented to have intercourse he could legitimately claim that she had returned to him as his wife and thereby invalidate her divorce suit, Bowes demanded sex. Equally resolved to resist, Mary swore that she would rather die than consent. Although she was plainly no match for Bowes's looming six-foot figure and renowned might, Mary threatened she would sue him for rape if he attempted to take her by force. No doubt aware that rape was a hanging offence, he relented and left her to sleep alone. Throughout the following day, Sunday 12 November, Bowes continued to threaten Mary with violence, harangue her with insults and cajole her with details of a fresh round of eviction notices he planned to serve on her tenants. Closely guarded by Bowes's confederates and served by Bowes's mistress, a maid called Mary Gowland who was pregnant with yet another of his illegitimate children, Mary remained resolute.

News that the Countess of Strathmore had been abducted in broad daylight from one of London's main thoroughfares spread rapidly through the streets of the capital and ultimately travelled even as far as India. 'The town was ringing about your old neighbour of the north Countess Strathmore and the enormous barbarities of her husband,' gossiped Horace Walpole to his friend Lady Ossory.[16] The Duchess of Brunswick, sister of George III, exclaimed to the Duchess of Argyll: 'What a shocking story this is of Mr Bowes carrying off Ldy Strathmore.' Despatching for good any remnants of Bowes's reputation, the sensational events also prompted many to reassess their assumptions about marriage. While Walpole considered that wealthy widows should in future prove 'a little cautious of Mac-Philanderers', the Duchess of Brunswick firmly pronounced: 'I seldom see love matches turn out well, love dose [does] make such havock.'

Eager to reveal the latest remarkable twist in the Bowes divorce, the press related the story in full. Rushing into print on the day after the kidnap, the *London Evening Post* announced: 'Yesterday, about two o'clock, Lady Strathmore was forcibly taken away from the house of Mr Forster [sic], brazier, in Oxford-street, where she had called on business, by five or six armed men, who violently seized and put her into her own carriage, which waited at the door.'[17] Describing the incident as an 'outrage', *The Times* averred that it was Bowes's 'unquestionable design' to carry the countess to Ireland. The *Gentleman's Magazine* carried the news in florid detail, reporting eye-witness accounts of Mary's struggles and appeals for help as her coach sped through villages 'at a most furious rate'. And finally catching up with the drama six months later, when the London news arrived by sea in India, the *Madras Courier* would astound its readers with 'the particulars respecting the forcibly taking away the Countess of Strathmore'.

Meanwhile Mary's friends and supporters lost no time in rushing to her aid. Appalled at seeing her beloved mistress and closest friend snatched from her side in Oxford Street, Mary Morgan had immediately dashed across town to find Thomas Lacey. But in an era seventy years before the existence of a nationwide police force, when even the most heinous crimes had to be pursued and prosecuted by the victims and their families, Mary's supporters were forced to rely on their own resources. Too late to seek legal redress that day, on the following day Morgan and Captain Farrer, who had trudged back to town footsore and shamefaced, swore an affidavit before Lord Mansfield to secure a writ of *habeas corpus* ordering Bowes to surrender Mary along with a 'Rule for Informations' demanding that he explain his actions.[18] A court tipstaff, Thomas Ridgeway, set off at once to serve the legal notices taking Captain Farrer as his guide. Together the pair galloped out of town, following the unmistakable trail of Mary's journey northwards. Reporting the tipstaff's quest, the *English Chronicle* confidently predicted, 'There is no doubt he will succeed as many accounts have arrived in town from the places they passed through, which point out and ascertain their route.'[19]

Left in London to rally forces, Morgan and Lacey rejoiced when they received Mary's damp-stained note revealing that she was heading for St Paul's Walden Bury. Relief quickly turned to anguish, however, when she and Lacey arrived at the house to find it empty. Now convinced that Mary was being taken to Ireland, the pair despatched express messengers to all the main seaports urging that Bowes be apprehended, and distributed handbills throughout the capital appealing for help in finding her. Warning of the legal measures taken, the leaflets urged, 'It is therefore hoped that all Persons will use their utmost Endeavours to stop their Progress, wherever they go, and prevent her being conveyed out of the Kingdom, and give every possible and speedy information thereof at her Ladyship's House in *Bloomsbury-Square*, London.'[20]

As predicted by the press, Ridgeway and Captain Farrer collected distressing reports of Mary's ordeal at every coaching inn they stopped at on the Great North Road; the information they gathered from witnesses would prove crucial. It was two days later, however, a full day behind Bowes, when their trail finally culminated in County Durham and the two crusaders were reliably informed that Mary was being held captive in Streatlam Castle. Joining forces with the resourceful Thomas Colpitts, the rescue party collected at the offices of a sympathetic local lawyer, Zachary Hubbersty, to consider their next move. 'I have to inform you by express that Capt. Farrer, Mr Colpitts & Mr Ridgeway arrived here this morning about 9 o'clock, after hearing of Mr Stoney all the way,' Hubbersty wrote in a dashed letter to Lacey in London.[21] Having likewise heard of the various weapons being brandished by Bowes and his lawless crew, Ridgeway reasonably concluded that he needed to raise reinforcements before proceeding. To that end, the tipstaff summoned help from law enforcers in the region and placed a 'strong guard' around the castle for, as Hubbersty presciently noted, 'there is no doubt but Mr B. will take Ly. S. off if any opportunity is given him so to do'.

With news of the extraordinary events radiating to every town and port, friends and allies throughout the country rallied to Mary's cause. Horrified to hear of Bowes's latest villainy, Robert Thompson, the sacked Gibside gardener, swore that he would save his mistress or 'dye on the spott'.[22] Receiving the alarming news in Cambridge, Mary's seventeen-year-old son John set off on horseback to rescue the mother he had not seen for six years. 'The young Earl of Strathmore', the *English Chronicle* told readers, 'has set out for the north, and is determined to liberate his mother out of her present disagreeable situation at the risk of his existence.'[23] Even the Duke of Norfolk, Bowes's old drinking chum and bail guarantor, sent messengers to friends in the north urging them to join the rescue efforts. And once they learned that Bowes had barricaded himself in at Streatlam, local miners besieged the house, hollering for Mary's release and lighting immense fires in an effort to prevent her being removed under cover of darkness. Watching the castle night and day, armed with guns, swords and bludgeons, the formidable force was variously estimated at two hundred, three hundred and even five hundred angry and determined men illuminated by 'great blazing coal fires' positioned in every avenue.[24]

While the miners were evidently prepared to risk their lives to deliver Mary from her ordeal, others were seemingly more resigned to her plight. Informed of events by Colpitts, Mary's aged aunt, Margaret Liddell, in Durham promised to launch inquiries in the neighbourhood to ascertain her niece's whereabouts but added lamely, 'I dare say he will send her abroad.'[25] Another correspondent, relating the news that had captivated the region, suggested, 'she is most likely a Prisoner for Life'. And one witness, reporting details of Mary's journey through Yorkshire, anticipated an even worse fate, writing, 'It's a dammed rascally affair . . . I hope he will not be vilain enough to do her away.'[26]

Although temperatures hovered close to freezing, the unyielding pitworkers gave a warm reception to Thomas Ridgeway when at last he approached Streatlam Castle with his documents in hand on 13 November. To nobody's surprise the tipstaff was gruffly refused entry by one of Bowes's hoodlums but when Ridgeway noticed a smartly dressed figure answering to Bowes's description at one of the windows, he pushed the writs underneath the castle door by way of serving them.[27] Powerless to take further action within the confines of the law but certain that his quarry was well and truly cornered, Ridgeway confidently awaited Mary's release.

With the castle surrounded by pitworkers, law officers and neighbours, its walls illuminated by giant bonfires, supplies of food stopped and even the water pipes cut, it seemed only a matter of time before the prison would be breached. Yet with no sighting of Mary for two days, her putative rescuers were growing apprehensive. Confirmation that the *habeas corpus* had been served took an inevitable two days to reach London, whereupon Mary's lawyers immediately requested that the King's Bench send an 'attachment', or posse of officers, to take Bowes into custody for failing to comply. It took a further frustrating day for the court to agree, on 16 November, to the plea. Accordingly a band of armed officers then set off from Bow Street, the pioneering police station founded in the 1750s by the novelist and magistrate Henry Fielding, with a warrant to arrest Bowes and rescue Mary. With the whole country now agog at the scandal, one newspaper duly reported, 'a party of peace officers, armed, in post chaises, went off with all expedition to Streatlam Castle', while the *Gentleman's Magazine* ruefully noted that fulfilling their task 'will prove a dangerous attempt to execute'.[28]

Meanwhile James Farrer, arriving hotfoot from Carlisle, had decided to take the law into his own hands – or at least those of local magistrates. Impatient at the interminable delays, he obtained a warrant from a local justice and with the aid of several sturdy supporters determined to force open the castle gates. As the assembled crowd watched with bated breath, on 16 November Farrer, Hubbersty and Colpitts burst through the doors, tripped over the *habeus corpus* writ lying unread on the floor and commenced a search of the building.[29] To their astonishment, and the subsequent amazement of the gathered assembly, there was no sign either of Bowes or Mary. Closely questioned by the lawyers, the handful of ruffians left behind refused to yield a single clue to their whereabouts. Since no carriages were missing the bewildered rescuers were stumped as to the means of Bowes's vanishing act and as there had been no sign of him since, they were equally flummoxed over his destination. Seriously alarmed that Mary might be irretrievably lost, it seemed, as one correspondent poignantly remarked, that Bowes had 'Arts & Contrivance enough to accomplish any thing he undertakes'.[30]

One step ahead, as ever, Bowes was long gone. For on the evening of Sunday 12 November, the day after arriving at Streatlam and a full four days before James Farrer broke in with his search warrant, Bowes had fled the castle under the very noses of the vigilantes. Having forced Mary to dress in a man's greatcoat and a maid's bonnet he had smuggled her out of a back door and, with Mary riding pillion, accompanied by his pregnant mistress and several armed accomplices, ridden stealthily away across the moors.[31] The next eight days would test Mary's powers of endurance to the limits. Suffering barely credible extremes of deprivation and brutality, exposed to intolerable conditions during the coldest autumn of the century, Mary would draw on a remarkable inner resilience and the long-buried physical strength which her father had instilled in her as a child.

Heading due west across the boggy moorland, aiming for Carlisle and probably Ireland, Bowes first halted at a rough cottage belonging to his mistress's father in a remote spot known as Roger Moor where the party laid low for the next two days. Here Bowes crammed Mary into a 'press bed' – a type of bed concealed in a cupboard commonly stored in eighteenth-century kitchens. When she still refused to sleep with him, he threatened her with his pistol, beat her about the head and shut her in. Enclosed in the darkness for most of the first day, she heard Bowes calling for padlocks and a hot poker but defiantly shouted that she was ready for whatever cruelty he might attempt. When finally the doors were opened Bowes laid her on her side then beat her severely with a rod.

Leaving the cottage once darkness fell the following evening, 15 November, Mary was placed on a horse behind Charles Chapman, a miner recruited as one of Bowes's heavies, and headed west again across the moors. 'It was a very windy, cold, dark night, when we left Roger Moor', Mary would remember, 'and travelled thro' part of the Yorkshire Highlands, scattered with occasional villages.' With sleet and snow beginning to fall, Mary's flimsy clothing and thin slippers rapidly became sodden, so that she felt so 'overpowered with the various fatigues, cruelties, want of sleep and the very wet condition I was in' that several times she almost fell from Chapman's horse. Breaking the ice on frozen rivers and trudging through deep snow drifts, the bedraggled party arrived in the early hours at the ramshackle cottage of Matthew Shields, a gamekeeper, in the hamlet of Arngill at the eastern foot of the North Pennine hills. That night Mary slept in a draughty loft with Mary Gowland while a fierce storm raged outside.

The following day, as James Farrer stormed Streatlam Castle, Mary was sitting on a wooden bench in Shields's hovel only fourteen miles away. Warmed by a feeble peat fire and sustained only by hot milk and water with a little bread, she met another of her husband's mistresses, Isabella Dixon, who was nursing the latest of his illegitimate children. Marooned in the cottage for a second night by the drifting snow, on 17 November Mary was encouraged when Henry Bourn arrived to inform Bowes that Captain Farrer and Thomas Colpitts junior, her agent's son, were now scouring the countryside for her. Fearful of being discovered, Bowes insisted that they set out again soon after dark.

With Mary mounted behind Chapman once more, the party was guided by Shields over the North Pennine hills. Known even now as 'England's last wilderness', the North Pennines form the highest points in the range which divides England down the centre, from Derbyshire in the south to the Scottish border in the north. As they rose forbiddingly before her now, capped with snow, Mary may well have echoed the judgement of the author Daniel Defoe that: 'This, perhaps, is the most desolate, wild, and abandoned Country in all *England*.'

Keeping to lonely country roads and treacherous moorland paths, the horses stumbled over the fells as sleet blinded their way. When they stopped briefly at a turnpike cottage near Brough, Shields told the tollkeepers that Mary was being taken to visit her daughter who was in labour. Arriving in the early hours at Appleby, a little medieval town on the road to Carlisle, Bowes installed Mary in one inn and sent his hoodlums to another in order to avoid suspicion. Again he tried to force her to have sex with him; again she swore she would prosecute him for rape if he persevered.

Anxious that Captain Farrer and young Colpitts might overtake them, Bowes forced the party to leave hurriedly the following morning, 18 November, so that in the rush Mary left behind her stockings. Bundling Mary into a chaise which Bowes had hired to reach Carlisle, they were stopped after only three miles by a man on horseback who warned them that they were being followed. Mary sank to her knees in gratitude that she was about to be rescued, but Bowes dragged her into the road, sent the carriage on towards Carlisle as a decoy and took off across the fields with the pregnant Mary Gowland riding pillion on his horse, Mary Eleanor mounted behind Chapman. When the determined Captain Farrer and his fellow pursuer hurtled past in their chaise in pursuit of the empty carriage only minutes later, Mary was being hidden in a cowshed a few hundred yards away.

Doubling back, Bowes now trekked east towards the steeply rising western escarpment of the Pennines, stopping only to find guides at remote cottages along the route. Never short of a ready fiction, Bowes told the country folk he encountered that he was a doctor and Mary a demented patient. Clinging to Chapman as their horse stumbled along the narrow passes, her bare legs numb from the cold, Mary gazed with awe on the 'stupendous rocks and mountains deeply covered with snow' and 'tremendous precipices' as they negotiated a route over the 2,454-foot peak of Burton Fell. So bleak was the terrain that even one of their guides lost his way. Weak from fatigue and cold, Mary fell from her horse when it plunged into a snowdrift but was promptly reseated by Bowes's henchmen. As they crossed a plain so immense and white that it 'perfectly resembled the wide Ocean', Mary recognised some rare alpine plants peeping out from the snow. Pointing them out to Bowes she shouted, 'that as I now saw them against my inclination, I would when released from him come there some future summer for my own pleasure and to indulge my Botanical passion'.

As the day darkened, Mary found that they had returned to Matthew Shields's house at Arngill where Isabella Dixon confessed herself astounded that they had survived the mountain crossing in such foul conditions. Yet before she had time even to dry her wet clothes by the fire, Mary was forced outside again, this time mounted behind Bowes, to press on towards Darlington. Creeping along the back roads through the night, the bedraggled group passed within three miles of Streatlam Castle where Bowes even had the gall to send one of his gang to glean news of the rescue efforts. The resulting information did not bring him comfort.

Having passed within yards of Mary's hideaway in the cowshed near Appleby, Captain Farrer and Colpitts junior had continued to Penrith, just as Bowes had hoped, but finding no trace of their quarry retraced their route with growing anguish.[32] Gathering jumbled reports of the fugitives as they went, they called at Arngill – missing Mary's second visit by hours – but were met with contemptuous silence from its inhabitants. In bewilderment they returned west as far as Carlisle, but discovering no sign of Bowes, doubled back again, their efforts now focused on County Durham. With armed officers arriving from London, every village watchman and country constable on the alert and sightings of the conspicuous group circulating widely, it seemed only a matter of time before Bowes would be cornered. 'Various & many are the reports of the Fugitives,' reported one correspondent following developments, '& a whole Country upon the Watch.'[33]

At last rising to the seriousness of the situation, Mary's aunt, Margaret Liddell, sent instructions to every coaching inn in the region to refuse fresh horses to Bowes's men. Conveying news to Colpitts, she lamented, 'This most melancholy afair has effected my nerves so much, that really I can hardly hold my Pen.'[34] At the same time James Farrer issued posters offering a £50 reward for any information leading to the arrest of Bowes and the rescue of Mary.[35] Pasted on tavern walls and turnpike gates throughout the north, the posters gave descriptions of Bowes, his accomplices and Mary herself in less than flattering terms. Bowes, one poster asserted, was 'above the middle size, sallow complexion, large Nose which stands rather one side, and lisps in his speech', while Mary was described as 'a little woman, a longish Face, with fine dark brown Hair, rather Bulky over the Chest'.

While Mary's lawyer was sparing no efforts to effect her release, Bowes's own lawyer was proving equally industrious on his client's behalf. An attorney in Darlington renowned for his sharp practices, Thomas Bowes – no relation to his defendant or to Mary – had acquired the soubriquet 'Hungry Bowes'.[36] It was Thomas Bowes who had masqueraded as his client when Ridgeway arrived at Streatlam Castle, and it was in the lawyer's own house that Mary was next imprisoned. Having arrived in the early hours of 19 November, she had been locked in a windowless room, or passage, without a candle before being allowed to sleep in a bedroom. That afternoon, however, the party was on the move again.

Plainly panicking as his pursuers closed in, Bowes and his crew took Mary in a hired chaise through Durham to Newcastle from whence he hoped to negotiate an alternative route to Carlisle. That night was spent at a coaching inn at Harlow Hill, just west of the city, where Mary was confined with Mary Gowland in the stableyard as wind and rain came in through the cracks in the chaise windows. But the perilous weather conditions, which had earlier proved almost fatal, now worked to her advantage when the postillions refused to continue on next morning so that Bowes had no alternative but to head back for Newcastle. Refused fresh horses at several coaching inns in the city, Bowes eventually found an amenable innkeeper. In a fury at the ingratitude of his former constituents and, for once in his life, seemingly devoid of any clear plan, Bowes now headed back south towards Darlington.

Nearing the town, Bowes realised that he was being followed – by one of Margaret Liddell's servants – so he promptly commandeered a horse from a fellow traveller on the road and, waving his pistol wildly in the air, chased the man for nearly two miles. Continuing in the chaise, a few miles further on they were met by Bourn who warned Bowes that a crowd had gathered in Darlington ready to seize him. Growing dangerously irrational in his panic, Bowes sent the chaise on to Darlington with Mary Gowland inside, seized Bourn's horse, and with Mary mounted bareback behind him and only his French valet, Mark Prevot, for protection galloped away across the open fields. It was mid-afternoon on Monday, 20 November, when Bowes arrived in the little village of Neasham, a few miles south of Darlington, beside the River Tees. Having travelled at least 180 miles in eight days, by coach, on horseback and on foot, with barely any nourishment in freezing conditions, Mary was now near exhaustion. Demented with fear and confusion, her captor was scarcely in any better condition.

*

Seated on his farm horse in his grubby workclothes, Gabriel Thornton, a ploughman who worked for Thomas Colpitts's son-in-law, bore little resemblance to a knight on a white charger. Yet from the moment he spotted the suspicious-looking couple riding through Neasham, he acted with chivalric courage and determination.[37] Although the woman riding pillion was unkempt, mired in dirt and dressed in a man's greatcoat with no stockings and only one slipper, he had no doubt that he had discovered the Countess of Strathmore. Well aware of the nationwide hunt to rescue the countess he initially followed at some distance. But knowing that Bowes was reported to be heavily armed and observing that the man who rode with him carried an unsheathed sword, he thought it prudent to summon assistance from the parish constable, one Christopher Smith. Together Thornton and Smith advanced towards their target and as they closed the gap, they were gradually joined by a growing number of farmhands and villagers. At last, as Bowes turned into a field, the little group of about a dozen men had him surrounded. Surprised at the ambush, Bowes immediately flourished one of his pistols and threatened to shoot out the brains of any man who tried to seize him. Although they were unarmed apart from a few sticks and farm implements, the villagers stood their ground. As Thornton stepped forward to challenge Bowes, an elderly man grabbed the bridle of his horse and Mary saw her chance. She slid to the ground and begged the gathered crowd for assistance. Staggering towards Thornton, she was grabbed by Prevot with his sword drawn but with her last ounce of strength she pinched his arm so severely that he dropped the weapon. Wrenching herself free, she was lifted by one of the farmhands on to Thornton's horse. In the confusion, Constable Smith seized Bowes's pistols and with the butt end of one of them gave Bowes a blow to the head that knocked him off his horse. Seeing her captor sprawled on the ground, disarmed and almost senseless, Mary now exclaimed with a flourish, 'Farewell, learn to amend your life', and with her gallant ploughman bearing her away she headed straight for London.

Safely back, at Farrer and Lacey's house in Bread Street Hill by the following evening, Mary was in little condition to celebrate. While Lacey scrawled a hurried letter informing Colpitts that Mary was 'just arrived safe at our House', Mary Morgan rejoiced 'at the blessed Restoration of my Dear & suffering Lady'.[38] Covered in bruises, severely affected by exposure and unable to walk, Mary Eleanor had to be carried into the court of King's Bench on 23 November to swear articles of peace against Bowes. A crowd gathered to watch her being lifted from her carriage and carried into the courtroom, limp, pained and exhausted. Spectators and reporters alike were then stunned to hear both the details of her suffering and her fortitude in surviving them. 'Lady Strathmore, from the extreme ill-treatment she has received since forced from this metropolis, is become an object of the most extreme pity, and compassion to every beholder,' pronounced the *English Chronicle* while the *Public Advertiser* reported that she had 'experienced the greatest hardships and distress, too tedious, and almost too dreadful to relate'.[39] Determined, nonetheless, to regale their readers with the details, newspapers from London to Madras devoted copious columns to the story while Grub Street publishers rushed into print with illustrated pamphlets and jaunty poems describing Mary's villainous abduction by her scoundrel husband and heroic rescue by a hardy band of country folk. In the meantime, Bowes had evaded his pursuers and taken refuge once more in his lawyer's house in Darlington where he was finally apprehended by the dogged Thomas Ridgeway. Now held firmly in the custody of the tipstaff, Bowes was conducted to London to face judgement. Naturally he still had a few tricks up his sleeve.

12
The Taming of Bad Wives

Westminster Hall, London, 28 November 1786

Dishevelled and pale, with a scarlet handkerchief bandaging the head wounds he had supposedly received at his capture, Andrew Robinson Bowes staggered into Westminster Hall just after 1 p.m. Limping through the cavernous medieval building, where William Wallace, Guy Fawkes and Charles I had once stood to hear their death sentences pronounced, Bowes was supported under each arm by the two tipstaffs who had finally put an end to his flight. The clamour in the noisy hall rose even louder as journalists, law students and spectators jostled for a view. 'Mr Bowes was dressed in a drab-coloured great coat, a red silk handkerchief about his head,' the reporter from *The Times* noted, while the correspondent for the *Gentleman's Magazine* observed that, 'he frequently appeared on the point of fainting, and his appearance on the whole was the most squalid and emaciated that could possibly be imagined.'[1] Depicted by James Gillray as stooping and dejected amid a sea of gawping faces in the caricaturist's last – and most truthful – contribution to the Bowes divorce saga, he cut a pitiful figure.

But if Bowes hoped to win public sympathy by his usual play-acting, this time he was gravely mistaken. Finally wise to his tricks and disguises, the crowds squashed into the courtroom hissed and jeered as he stumbled towards the bench and the newspaper writers cynically dismissed his sickly pallor. 'Mr Bowes had dressed his person to draw pity from the multitude,' the *Morning Chronicle* wryly informed its readers and added: 'It is said by some of the persons who attended Mr Bowes into town, that he did not appear to be much in pain from the ill-treatment complained of in his affidavit, till he came into town, and then he began to rehearse his part.' Indeed, as Jessé Foot would later reveal, Bowes had manufactured his deathly countenance by taking an emetic. Having vomited twice as he was conveyed to Westminster Hall, he had persuaded the ever-willing surgeon to plead that he was unfit to attend. Only the dissent of a second, less corruptible, doctor had prevented Bowes from evading his appointment with justice.

Held firm by the two tipstaffs, Bowes was brought before the notorious Judge Francis Buller. Presiding over the King's Bench in place of the ailing Lord Mansfield, Justice Buller had made himself as unpopular with the lawyers who argued their cases under his withering gaze as with the cowering defendants who stood before him. Having scaled the legal ladder with unprecedented agility, Buller was the youngest judge ever to be appointed to the King's Bench at the tender age of thirty-two.[2] Arrogant and brash in his manner, stubborn and impetuous in his judgements, at fifty he was now tipped to succeed the mentor he idolised yet made seemingly little attempt to emulate. Where Mansfield had been acclaimed for his liberal stance, Buller had become a laughing stock by suggesting that a husband could lawfully beat his wife as long as he used a stick no thicker than his thumb. Yet even 'Judge Thumb' was scandalised at the depraved extremes of Bowes's conduct which now unfolded before the court.

In an era of public hangings, child labour and routine domestic violence, there was little that shocked Georgian sensibilities. But the extent of Bowes's sadistic ill-treatment of his own wife, described in the articles of peace read by Mary's lawyers, appalled reporters and spectators alike. Recording the beatings, floggings, murder threats, attempted murder, attempted rapes and unspeakable deprivations Mary had suffered during her abduction and confinement, the charges were described by *The Times* as containing 'a detail of barbarity that shocks humanity and outrages civilisation', while the *Morning Chronicle* referred to 'a scene of the utmost inhumanity and brutality'.

As Bowes swooned from his pretended injuries, his lawyers made a pathetic effort to present him as a wronged man who had only abducted Mary to rescue her from her manipulative servants. Having left Streatlam Castle before the *habeas corpus* had been served, Bowes had been oblivious to the nationwide quest to rescue her until several days later, they claimed, at which point he had dutifully headed south to deliver her in person. It was while endeavouring to return her to London, his lawyers insisted, that Bowes had been apprehended by a rough band of labourers who had mercilessly bludgeoned him over the head. Producing a sworn statement from a surgeon in Darlington who asserted that Bowes had sustained a serious head wound, his lawyers feared that even now his injuries might prove fatal.

Bowes's version of events received short shrift from the formidable Buller. Briskly dismissing the concoction of excuses over the *habeas corpus*, the judge remanded Bowes in custody until a full hearing, with bail set at the colossal sum of £20,000, possibly the largest bail figure to date in such a case.[3] When Bowes's counsel pleaded that a spell in jail might endanger his life, the judge promptly retorted that there were apartments in prison 'sufficiently commodious' for Bowes to receive medical treatment, at which point the marshal of the prison confirmed – to uproarious laughter – that he 'could accommodate him very properly'.

As Bowes was conveyed out of court by the tipstaffs, a vast mob surged forwards, hissing, howling and shouting abuse, while the tipstaffs forced a path to the waiting hackney carriage.[4] Bundled inside the waiting coach, Bowes was driven the short distance to the King's Bench prison in Southwark where he arrived at 3 p.m. At last the captor was captive. The man who had variously imprisoned his wife, his sister, his stepdaughter, his mistress and her child, was himself finally under lock and key. And as *The Times* drily remarked: 'It is an uncomfortable reverse of situation, to be forced from the elegant apartments of a noble house in Grosvenor-square, to a room twelve feet by eight in a prison.'

For satirists and cartoonists ever on the lookout for a fresh victim to lampoon, Bowes's dramatic plunge from preening country gentleman to lowly prison inmate was a gift. Seizing the opportunity to rake over Bowes's chequered past while milking popular prejudice against the Irish, one anonymous writer turned the drama into a short play, entitled 'The Irishman in Limbo, or, Stony Batter's Lamentation for the loss of his Liberty'.[5] In an imagined dialogue between Bowes and an Irish jailor, Bowes declares: 'One wife I ingeniously tormented out of her life, and the other I would have done the same by, but she, with her sage advisers, has proved too many for me, and prevented my scheme from taking.' Another attack, under the title 'Who Cries Andrew now?' recalled Bowes's horse-racing and political heyday in nine jaunty verses, including the lines: 'No more at ELECTIONS his Name we repeat,/Like his Galloper jaded, he's down at each heat;/Tho' this bold Irish Hero, this Bruiser of Wives,/the Gallows Escapes, like a Cat with Nine Lives.' A third, called 'Paddy's Progress', described Bowes's dazzling ascent from army ensign to popular MP and his equally spectacular descent in a rollicking ballad spanning twenty-four pages. Its final verse concluded: 'Doom'd to a room, twelve feet by eight!/Who could but say – they serv'd him right?/Thus he who cry'd up Freedom's laws,/His freedom lost in Freedom's cause!'

In reality, however, Bowes's new life in captivity brought little hardship. Far from being incarcerated in a tiny cell, Bowes ranged around a comfortable house adjacent to the prison which he rented from the obliging marshal. Here he lived in comparative luxury with four-year-old William, the pregnant Mary Gowland and several of his stooges, dining on the Bowes silver plate and entertaining friends. Attended daily for his feigned injuries by Foot, Bowes feverishly attempted to raise the bail necessary to secure his release while masterminding his legal defence. With the abduction case, divorce suit and deeds challenge simultaneously lumbering to their conclusions through the tortuous Georgian legal system he had plenty to keep him busy.

In the meantime, it was Mary who was confined to a single room, forced to remain upstairs in Farrer and Lacey's house in Bread Street Hill through the ill effects of her ordeal. According to the apothecary who examined her after her rescue, Mary had sustained a 'great pain' in her right shoulder from her fall from the horse during her trans-Pennine trek, as well as bruises to her neck, chest and feet, and a severe cough.[6] 'From the severity of the weather and the ill-treatment she had suffered,' he reported, 'I thought her life in great danger.' It would be a full month before she could stand up and six weeks before she could walk across the room with the aid of a stick. On Christmas Day she was carried downstairs for the first time to enjoy Christmas dinner with friends.[7] While her physical symptoms slowly improved, her emotional state took longer to recover. Relating to Colpitts the after-effects of the ordeal – in a far-sighted description of post-traumatic stress disorder – Mary explained: 'I know by experience, that . . . one begins to feel the Effects of Terror, etc, in a manner that the false spirits & activity necessary whilst our exertions were required prevented our being sensible of 'till the storm has subsided.' Those symptoms might well continue, she speculated, confessing to Colpitts that, 'I shall not be very willing, I think, ever to go out of Doors again, as I have experienced that there is no personal security in this Kingdom even at noon.' Since Bowes's hoodlums remained at large she had every reason to fear for her safety.

Yet if Mary endured lasting anxiety in her liberty, she could at least rejoice in the strength of support she now received from friends and family. Mary Morgan remained her closest friend and staunchest ally, while Colpitts and her other supporters in the north would continue to prove their worth. Putting on record her gratitude to the miners, tenants and farmworkers who had collaborated in her rescue, Mary placed an emotional notice in the Newcastle and Durham newspapers at the end of December. 'Lady Strathmore returns her most sincere & hearty thanks to her friends in Yorkshire, Durham, Northumberland, Westmoreland, Cumberland, & many other counties, for their humane & spirited exertions towards the Restoration of her Liberty, & the Preservation of her Life.'[8] Back from the north after playing his own part in the rescue mission, the assiduous Captain Farrer resumed his romantic attentions while well-wishers deluged the house to congratulate Mary on her release.

At the same time, Mary painstakingly began to rebuild relations with her scattered young family. George and Thomas, her Eton boys, were the first to arrive at her bedside in early December. A few days later Mary was overjoyed when her two eldest children, Maria and John, came to visit. It had been six long years since she had last seen her eldest son, the young Lord Strathmore. She had left a nervous boy of eleven in thrall to his tutors and guardians; now she met a tall, handsome and self-confident young man who had just enrolled as a cornet, the cavalry's equivalent of an ensign, in the Royal Horse Guards.[9] Although she would never fully be reconciled with Maria, at one time her favourite child, Mary belatedly forged a strong and loving bond with the son for whom she had once confessed an 'unnatural dislike'. As she followed his military career with maternal pride, pasting newspaper cuttings on his activities into a scrapbook, so he endeavoured to reunite the dispersed family and revive its disparate fortunes.

This was no simple task. Although their father languished in prison, accused of kidnapping, attempted murder and attempted rape, Mary's two youngest children remained firmly and legally under his control; young William even shared his father's captivity while nine-year-old Mary was being held in a secret location on his orders. And there was no record of a visit to her mother from Anna, now sixteen, who continued to behave as precociously as ever despite the hawk-like scrutiny of her governess, the sanctimonious Mrs Parish, who had recently confiscated a book she deemed 'not fit for the reading of a young Person'.[10] In future, Anna would take care to keep her pleasures better hidden. And although Thomas Lyon had mellowed sufficiently to allow Mary at least some access to her children, he remained largely immune to her plight. As Mary commented archly to Colpitts, 'I must say, that Mr Lyon has not departed from his usual Supineness & Indifference in <u>any</u> particular.'[11]

Bolstered by the kindness of friends and family, Mary

Eleanor moved into a rented house in Holles Street, just off Oxford Street, with Morgan and a few trusted servants in January 1787. A small terraced house, with just one spare room, it was a far cry from the opulence of her former homes, which now lay abandoned and neglected, yet it was 'very neatly furnished' and she could now manage the stairs without a stick. With her strength steadily returning, her determination to sever all links with Bowes remained undiminished. 'I am resolved at all events', she told Colpitts, 'to trust alone to a legal & Public Decision, & that I would beg my bread or earn it by sweeping the Crossings of a street, sooner than enter into any amicable Terms with Mr Stoney & I feel that the Resolution wch. supported me in the Highlands wd not desert me upon the Occasion.' As the appeal against her divorce suit approached, she would need every ounce of her willpower.

Bowes had filed his formal response to Mary's divorce victory to the Court of Arches, the ecclesiastical appeal court for the province of Canterbury, on 30 November, just two days after his enfeebled appearance in Westminster Hall. But there was nothing feeble about its contents. He had already given a broad hint that he was preparing a robust case in a testimony signed on the day of his capture which referred to certain 'papers' with which Mary had presented him soon after their marriage 'containing such a scene of iniquity as this deponent believes is not to be paralleled in any history on life'.[12] Having purchased an interest in *The Times*, or *Daily Universal Register* as it was still known, that same month, Bowes made it plain he intended to fight his corner in the full glare of publicity.[13] Orchestrating his campaign from his roomy prison quarters, he fed titillating clues about the revelations his forthcoming appeal would furnish to an eager press.

World promised its readers that
s against Mary were 'perhaps, the
cedented ever exhibited before
fterwards *The Times* tamely
dice had 'never run with
l' than it had against
at 'the stream will
colour, on
hich that
e

es's fam
sserted tha
ravagant, lus
osition' who ha
ntempt and disobedi
lecency' which had forced
behaviour and 'by argument
pt to 'give her a proper sense
Yet despite his heroic efforts
she had embarked on three

eged, had been her footman
she had 'very frequently' com-
ummer of 1777. Discovering this
, Bowes had instantly dismissed
e fact that Mary had been on the
is own contention, that summer
ally been dismissed at the end of
caped his memory. His only evi-
ffair was the testimony of another
the former Eliza Planta who had
nistress at the time. She claimed she
with Mary in her bedchamber. The
urse, was pure revenge for Walker's
ary's prenuptial deed. In a vehem
er relationship, Walker would

followed was a bizarre confectio
from the furthest reaches of Bow
which would have been comical w
to Mary and several of her friends.
filed by Bowes, the presiding judge S
four outright but the five that he allo
were more than sufficient to satis
gathered journalists. Peddling Bow
indulgent husband, his allegations a
more is a woman of the most ext
and abandoned temper, and disp
Bowes with 'the most insolent co
It was this 'impropriety and in
Bowes to lay 'restraints' upon her
and gentle remonstrances' attem
and abhorrence of those vices'.
to reform his wife's character,
successive affairs.

Her first lover, Bowes all
George Walker with whom
mitted adultery during the s
liaison at the end of the yea
the servant, he claimed. Th
point of giving birth, by h
and that Walker had actu
March, had seemingly es
dence for the supposed a
servant, Eliza Stephens,
probably been his own r
had found Walker alon
entire allegation, of co
role in safeguarding M
denial of any improp

In January, therefore, *The World* promised its readers that Bowes's expected allegations against Mary were 'perhaps, the most extraordinary and unprecedented ever exhibited before a Court of Judicature'.[14] Shortly afterwards *The Times* tamely observed that although popular prejudice had 'never run with greater rapidity against any individual' than it had against Bowes, there was now reason to believe that 'the stream will turn with the tide, and public opinion change its colour, on the full disclosure of every circumstance under which that Gentleman has acted'. And so when the appeal finally came up for its hearing, on 20 January 1787, the great hall at Doctors' Commons, where the Court of Arches also met, was packed with excitable journalists and shorthand writers. As the hacks listened, their quills poised, the court deliberations hinged on precisely how much of Bowes's explosive case could be aired in public.

His own reputation irreparably ruined, having been denounced as an adulterer, rapist and bully, Bowes had determined that his best line of defence lay in traducing Mary's name to an equal degree. If he could prove that Mary had committed vulgar and unnatural acts at least as shocking as the charges laid against him, then he was convinced her case would founder. And to achieve that end, he knew he possessed the ultimate secret weapon.

First he set the scene, lodging with the court a series of remarkable 'allegations' that accused Mary of brazen and repeated adultery with a succession of male acquaintances.[15] Deviously entwining fact with fiction, this document described her adulterous affair with George Gray, subsequent abortions and concealed pregnancy in salacious detail. That these events all predated her marriage to Bowes, and that Gray's death six years previously prevented any effective challenge, made little difference to their deleterious effect. What followed was a bizarre confection of outrageous claims culled from the furthest reaches of Bowes's degenerate imagination which would have been comical were they not so destructive to Mary and several of her friends. Of the nine allegations filed by Bowes, the presiding judge Sir Peter Calvert rejected four outright but the five that he allowed to be read in court were more than sufficient to satisfy the appetites of the gathered journalists. Peddling Bowes's familiar image as the indulgent husband, his allegations asserted that 'Lady Strathmore is a woman of the most extravagant, lustful, wicked, and abandoned temper, and disposition' who had treated Bowes with 'the most insolent contempt and disobedience'. It was this 'impropriety and indecency' which had forced Bowes to lay 'restraints' upon her behaviour and 'by argument and gentle remonstrances' attempt to 'give her a proper sense and abhorrence of those vices'. Yet despite his heroic efforts to reform his wife's character, she had embarked on three successive affairs.

Her first lover, Bowes alleged, had been her footman George Walker with whom she had 'very frequently' committed adultery during the summer of 1777. Discovering this liaison at the end of the year, Bowes had instantly dismissed the servant, he claimed. The fact that Mary had been on the point of giving birth, by his own contention, that summer and that Walker had actually been dismissed at the end of March, had seemingly escaped his memory. His only evidence for the supposed affair was the testimony of another servant, Eliza Stephens, the former Eliza Planta who had probably been his own mistress at the time. She claimed she had found Walker alone with Mary in her bedchamber. The entire allegation, of course, was pure revenge for Walker's role in safeguarding Mary's prenuptial deed. In a vehement denial of any improper relationship, Walker would reveal that Bowes had tried to bribe him to support his cause but declared, 'I despised his offers! as I despised the Man!'[16]

Mary's second lover, the fiction continued, was a house guest named Edward Llewellin who had apparently stayed with the family at St Paul's Walden Bury in August 1783. The pair had been discovered 'in the very act of carnal copulation' on a bench in the garden, Bowes claimed, although he had only learned this shocking revelation after Mary had left him. Scarcely bothering to substantiate this charge, Bowes produced no evidence and no witness. And, of course, there were none since in August 1783, when Bowes was conducting an affair with his son's wet-nurse Mrs Houghton, Mary was not permitted so much as to walk alone in the garden to view her flowers, let alone cavort there with a lover. In all probability, since nobody in Mary's acquaintance had any recollection of the name, Llewellin did not exist. But of all the allegations, the most ludicrous, and the most cruel, was the claim that Mary had enjoyed an intrigue with the Gibside gardener Robert Thompson.

According to the charges, Mary had conducted a tempestuous affair with her gardener during the spring of 1784 such that 'many great and indecent familiarities were seen to pass' between the pair and they were spotted by two witnesses 'in the very act of carnal copulation' in the greenhouse, the garden house and various parts of the garden. Describing this improbable coupling, Joseph Hill, an ostler to the pit ponies, attested that he and his fellow colliery worker, Charles Chapman, had spied on Thompson through a window of the garden house 'lying upon the body of the said Mary Eleanor Bowes'.

It would have been hard to find a more doting or devoted admirer of Mary than Robert Thompson. Since his appointment in 1782, he had loyally tended her rare botanical specimens, once risking Bowes's wrath by allowing her to pick a single bloom, and ultimately defying his orders by continuing to nurture her gardens after his dismissal. Equally, it would have been hard to imagine a less likely lover. Wretched with poverty and sickness, infested with lice and racked with rheumatism, Thompson could barely manage to tend the plants let alone engage in athletic couplings between chores. According to fellow servants, Thompson was so unwell in 1784 that he 'walked almost double' and was frequently seen to 'pick the Lice from off his Body and his Cloaths'.[17] Utterly in awe of Mary, and having sworn that he would 'dye on the spott' in his desperation to rescue her when abducted, Thompson's highest ambition was simply to serve her by cherishing her garden. Mortified by the accusation, Thompson would attest that he had never once been alone with Mary or even touched her garments except, he poignantly admitted, 'when her Ladyship might Hand me a pott of Flowers out of her hand which by Chance I might touch her Fingers but never otherwise'.

Transparently, Bowes's outrageous slander was punishment for Thompson's unbending loyalty. The conniving Hill had plainly been bribed to make his testimony while Chapman had only recently been captured for his part in Mary's abduction. Yet unbelievable as the claim was, the humiliation may well have been the last straw for the poor gardener. Thompson died less than two months after the allegations were broadcast and on his deathbed told a fellow ex-servant, James Smith, that the charge 'had almost broken his Heart'. So impoverished that he left not even enough money for a funeral, the last rites were paid for by Smith.

Notwithstanding this lurid catalogue of vice, Bowes still maintained his insistence that he wished to stay wedded to his errant spouse. Even more staggering, given the criminal trial hanging over him for abduction, he contended that since their separation – during the very ten days of the countrywide hunt to rescue Mary – they had 'lived and cohabited together', sharing bed and board, 'with mutual consent and forgiveness towards each other'.

Yet if Bowes's allegations seemed incredible, not to mention his undiminished zeal for the institution of matrimony, his lawyers now produced shocking evidence to support their case: Mary's own 'Confessions'. Extorted under threat of violence nine years earlier and jealously guarded by Bowes ever since, Mary's frank account of her youthful flirtations and adulterous affair with Gray, her several abortions and her secret pregnancy, was ample ammunition to condemn her by her own pen. And it was not only Mary Eleanor whom the revelations could harm, for by exposing the illegitimacy of little Mary in public, the document effectively tainted her reputation too. Previously lodged with the court, it was this extraordinary hundred-page testament that Bowes wished to be read verbatim and had primed the assembled hacks to expect. Unparalleled in their honesty, unprecedented in their first-hand description of attempted and successful abortions, the confessions could easily sway public opinion in Bowes's favour, as Mary and her followers were only too well aware.

Since the confessions were irrefutably in Mary's handwriting, there was no question but that they were genuine. Precisely how they had come to be written, however, was the question that exercised the court. Mary Eleanor had already dismissed the document as 'spurious, most false and scandalous', while Mary Morgan called it 'that vile paper extracted from her Ladyship by force & partly dictated by his [Bowes's] own malicious invention'.[18] Mary's steadfast attorney, James Farrer, had no less hesitation in disregarding the document.

In an impassioned defence, sent to his partner Thomas Lacey, Farrer argued: 'The narrative ascribed to be writ by Lady S. is certainly in her own Hand Writing, which was procured from her Ladyship by threats and menaces, and the fear of Death, at a time her Ladyship was regardless of any thing but quietude, and the wish to avoid that severity of treatment she almost daily experienced, or at least to have it mitigated in some measure, when she was worn down in her spirits, depressed in the extreme, and in a state of despondency from an ill state of Health and a succession of cruelty, which occasioned.'[19] Most of the paper had been dictated by Bowes, or at least instructions given as to what it must include, Farrer wrote. And its purpose, he said, was plain. It was a 'pocket pistol' kept by Bowes 'to destroy her Ladyship's fame, and to harden and steel the Hearts of every one against her Ladyship'.

For the moment, at least, that pistol had misfired. For no sooner had the clerk to the court solemnly read aloud a few pages than the presiding judge ordered him to halt. Decreeing that the document had been obtained under duress and was furthermore unrelated to the facts of the case, Calvert banned any further reporting of its contents. At that point, as the *Newcastle Journal* related: 'A little murmur ensued, and three or four short-hand writers, who had seated themselves to take the contents of this choice MS. put up their papers, and marched out of the hall.'[20]

Yet the bullet still managed to reach its mark. For even the limited details which had emerged and which were greedily repeated in the media were sufficiently scandalous to divide public opinion. 'A few pages of this extraordinary performance were read in Court,' the *Journal* reported, 'in which her Ladyship confesses she had been guilty of *five* mortal crimes.' Leaving its readers to speculate on the precise nature of her sins, the newspaper added: 'However foreign to the present contest between the Countess and Mr Bowes . . . that part of her narrative, which was recited on Saturday, appeared to be written with a peculiar degree of candour and correctness, and those who have perused it, in general agree, that it is by no means a partial *apology* for her conduct; but a sincere penitential confession of her transgressions.' Other newspapers spared their readers no blushes in relating the 'crimes' to which Mary had confessed. Inevitably these included *The Times* which proclaimed: 'The confession drawn up and signed by Lady Strathmore . . . was perhaps the most extraordinary that ever came before a court of justice.'[21] And even though Mary inserted a letter in several newspapers condemning the 'scandalous paragraphs which have, for a considerable time, daily appeared against me', the damage was done. The *Rover's Magazine*, which published Bowes's steamy allegations in full, along with a saucy cartoon depicting said countess and gardener *in flagrante* in the conservatory, sneeringly remarked that Mary had endeavoured to 'exculpate herself and to intimate that she is almost immaculate'.

Just as Farrer had predicted, airing the confessions succeeded in hardening the hearts of some of Mary's erstwhile sympathisers. Learning of the latest revelation in his estranged son's colourful life, George Stoney told a relation that, 'Lady S. is exerting every possible means to acquit herself of severe charges made against her' while adding, 'there certainly has been many faults on both sides'.[22] Growing increasingly pious in his advancing infirmity, he argued that divorce was 'a dangerous Precedent'. Yet when he died the following month, George Stoney's will divided his sizeable estate among his large family and bequeathed Bowes, his eldest son, a derisory one-ninth share of only £2.

*

Growing increasingly frustrated by his containment, as he awaited the decision of the Court of Arches, Bowes directed his energies to raising bail. Trying to tap his usually amenable source, he wrote an unctuous letter to the Duke of Norfolk in March. In a cringing attempt to justify his abduction of Mary, he explained: 'I adopted it, with all the Inconvenience it threatened to myself, merely to remove an Infatuated Woman from the Public Infamy which I knew she must finally suffer, if I did not snatch her from it.'[23] Although the scheme had been 'abhorrent' to him, he had been persuaded to carry it out by the 'ardent, persuasive zeal' of certain friends, he wheedled. Insisting that all Mary's allegations against him were completely false – 'sportive dalliance excepted' he added with an obvious wink to the philandering duke – Bowes implored him to guarantee the necessary sum for his bail. For although he was impatient to prove his innocence at the forthcoming trial, his presence in the north was 'most essentially necessary in matters of the utmost Importance to my concerns'. Evidently not persuaded by Bowes's raving protestations of innocence – nor probably by his assurances of a timely return – the duke declined to stump up the cash.

Yet Bowes could still muster wealthy friends with even fewer scruples than the debauched duke. By the end of March he had procured two financiers who were willing to pledge the funds needed to secure his release and, just as he had so ominously declared, he immediately sped north. News that Bowes was once more at liberty came as a severe blow to Mary, already demoralised by her degrading treatment at the hands of the press. 'The present agitated state of my Mind upon hearing that Mr Stoney has procured Bail, renders me scarce capable of writing coherently,' she told Colpitts, while

Morgan gravely warned him that, 'you may expect him as soon as horses can bring him to the North'.[24]

Sure enough, within days Bowes and his cronies had unleashed a new wave of intimidation among Mary's allies in the north-east, offering bribes to persuade vital witnesses to change their evidence and, if these failed, indicting them for perjury. Thomas Ridgeway, the redoubtable tipstaff, and Gabriel Thornton, the valiant ploughman, were among those Bowes charged with perjury; both held firm. Susannah Church, Mary's former maid, was less resilient; she swore a testimony that Mary lived in fear of Mary Morgan who had organised Mary's escape for her own pecuniary ends.[25] Bowes even pressed perjury charges against Mary Eleanor herself. She only narrowly escaped being arrested to face this allegation by the quick-thinking of James Farrer who hared into court just in time to secure her bail. While the perjury charge further undermined Mary's credibility in the eyes of the general public, in reality Bowes's case hinged on the most laughably trivial errors in her testimony. She had accused him of locking her in a 'dark room' when Bowes claimed it was a 'passage', and of keeping her in a 'pig sty' which Bowes insisted was a 'stable yard'. Ultimately, he would quietly drop the charge.

Swaggering around the north-east flanked by his gang, Bowes convened a bizarre series of hearings – a kind of show trial – which opened on 13 April at the Wheatsheaf Inn in Durham. Over the next ten days he paraded his usual accomplices to swear testimonies invoking his virtues – and Mary's vices – as evidence both for the divorce case and the abduction trial. Yet the image he strived to create of a loving and faithful husband was somewhat undermined by the fact that his mistress, Mary Gowland, went into labour in the middle of the sessions.[26]

When Bowes's legal team won a reduction of his bail term from fourteen years to two in early May it seemed as if the tide had turned his way. Certainly *The Times* thought so, unable to resist the comment that 'it appears, that, in spite of public prejudice, the cause of her Ladyship is not so immaculate, as the world at large have been taught to believe'.[27] Even when the Court of Arches found in Mary's favour on 7 May, confirming her divorce and alimony payments, he was undaunted. Determined never to release Mary from her marital shackles if he could possibly avoid it, nor pay her a penny, he immediately launched a further appeal, this time to the High Court of Delegates, the ultimate place of appeal from the ecclesiastical judicial system, on the spurious ground that he had not been allowed time to produce all his witnesses.[28] As he headed back to London to face his trial for abduction with bullish self-confidence, Bowes inserted a notice in *The Times* announcing that a 'certain society of married Gentlemen' planned to celebrate his expected victory by erecting a memorial to Bowes 'in honour of his meritorious services to the enemies of *petticoat government*, and the friends of matrimonial subordination'.[29] Referring to the social reformer John Howard, who had just begun his final tour of the foul conditions endured by the majority of England's prison population, if not Bowes himself, the article added: 'It is thought that this subscription will be much larger than that which was made to give a statue to Mr Howard; as the taming of bad wives is a matter of infinitely greater importance to society than a casual improvement in the police [government] of a prison.' So, by the time Bowes appeared before Judge Buller and a special jury at the King's Bench on 30 May 1787, he cut a far more jaunty figure than the reviled character of six months earlier.

Charged with five counts of conspiracy that essentially accused him of seizing, assaulting and imprisoning Mary in order to compel her to drop her divorce suit, Bowes appeared with eight of his partners in crime.[30] These were the corrupt constable Edward Lucas, the hackney coach driver John Bickley, the pitworkers Charles Chapman and William Pigg, the coal merchant Francis Peacock, Bowes's valet Mark Prevot, his steward Henry Bourn and his attorney Thomas Bowes. Doubtless feeling secure in the knowledge that numerous husbands had previously stood on that very same spot and successfully defended their ancient right to chastise and confine their wayward wives, Bowes listened impassively as the charges were read. And since he had engaged probably the best criminal defence barrister of the Georgian era, Bowes had every reason to feel confident.

At 37, Thomas Erskine was a rapidly rising star in the legal profession whose services were heavily in demand among those unfortunate or uncouth enough to find themselves before the King's Bench.[31] The youngest son of a straitened Scottish earl, Erskine had joined the navy and then the army before trying his hand at the law, at which point he had enrolled as a pupil with Francis Buller. Having finally found his metier, he immediately proved himself an audacious advocate and sparkling orator by winning a string of acclaimed legal victories. A lifelong radical and fervent advocate of free speech, Erskine was briefly elected an MP during the Fox–North coalition in 1783–4; in future years he would defend Thomas Paine, unsuccessfully, in the state trial over publication of *The Rights of Man* and secure the acquittal of the radicals Thomas Hardy, John Horne Tooke and John Thelwall in their dramatic trial for high treason in 1794. Ultimately, in 1806, he would become Lord Chancellor. Defending political agitators from charges of treason notwithstanding, his brief to defend Bowes would prove one of the toughest challenges of his career.

Faced with the bar's most popular and esteemed advocate, Mary's barrister James Mingay had every excuse to feel apprehensive as he rose to open the case for the prosecution. The son of a country surgeon from Norfolk, raised in 'the most humble obscurity' as one contemporary would term it, Mingay had lost his right hand in an accident in his youth and subsequently sported an iron hook. Stymied from following his father's profession, the young Mingay was given financial help by the Duke of Grafton to enter Cambridge and subsequently join the bar. Rising rapidly, Mingay had soon found himself pitched against Erskine in the King's Bench where their fiery sparring matches provided entertainment for law students comparing their oratory styles. Concise, bold and forceful where his adversary was polished, flowery and verbose, 35-year-old Mingay was widely regarded as 'the *second* person in professional estimation' to Erskine himself. Strident rivals in court, the two had become firm friends at leisure.

In a court packed with students, journalists and spectators, as eager to hear the expected duel of words between the two advocates as to witness the long-awaited battle between Mary and Bowes, Mingay began by addressing the jury. Adopting the grave tone which the alleged crimes certainly merited, he solemnly warned the jurors that it 'will be necessary for me to state to you a transaction that I hope never, or any thing like it, existed before in a Christian country'. And as he proceeded to outline the details of Mary's kidnap and subsequent ordeal with the clarity and verve for which he was renowned, he did not disappoint them.

With studied restraint, Mingay described how Mary had fled her marital home and instituted divorce proceedings after 'eight long and miserable years' following 'treatment that I should have thought no man could possibly have adopted against any woman, and that no woman, thank God, is bound to bear in this country from any man'. Fully cognisant that Bowes was likely to argue his right reasonably to chastise and confine his wife, Mingay concentrated on demonstrating that Bowes's conduct had been neither reasonable nor justifiable. Having seized Mary from a public street in the middle of the day, Bowes had dragged her 'near three hundred miles, through the heart of this kingdom' and attempted to force her to drop her divorce 'by means as savage as they were uncommon and unheard of'. Met at Streatlam Castle by her husband's pregnant mistress, who had since 'been brought to bed of a bastard child by the husband', Mary had been ordered to sign a paper revoking her divorce suit with a pistol at her head. Yet still she had refused to drop her case and even ordered Bowes to fire with, Mingay proclaimed, 'a courage that to me is astonishing!' Subsequently bundled up the stairs by Chapman and Pigg – 'people that were accustomed to deeds of darkness by living in a mine' – Mary had resisted Bowes's attempts to rape her. At this point Mingay felt compelled to advise the jurors, no doubt to their incredulity, that there were indeed cases where 'a husband is liable to be tried for a rape even on his own wife' – although in this respect his legal history was optimistic at best, since rape within marriage would not finally be recognised as a crime until 1991.

Detailing Mary's torment over the next eight days as she was compelled to trek over mountains covered in snow, Mingay told the jury 'she was very near dead, she was very near frozen'. Yet far from hanging his head in shame at the treatment he had meted out to his own wife, Bowes had since had the audacity to accuse her of perjury by disputing whether she had been kept captive in a dark room or a dark passage. Rising now to a crescendo, Mingay asked the jury: 'I will, for a moment, suppose her the most abandoned prostitute that the earth ever produced, but for a man to treat a woman thus, what must be every honest man's sensations?' Leaving unsaid the obvious fact that the victim of this crime was not a resident of a brothel, but rather the only daughter of an ancient landed family, Mingay left the jurors in no doubt as to what he considered should be the response of an 'honest man' with his simple question: 'Gentlemen, I ask whether she is not the most persecuted woman that ever was?' Finally inviting the jury to identify with the simple but courageous country folk who had rescued Mary from such abominable maltreatment, Mingay concluded with a virtuoso flourish, declaring that, 'a straw in the hands of an honest countryman is equal to all the fire arms in the hands of Bowes'.

Having brilliantly set the scene of Bowes's outrage, Mingay produced a succession of turnpike keepers, tavern landlords and servants who testified to Mary's suffering at every stage of her journey north and subsequent cross-country expedition. They included the innkeeper of the Red Lion at Barnet who thought that Mary looked such a 'subject of pity' on her return homewards that she reminded him of 'a woman that was sifting cinders in Gray's Inn Lane'. None of them could have been more stolid in their support than Mary Morgan who said when she was reunited with Mary Eleanor: 'I can scarcely describe her condition, she was so altered, so full of mud, and dressed in an old bed gown.' Producing in court those very clothes – a red petticoat, bed gown and old bonnet – Morgan described the bruises Mary had revealed on her breast and at her temples. Asked whether her mistress had full command of her reason, in anticipation of Bowes's defence, Morgan retorted adamantly: 'I do not know any

Lady that has so much possession of her mind.'

Given the enormity of the allegations so fluently described by his old adversary, even the renowned Thomas Erskine faced an uphill struggle to defend his client's actions. Just four years earlier in a libel case, Erskine had famously upstaged Judge Buller, his former teacher, when he had refused to concede that Buller could overrule the jury. Now, it appeared, positions were reversed as the renegade pupil rose before his erstwhile master to plead a virtually impossible case. Indeed, it almost seemed that Erskine had concluded that the allegations were indefensible when he began by admitting that, 'a man must be lost, not only to all Christians, but, I should apprehend, to all human feelings, who does not feel infinitely hurt by everything that has been stated this day.'

Having effectively confirmed his client's guilt – and quite possibly betraying his true feelings – Erskine made no attempt to deny the acts alleged beyond suggesting that many statements were 'fabrications of Lady Strathmore'. Neither did he endeavour to argue the usual abusive husband's justification, despite the fact that it would remain a stock defence for a further century, when he gamely asserted that a 'wife has a right to the protection of the law to keep herself from violence even against her husband' and that although the husband enjoyed the right to the 'possession of her body' this did not permit him to seize or detain her by force. In an uncharacteristically lacklustre oration, Erskine merely claimed that Bowes's actions stemmed from 'just and pure motives' in his determination to remove Mary from the hands of people 'conspiring to ruin her with fortune-tellers, to widen the breach with her husband'. Instead, with Bowes seemingly a lost cause, Erskine concentrated his legal aplomb on attempting to exculpate his fellow accused by insisting that they were innocent of conspiracy since they had had no knowledge of Bowes's aims. Channelling his energies in particular into absolving his colleague, Thomas 'Hungry' Bowes, Erskine called as a character witness the former attorney general 'Honest' Jack Lee who earnestly swore that: 'I never did know a man of his profession, bear a fairer or more honourable character in my life.' As Erskine sat down after one of the least inspiring speeches of his career there was little doubt that Bowes's fate had been sealed.

Summing up the case for the jury, Judge Buller made no effort to disguise his disgust for the nine defendants or their misdemeanours. Taking particular exception to their exploitation of fundamental planks of the law for their criminal ends, by trumping up a charge against Mary's servants, pretending to carry her to Lord Mansfield and even abusing the role of a constable, Buller had no hesitation in declaring that all nine had 'knowingly engaged in criminal acts'. After seven hours of testimony, it took the all-male jury just minutes to decide that Bowes and his entire gang were guilty of every charge.

With sentencing deferred to a future date Bowes and his confederates remained on bail and at liberty. Inevitably, the entire pack absconded so that two weeks later writs had to be issued to bring them back for sentencing. When Bowes was seized, on 16 June, he claimed, of course, that he was on his way to court. All charges having been dropped against Thomas Bowes – there being as much honour among lawyers as thieves – and with Chapman, Pigg and Bickley still on the run, only Bowes and four of his accomplices now appeared at the King's Bench on 26 June 1787 for judgement before Buller, Sir William Ashhurst and Sir Nash Grose.[32]

Although nearly two hundred crimes, from stealing a

handkerchief to cold-blooded murder, carried the death penalty in eighteenth-century Britain, conspiracy was not among them. Nonetheless, while Bowes might escape the rope for his various acts of attempted murder, attempted rape and repeated assaults, he finally had to face the very real prospect of a lengthy imprisonment. Desperate to retain the liberty he had denied so many others, he now pulled out all the stops in his bid to mitigate his sentence. Maintaining the tired fiction of the tender husband trying to rein in his sinful wife, he had collected stacks of affidavits from the usual dubious suspects to justify his actions. Several of the testimonies even claimed that Mary had enjoyed boisterous sexual relations with Bowes throughout her abduction. So Bowes's mistress Mary Gowland swore that she had heard them 'whispering and laughing' in bed, while the gamekeeper Matthew Shields attested that Mary 'went to bed very willingly'. Yet even as he portrayed Mary as his devoted bedmate, Bowes continued to accuse her of wanton and lewd behaviour. The judges were having none of it. Tersely, Grose remarked that rather than explain why Bowes wished to halt his divorce his evidence 'would seem to make it rather a desirable thing'. His key evidence rejected, Thomas Erskine was forced to fall back on the argument that Bowes had been exercising his power, indeed his duty, as a husband to protect his wife when she was incapable of governing herself.

Fully prepared for this age-old defence, James Mingay called on the justices to make an example of Bowes in order to deter similarly abusive husbands by issuing a 'heavy sentence'. Finally losing his temper with his legal colleagues, he exploded: 'How the Gentlemen can reconcile the evidence of the trial with the duties of a husband, seems to me to be a paradox!' And in a bravura performance which went to the heart of the debate on husband's rights, Mingay asked: 'Are the powers of a husband in this country such, that women that are ill-used are not to complain?' Women who had left their husbands to pursue divorce suits through the ecclesiastical courts required the protection of the law from such men who tried to seize them, not its connivance, he insisted. And in a clear swipe at the stereotype of the Irish fortune hunter, he added: 'Is this the way Mr Bowes thinks English husbands are to protect their wives?'

Certainly the judges thought not. In a stinging indictment, Justice Ashhurst branded Bowes's crimes 'as atrocious and daring a nature as ever appeared in a Court of Justice'. Had not the facts been incontestably proven it would scarcely have seemed credible that 'in a civilized country, governed by such laws, any set of men would have been found hardy enough to take away a Lady of rank and fortune, from one of the most publick streets of this great town, at mid-day, in defiance of all law, order, and government, and to drag her through the heart of the kingdom 240 miles'. What was worse, the judge added, was that Bowes's intent had been to pervert the course of justice by preventing the progress of a properly instituted lawsuit. Bowes was fined £300 and sentenced to three years' imprisonment, at the end of which he would be required to find securities totalling £20,000 for the ensuing fourteen years. His fellow conspirators were likewise sentenced to prison with heavy fines.

Widely reported in the press, the Bowes trial was a landmark case which signalled a warning to violent husbands everywhere that the powers they might have assumed were absolute over their wives were actually curtailed by law. It gave hope to abused wives throughout the country that they could expect the protection of the courts when pursuing divorce claims. At the same time, Bowes's conviction and sentence were symbolic of a subtle shift in society's perceptions of the balance of marital power and represented another step in the slow march towards the outlawing of domestic abuse and wrongful confinement. Sadly, however, it would be more than a century before the defence of reasonable confinement was finally declared obsolete. In a case remarkably similar to Mary's, Emily Jackson was kidnapped in 1891 by the fortune-hunter husband she had fled yet her family's application for a writ of *habeas corpus* was refused by the High Court on the usual basis of the husband's right to detain his wife. The Court of Appeal, however, firmly rejected this defence as stemming from 'quaint and absurd dicta' which no longer applied in a civilised country.

Incarcerated but unrepentant, Bowes pursued his remaining legal challenges with undiminished zeal, determined at all costs to hang on to his fortune whether by scuppering the divorce or affirming his deed. Still a wealthy man, by virtue of the income from Mary's estate, he continued to live in the marshal's best apartments where he entertained his friends and mistresses. His decadent lifestyle prompted the *Morning Post* to observe: 'To some people ... a commitment to BANCO REGIS [the King's Bench] is no great punishment. A certain delinquent daily eats, drinks, and gets merry, and though surrounded by as many wives and children as MACHEATH, keeps them all in good order.'[33] In the meantime, Mary remained penniless, dependent on the goodwill of friends and powerless to prevent the once grand homes of her childhood from sliding into decay. At Streatlam, Colpitts's son reported that October, the meadows were overgrown, the deer had not been culled and 'the Castle is uninhabited except by pigeons and jackdaws'.[34] At Gibside, where the snooping ostler Joseph Hill had set up quarters, James Smith lamented that 'the Chapell, Greenhouse,

Banquiting House, Bath, Gardens, and Walks, [and] pleasure Grounds are all gone to Ruin'.

Pressing on resolutely with her legal cases from her house in Holles Street, Mary was distraught in December when Morgan fell sick with a fever. Afraid the illness might carry off her friend, she told Colpitts: 'You will easily imagine what I must have suffered; indeed it has cast a desponding Languor upon my spirits & a tremor upon my nerves.'[35] As Morgan recovered, Mary's nerves remained on edge. Still watched and harassed by Bowes's hoodlums, who had recently tried to abduct two of her servants, she wrote: 'I believe really that, instead of being tamed, Stoney will grow more & more desperate, I am therefore doubly cautious.'

There was fresh anxiety in the New Year but from an unexpected quarter. Despite the waspish vigilance of Elizabeth Parish, her seventeen-year-old charge Anna had been secretly exchanging love letters for almost a year with a debt-ridden young lawyer called Henry Jessop who lived opposite their house in Fludyer Street, a narrow thoroughfare parallel to Downing Street.[36] Growing impatient to consummate her clandestine passion, at the end of January 1788 resourceful Anna placed a plank from her bedroom window to that of Jessop's and crawled across to his waiting arms. Heading straight for Gretna Green the couple married on 28 January.

News of the daring elopement reverberated around the capital. A few days later Mrs Parish's embarrassment was compounded when the gossip reached the north and the *Newcastle Journal* revealed: 'It appears that a correspondence has been carried on for near a twelvemonth past, by means of the servants in each family, yet not the least suspicion was ever entertained by Mrs P.' With Anna still a ward of Chancery due to inherit a substantial fortune when she came of age – put at £13,000 by one newspaper and £20,000 by another – the scandal brought renewed frustration for Thomas Lyon which for once he could not lay at the feet of his sister-in-law. Forced to make the best of a bad match, he negotiated a generous marriage settlement to help clear young Jessop's debts.

As Anna rushed blindly into wedlock with a man she scarcely knew, her mother was still struggling to undo the damage wreaked by her own impetuous marriage. It was 8 March, as the spring bulbs pushed defiantly through the overgrown lawns at Gibside and Streatlam, when the fate of the Bowes estate finally came up in Chancery. No stranger to the family's wrangles, Lord Chancellor Thurlow had previously ordered the couple to return Anna from France; four years later he was faced with their competing claims to the Bowes fortune. Unable to launch a petition in her own name, since wives of course were not normally entitled to own property, Mary had lodged a bill in the name of her trustee, George Stephens, seeking to restore her prenuptial deed of 9 and 10 January 1777. Countering this, Bowes had filed a cross bill claiming that the document was fraudulent since it had been kept secret from him before their marriage and instead asked to confirm the deed of 1 May. Evidently eager to evade the thorny problem, Thurlow referred the case to the Court of Common Pleas for a jury decision – a not uncommon move – on whether the later deed had been extracted under duress.

Two months later, on 19 May, the dispute came before a jury in Westminster Hall. Providing further entertainment for the assembled journalists, Mary's lawyers rehearsed the sorry story of her marriage and its immediate aftermath. As the hacks scribbled furiously, a succession of witnesses described how Bowes had tricked Mary down the aisle by pretending he was mortally wounded in a 'sham duel' then as soon as they were married had subjected her to brutal abuse, forced her to endure the company of prostitutes and curtailed her freedom with tyrannical control.[37] Bowes's former valet, Thomas Mahon, revealed how his erstwhile master had faked his wounds while past servants from the Bowes household described the tell-tale signs of domestic abuse that they had witnessed from the earliest days of the marriage.

By comparison, Bowes's case was flimsy. Scarcely bothering even to sustain the pretence that the duel had been genuine, Bowes's lawyer shrugged that since he had been competing for Mary's hand with his rival Gray then 'stratagem was fair in love, as well as in war'. Effectively admitting the marital brutality, he argued that even if 'one or two blows had been given' that did not prove the deed had been obtained under duress. And resorting again to the medieval principle of the husband's exclusive power over his wife's property the lawyer insisted that by Mary's prenuptial deed Bowes had been 'defrauded of that absolute power which the law gives the husband over the personal estate of his wife'. But the argument was wearing thin. Any sympathy Bowes might once have evoked for his patriarchal privileges from the all-male jury had long since evaporated in the black cloud of infamy over his well-publicised conduct. His downfall was plainly cast when Lord Loughborough, the Lord Chief Justice, weighed up the two sides united on the fateful day of the marriage: 'On one side, was a lady, family, and great estates; on the other, a half-pay lieutenant, without fame or fortune.' He left the jurors in little doubt of the verdict they should bring in when he added: 'It was a marriage brought about by a fraud; a fraud of such a kind, that had it been practised to obtain a hundred pounds from Lady Strathmore, Mr Bowes must have answered for it criminally.' Sure enough, without pausing to retire, the jury delivered its verdict that Bowes's deed of 1 May had been obtained under duress. At that point, the *Gentleman's Magazine* related, the entire court erupted in cheers.[38] It only remained for Chancery to receive and confirm the verdict, which it did on 19 June, with the ubiquitous Buller standing in for Lord Thurlow. Bowes's case was dismissed and costs were levied against him.

For married women everywhere, the Chancery decision marked a significant victory in the lengthy progress towards wives' rights to retain their own property, although it would take almost another century before they could automatically keep any money they had earned during marriage, when the 1870 Married Women's Property Act was passed, amended twelve years later to encompass all property.[39] For Mary, of course, the verdict was monumental, restoring to her and her heirs the vast and valuable estate which she had inherited from her father at the age of eleven. Finally able to begin paying the substantial accumulated debt due to her lawyers and friends, Mary now enjoyed an independent income for the first time since her widowhood – although naturally Bowes would fight over every penny he owed. And for the tenants, pitworkers and other families so long dependent on the Bowes estate, the outcome was equally vital, bringing security of employment and tenure as well as freedom from intimidation for generations to come. It was little wonder that the verdict was greeted in County Durham with 'great Rejoycing', as one of Mary's supporters, William Watson, gleefully reported.[40] No sooner had they heard the news than Watson and his friends marched up to Gibside Hall and threw Joseph Hill out of the house. Taking possession of the mansion in Mary's name, Watson wrote, 'we clapd on 15 or 16 Locks'. Turning next to the unpaid pitworkers at the abandoned collieries, Watson set the wagons rolling to transport coal towards the Tyne once again.

Her fortune restored, her safety assured, if not altogether certain, Mary was still legally tethered to Bowes. As the final appeal in the divorce suit loomed, Bowes summoned his usual talents for media manipulation by luring into his power Mary Farrer, the estranged wife of Mary's sea captain. Having been forced to fend for herself during the captain's two-year sojourn at sea, Mary Farrer had scarcely seen more of her husband since his return in October 1785. Just as he had spent much of his time with the new object of his affections, Mary Eleanor, so Mrs Farrer had apparently filled her days with admirers of her own. In November 1787, possibly encouraged by Mary Eleanor's recent legal successes, the captain had persuaded his inconvenient wife to sign a private separation arranged by Thomas Lacey which guaranteed her £100 a year provided she kept at least a hundred miles from London. Realising belatedly that she had been paid off rather too easily, Mrs Farrer had now thrown in her lot with Bowes.

Tirelessly marshalling his affairs from his prison suite, in October 1788 Bowes helped Mrs Farrer publish a pamphlet entitled, with breathtaking irony, *The Appeal of an Injured Wife against a Cruel Husband*.[41] Bearing every hallmark of Bowes's shameless hand and dedicated 'To the right Honourable the Countess Dowager of Strathmore', the sixty-six-page tract spins the story of an innocent wife made wretched by her penny-pinching, violent and philandering husband. Clearly drawing heavily on Bowes's considerable experience, the pamphlet described the cold-hearted captain striking his wife, threatening her with his pistol and attempting to rape her three sisters while gaily conducting a rapturous affair with his countess. Laughably, at one point, the document even related that Captain Farrer had wished his wife married to Bowes, 'that I might know the difference between the good treatment I received from him, and the cruel usage, the poor dear woman, meaning Lady Strathmore, had experienced from Captain Stoney'. Blaming Mary as the 'principal cause' of all her anguish, Mrs Farrer ended by swearing that she would prevent any union between the couple. Two months later, on 22 December 1788, Bowes staged a benefit performance for his protégée at the Theatre Royal in Haymarket of Nicholas Rowe's *Tamerlane* in which Mrs Farrer herself played the leading role of the stoical heroine Arpasia who chooses death rather than yield to the tyrannical Turkish emperor Bajazet.[42] No doubt audiences relished the unintended farcical elements of Rowe's tragedy as the captive Arpasia addresses her jailor as 'brutal ravisher' and the 'king of terrors'. Fittingly, the evening concluded with the comedy *Who's the Dupe?*

While Bowes championed Mrs Farrer's cause against her supposedly cruel and adulterous husband, he was also busy limbering up for his last stand against Mary's case for divorce on grounds of his cruelty and adultery in the Court of Delegates. Established in the aftermath of Henry VIII's marriage annulments to provide a final point of appeal for ecclesiastical cases once the route to Rome had been severed, the Court of Delegates was an ad-hoc system usually consisting of six judges from both common law and ecclesiastical courts who were appointed to hear each specific case.[43] Expensive and rarely used, the delegates' court heard only eleven divorce appeals during a 30-year period in the mid-eighteenth century and few more in later years. Inevitably, Bowes had determined to avail himself of this last-chance opportunity to contest his divorce and, accordingly, six judges had been appointed soon after he had lodged his appeal in 1787. But since the delegates' system was at least as labyrinthine and laborious as the ecclesiastical courts, it took more than a year for the various witnesses on each side to be interviewed and cross-questioned before finally the case came up for its hearing before the chosen justices on 13 February 1789.

For all Bowes's excuse that he had previously been denied sufficient time to produce all his witnesses, it was, of course, the familiar line-up of bribed and degenerate characters spouting the usual litany of half-baked claims and outrageous smears that appeared before the judges on the appointed day. Making no attempt to defend himself against the charges of serial adultery and life-threatening abuse, Bowes focused his attack on undermining Mary's witnesses by branding them prostitutes or alleging that they had been bribed. At the same time he produced the weary round of allegations of extravagance and promiscuity levelled against Mary. In the face of an even longer queue of witnesses for Mary, including servants, estate staff, rape victims as well as several of Bowes's former friends, such as William Davis, who had grown understandably tired of his incessant cheating and debts, Bowes's case looked feeble. If even Mary's own lawyer remarked that 'broken heads and bloody noses are rather the common consequences of the marriage state',[44] it was no longer deemed reasonable for women to live in a state of abject terror of their husbands. When they reconvened on 2 March, it took the six judges only half an hour to agree that Bowes had committed 'several acts of cruelty' as well as 'the heinous crime of adultery'. And the court duly issued the now incontestable decree that, 'Andrew Robinson Bowes and Lady Strathmore be divorced, and live separate from each other: but that neither of the parties marry during the natural life of the other of them.'

Still Bowes clung to the last straw of hope having

demanded that his Chancery case be reheard under his statutory right of appeal. But the very next day, 3 March, the decision to reinstate the prenuptial deed was confirmed by Lord Chancellor Thurlow. 'Thus,' reported the *Gentleman's Magazine*, 'is Lady Strathmore, at length, fully restored to the large possessions of her family, and divorced from a marriage contracted in an evil hour'.[45] Blankly refusing to pay the accumulated alimony, legal costs and backdated rents that he now owed, Bowes clung grimly to the Bowes family plate as he sank into a slough of drink and depression. With his debts steadily mounting, he was finally forced to exchange his comfortable and spacious rented house for a room inside the King's Bench prison.

As news of the double victory reached the village of St Paul's Walden, the scene of some of Mary's worst abuses, villagers rang the church bells and struck up music.[46] Released at last from the bonds of wedlock, Mary sent an epitaph to Bowes in prison. 'He was the very enemy of Mankind;/Deceitful to his friends, ungrateful to his benefactors,/ Cringing to his superiors and tyrannical to his dependents.'[47] Twelve years after she had been hoodwinked into marrying her charming captain, four years after fleeing her marital home and just a week after her fortieth birthday, Mary was finally free to live as she pleased. Only one challenge remained.

13
Out of the World

Southwark, London, 5 March 1790

Denied all contact with her mother for the past five years, twelve-year-old Mary could hardly believe the news. All her life she had been hidden away. Born in secrecy, a source of bitterness to her bullying stepfather as she grew up, she had borne silent witness to her mother's cries when she was beaten and to her father's grunts as he seduced or raped the maids in the nursery where she slept. At six she had been despatched to boarding school and left there while Bowes took her stepsister Anna to France. When her mother fled a year later Mary had been seized by Bowes and removed to a secret location in the care of his stooge Eliza Stephens. And even after Bowes had disowned her as his daughter and exposed her illegitimacy to the world by publicising her mother's 'Confessions', he had kept her close. Now her life was about to change.

Ever since Mary Eleanor had escaped in February 1785, Bowes had bluntly refused her any access to or news of her two youngest children. While he publicly bemoaned the fact that Mary had left him with 'two poor little helpless Children' he vindictively deprived them of any communication with their mother. In this, of course, he was entirely within his rights since eighteenth-century law gave fathers absolute control over their children up to the age of twenty-one. Unless separating couples signed a private agreement which specified a right to custody or access, mothers had no recourse in law to see their children – and even then such clauses were sometimes overruled by the courts. So although Bowes was serving a three-year sentence for abduction and had been found guilty of cruelty and adultery, he was acting in full accordance with the law when keeping little William incarcerated in his prison quarters and young Mary under careful guard. Naturally he had no particular interest in William or Mary themselves – any more than he cared about the ever-growing brood of illegitimate children he continued to father. Their value was simply as a bargaining tool with their mother; they were, quite literally, hostages to fortune.

Nevertheless, despite the centuries of legal precedent and the sorry experiences of countless grieving mothers, Mary Eleanor was now resolved to win back her children. Approaches by her lawyers during the several stages of the divorce had come to nothing; Bowes had adamantly refused to relinquish any hold on his charges. But gradually, after her legal victories in 1789, Mary had begun to win a number of important figures to her cause.

First and foremost, her eldest son, the 20-year-old Lord Strathmore, had pledged to reunite the family. A sensible and sensitive young man, who had spent several years abroad with his regiment, the earl had grown increasingly close to his mother; after a visit from the Continent in early 1789, she had noted plaintively in her scrapbook, 'my son did come over for 10 days, just to see me.'[1] No doubt remembering his own lonely childhood, when he returned to England on army leave that summer, John lent his weight to his mother's battle to regain William and Mary. As well as the stoical James Farrer, championing her legal business as ever, Mary had won the support of the influential magistrate Sir Sampson Wright. Having succeeded his former boss, Sir John Fielding, as magistrate of the famous Bow Street police office, Wright was a justice of the peace for Middlesex, Essex and Surrey. Even Thomas Lyon, her oldest adversary, now condescended to help her claim. And crucially, that autumn, Mary had secured the help of one of Bowes's most loyal collaborators.

Once Mary's closest confidante, later her fiercest critic, the treacherous Eliza Stephens had not hesitated to testify to the illegitimacy and secret birth of the little girl with whose welfare she had been entrusted from the age of seven. In the wake of Bowes's court defeats, however, which jeopardised the £200 annuity she had received since leaving the family in 1778, she had evidently surmised that her best interests lay elsewhere. Secretly meeting with Mary and Lord Strathmore at her home in Plympton, Devon, Eliza had been persuaded with the help of a generous donation to divulge vital information about little Mary and her whereabouts. So Mary gleaned that her daughter was being held in a private school, run by a certain Mrs Gilbert, in the hamlet of Newington, just a stone's throw from Bowes's prison quarters in Southwark. Since the neighbourhood boasted four prisons, whose inmates were commonly given leave to frequent the abundant local taverns, as well as the Magdalen Hospital for prostitutes, Bowes had evidently not chosen the school for its salubrious surroundings. Rather it allowed him to maintain a rigorous watch on his daughter and her visitors. Vigilantly guarded, Mary was permitted to see only Bowes, her little brother William on occasional excursions from his prison home, and an older sister of Eliza's referred to as Mrs Baddiley. Her holidays were spent with Eliza in more peaceful environs, if no less degenerate company, in Devon. But now that Bowes no longer received sufficient income to pay her school fees, little Mary's future seemed uncertain.

In a series of fawning letters sent covertly to Mary Eleanor from October 1789, Eliza voiced her dread that Bowes might discover her betrayal and then remove Mary to 'where perhaps neither of us might be able to discover her'. Agreeing nonetheless to act as go-between, Eliza hoped that 'Happier Prospects' were in store for her former charge. Writing again two months later, Eliza reported that Mary was well and declared, 'our wishes for your getting Possession of both your Children, are more earnest than I can express.' A few weeks later, having ominously heard no further news from young Mary, Eliza hoped that she would stay safe at her school in Newington 'till the happy Period which will I trust restore her to her Mother'. The New Year brought new information as Eliza forwarded several letters from little Mary which revealed that she had spent the Christmas holidays at school, '& not in Scenes of Wretchedness & Impropriety', by which Eliza apparently referred to Bowes's prison rather than her own pastoral abode. But with the half-year's school bill expected imminently, the child's prospects were in the balance.

By the end of January 1790, Bowes was decidedly feeling the pinch. Saddled with costs from his various lawsuits, alimony payments due to Mary and claims for backdated rents and profits from her estate, he appeared before the Court of Delegates pleading his inability to pay the divorce suit costs due to his responsibilities to his two children. If forced to pay, he argued, not only would he remain 'a Prisoner for Life' but his children would 'with himself be reduced to very great distress if not absolute Want'.[2] There was an obvious solution to this predicament, as Mary was quick to point out, assuring the court in person that she was 'now willing to receive the said two Children and will at all times hereafter be ready to receive, maintain, Cloathe and Educate the said two Children in a suitable and proper manner'. With no jurisdiction over child custody, the judges simply confirmed that Bowes must pay. When he still refused, with more than £500 outstanding, on 5 February 1790 he was excommunicated for contempt of court.[3] On news of the order reaching Newcastle, the city's former MP was solemnly denounced from the pulpit of St Nicholas's Church by the curate John Ellison, son of the Reverend Nathaniel Ellison who had married Bowes to Hannah Newton twenty-two years earlier.

Unable to pay for the children's upkeep or settle his debts, and therefore condemned to remain in prison, Bowes's grip on William and Mary seemed increasingly weak, as Eliza noted. 'I should imagine that the last decision relative to the Costs of Suit must produce such consequences as must remove every fear of a party being ever at liberty to again give us any cause of apprehension,' she wrote to Mary Eleanor in February, adding, 'His Declaration of inability to maintain them must surely accelerate the restoration of both your Children to you.' By early March, Mary had secured the consent of Sir Sampson Wright and Thomas Lyon to stand as trustees with Lord Strathmore in settling £5,000 each on William and Mary if they could be made wards of Chancery. Unable to finalise the agreement until the earl's twenty-first birthday, just a month away, she remained on tenterhooks. As James Farrer briefed counsel for a hearing to determine wardship with Lord Chancellor Kenyon – no friend to separated women – Mary urged him to cite Bowes's lifestyle and stress that 'he is not only a Prisoner for Cruell & illegal Acts, but is living in public Infamy continually Inebriated, surrounded with prostituted Women, which in its best representation must be a horrid Scene for an Innocent Mind'.[4] Yet since such considerations had rarely given the courts pause for thought in previous cases, Mary decided to take the law into her own hands. Playing Bowes at his own game, she had resolved to seize her daughter from her hiding place in south London. With the city's leading magistrate on her side, and the child's keeper, Mrs Gilbert, won over to her mission, Mary laid plans to bring her daughter home.

Told on 5 March, at her school in Newington, that she was to be reunited with her mother the very next day, young Mary was ecstatic. The touching letter that she wrote, the first communication with her mother for more than five years, survives to this day. 'My Dear Mama', she began, 'It is with the greatest satisfaction I understand that you will be glad to hear from me. It is so long a Time since I have had the Happiness of either seeing or hearing from you, that I cannot express the Joy it was to me to be informed by my Lady Wright of my turn of Fortune in being now I hope under your Protection. When I parted from you I was much too young to know the loss of a Mother. I am sensible of the duty and affection I owe to you and my Brother.'[5] With no hint of resentment at her mother having left her behind, Mary added: 'I long very much to see you and hope there is nothing now more wanting to complete my happiness.' Loyally she did not forget to mention: 'I am sure you will be very glad to see my dear little Brother William indeed he is a very fine Boy.' And despite the five years' absence, she assured her mother, 'I have not forgot any place where I spent my Infancy and I believe I could find my way over one half of Paulswalden and Gibside Houses &c.'

It was an emotional reunion. So flustered that she could barely manage the usual pleasantries with Thomas Lacey, Mary later apologised that her 'flurry' was 'nothing but the circumstance of being restored to the sight of a long lost Child could excuse'.[6] But it was still a highly risky manoeuvre. Immediately discovering the breach in his security, Bowes obtained a *habeas corpus* writ demanding Mary surrender her daughter. She in turn urged her lawyers to press Lord Kenyon to 'grant a protection for the child, on acct. of her age, & sex, till proper Trustees can be appointed'.[7] All depended on the anticipated hearing in Chancery.

By 13 April, when Lord Strathmore celebrated his twenty-first birthday and inherited his late father's estate, the younger children's futures remained unclear. With snow heavy on the ground at Gibside, tenants and staff caroused in the great hall into the night, consuming vast quantities of rum, port, ale and punch as they toasted the young earl's health. Celebrating more soberly at her recovered home of St Paul's Walden Bury, Mary set in motion a legal settlement under the terms of her re-established prenuptial deed to hand the remaining estate to her eldest son. Having regained control of her fortune less than a year earlier, she planned to give it up in order to place it out of Bowes's reach for good. Hurrying Farrer to conclude the agreement she hoped that, 'afterwards you & my Son will have leisure to consult together upon the steps to be taken by the latter to finally crush all Mr Stoney's Hopes'.[8]

Five months later the settlement was finalised and 'in Consideration of the Love and Affection which the said Countess beareth to her Son' Mary transferred the Gibside and Streatlam estate to the earl in return for a £2,000 pension and future allowances totalling £10,000 for William and Mary.[9] His hopes duly 'crushed', Bowes had no alternative but to relinquish his claim to the children and they were finally free to live with their mother. For William, now eight, it was literally the end of a prison sentence since he had spent most of the past three years in jail with his father. In this he was not alone; numerous children were brought up in the King's Bench or Fleet prisons in desperate conditions during the eighteenth century. His education directed by the prostitutes, mistresses and debtors of Bowes's acquaintance, the move to his mother's instructive care and spacious home would require some adjustment. For Mary, now thirteen, the ordeal she had endured had apparently left no deleterious effects. The sunny, curly-haired infant on whom her mother had doted had grown into a sensible and dutiful young girl but her cheerful good nature and lively spirits remained as buoyant as ever.

Her last major legal victory, and in some ways the most significant, Mary's triumph in regaining her children, albeit through male trustees, was remarkable for its time. Only in the most extreme circumstances, when deemed to have exceptionally depraved morals or irreligious views, did fathers ever lose custody of their children. In 1765, for example, Chancery had enforced a private settlement awarding Lady Anne Boteler custody of her daughter Elizabeth following extreme abuse against both of them; at one point Sir Oliver had threatened to drop his daughter down a stairwell.[10] Likewise, in 1817, the poet Percy Bysshe Shelley would be denied custody of his children – by Bowes's former crony Lord Eldon – after their mother's death for fear that his atheism would lead to 'immoral and vicious' conduct.

These remained isolated examples, however, and Mary's success did not prove a turning point. While mothers had enjoyed limited progress in asserting their right to access to their children under the liberal regime of Lord Mansfield, the next fifty years would see a crackdown led by the arch conservative forces of Lords Eldon, Kenyon and Ellenborough. Only a sustained campaign by the author Caroline

Norton, herself denied access to her three children by their abusive father, would ultimately lead to reform. In 1839 the Infant Custody Act gave courts discretion for the first time to award custody of children under seven to their mothers, although this was still denied to wives found guilty of adultery. In 1873 this discretion was extended to children up to sixteen and the adultery rule abolished. But it would be 1925 before mothers and fathers were viewed equally in custody battles. It was little wonder, therefore, that at the end of the eighteenth century, when pregnant with her first child, Mary Wollstonecraft would write to her lover: 'Considering the care and anxiety a woman must have about a child before it comes into the world, it seems to me, by a natural right, to belong to her ... but it is sufficient for man to condescend to get a child, in order to claim it. – A man is a tyrant!'

Finally free to govern her own life with a modest but independent income, Mary now devoted herself to the seven children she had variously neglected or been separated from in their early years. The suffering she had endured had evidently given her the maturity and compassion to value her children in a way she had not as a young mother. In some ways it was too late for the five children of her first marriage. Effectively they had been failed by Mary in their infancy when she had ignored her sons and favoured her daughters; after they had come under the harsh rule of their guardians and were denied all but the briefest of interludes with their mother, they had been failed by the prevailing legal and social mores. But although she could never replace those lost years, Mary did now try her best to mend the fractured bonds.

Rebellious Anna would remain the most distant. Having failed to learn from her mother's mistakes, her hasty Gretna Green marriage soon proved unhappy. Her debt-ridden lawyer would die young and leave her with two small daughters, Anna Maria and Susan, to bring up alone. Although she patched up her past differences with Mary their relationship would always be fraught; at one point a friend would report that, 'Lady Anne Jessup [sic] & her family have been staying some time with her mother, but they have had a fall out, so Lord Strathmore has taken them all to him.'[11] Her elder sister Maria, having adhered closely to the rules of social etiquette as defined by the Lyons, had married rather more conventionally shortly after her twenty-first birthday in May 1789 to a well-heeled army officer, Captain Barrington Price.[12] She too would have two daughters named, with customary Georgian lack of imagination, Maria and Anne.

With both her eldest girls now married and starting their own families, Mary lavished her maternal pride on her three Strathmore boys. Making up for her lack of interest when they were little, she fondly followed their various careers by pasting news cuttings into her album. Finally released from the stranglehold of frugal Uncle Thomas, and now a wealthy aristocrat in his own right, the tenth earl rose to his new responsibilities. A kindly and generous head of the family, John welcomed his two half-siblings into the fold and applied himself to healing old rifts and circumventing new ones, as his intervention in the tiff between Mary and Anna would reveal. A diligent landlord, he took possession of Gibside and threw himself into restoring the buildings and grounds which his grandfather had so lovingly crafted. The woods having been devastated by Bowes, the earl immediately began replanting. One bill for 1790 reveals an order for 1,000 young oaks, 16,500 oak saplings and 5,000 elm seedlings.[13] The Gothic buildings and glasshouses having been neglected or vandalised by Bowes, the earl initiated renovations. Shutters were replaced in Mary's greenhouse, frames fixed in her hothouse, the banqueting house was whitewashed and the time-worn figure of Lady Liberty on top of the great column was restored once more to her gilded glory. The earl would even complete the chapel which had been abandoned at George Bowes's death thirty years previously and re-establish the stud his grandfather had once maintained at Streatlam. At Glamis, he was no less active. All work at the castle having been halted on the death of the ninth earl in 1776, the planned new west wing remained half-built and the grounds overgrown. Immediately, John drew up plans for renovations and embarked on a lengthy programme of rebuilding and repairs. Yet he would visit his Scottish seat only rarely – for the earl's thoughts were soon preoccupied by events closer to home.

If he had inherited the good looks of his father and the good taste of his grandfather, the tenth earl also possessed the impulsiveness and passion of his mother in her youth. Invited in early 1791 to a theatrical evening at Seaton Delaval, the magnificent home of Lord Delaval on a wild stretch of the Northumberland coast, 21-year-old John fell in love with the earl's youngest and favourite daughter, Sarah.[14] Six years his senior, golden-haired Sarah Hussey Delaval had married her father's friend, the second Earl of Tyrconnell, when she was just sixteen and the earl, recently divorced from his first wife, twenty-nine. Having provided the earl with two children, the young Countess of Tyrconnell had been indulged by her accommodating husband and encouraged by her doting father to conduct an affair with Frederick, Duke of York. Lord Delaval had even bought his daughter Claremont House near the duke's home at Weybridge so that the Tyrconnells could live hand in glove with the prince's household.

In an age notorious for scandal and eccentricity, the

Delavals were a class apart. Devoted to amateur dramatics, Sarah's profligate uncle Francis had once hired Drury Lane theatre to stage a family performance for which the House of Commons adjourned early so that MPs could enjoy the spectacle. Later running his own private theatre he persuaded his friend, the playwright Samuel Foote, to undertake an ill-advised stunt on horseback in which poor Foote lost a leg. Sarah's father, who had assumed the family estate in return for settling Francis's debts, had only recently taken a sixteen-year-old mistress following the death of his wife. And Sarah, known in the family as 'Hussey', had reputedly once appeared at dinner on a hot day naked to the waist.

Stunningly beautiful, with white-gold hair which fell in voluminous curls to her waist, 27-year-old Sarah had just ended her affair with the duke, whose marriage had been arranged with a Prussian princess, with a very public renunciation. Having persuaded her father to stage Nicholas Rowe's *The Fair Penitent* at Seaton Delaval, Sarah gave a virtuoso performance as the unfaithful wife atoning for her adultery by killing herself. Taken to a performance by his friend, the travel writer Henry Swinburne, Lord Strathmore was bewitched. When Swinburne returned to the north-east a few weeks later he was somewhat peeved to discover 'that my introduction of Lord Strathmore at Seaton Delaval had been followed up, and that he was now completely *domicilié* with the family'. Meeting this extended family for supper in Newcastle, Swinburne wrote: 'I was rather surprised to see the intimacy which had struck up so suddenly; and a fine scene between Lady Tyrconnell and Lord Strathmore afforded me great amusement.' Ruefully he added: 'The poor man is desperately smitten.' With little talent for subtlety, the family next staged *Othello* with Lord Tyrconnell in the lead role, his wife as Desdemona and Lord Strathmore playing Cassio, the loyal friend suspected of an affair with the Moor's wife.

Captivated by the alluring Lady Tyrconnell and befriended by her broad-minded husband, Lord Strathmore became absorbed into the family's pleasure-seeking schedule, becoming a regular racing companion for the earl by day and a regular bedtime companion for his wife by night. Inevitably, before the year was out, the young earl found himself the butt of gossip writers and satirists. In December *The Bon Ton Magazine* reported that Lady Tyrconnell had left her husband to live with Lord Strathmore at Gibside. That same month, a cartoon by Isaac Cruikshank, entitled 'A Strath Spey or New Highland Reel as Danced at Seaton D–l', depicted Lord Tyrconnel bursting in on his wife as Lord Strathmore hides beneath her bed. Upsetting a chamber pot over a portrait of the Duke of York, the young earl explains his indiscretion in mock Scottish dialect by reference to his mother's colourful past with the words: 'My Mither did sa before me.'

Passing no judgement on her son as he embarked on his own tragic journey, Mary kept track of his increasingly indiscreet travels around the country with the Tyrconnells in her scrapbook. The summer of 1791 had seen the threesome visiting the Lakes while December found Lady Tyrconnell in Northumberland; in January 1792 the theatre season had resumed at Seaton Delaval with the entire family performing *The Fair Penitent* and *Othello.*[15] As Lord Strathmore chased his mother down the bumpy road of society scandal, George and Thomas followed somewhat more staidly in his and their father's footsteps to Pembroke College, Cambridge.[16] As soon as George reached twenty-one, in November 1792, Mary handed him ownership of St Paul's Walden Bury and took for herself a quiet country house, Purbrook Park, near

Portsmouth. Writing a poem in honour of George's birthday, she hoped his future would bring 'a loving Wife, a faithful friend,/and Children who may fondly pay to you/That filial tribute which is justly due'.[17]

For Mary, domestic contentment now ran personal ambition into a poor second place. This was the first time since her brief widowhood that she was truly at liberty to indulge her twin passions of botany and literature, as well as to enjoy the social whirl, witty conversation and male admiration that she had so loved as a girl. Yet although she composed a few poems, tended her museum, painted occasional flower pictures and corresponded with friends, she would never fulfil her original literary or scientific potential nor fully enter society again. A poignant little note in her album in 1791 recorded that, 'In sept I heard but did not see a paragraph about my being at Weymouth & in favour with their Majesties there.' [18] For all that the royal couple might deign to notice her on their seaside jaunt, Mary's high-profile divorce and the irreparable damage her reputation had suffered ensured that she could never regain her place within society. There would be no more routs or assemblies, no more lovers or suitors. And with her wealth now safely in the hands of the next generation, she was finally free from fortune hunters too.

Having ardently maintained his attentions throughout Mary's kidnap ordeal and subsequent courtroom dramas, Captain Farrer had faded from the scene. Whether the revelations about his marriage had tarnished Mary's interest or the adventurer had simply decided to seek his fortune elsewhere, in December 1790 the captain resumed his position at the helm of the *True Briton* and set sail for Madras.[19] On his return, in 1792, he paused in Britain long enough to sue his wife successfully in the ecclesiastical court for separation on the grounds of her adultery; after a further two-year absence at sea he would win a full divorce in the House of Lords in 1796. In any case, even if the captain would eventually free himself from his marital ties sufficiently to marry again, Mary Eleanor would never be granted that privilege; while Bowes was alive, she was not permitted to remarry. Her captain having disappeared over the horizon, there would be nobody to replace him. Instead, Mary relished the quiet triumph of her newfound independence in the carefree company of her two youngest children, her indispensable companion Mary Morgan, a small band of faithful servants and an assortment of pets. In her last portrait, painted by an unknown artist in the grounds of St Paul's Walden Bury in 1791, she stands relaxed and smiling wearing an elaborate gown and sporting an improbably tall hairstyle, with a favourite dog at her feet and a flowering sprig in her hand.[20] Yet if Mary hoped to fade quietly from public scrutiny, Bowes would make sure that she did not.

Losing his liberty, his income and his children had done nothing to improve Bowes's temper. Since losing his claim to Mary's fortune, he had sunk into a 'complete state of despondency', according to Foot, still pandering to his patient's pretended ailments.[21] The final divorce decision had been 'another deadly blow' and he had then been 'stunned with the thunder of excommunication', the surgeon recorded. Yet for all his genuine or feigned melancholy, Bowes still commanded the best room in the prison where he divided his time between corrupting vulnerable young women and enticing gullible young attorneys into continuing his legal battles.

Having abandoned Mary Gowland shortly after she had given birth to his latest offspring, Bowes had soon found a new target for his lust. The teenage daughter of a fellow prisoner, who happened to own a considerable estate, Mary or 'Polly' Sutton had caught Bowes's eye when she visited her father. Applying his customary seduction technique, he charmed his prey with flattery and presents. When Polly fell ill with a fever, he sent Foot to tend her; the surgeon found her 'feeding a pigeon with split peas out of her mouth' and described her as 'a girl of perfect symmetry, fair, lively, and innocent'. Making no attempt to preserve Polly's innocence by warning her of her admirer's depravity, Foot observed silently as Bowes duly seduced the girl and brought her to live with him in jail. If his treatment of Mary had made Bowes notorious, his most pitiful victim must surely have been young Polly whose voice would never be heard. Hiring a room for her, to which Bowes alone had a key, he kept Polly confined day and night; she was, effectively, the prisoner of a prisoner. In her lonely cell, she bore Bowes five children, all of whom shared her confinement. Never permitted to attend the dinners Bowes threw for fellow inmates, she lived the life of a recluse. Occasionally Foot caught a glimpse of her, when Bowes called him to treat one of the children, but found it impossible to speak to her since 'Bowes was always present, hurried the visit as much as possible, locked the door, and took the key in his pocket'. Polly, who would remain with Bowes for the rest of his life, effectively became his third wife and was treated accordingly – subject to extreme domestic violence and blatant infidelity. But Bowes had not yet forgotten his second wife.

Sustained only by his army half-pay and a paltry income from his Irish property but with mounting debts and more mouths to feed, Bowes was desperate to raise funds. With his usual flair for media exploitation, in April 1793 he published in full Mary's 'Confessions'. Reproduced from the original lodged at Doctors' Commons six years earlier, *The Confessions of the Countess of Strathmore* sold for 2s 6d. Parading Mary's 'crimes' and 'imprudencies' for public titillation once again, Bowes's marketing campaign dug up the names of a host of other characters who would no doubt have preferred their roles in the Bowes drama to have been forgotten. An advertisement in *The Star* announced that the book promised 'many curious Particulars' on a cast of notables including the Duke of Buccleuch, Charles Fox, Joseph Planta and Thomas Lyon.[22]

Refusing to rise to the bait, Mary inserted notices in London and regional newspapers attempting to draw a line under the entire sorrowful episode. 'Having too long trespassed on the Public relative to matters in which I reluctantly intrude myself upon them,' she wrote, 'I shall take leave of Mr Bowes and his productions for ever; not thinking it necessary, in future, to take the least notice of any subject which may be introduced into print, either by himself, or through any other channel he may think proper to employ.'[23] She stayed true to her word. But although Mary tried her utmost to ignore the fresh reminder of her past indiscretions, publication of the unexpurgated 'Confessions' fostered an image of her as a licentious, extravagant and flighty fool with which she would be branded for posterity.

For her daughter Mary, who reached sixteen in 1793, the timing could not have been worse. Her illegitimacy and clandestine birth exposed again at the very moment that she was ready to make her debut on the London scene most probably scuppered her chances in the marriage market for good. Young Mary had gone to stay with a family friend, called Mrs Ogilvy, in fashionable Chelsea for the winter season of 1793–4; although her mother eschewed the gossip-driven metropolitan social life, she evidently did not want to deprive her daughter of her introduction into society. The artist Joseph Farington bumped into the debutante at a dance in April 1794 and recorded in his diary: 'Miss Bowes, a daughter of Lady Strathmore by Mr Bowes, came with Mrs Ogleby [sic] of Chelsea, with whom she resides.'[24] Yet while she would continue to enjoy a party well into her old age, Mary would never marry.

Studiously avoiding city revels and society gossip as incredulous readers pored over her past, Mary Eleanor absorbed her days with her pets and her poems at Purbrook Park. Her eclectic collection of animals included numerous cats and dogs, a donkey, a talking parrot and a tame robin named 'Bob' that lived uncaged in her bedroom. With Morgan as her amanuensis, she composed poetry on mundane domestic issues and topical current affairs, ranging from a ditty on Mrs Ogilvy's four kittens to a translation into poetry of Thomas Erskine's speech defending Thomas Paine.[25] In early 1794 she struck up a poetical correspondence with Katherine Bentley, whose daughter shared lodgings with young Mary in town, which continued in verse for the next eighteen months. While Mary regaled her new literary friend with news of her family, her animals and her health, Mrs Bentley responded with titbits on their daughters and city affairs – all in light-hearted doggerel. Detached from society, Mary acknowledged her increasing estrangement from contemporary life. Confessing that she no longer took any interest in fashion, she declared: 'How eccentric I am you can't think,/(How wide from the Bulk of Mankind,)/At many Great faults you must wink,/And some virtues I trust you will find.' Instead of binding curls, Mary revealed, her maid was now kept busy binding manuscripts.

Evidently the strain of her past torments was still being felt, exacerbated by a serious coach accident the previous year in which Mary had lost three teeth, Morgan had been badly hurt and a fellow passenger had been killed.[26] Apologising to Mrs Bentley for her indisposition, Mary revealed in April 1794 that her legs were so painful that, 'I seldom can Walk'. And in an affecting description of the long-term consequences of her abuse, she wrote: 'I fear you would shrink/Could you only once think/What Object you'll meet with in me;/Who, tho' not very old,/Am by Blows & by Cold,/More batter'd than Ships come from Sea./Some years 'twas my potion/to sail on an Ocean/Of Horrors, of Tears, & of Grief,/When I lost my Main-mast/But was landed at last/Too late, though, I found for relief.'

That summer, as Europe was engulfed in war and her sons George and Thomas both enlisted in the army, Mary moved temporarily back to St Paul's Walden Bury where she was joined by 'my Girls' – most probably Mary and Anna. In September Mrs Bentley came to stay, although their lyrical exchange continued throughout the visit and carried on after Mrs Bentley returned to London. When the whole household was stricken by sickness in December, Mary's physicians feared she would not recover but by Christmas she was sufficiently restored to embrace the New Year with a cheery: 'Let gay ninety-five with fresh garlands be crown'd.'

Reliving the past trials she had suffered at St Paul's Walden Bury and elsewhere, Mary now embarked on a 'narrative' which described in more than three hundred pages of harrowing detail the barbarities she had suffered during her marriage and abduction. Prefaced with a warning that the events she related were 'so uncommon as to stagger the belief of Posterity', she may have intended the text for publication, perhaps as a counterpoint to the 'Confessions'. Finishing her narrative in February 1795, as she packed to move one last time, Mary looked forward to 'a period not very distant, when I have the best prospect of being able to seat myself in some pleasant and cheerful retirement for the remainder of my days, in the Enjoyment of every Comfort, and amusement, a rational Being can desire, and with a most consummate Contempt for all those airy, and what perhaps may be justly stiled those vicious Bubbles, which the Fools and Rogues of the present age, agree to decorate with the false name of Pleasure'. After a summer spell in seaside lodgings, Mary moved that autumn into Stourfield House, a rambling mansion on a remote country estate bordering the Hampshire coast, where she hoped she would find the peace that she craved.

Built in 1766 as the country seat of a wealthy barrister, Stourfield House suited Mary's purposes perfectly. Sitting on a small rise about half a mile from the beach, with a fine view of Christchurch Harbour nearly three miles to the south-east, the house was sheltered by a plantation of trees.[27] Bounded by the sea to the south, the River Stour to the east, the estate stretched twelve miles northwards across farmland and heath towards the chalk hills of Dorset and the fringes of the New Forest in the distance. An isolated and romantic spot, almost impregnable to unwelcome visitors and remote from prying neighbours, it proved ideal. Here, Mary told one friend, she could feel 'as if she were out of the world'.

Arriving in her coach in October 1795, accompanied by her daughters Anna and Mary, her friend Mary Morgan and her establishment of servants, Mary caused something of a stir in the usually uneventful life of the quiet neighbourhood. Inevitably, her reputation had preceded her. Mary Dale, the wife of a tenant farmer, Henry Dale, was already aware that Mary had suffered 'great trials' on account of her 'very cruel and unkind husband'. Cut off from friends and family in

London and Durham, Mary had few visitors. Her sons came occasionally; Anna sometimes stayed with her girls. But with her beloved daughter Mary by her side, Morgan as her companion and a brood of dogs at her feet, she needed no further company. Although she remained aloof from the local gentry, Mary won hearts and minds among the country folk for her generosity, making firm friends with the Dales and distributing soup among the poor several times a week.

Yet Mary had scarcely settled into her coastal idyll before her newfound serenity was shattered. After indifferent health for several months, on 17 January 1796, Mary Morgan died, aged just forty-six. She was buried in the Lady Chapel of Christchurch Priory where Mary erected a memorial to the 'Heroic Qualities', the 'Cool, deliberate Courage' and the 'matchless persevering Friendship' of the faithful maid who had rescued her from the depths of misery.[28] According to Mrs Dale, Mary 'never could get over' Morgan's death, 'it seemed to press so heavy on her mind'.

Further distress arrived that October when Mary heard that Bowes was launching a fresh legal assault. Living 'out of the world' just like Mary, though not through choice, Bowes fretted over his depleted finances and his claim to Mary's former fortune. Changing his attorneys as often as he changed his mistresses, he now appealed to the House of Lords against the Chancery decision on the prenuptial deed. It took the peers little time to affirm the Chancery verdict at which point they made clear their disdain by charging Bowes £150 costs and issuing a vituperative indictment of his challenge. Remarking that every step he had taken to acquire his marital rights had been 'grossly fraudulent', the law lords asserted: 'That if it be possible to conceive the Husband, of all others, who ought the least to be permitted to question any such Dispositions made by a Wife, the Appellant is that Husband.'[29]

Merely emboldened by their contempt, in December Bowes concocted a new suit to Chancery based on another supposed deed of revocation which, apparently, he had just remembered that Mary had signed in November 1781 in front of a witness who was conveniently now dead. This deed, which Bowes had subsequently lost, entitled him to a third of two farms in County Durham, or so he claimed. Ludicrous as his case might seem, inevitably the challenge involved further legal wrangling, renewed witness statements and more anxiety for Mary. Struggling to remember where she was on the days in question, Mary despaired that many of her former witnesses – including poor Morgan – were now dead. Keen to avoid a trip to London on account of 'my deranged finances & present bad health', she hoped the case would quickly be quashed.[30] Incredibly, the arguments would rumble on for a further ten years. Hinging on a legal loophole concerning a codicil to George Bowes's will, the case was referred in 1798 to the King's Bench, which found in Bowes's favour. An appeal by Mary and Lord Strathmore to the House of Lords the following year failed so that once again Bowes had his hands on a share of Mary's fortune and a claim to unpaid rent. Ultimately, when Bowes reasserted his claim to the farms – Lord Strathmore having ignored the outcome – the case would come before the Court of Common Pleas in 1807 when the entire story of the sham duel would be thrashed out once more and Bowes's suit finally dismissed.

Her peace of mind fractured by Bowes's tireless legal challenges, her health still scarred by his years of abuse and her spirits sapped by the loss of her companion, Mary was becoming increasingly frail and eccentric. Lavishing attention on her many dogs, Mary ensured that each had its own bed and was treated to a hot dinner every day. When one went missing in 1798, she circulated handbills offering £10 reward. The poor animal was found dead on the heath by Farmer Dale and was tenderly carried back to the house in a basket. When Dale declined the reward – 'because of the great kindness she had always shown his wife and himself' – Mary insisted that he take refreshments at the house whenever he wished. From that point on she frequently ordered her servants to take a cooked dinner and beer to the farmer when she saw him working in the fields nearby. And for all her strange ways, the farmer's son, Richard Dale, insisted, 'no person could be more respected and beloved than Lady Strathmore'.

That same year Mary was reported to be so ill that doctors despaired of her survival; one newspaper reported that she had been 'given over by her Physicians'.[31] Although she confounded the doctors, she was becoming increasingly preoccupied with her health. Her spirits depressed, she began inviting Mary Dale to the house for frequent discussions about the arrangements for her funeral. In 1799, she asked the Dales and her gardener, George White, to witness amendments to her will. The dawn of the new century brought no improvement, and on 28 April 1800, at Stourfield House, Mary died. Her final illness unrecorded, her cause of death would remain unknown, though her weakened health would have left her easy prey to any number of the period's lethal contagious diseases. She was just fifty-one years old. Days later Richard Dale, an observant boy of five, watched in wonder as the horse-drawn hearse bearing Mary's body, followed by three mourning coaches containing her grieving family, clattered slowly down the winding drive to begin the long journey to London.

Mary was buried, at her own request, in Poets' Corner of

Westminster Abbey, close to the graves of Chaucer, Spenser and Dryden, on 10 May.[32] If she could not achieve greatness as a poet in life, she would dwell with great poets in death. Curiously, for someone who had suffered two wretched marriages, she was buried – at her own wish – in the magnificent jewelled wedding dress she had worn for her first marriage at the age of eighteen. One further request, by far the most fitting, was never carried out. In her will Mary had asked for a statue to be erected at her grave. Although she had grown up under the gaze of Lady Liberty on top of her majestic column, it was not a statue to liberty but the blindfolded figure of Justice that Mary desired to stand guard at her tomb. Having lost and regained her freedom in the most extraordinary circumstances over the course of her remarkable lifetime, few could have set a higher price on the value of liberty. And yet, as she was well aware, it was only through the fundamental principles of justice that her liberty had finally been secured.

In the Age of Enlightenment, when brilliant thinkers and daring innovators, both men and women, were rightly revered, Mary Eleanor Bowes had the potential to achieve great things. Having been born into wealth, blessed with the best education of the day and, encouraged by her progressive father, grown up confident and ambitious, she could have won acclaim as a talented writer and linguist, an accomplished botanist or a prominent scientific patron. But if her personal aspirations were stifled by her first husband, they were strangled by the next.

Instead, Mary Eleanor achieved something of much more significant and far-reaching importance. After suffering eight years of barely imaginable brutality, which reduced her to a petrified and cowed spectre of her former self, Mary somehow found the strength to embark on an audacious counter-attack. Despite having once enjoyed the position of Britain's richest heiress, for all that she had married into the aristocracy, she could rely on neither money nor connections in her struggle. And yet through sheer tenacity and courage, and the kindness of those on the bottom rungs of the Georgian social scale, Mary successfully pitted her wits not only against one of history's vilest husbands but also the might of the entire legal and religious establishment. At a time when women enjoyed pitifully few rights in law, either in marriage or in general, Mary Eleanor Bowes won an unprecedented series of victories, amounting to a remarkable triumph, which would stand as a beacon of hope to inspire writers and encourage campaigners in the continuing battle for reform.

Unjustly, although she had well and truly outsmarted him, Mary was outlived by Andrew Robinson Bowes. His unpaid debts, including the alimony he never paid to Mary or her descendants, meant that he would remain under the jurisdiction of the King's Bench, spending the last twenty-two years of his life a prisoner. But following Mary's death he was allowed to live outside the prison walls, in the area surrounding the jail known as 'the rules'. And so, with the long-suffering Polly, their two girls and three boys, and a straggle of mangy cats and dogs, Bowes took a house in London Road, close by the jail. Investing his remaining time in evading the lawyers and tradesmen to whom he owed money, Bowes perfected his customary deceit in feigning illness – pretending to suffer fits, loss of memory and deafness – and dressed himself and his offspring in rags. According to Foot, Bowes insisted that the children never wore shoes or stockings. As he refused even to buy a broom to keep the house clean, his daughters had to go down on their knees to collect the dust with their hands.

Despite living outside the prison walls – the family moved to a second house in Lambeth Road by 1807 – Bowes continued to treat Polly as his personal prisoner. He kept her locked in a room, denied her all visitors and allowed her only one meal a day. And so it came as a surprise to Foot, calling at the house on 10 January 1810, when Polly answered the door for the first time in her life. Inside he found Bowes in bed, for once genuinely ill. With his family crowded around him, Foot learned that Bowes's will left nothing to his common-law wife of more than 20 years. It was only after the pleas of his children, his attorney and Foot himself, that Bowes was finally persuaded to grant Polly a measly £100 a year.[33]

Six days later, on 16 January 1810, Bowes died. He was buried in the vault of the nearby St George's Church, where he would spend eternity within the prison rules. His chief apologist during life, his chief mourner in death, Foot dolefully followed Bowes's coffin to its resting place. Yet just two years later the surgeon published an excoriating exposé of his erstwhile patron's life in which he cheerfully proclaimed: 'He was a villain to the backbone!' Relating the epic tale of his friend's trickery, violence, sexual assaults and depravity, Foot concluded: 'To sum up his character in a few words, he was cowardly, insidious, hypocritical, tyrannic, mean, violent, selfish, jealous, revengeful, inhuman and savage, without a countervailing quality.'

None of Mary's children enjoyed particularly fulfilling lives or found lasting happiness in marriage. William, the youngest, joined the navy and survived one naval disaster, becoming icebound in the Elbe on the *Proserpine* in 1799, only to perish in another, at the age of twenty-four, when a storm wrecked the *Blenheim* off the coast of Madagascar in 1807.[34] His half-sister Mary settled in Bath and though she never married, she retained her mischievous humour and happy-go-lucky nature to the last, becoming a favourite aunt to her nieces and nephew. She died in 1855, aged seventy-eight.

Maria, the giggling toddler who had once charmed Thomas Gray, lived comfortably in Gloucestershire with her family, but died in 1806 at just thirty-eight. Her brother George died the same year, aged thirty-five, after being married only eighteen months, and since he left no heirs St Paul's Walden Bury descended to younger brother Thomas. George's widow, Mary, and Maria's widower, now Colonel Price, consoled each other in their grief by getting married in 1811.[35] Thomas fared better, marrying three times and outliving two of his wives but also his only child. Headstrong Anna, herself a widow after her husband's early death, lived with her two girls at Bird Hill House, a lodge on the Gibside estate. Never marrying again, she died in 1832, aged sixty-one. But, least lucky of all in marriage, the tenth earl achieved only one day of marital bliss.

Unperturbed by society gossip, John and the beautiful Sarah had remained inseparable yet powerless to cement their union. While their families condoned their affair as long as it remained covert, any move to make the relationship public or legal was immediately frowned upon. So the devoted pair continued to live in perfect harmony out of wedlock. When Sarah began to exhibit the tell-tale signs of tuberculosis, John spared no expense in bringing the best doctors to Gibside. Sadly, nothing the Georgian medical fraternity had to offer could help Sarah and she died in October 1800, aged thirty-seven, with her lover at her side. Having lost his mother and his lover within six months, the distraught earl arranged Sarah's long hair, painted her face, dressed her in lace and adorned her with jewels then accompanied her body for burial in Westminster Abbey.[36]

It would be nine more years before Lord Strathmore could face another entanglement. Confounding social conventions once again, he fell for Mary Milner, a 22-year-old maid who worked at his Yorkshire hunting lodge, Wemmergill Hall.[37] Living together at Streatlam Castle, the earl treated Mary as his wife and when she gave birth to their son, baptised John Bowes, in 1811, he instantly acknowledged him as his heir. With his health precarious, the earl married Mary on 2 July 1820 in a last-minute effort to legitimise their son. The following day Lord Strathmore died. Yet although John Bowes duly inherited Gibside and Streatlam, by virtue of his father's will, his claim to the Strathmore title and Scottish estate was immediately challenged by his father's younger brother, Thomas. Backed by the redoubtable James Farrer, John's claim was based on the principle in Scottish law that his parents' marriage legitimised him retrospectively. Yet Uncle Thomas, as sharp as his namesake, successfully argued in the House of Lords the following year that since the tenth earl had not lived in Scotland his son must abide by the English principle that, despite his parents' marriage, he remained illegitimate. So Thomas, Mary Eleanor's third son, became the eleventh Earl of Strathmore, the great-great-grandfather of Elizabeth Bowes Lyon, the late Queen Mother.[38]

It was John Bowes, however, who maintained the Bowes family estate and upheld the family traditions, ultimately creating a remarkable legacy, the Bowes Museum at Barnard Castle, to house his fine art collection along with Mary's botanical cabinet. It was also John Bowes who continued Mary's literary connections. In the summer of 1841 he invited a friend, the young writer William Makepeace Thackeray, to stay at Streatlam Castle.[39] Hearing the story of John's grandmother, imprisoned in the castle by her husband more than fifty years earlier, Thackeray was entranced. Here was the perfect subject for a book. Soon afterwards Thackeray began writing his first significant work of fiction, *The Luck of Barry Lyndon*, which spun the tale of a wily, brutish and philandering Irish soldier who was ultimately outwitted by the titled heiress he had duped into wedlock. An outlandishly fantastical story, only the truth could be more astonishing.

Acknowledgements

It is only through the unstinting help and generous advice of numerous people and institutions that this book has been possible. Firstly, for his kind permission in allowing me access to the Strathmore archives at both Glamis Castle and Durham County Record Office, I would like to thank the eighteenth Earl of Strathmore and Kinghorne. For permission to view Mary Eleanor Bowes's album, portrait and other materials at St Paul's Walden Bury, and for their hospitality during my visits, my thanks are due to Simon and Caroline Bowes Lyon. I would like to thank His Grace the Duke of Norfolk for permission to use the Arundel Castle archives. My thanks are due to the Bowes Museum for permission to view archives and other materials there, and to William Baker Baker and Durham University Library for permission to access the Baker Baker archive at that library. I wish to acknowledge the permission of Her Majesty Queen Elizabeth II to quote from material in the Royal Archives.

Many archivists, curators, librarians and other staff have been crucial to my research. In particular I wish to thank Jane Anderson, archivist at Glamis Castle, for her diligent and efficient help on my repeated trips to view the Strathmore archives. My thanks are due also to Lady Mary, Dowager Countess of Strathmore, for her interest in my research and to Hamish Howe, guide at Glamis, for his advice. For their unerring hospitality and help, I wish to thank all the staff at Dundee University Archives Department, who provided facilities for me to view the Strathmore archives and always made me welcome during my many visits, keeping me fuelled with biscuits and enthusiasm. I especially wish to thank Dr Mary Young, archivist for the Glamis Project at Dundee University, who has proved my invaluable guide and delightful friend throughout my research, making my trips north an inspiration and a pleasure. In Durham, I wish to thank all the staff of Durham County Record Office and Durham University Library. At the Bowes Museum, I am indebted to the help and advice of curator Howard Coutts and Claire Jones, former keeper of furniture, during my several enjoyable visits. Peter Donnelly, curator of the King's Own Royal Regiment Museum, Lancaster, provided much appreciated advice on army life. Anne Wheeldon, archivist at Hammersmith and Fulham Archives and Local History Centre, kindly advised me on Craven Cottage. In addition I would like to thank everybody who has helped me at the British Library, National Archives, Royal Society, Wellcome Library for the History of Medicine, Linnean Society, Kew Gardens Library, Westminster Cathedral Library, Royal Pharmaceutical Society, Royal Society of Arts, Fitzwilliam Museum, Arundel Castle archives, London Metropolitan Archives, City of Westminster Archives Centre, Guildhall Library, Kensington Library, Hammersmith and Fulham Archives and Local History Centre, and the Huntington Library, California. My thanks are also due to everyone involved with the National Trust at Gibside, especially former property manager Tony Walton and advisers Hugh Dixon and Chris Gallagher.

I have been hugely privileged to benefit from advice in

specialist areas from a large number of individual experts. I would particularly like to thank Elizabeth Foyster for sharing her expertise on the history of domestic violence, Michael Bundock for his advice on eighteenth-century law, Caroline Chapman for her insights on John Bowes and her hospitality in Yorkshire, John Brown for his expertise on eighteenth-century economics, Margaret Wills for her advice on Gibside, Alexander Huber for his advice on Thomas Gray, Dr Donald Stevens for information on Priory Church in Christchurch, and Gina Douglas for her botanical help. For sharing their knowledge of Cole Pike Hill and kindness during my visit I am grateful to Alan and Marjorie Hopps, Paul Shepherd and Stuart Wright. For advice on South African geography and culture, my thanks are due to Catherine Goodwin, and for their generous help in checking my Cape botanical references, I am extremely grateful to Peter Goldblatt and Dr John Manning. For help in French translation my thanks are due to Rachel Hall. For his much-appreciated help in technological emergencies, my grateful thanks to Mike Cudmore. And for pointing me towards Mary Eleanor Bowes in the first place, heartfelt thanks to Simon Chaplin, curator of the Hunterian Museum.

As always, I have been extremely lucky to work with some of the best people in publishing. First and foremost, I wish to thank my unbeatable agent Patrick Walsh for encouraging and guiding me throughout the journey of this book. I am grateful to all the staff at Weidenfeld & Nicolson who have welcomed me into their fold as one of the family and especially to my editor Kirsty Dunseath for her expert and sensitive oversight from start to finish. My thanks go also to copy-editor Marian Reid.

Finally, I want to record my enormous gratitude to all my family and friends who are a constant source of support, keeping me generally on the right track and sometimes providing much appreciated diversions. I am only sorry I cannot name everyone individually. And, as ever, I want to thank Peter, my partner, first reader and – despite the subject of my book – now my husband, for his skilful judgement and unwavering faith in me and my work.

WEDLOCK

Reading Group Notes

How did you come to write Wedlock?

Wedlock is my second book and also my second relating the life of an eighteenth-century personality. After writing my first book, *The Knife Man*, about the eighteenth-century surgeon John Hunter, I was scouting around for another idea. I was still drawn to the colourful world of medical history and spent many weeks pottering around dusty medical archives when suddenly Mary Eleanor Bowes burst into my life.

I had had a brief encounter with Mary Eleanor Bowes, the Countess of Strathmore, when writing my first book. She was a friend of John Hunter and donated to him the skin of a giraffe that had been brought back from an expedition she had sponsored to southern Africa. I knew no more about her until the curator of the Hunterian Museum in London, where John Hunter's human and animal body parts are exhibited, mentioned that the countess had a fascinating story of her own. Not expecting much, I ordered a few books – accounts of the divorce case and the kidnap trials published at the time – when I next visited the British Library. I could scarcely believe what I read. The shocking story of an accomplished heiress who was tricked into marrying an Irish scoundrel by a fake duel, her wretched married life, her audacious escape and landmark legal battles and – most staggering of all – her abduction by her estranged husband from a busy London street, seemed like the stuff of fiction. I was hooked. Immediately I dropped the other ideas I had been exploring and began a detective trail exploring Mary Eleanor Bowes's life and times.

For the next two years, I devoted myself to researching and writing Mary Eleanor's story, visiting her childhood home of Gibside in north-east England – where her house is still in ruins and the romantic Glamis Castle belonging to her first husband in Scotland – where the late Queen Mother was brought up – as well as trawling through countless boxes of letters, diaries, bills and even school books in various archives. It has been an enthralling journey.

What made you want to write a book about the Countess of Strathmore?

Above all, it was the action-packed story which initially inspired me to write about Mary Eleanor. I'm a journalist by training and I know a good yarn when I hear one. But as I got deeper into my research, I became fascinated by

the themes which the story illuminated – how our ideas about marriage have changed, why divorce has risen from the eighteenth century onwards, arguments about child custody and women's rights – all issues which are just as topical today. I find the eighteenth century compelling for this contradiction: so many of the customs, fashions and characters seem bizarre and eccentric to us today and yet so many of the concerns – celebrity, relationships, media obsession – are exactly the same.

What original sources did you use in the research?

I was extremely lucky to find a rich treasure trove of material in archives, particularly at Glamis Castle. I made seven trips to Scotland, where I ploughed through dozens of boxes of neatly tied bundles of letters, accounts and legal documents which had to be transported for me from Glamis Castle (where they are kept in a cold and inhospitable turret) to Dundee University. Reading Mary's letters and the replies to her from her lawyers, her family, her tenants and her friends helped me piece together the jigsaw puzzle of her marriage and divorce. In earlier biographies – all by male authors – she had been depicted as vain, selfish and gullible, and it was reading the descriptions of her ordeal in her own words that brought to life the intelligent, compassionate and much-wronged woman to whom I felt a strong connection. Some of the items – particularly the little bills for shoes, clothes and medical treatment for the five Strathmore children – were very poignant. Often it is a small specific detail – like the bill which mentioned lettuce for the young 10th earl's tortoise – that can bring out the human element in a story.

Were there any problems in writing the book?

One of the difficulties was trying to understand what attracted people – women and men – to Andrew Robinson Stoney when obviously he was such a villain. How could they be so easily fooled? It helped to read the desperate letters of Anne Massingberd, whom he seduced between his two marriages, which plainly revealed that women were totally besotted with him. Evidently, he possessed some strong magnetism that women found hard to resist. It was also challenging to unravel the complexities of the eighteenth-century legal world and understand the botany of southern Africa but I was lucky to find experts in both fields who helped me.

Were you surprised to discover the limits on women's freedom and rights?

My last book centred very much on the men's world of eighteenth-century medicine and science. Researching *Wedlock* brought home to me that the eighteenth century in general was indeed a man's world. I hadn't realised the extent to which girls and women were effectively ruled by their fathers and then their husbands. Not only were women's lives generally governed by men, they really had no legal status at all so that their property, their income and even their children all belonged to men. The stories of babies and young children being taken from their mothers and handed over to their fathers when couples divorced – often never seeing their mothers again – were harrowing to read, especially as a mother myself. What was perhaps more surprising, though, was how many women spoke out against their lack of rights and how many became celebrated, respected and powerful figures, despite the legal and society restraints. I have huge admiration for women like Mary Wollstonecraft, Lady Mary Wortley Montagu and Mary Eleanor Bowes, who refused to accept the status quo and stood up for their principles.

What was life like for an intelligent, highly educated, wealthy woman in mid-eighteenth-century Britain?

Highly frustrating, I imagine. The few women like Mary Eleanor, who were sufficiently privileged to enjoy a full and rounded education, could hold their own in salon conversations about science and the arts. But they were barred from any serious involvement in either the scientific or arts worlds, unable to join organisations like the all-male Royal Society and disparaged if they tried to compete on equal terms in writing poetry or books. Several women, like Hannah More, Elizabeth Carter and Mary Wortley Montagu, did earn respected reputations for their learning but they were also viewed as oddities and unfeminine. As the Bishop of London said: 'Nothing, I think, is more disagreeable than learning in a female.' Having said that, Mary Eleanor would probably have been relatively happy had she been allowed the freedom at least to pursue her passion for botany and her love of writing; both were stifled by her successive husbands.

Questions for readers

1. Mary Eleanor Bowes was brought up by her father to be a self-confident, ambitious and clever girl. Thanks to him she enjoyed an education only normally provided for the sons of aristocratic families and through his wealth she enjoyed a pampered, privileged youth.

Was this upbringing and education her downfall? Did it make her a poor judge of character, naively assuming that those who pandered to her needs had genuine affection for her? Or was it her final strength which gave her the self-belief to escape and fight back against her bullying second husband?

2. Mary Eleanor married her first husband, the 9th Earl, with romantic expectations of a loving, harmonious marriage. She was just 16 when they became engaged and had led a largely closeted life. Steeped in romantic fiction, she was captivated, she said, by his 'beauty' and a 'vision' in which he appeared to her (p. 55). He was older, sexually experienced and worldly-wise, having enjoyed a tempestuous affair with an Italian contessa (p. 93–4).

Was their marriage doomed from the start? Whose fault was it that the marriage failed and Mary ultimately sought affection in an affair? Did you feel any sympathy towards the earl? What role did the earl's brother, Thomas Lyon, play in the relationship and was the two brothers' closeness perhaps a factor in the failure of Mary and the earl's marriage?

3. Mary Eleanor herself confessed she was not fond of her three sons, although later in life she tried to patch up her relationship with them.

Was her initial distance from them an inevitable result of customs in eighteenth-century wealthy families? The children were wet-nursed, looked after by nursemaids and governesses, then sent away to boarding school. Was it perhaps a flaw in Mary's personality or a result of her own pampered upbringing?

4. Andrew Robinson Stoney, later Bowes, was undoubtedly one of history's worst husbands and biggest scoundrels: a liar, a cheat, a womaniser, a bully and a fraud. He seemingly had a relatively normal upbringing for the period in a generally happy family with fairly liberal parents. His own father called him 'the most

wretched man I ever knew' (p. 306), yet the poignant letters from Anne Massingberd (p. 140–41 and p. 183–4) reveal his obvious attrac tion to women.

What could possibly have caused his extraordinary personality traits? How would someone like him operate today? Would he perhaps have been diagnosed with a psychotic personality disorder? And why was he so successful in seducing women? Are men like him still attractive to women today?

5. Mary Eleanor Bowes was vilified during the divorce cases as an outrageous libertine, an ungrateful wife and a hard-hearted mother. In biographies since her death she has been portrayed as a silly, vain and naive female who, to a greater or less extent, received her just desserts in her miserable second marriage.

Is there any justification in these descriptions or are these just male interpretations of a woman who sought a liberated lifestyle? Did she bring her misfortunes on herself? How would a woman today who followed a similar lifestyle be treated?

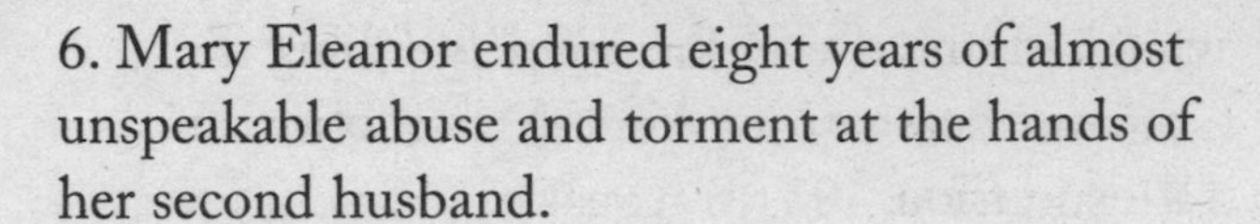

6. Mary Eleanor endured eight years of almost unspeakable abuse and torment at the hands of her second husband.

Why did she not confide in anyone for most of this time? Why did she wait so long before leaving him? Was this mainly a result of her reluctance to leave her children, her fear of society's condemnation and the financial deprivations she knew she would incur or was there any element of hoping her husband would change? When writing her 'Confessions', she seemed hopeful she could convince him of her devotion while mindful of her duty to 'obey him' (p. 194). Was she still partly in love with him or was she terrified he would come after her? Why do some women today continue to live with abusive husbands?

7. Most marriages among wealthy and landed families in the first half of the eighteenth century were arranged by parents as advantageous financial matches. Some were forced on young people. Gradually over the century, views changed so that the idea of marrying for love and the ideal of a harmonious companionate marriage – our modern Western idea – became the norm. Some commentators blamed this

change on the rise of the novel pedalling romantic ideas of love and the promotion of self-expression.

Can novels have such a profound impact on society? Did the ideal of a blissfully happy marriage – the novel's perfect ending – set up unrealistic expectations in couples? Was this the reason for rising divorce rates from the eighteenth century onwards and is it necessarily a bad thing?

8. During the eighteenth century, reading and writing books and other forms of literature became an important vehicle for enabling women to express their views. Women met in literary salons like the famous 'blue-stocking club' – prototypes for today's reader groups – and some women enjoyed success in writing poetry and especially novels.

So how do books play a role, then and now, in empowering women? Can literary gatherings or reader groups help in emancipating – or subverting – women?

Notes

ABBREVIATIONS

ARB Andrew Robinson Bowes
ARS Andrew Robinson Stoney
BBP Baker Baker Papers
BL British Library
BM Bowes Museum
CWAC City of Westminster Archives Centre
DCRO Durham County Record Office
DCRO SEA Durham County Record Office, Strathmore Estate Archives
DUL Durham University Library
GL Guildhall Library
HL Huntington Library, San Marino, California
HMC Historical Manuscripts Commission
LMA London Metropolitan Archives
MEB Mary Eleanor Bowes
NA National Archives
NT National Trust
ODNB Oxford Dictionary of National Biography
RA Royal Archives
RS Royal Society
SPG Strathmore Papers, Glamis
SPWB St Paul's Walden Bury

MONEY

Making comparisons between the purchasing power of money in the eighteenth century and today is far from straightforward. However, since money is obviously a significant factor in this story, some comparisons are clearly helpful. Where I have given comparative figures these have been made using the Bank of England inflation calculator: *www.bankofengland.co.uk/education/inflation/calculator/index1.htm*

All dates are given according to the new calendar. All descriptions of weather are from the meteorological reports published monthly in the *Gentleman's Magazine* or other contemporary accounts.

CHAPTER 1: AN AFFAIR OF HONOUR

Information on the Adelphi Tavern is from Allan, *passim*; London County Council, vol. 18, pp. 99–100. Originally 18 Adam Street, the Adelphi Tavern adjoined the new headquarters of the Society for the Encouragement of Arts, Manufactures and Commerce, now the Royal Society of Arts. In 1957, the RSA absorbed the tavern building. The original first-floor dining room and ground-floor coffee room can still be viewed. Background information on duelling is from Millingen; Melville and Hargreaves; anon, *The British Code of Duel* (1824); Baldick; and Landale.

1 Details describing the duel and quotes about it are from the statements by J. Hull, John Scott, Caesar Hawkins and Jessé Foot in *The Gazetteer and New Daily Advertiser*, 24 January 1777, and from anon, *A full and accurate report of the trial*, p. 9 unless otherwise specified. Hull's first name is given as John, and his post as clerk, in *The Royal Kalendar*, 1776, p. 121.

2 Boswell, p. 484.

3 Sir Henry Bate Dudley (he adopted the name Dudley from an uncle who left him a large legacy in 1780 and was made a baronet by George IV when Prince of Wales in 1812) was editor of the *Morning Post* from 1775 to 1780. The *Morning Post* merged with the *Daily Telegraph* in 1937. Fyvie, pp. 79–104; Hindle; Aspinall; Barker; all *passim*.

4 Walpole to Lady Ossory, 13 November 1776, in Lewis, W. S., vol. 32, pp. 331–2.

5 Boswell, p. 1,295.

6 Foot, p. 5.

7 A report of the duel and events leading up to it, agreed between Bate and Stoney, was published in the *London Chronicle*, 18–21 January 1777. Details were given in shorter form in the *Morning Chronicle*, 15 January 1777, as well as in other newspapers. The subsequent details describing the duel and its causes are taken from the *London Chronicle* report.

8 *Morning Post*, 10 December, 23 December and 24 December 1776, and 11 January 1777.

9 Foot, p. 45.
10 Donellan would elope with and marry the young heiress Theodosia Boughton later in 1777. In 1780 he was accused of poisoning her twenty-year-old brother, Sir Theodosius, whose fortune went to his sister if he died before the age of twenty-one. An inquest pointed to Donellan's guilt, despite objections on scientific grounds by the surgeon John Hunter, and Donellan was hanged for murder in March 1781. Moore, pp. 288–291; ODNB, vol. 16, pp. 521–2.
11 Information on Wogdon is from Atkinson, pp. 33–48.
12 Foot, pp. 27–8; anon, *A full and accurate report of the trial*, p. 5.
13 Testimony of MEB in copy of evidence for House of Lords appeal 1796: SPG, volume C.
14 Foot, p. 28.
15 *Annual Register*, 1760, vol. 3, p. 131.
16 Foot, p. 13.
17 Testimony of MEB ... 1796: SPG, volume C.
18 Fyvie, pp. 118–119.
19 Parish register, St James's Church, Piccadilly, 17 January 1777, CWAC. Stoney had obtained a licence to marry at short notice from the Bishop of London: Bishop of London's marriage allegations, GL MSS 10091/138.

CHAPTER 2: DOWNRIGHT GIRLISHNESS

Information in this chapter on the ancestry of the Bowes family is from Wills, and Durham County Council, *passim*. Biographical details on George Bowes can be found in Wills, and ODNB, vol. 6, pp. 931–4. Background on the history of the north-east England coal industry is from Flinn and Stoker; and Atkinson, both *passim*. For information on the Gibside estate, now NT, see Wills and Garnett, and Wills, both *passim*. My thanks to Tony Walton, former NT property manager of Gibside, for kind help and advice during my visit 23 October 2006. The contents of Gibside Hall at the time are from two sources: Inventory of the household goods, etc, at Gibside, 29 Oct 1761: SPG, box 185, bundle 5; and an inventory of the contents of Gibside, listing furniture, linen, plate, china, art and books bequeathed by George Bowes to MEB produced in 1779 in answer to a case in Chancery begun in 1777 by Thomas Lyon on behalf of MEB's five children by Lord Strathmore: NA Chancery Records, C12/1057/31 (schedule). A list of paintings purchased by George Bowes is preserved as DCRO SEA D/St/E5/2/18.

1 William Blakiston Bowes to Lady Elizabeth Bowes, 20 March 1718: BL Add. MSS 40747 ff. 164–5.
2 MEB describes her father and her childhood in Bowes, p. 49.
3 Miss Verney's poems: SPG, vol. 338.
4 Letters regarding the marriage of George Bowes and Eleanor Verney: SPG, Bowes-Lyon Letter Books, vol. 39, ff. 71–153
5 Marriage settlement of George Bowes and Eleanor Verney, 29 and 30 September 1724: DCRO SEA D/St/D13/5/22.
6 Halsband (1956), p. 123; Perry, p. 504.
7 Chester, vol. 9, p. 312; Sykes, vol. 1, p. 141.
8 George Bowes to Henry Vane, 9 March 1743, cited in Durham County Council, p. 7.
9 Marriage settlement of George Bowes and Mary Gilbert, 10 June 1743: DCRO SEA D/St/D13/5/32. Mary Gilbert's date of birth is unknown but her age is given as sixty when she died in January 1781 on the inscription in the mausoleum at Gibside, suggesting that she was born in 1720 or 1721.
10 'March 28 Mary Eleanor Daughter of George Esqr. and Mary Bows [sic], Born Feb 24th': Parish register St George's Church, Hanover Square, baptisms 1749, CWAC.
11 Mrs Bowes's Cash Books, 16 March 1749: DCRO SEA D/St/E15/5/98. The household accounts date from 1744 to 1760; all details of family purchases are from this source.
12 Captain William FitzThomas to George Bowes, 3 March 1749, and Fra. [Francis] Oneal [sic] to George Bowes, 4 June 1749: BL Add. MSS 40748 ff. 103–4 and 105.
13 Hester Chapone, cited in Hill, Bridget, p. 74.
14 Will of George Bowes, 7 February 1749 [old style, ie 1750], proved 12 December 1761, Borthwick Institute of Historical Research, York University.
15 Mrs Bowes's Cash Books, 29 August 1750 and 22 May 1751: DCRO SEA D/St/E15/5/98. Cash book of Gibside receipts and expenditure, 1748–54, 11 August 1750: DCRO SEA D/St/E5/5/7.
16 Brand, vol. 1, pp. 434–5.
17 Lancelot [Capability] Brown to George Bowes, 22 October 1750: DCRO SEA D/St/C/3/11. More information on the column can be found in Wills, pp. 43–7, and Hudson, pp. 2,460–1. Estate accounts list various stages of the work in Cash book of Gibside receipts and expenditure, 1748–1754: DCRO SEA D/St/E5/5/7.

18 Climenson, vol. 2, pp. 36–7.
19 Angerstein, pp. 273–4.
20 George Bowes's memo books 1754–6: SPG, box 186, bundle 3.
21 George (1976), p. 399. Figures quoted from the London Bills of Mortality show that 63 per cent of babies born in London between 1750 and 1769 died before the age of five.
22 Foot, p. 14.
23 Bowes, pp. 49–50. Subsequent quotes are from the same pages.
24 Thomas Sherlock, Bishop of London, to Elizabeth Montagu, 1 September 1760, in Climenson, vol. 2, p. 198; Myers, p. 246.
25 Lady Mary Wortley Montagu to Lady Bute, 28 January 1753, in Halsband (1965), vol. 3, pp. 20–4.
26 Hill, Bridget, p. 44.
27 de Salignac, pp. 2, 3 and 14.
28 SPG, box 243.
29 Mrs Bowes's Cash Books: DCRO SEA D/St/E15/5/100. Andreas Planta was paid his 'entrance money' on 29 January 1757; a pair of stays was bought on the servants' account for his daughter Elizabeth Planta on 10 March 1757.
30 Gibside Cash Book 1758–60, quarrying for the chapel, 5 January 1760, digging the foundations, 19 July 1760: DCRO SEA D/St/E5/5/9. The chapel and Gibside estate are described in Paine.
31 Sykes, vol. 1, p. 229.
32 *Annual Register*, 1760, vol. 3, p. 131, *London Magazine*, 1760, vol. 29, p. 556, and Sykes, vol. 1, p. 229, all put MEB's inheritance at £600,000. Barlow, vol. 2, p. 464, puts her inheritance at £1,040,000. Other, later, sources also value her inheritance at £1,040,000, for example, Vincent, p. 702 and anon, *The Monthly Chronicle*, vol. 1, p. 196.
33 Will of George Bowes, York University.
34 Bowes, p. 52. Parish rates books, St James's Church, Piccadilly, CWAC. Mrs Bowes paid rates at no. 40 from 1763 to 1767.
35 Clark, vol. 3, p. 61.
36 Bowes, p. 53.
37 MEB to Elizabeth Montagu, Saturday 29 March [1760]: HL MO 623.
38 Blunt, vol. 1, p. 65–6.
39 Lord Lyttelton to Elizabeth Montagu, 11 October 1760 in Climenson, vol. 2, p. 203.
40 Grosley, vol. 1, pp. 22, 34, 35 and 44–5.

41 Ilchester and Stavordale, vol. 1, p. 188.
42 Bowes, p. 54.
43 For information on the history of marriage (and divorce) see Stone (1977) and (1995); and Habakkuk.
44 London County Council, vol. 39, p. 3.
45 Sir William Temple in *Popular Discontents*, 1680, cited in Habakkuk, p. 144.
46 Savile, p. 25.
47 Astell, p. 12.
48 Lady Mary Wortley Montagu to Philippa Mundy, April 1712, in Halsband (1965), vol. 1, p. 122.
49 George (1976), p. 305.
50 Foreman, p. 74.
51 Papendiek, vol. 1, p. 9; Sarah Scott to Elizabeth Montagu, March 1762, in Doran, p. 110; Papendiek, vol. 1, p. 75.
52 Bowes, pp. 54–5.
53 Ilchester, vol. 1, pp. 202–3.
54 ODNB, vol. 20, pp. 609–22.
55 Blunt, vol. 1, pp. 65–6.
56 John Stuart, First Marquess of Bute (1744–1814), ODNB, vol. 53, pp. 182–3; Ilchester, vol. 1, p. 180.
57 Bowes, p. 65.
58 Walpole to Horace Mann, 13 November 1766, in Lewis, vol. 22, p. 465.
59 Hare, vol. 2, p. 172. Hare was the great-grandson of Lady Anne Simpson, sister to the ninth earl.
60 Osborn, pp. 132–3; Toynbee and Whibley, vol. 3, p. 925.
61 Colman and Garrick, p. 42.
62 Account of Miss Bowes's wedding clothes on her marriage with the Earl of Strathmore: BM Archives. Marriage settlement on intended marriage of Mary Eleanor Bowes and John, Earl of Strathmore, 6 and 7 October 1766: DCRO SEA D/St/D13/5/43. Parish register, marriages, St George's Church, Hanover Square, 1760–8, 24 February 1767, CWAC.

CHAPTER 3: A WORTHY LITTLE WOMAN

The main source for the Stoney family's history is Stoney, *The Annals*, which is based on private family papers, including the family bible which bears the date of ARS's birth, and also transcribes the diaries of

George Stoney (ARS's father) for 1765 and 1781. Information on family life is taken from these diaries and letters unless otherwise stated.

1 Sykes, vol. 1, p. 191.

2 Extract of William Newton's will: DCRO D/X540/1; Newton v Stoney, Chancery bill 14 April 1773: NA Chancery Records C12/1626/23.

3 Baptism 11 November 1747 of 'Hannah daur. of Wm Newton Burnopfield', baptism register, St Margaret's Church, Tanfield, DCRO.

4 Foot, p. 7, citing a letter from 'a mother in Bath to her daughter in London'.

5 Army Commission Book 1763–7, NA WO 25/30. Stoney enlisted on 28 November 1764.

6 ODNB, vol. 2, pp. 427–8.

7 John Scott to George Stoney, 13 February 1746, in Stoney, p. 9.

8 Thomas Johnston to Lieutenant Robert Johnston, 20 April 1765, in Stoney, p. 16.

9 Thomas Johnston to Lieutenant Robert Johnston, 20 April 1765, in Stoney, p. 16. Details of the movements of the King's Own Regiment and other background information are from Cowper, vol. 1, pp. 190–225.

10 Colonel Andrew Robinson to George Stoney, 17 September 1765, in Stoney, p. 17.

11 Lieutenant Colonel George Maddison to Colonel Robert Brudenell, June 1766, in Stoney, p. 17.

12 General Bigoe Armstrong to George Stoney, 12 July 1766, in Stoney, pp. 17–18.

13 Elizabeth Montagu to Sarah Scott, n.d. [1758], in Climenson, vol. 2, p. 138. Sophia Curzon (née Noel) to Mary Noel, 28 September 1779, in Elwin, p. 145. General information on eighteenth-century Newcastle can be found in Brand; Ellis; and Middlebrook, all *passim.*

14 *Newcastle Chronicle* and *Newcastle Journal*, 1767–8, *passim.*

15 Elizabeth Montagu to Lord Lyttelton, n.d. [October] 1760, in Climenson, vol. 2, pp. 205, 207–8.

16 Stoney, p. 19.

17 Foot, pp. 5–6.

18 Extract of William Newton's will: DCRO D/X540/1.

19 ARS to George Stoney, 23 April 1768, in Stoney, p. 19.

20 Anon, *The Irish Register.* The phenomenon is discussed in Habakkuk, pp. 203–4.

21 The letters, all reproduced in *The Annals*, are ARS to George Stoney,

23 April 1768, 19 June 1768, 2 August 1768 and 10 September 1768, in Stoney, p. 19–22.

22 *Newcastle Chronicle*, 12 November 1768; *Newcastle Journal*, 5–12 November 1768; *Newcastle Courant*, 12 November 1768.

23 ARS to George Stoney, 7 November 1768, in Stoney, p. 19. The letter is dated 7 November – perhaps the date it was posted – although it was written on his wedding day, which was 5 November.

24 Dating from at least the fourteenth century, the house and estate of Cole Pike Hill were acquired by the Newton family in the early eighteenth century. The original hall was extended in 1854 and the house is now divided into three homes.

25 The horse-whipping incident must have happened in 1769 since this is when the regiment was stationed in Perth. 'Answers for Mr Stoney Esq, Ensign in the 4th regiment of foot, to a complaint preferred agt. him by John Smith his servant', n.d., SPG, Bowes Papers, vol. 41. Stoney was promoted to lieutenant on 22 December 1769 (private communication, Peter Donnelly, curator of the King's Own Royal Regiment Museum, Lancaster). He exchanged places with a Lieutenant Rooke in the 30th Regiment at some point after April 1770. S. Hodgson to ARS, 9 April 1770: SPG, Bowes Papers, vol. 41.

26 Letters addressed to Stoney in Ireland, George Forbes, 27 October 1769 and S. Hodgson, 9 April 1770: DCRO SEA D/St/C1/13/1; SPG, Bowes Papers, vol. 41.

27 Accounts of Rowland Stephenson's receipts and expenditure for Cole Pike Hill and Twizedale estates, 1767–9: DCRO SEA D/St/E8/18.

28 Robert Morrow to ARS, 17 March 1772: SPG, Bowes Papers, vol. 41. Morrow succeeded Stephenson when he died in 1770.

29 Eight letters to ARS asking for payment of bills 1769 to 1775: DCRO SEA D/St/C1/13/1.

30 SPG, vol. 33, p. 128.

31 Foot, pp. 6–8.

32 Foreman, p. 97.

33 Robert Johnston to ARS, 19 August 1771: SPG, Bowes Papers, vol. 41.

34 Will of Hannah Stoney: DUL, 1776/523/1.

35 Newton v Stoney, 14 April 1773: NA Chancery records C12/1626/23. No outcome is recorded. The trees were advertised for sale in the *Newcastle Chronicle*, 13, 20 and 27 March 1773.

36 ARS to George Stoney, 21 June 1775, in Stoney, pp. 28–9.

37 Bill for ARS, 20 July 1775: DCRO SEA D/St/C1/13/1.
38 *Newcastle Journal*, 16 March 1776. The burial register reads: '14 Mar 1776 Hannah wife of Andrew Robinson Stoney Esq., Coltpighill', burial register, St Margaret's Church, Tanfield, DCRO.

CHAPTER 4: MY IMPRUDENCIES

Mary's first marriage and various flirtations are described in her *Confessions*. For background information on the study of botany in the eighteenth century see Shteir; Desmond (1995); Lemmon, all *passim*.
1 *Newcastle Chronicle*, 4 April 1767.
2 Young, vol. 4, p. 584.
3 MEB said she had been ill before leaving Hertfordshire. The poet Thomas Gray had written that MEB was 'with child, and not very well, as I hear' in June. Bowes, p. 66; Gray to Brown, 2 June 1767, in Toynbee and Whibley, vol. 3, p. 961.
4 Bowes, p. 65–6.
5 Bowes, p. 8.
6 *Annual Register*, 1767, p. 81. The bill was given royal assent on 3 April.
7 Lord Chesterfield to the Duke of Newcastle, 20 June 1766, in Dobrée, vol. 6, p. 2,744.
8 Details on the Strathmore family history are from Cokayne, vol. 12, pp. 395–403; Surtees, Robert, vol. 4, p. 109; Slade, *passim*; Innes-Smith, *passim*.
9 Minutes of curators 1753–61: SPG, box 102.
10 Venn, vol. 1, p. 342; James was admitted in February 1756 and Thomas in 1758. Lord Strathmore's bills for his time at Cambridge are in SPG, box 144, bundle 4.
11 William Mason to Thomas Gray, 1 March 1755 and Gray to Thomas Wharton, 9 March 1755, Toynbee and Whibley, vol. 1, pp. 419 and 421.
12 The official history of Pembroke College argues that Tuthill was sacked for absenteeism, when the record plainly shows that he was absent having been suspected or found guilty of 'great enormities'. The latest biography of Gray takes the view that the poet was probably homosexual and that Tuthill was probably sacked for homosexual acts. Attwater, p. 97; Mack, pp. 33–5, 490–1. My thanks to Alexander Huber, editor of the Thomas Gray Archive www.thomasgray.org at the University of Oxford for advice.
13 Gray to Wharton, 17 February 1757, Toynbee and Whibley, vol. 2, p. 495.

14 Gray to Wharton, 23 January 1760, Toynbee and Whibley, vol. 2, p. 660.

15 Lord Strathmore to the Dowager Countess, 2 February 1760: SPG, box 144, bundle 4; Lord Strathmore to George Bowes, 27 January 1760: SPG, box 187, bundle 3.

16 Thomas Pitt and Lord Strathmore, 'Observations in a Tour to Portugal & Spain 1760 by John Earl of Strathmore & Tho. Pitt Esqr.': BL Add. MSS 5845. Although the two authors are named, it is clear from the journal that Pitt was the writer.

17 Lord Strathmore to Thomas Lyon, n.d. [March 1760]: SPG, box 254, bundle 4.

18 SPG, box 145, bundle 1. Lord Strathmore's time in Italy is also detailed in Ingamells, p. 907. For general information on the grand tour to Italy see Black (1992).

19 Lord Strathmore to William Henry, Marquess of Titchfield, 10 February 1761, in Turberville, vol. 2, p. 37.

20 Mann to Walpole, 15 August 1761, in Lewis, vol. 21, p. 524. The later comments are HM to HW, 10 April 1762, vol. 22, pp. 22–3 and 28 May 1763, p. 145. Details of the Sanvitale family can be found in Litta.

21 Walpole to Mann, 30 June 1763, in Lewis, vol. 21, p. 152. By 'Celadonian' Walpole was referring to the character Céladon in the play 'L'Astrée' by the seventeenth-century French novelist Honoré D'Urfe, which was fashionable at the time.

22 Foot, p. 13.

23 Lord Strathmore to Thomas Lyon, 6 June 1766: SPG, box 199, bundle 2.

24 Foot, p. 27; Lord Chesterfield to his son, 13 February 1767, in Dobrée, vol. 6, pp. 2,795–6.

25 SPG, box 150, bundle 7.

26 Lord Chesterfield to his son, 13 February 1767, in Dobrée, vol. 6, pp. 2,795–6.

27 Draft marriage settlement MEB and Lord Strathmore, September 1766: SPG, box 102, bundle 2.

28 Blackstone, vol. 1, p. 430; vol. 2, p. 433. It would be 1870 before married women were allowed separate use of their earnings and 1882 before they were entitled to acquire, keep and sell property in their own right. The novelists' quotes given below are from Wollstonecraft, p. 118 and Dickens (2004, first published 1838), p. 402.

29 Gray to Wharton, c. 30 September 1765, Toynbee and Whibley, vol. 2, pp. 887–95.
30 Thomas Lyttelton to Elizabeth Montagu, in Climenson, vol. 2, p. 168.
31 Bowes, p. 67. Thomas Lyon was MP for Aberdeen Burghs from 1766 to 1778. Details of his parliamentary career can be found in Namier and Brooke, vol. 3, pp. 73–4.
32 Accounts for masonry, carpentry and painting 1767–8: SPG, box 150, bundle 7; improvements by James Abercrombie 1767–8: SPG, box 148, bundle 4.
33 Lord Strathmore's medical bill with Dr William Farqeson, 1772–4: SPG, box 145, bundle 4.
34 Gray to Mason, 9 August 1767, and 11 September 1767, in Toynbee and Whibley, vol. 3, p. 973 and pp. 976–7.
35 Mary Bowes to Thomas Colpitts, 21 April 1768: SPG vol. C; Parish register St George's Church, Hanover Square, baptisms, CWAC, 19 May 1768, 'Maria Jane, born 21 April'. Bells were rung at Gibside a week after the birth, suggesting the news had just arrived from London.
36 Mary Bowes to Thomas Colpitts, 13 May 1768: SPG, volume C; Parish register St George's Church, Hanover Square, CWAC, baptisms, 11 May 1769, 'John, born 13 April'; Mrs E. Rickaby to anon [William Leaton] 12, 13 April and 26 September 1769: DCRO SEA D/St/C2/3/59.
37 Gray to Brown, 22 May 1770, in Toynbee and Whibley, vol. 3, p. 1,135.
38 Bowes, p. 67. The children's baptisms are recorded as follows: Parish register St George's Church, Hanover Square, CWAC, baptisms, 2 July 1770, 'Anna Maria, born 3 June'; 16 December 1771, 'George, born 17 November'; 31 May 1773, 'Thomas, born 3 May'.
39 Foreman, pp. 48 and 265; Lewis, Judith Schneid, p. 42.
40 Home, vol. 3, p. 30. The comment is recorded by Lady Mary Coke in her journal in 1769.
41 Lord Strathmore to MEB, n. d. [1776]: BM Archives.
42 Bowes, p. 5. Her alleged preference for cats and dogs is from Testimony Revd Henry Stephens: NA divorce appeal to Delegates, DEL 2/12/. The cartoon is Gillray, 'The Injured COUNT..S' [1786 or c. May 1788]. See George, vol. 6, no. 7013, pp. 335–6.
43 Foreman, p. 122; *Rambler's Magazine*, 1783, p. 318.
44 Bowes, p. 5.

45 Foreman, p. 122.
46 SPG, box 83, bundle 3; box 68, bundle 8.
47 Lord Strathmore to MEB, n. d. [1776]: BM Archives.
48 Bowes, pp. 53–4.
49 MEB, *The Siege of Jerusalem* (London, 1774). The play is stated in the published text to have been written in 1769 but a letter from Elizabeth Planta to MEB in May 1771 refers to her having just finished her 'literary work' and a subsequent letter in June offers criticisms on the play. Elizabeth Planta to MEB, 30 May and 15 June 1771: RA, Geo/Planta 6. The letter regarding the post of governess to the princesses is Elizabeth Planta to MEB, 14 July 1771: RA, Geo/Planta 6.
50 Bowes, p. 90. Background on James Lee is from Willson.
51 Bowes, p. 96. For information on John Hunter see Moore (2005). Solander is mentioned in Bowes, p. 36.
52 Lomas; Græme, pp. 616–36; Ewing and MacCallum, *passim*; Mudie and Walker, *passim*; obituary of James Graham, aged 23, *Scots Magazine* 1779, p. 110.
53 Bowes, pp. 8, 69–76, 9–11.
54 Bowes, pp. 68. Family accounts show that Mary stayed in Edinburgh for two weeks from 7 August 1774: Glamis accounts 1774–5, SPG, box 146, bundle 1.
55 Walpole to Conway, 27 November 1774, in Lewis, vol. 39, p. 220; Mary Bowes to anon [?Peter Proctor, Glamis Castle], 9 August 1775: SPG, box 142, bundle 4.
56 James Menzies to Lord Strathmore, 24 December 1775, cited in Slade, pp. 62–3; Peter Nicol to Thomas Lyon, 14 November 1775: DCRO SEA D/St/C1/7/2.
57 Information on Gray is from Sherwen; Letter books of George Gray senior, 1760–1779: BL India Office, MSS EUR c 439 and D691. His baptism is recorded in Christenings in Calcutta 1737, George Gray baptised 1 September: BL India Office, microfilm N/1/1–3, f. 202. Background on Gray's argument with Clive can be found in Bence-Jones, pp. 226–9 and 273; and Khan, pp. 69–98.
58 Gray to Brigadier-General John Carnac, 13 November 1761: BL India Office, Sutton Court Collection, papers of Brigadier-General John Carnac, MSS EUR/F128/35. Gray has been mistakenly credited as the author of an anonymous poem, *A Turkish Tale*, said to be dedicated to Mary and published in 1770. The poem was actually written by George Grey, the father-in-law of the first Earl Grey. A handwritten note inside

the text credits the poem to 'George Grey Esquire of Southwick'.
59 Bowes, pp. 15–22.
60 Apothecaries' accounts 1774–8: SPG, box 202, bundle 6.
61 William Farqeson to James Menzies, 4 April 1776: SPG, box 83, bundle 6.

CHAPTER 5: A BLACK INKY KIND OF MEDICINE

Most of the events in this chapter are drawn from Foot and Bowes, unless otherwise indicated. Background on women and property rights is from Habakkuk, p. 83. Details of the sale at Glamis in June 1776 are from SPG, box 188, bundle 3 and the ninth earl's debts in SPG, box 83, bundle 6. Details of the sale at Gibside in November 1776 are from SPG, box 142, bundle 8. For information on the history of abortion see Bullough; Shorter; Riddle, all *passim*.
1 Lord Strathmore to MEB, n. d. [1776], BM Archives.
2 Elizabeth Planta [on behalf of MEB] to anon [James Menzies], 6 April 1776: SPG, box 83, bundle 6.
3 Unknown artist, 'Mary Eleanor Bowes, Countess of Strathmore', c. 1776, Glamis Castle. Doubts exist as to whether this is really Mary since it was only attributed to her relatively recently. However, there is a marked similarity between this portrait and that by John Downman drawn in 1781.
4 Gay, p. 64; Home, vol. 1, preface, p. lxxii.
5 Anon, Allegations against the Countess of Strathmore, p. 5 in Anon, *The Trial of Andrew Robinson Bowes, Esq; first heard in the Arches*. According to figures from Joseph Massie, estimating annual incomes in 1759, the top twenty families enjoyed £13,470 pa. Cited in Hay and Rogers, p. 20.
6 Thomas Lyon to anon [James Menzies], 29 April 1776: SPG, box 83, bundle 6.
7 Testimony of Ann Eliza Stephens [née Planta], 23 February 1788: NA DEL 2/12.
8 The letters from Thomas Lyon to anon [James Menzies], are 29 April, 21 April and 19 April 1776: SPG, box 83, bundle 6. The letter from Elizabeth Planta [on behalf of MEB] to James Menzies, is 19 May 1776: SPG, box 83, bundle 6.
9 Legal bill, Joshua Peele, 1776: SPG, box 142, bundle 9; Letters of administration appointing Thomas Lyon administrator for Lord Strathmore's estate, 23 July 1776: SPG, box 101, bundle 5.

10 Stone (1993), pp. 139–61; the story of Elizabeth Foster is described in Foreman, p. 100 and Chapman, p. 28. The case of Elizabeth Vassall, who married Sir Godfrey Webster but in 1796 eloped with and later married Lord Holland, is cited in Lewis, Judith Schneid, pp. 43–5.
11 Earl of Strathmore v Bowes, 1777, Chancery case: NA C12/1057/31. This case, pursued by Thomas Lyon on behalf of the tenth earl and his siblings, referred to the guardianship document dated 14 October 1774.
12 Lady Maria Bowes to Mary Lyon, 25 May 1776: SPG, box 202, bundle 10.
13 Bowes, p. 22. Details of her affair with Gray and abortions are all from the *Confessions*.
14 Pottle, p. 227. The advertisement is cited in Stone (1977), p. 266.
15 Anon, *Trials for Adultery*, vol. 3, pp. 3–6.
16 Hicks, p. 176. Mary's description of her abortions is from her *Confessions*, Bowes, p. 89.
17 Bowes, pp. 88–9.
18 Foote, pp. 17–18 and 37.
19 Bowes, pp. 79–80 and 36; bond between MEB and Joshua Peele, 22 April 1776: DCRO SEA D/St/D1/14/31.
20 Bowes, p. 27.
21 The hon. Mrs Boscawen to Mrs Delany 1776 [c. June/July], cited in Llanover, vol. 2, p. 237; Foot, p. 16.
22 Bowes, pp. 92–3.
23 Bowes, pp. 11–12. Graham's death is recorded in *Scots Magazine* 1779, obituary of James Graham, 31 January 1779, p. 110.
24 Journal Book Copy, RS, vol. 28, 1774–77, pp. 368–72; 388–91; 393–6. Masson's account was read at three meetings of the RS, in February 1776, in the form of a letter to the president, Dr John Pringle.
25 Journal Book Copy, RS, vol. 28, 1774–77, p. 444. Background on Penneck (1728–1803) and Planta (1744–1827) can be found in ODNB, vol. 43, pp. 573–4 and vol. 44, pp. 519–21.
26 O'Brian, pp. 100 and 130; Beaglehole, pp. 140, 232–3. Information on his brother, Captain Magra, is from Millan, p. 70.
27 There were at least five Planta daughters: Frederica (c. 1751–1778) and Margaret, who were both governesses to the royal family; Elizabeth Planta (later Mrs Parish), the second eldest daughter, who worked for MEB and must have married John Parish between 1776 and 1778; Ann Eliza Planta (c. 1757, still alive 1807, later Eliza Stephens), who replaced her sister as governess to MEB in July 1776; Ursula Barbara Planta, who

was left money in Mrs Bowes's will; the latter may have become Mrs Minnicks, who emigrated to America, or this could have been a sixth sister.

28 Foot, pp. 11–12.

29 Bowes, p. 6.

30 Details of Stoney's life at this point are from Foot, p. 9.

31 Massingberd, pp. 178–81.

32 Anon [Anne Massingberd] to ARS, 1 November 1776: SPG, volume C.

33 Documents relating to an appeal by ARS to the House of Lords against a Chancery decision: SPG, volume C. Anon, *A full and accurate report of the trial*, p. 2. Individuals could not be declared bankrupt unless they traded in some manner.

34 Anon, *A full and accurate report of the trial*, p. 10.

35 David Walson [tailor] to ARS, 20 July 1775: DCRO SEA D/St/C1/13/1.

36 Bowes, p. 29.

37 ARB to MEB, 24 July [1776]: SPG, volume C.

38 Anon [Anne Massingberd] to ARS, 1 November 1776: SPG, volume C.

39 Testimony of Ann Eliza Stephens (née Planta), 23 February 1788: NA DEL 2/12; Bowes, p. 7. The legal case is cited in Hill, Bridget, p. 140.

40 Foot, p. 18.

41 Thackeray, p. 143.

42 Anon [Anne Massingberd] to ARS, 1 November 1776: SPG, volume C.

43 Rate book, Chelsea, 1775–80, Kensington Library, 13 March 1777; Foot, p. 13. Most references to Stanley House state that MEB bought the property from Mary Southwell in 1777. However, the rate book for March 1777 shows that MEB had paid the previous three months' rates ie since December 1776. This agrees with Foot's assertion that she owned the house prior to her marriage with ARS. For information about Stanley House see London County Council, vol. 4, pp. 43–4; Faulkner, vol. 1, pp. 55–60. Stanley House was sold, reputedly to a Russian millionaire, in 2004 (personal communication, Hampton estate agents, May 2007).

44 No definite date for the marriage has been found but Eliza would

later say she was married in November 1776. Anon, *A full and accurate report of the trial*, p. 29.
45 Thomas Mahon, Bowes's valet, would testify to seeing Bowes emerge from Eliza's bedroom at Gibside at 5 one morning in early 1777. Anon, *A full and accurate report of the trial*, p. 29.
46 Anonymous letter [MEB and Eliza Planta to Revd Henry Stephens], n.d. [December 1776], submitted by ARS in evidence in divorce case: LMA, DL/c/561/4. The letter refers to Eliza being then nineteen. Bowes, p. 26.
47 Anonymous letter [MEB and Eliza Planta to Revd Henry Stephens], n.d. [December 1776], submitted by ARS in evidence in divorce case: LMA, DL/c/561/4. This comment would later be produced as evidence that Hunter had helped her attempt an abortion. Evidence of John Hunter, anon, *The Trial of Andrew Robinson Bowes, Esq; first heard in the Arches*, pp. 96–103.
48 Foot, pp. 22–4.
49 Vickers, p. 59.

CHAPTER 6: BOWES AND FREEDOM

Events leading up to MEB's marriage with ARB and immediately after are related in Foot, pp. 45–9 and 'Lady Strathmore's Narrative from the time of her Marriage 'till she left Mr Stoney': SPG, vol. 332. The latter, which is the first of two volumes handwritten by MEB describing events in her life, is undated but was completed by MEB c. 1795. It is hereafter referred to as Narrative.
1 *Morning Post*, 12 December 1776. The other letters appeared as follows: Monitus, 24 December 1776; Hamlet, 3 January 1777; Monitus, 7 January 1777.
2 Narrative, p. 1. She explains her decision to marry ARB on p. 6. His application for a marriage licence can be found as Marriage allegation, Andrew Robinson Stoney, 16 January 1777: GL Ms 10091/138.
3 Anon, Allegations against the Countess of Strathmore, p. 8 in anon, *The Trial of Andrew Robinson Bowes, Esq., first heard in the Arches.*
4 *Gazetteer and New Daily Advertiser*, 24 January 1777.
5 Evidence of Jessé Foot, anon, *The Trial of Andrew Robinson Bowes, Esq., first heard in the Arches*, pp. 90–2; Foot, pp. 12 and 8.
6 Narrative, p. 12; Bate's comment is from Fyvie, p. 91.
7 Fortescue, vol. 5, p. 471 and vol. 6, p. 7. In 1782 George III refused to

pay a final pension to 'that worthless man' who by that point vocally supported the Prince of Wales.

8 'A Baite for the Devil', 1779, cited in George, vol. 5, no. 5550, p. 332.

9 Sheridan; Rhodes, pp. 40–5, 71–2. Foot reveals that Bate had met Garrick shortly after the duel: Foot, pp. 39–40.

10 Evidence of Thomas Mahon, anon, *A full and accurate report of the trial*, pp. 9–10.

11 *Newcastle Journal*, 31 May 1788.

12 Narrative, p. 4. She describes Bate's letter in MEB, 'An Account of the Inns when I was carried off and a comparison between Major Semple and Mr Stoney': SPG, vol. 333, p. 128.

13 William Scott to Henry Scott, postmarked 20 March [1777] in Surtees, William, p. 48; Foot, p. 53. Foot describes the revived argument with Bate as happening during the summer but this letter shows it took place earlier. The quote from Bate is from Foot, p. 57. The description of ARB as a 'coward' is from Foot, p. 9.

14 Arnold, pp. 63–70. Arnold argues that MEB conspired with Stoney to stage the duel in order to provide an excuse for marrying him rather than Gray but that Bate was an innocent party in the ensuing encounter. However, there is no direct evidence for her role, later trials found that the conspiracy was all Stoney's and various reports point to Bate's guilt.

15 Narrative, pp. 2–3.

16 Evidence of George Walker, anon, *A full and accurate report of the trial*, p. 6.

17 Narrative, p. 9; Evidence of George Walker, anon, *A full and accurate report of the trial*, p. 6; Narrative, pp. 10–11.

18 MEB to George Stoney [n.d.] in Stoney, pp. 34–5.

19 Narrative, pp. 92–3.

20 Mary Bowes to MEB, 12 April 1777: BL Add. MSS 40748.

21 Foot, p. 50.

22 Narrative, p. 10.

23 Evidence Ann Mahon, anon, *A full and accurate report of the trial*, p. 12. The maid married Thomas Mahon soon after Mary's marriage. Her husband's statement is from Evidence Thomas Mahon, anon, *A full and accurate report of the trial*, p. 10.

24 Narrative, pp. 17–18.

25 George Selwyn MP to Lord Carlisle, February 1777, HMC Carlisle, p. 319.

26 Anon [James Perry], 'The Torpedo, a poem to the electrical eel' (London, 1777), p. 6.
27 Anon, 'The Diabo-Lady' (London, 1777), pp. 8–9.
28 Anon, Allegations against the Countess of Strathmore, p. 6 in *The Trial of Andrew Robinson Bowes, Esq., first heard in the Arches.*
29 Trust document, signed George Walker and Joshua Peele, 9 and 10 January 1777: DCRO SEA D/St/D13/4/22.
30 Bowes, pp. 29–30.
31 Evidence George Walker, anon, *A full and accurate report of the trial*, p. 7.
32 Background on the 1777 by-election can be found in Namier and Brooke, vol. 2, pp. 106–8 and 350–1; Knox (1985). Stoney was granted royal licence to change his name to Bowes on 11 February 1777. *Gentleman's Magazine* 47 (1777), p. 93.
33 ARB to Mayor of Newcastle et al, 17 February 1777, in Stoney, p. 37; Isaac Stoney to Thomas Bowes, 8 February 1777, in Stoney, pp. 35–6.
34 Handbill, 'Bowes and Freedom!': SPG, box 78, bundle 13; *Newcastle Chronicle*, 5 March 1777: BM Album.
35 Foreman, p. 147.
36 *Newcastle Chronicle*, 8 March 1777: BM Album.
37 Copy of letter or note by Edward Montagu, 1777: BM Archives.
38 Evidence Francis Bennett, anon, *A full and accurate report of the trial*, pp. 17–18. The pamphlets are Handbill, 'Bowes and Freedom!': SPG, box 78, bundle 13; 'A New Song on the Countess of Strathmore's Birth-day', n.d. [1777]: SPG, volume C; and Handbill, 'To the Worthy Freeman in Newcastle', n.d. [1777]: BM Album.
39 Lady Maria Bowes to Mary Lyon, 7 April 1777: SPG, box 202, bundle 10.
40 Copy of letter or note by Edward Montagu, 1777: BM Archives.
41 ARB to Thomas Bell, 19 May 1777: SPG, Bowes Papers vol. 41. Bowes reported the figure at a public meeting: *Newcastle Courant*, 27 May 1780.
42 Testimony Ann Eliza Stephens (née Planta), 23 February 1788: NA DEL 2/12.
43 Testament Thomas Mahon, anon, *A full and accurate report of the trial*, p. 29.
44 ARB to Henry Stephens, Good Friday [28 March 1777] and MEB to Henry Stephens, 28 March 1777, submitted as evidence by ARB: NA DEL 2/12.

45 Anon [ARB to Gibson Gorst] n.d. [1777]: SPG, volume C.
46 Evidence Henry Stephens and Ann Eliza Stephens, anon, *A full and accurate report of the trial*, pp. 27 and 29.
47 George Walker to Mary Morgan, 31 March 1788: SPG, box 69, bundle 6.
48 Bowes, pp. 12–13.
49 Deed of revocation 1 May 1777, signed by ARB and MEB, witnessed by John Scott, John Hunter and William Gibson: DCRO SEA D/St/D13/4/23; Evidence of John Hunter, anon, *A full and accurate report of the trial*, p. 26; MEB [to Farrer and Lacey] n.d.: SPG, box 185, bundle 2. The Bowes fortune was still held in trust, so that no land, property or heirlooms could be sold off and the estate kept intact for future generations, but all profits and income accrued to the life tenant (originally MEB, now ARB) for their lifetime.
50 Narrative, p. 19.
51 Sherwen.
52 Anon [ARB to Gibson Gorst] n.d. [1777]: SPG, volume C.
53 Hicks, p. 173; Hill, G. B., vol. 2, p. 247. The Duchess of Grafton's delivery is described in Stone (1993), pp. 139–56. William Hunter's anecdote is given in Wadd, p. 283. The Bristol incident is from *Jackson's Oxford Journal*, 29 March 1755, cited in Hill, Bridget, p. 35.
54 Anon, Allegations against the Countess of Strathmore, p. 10 in anon, *The Trial of Andrew Robinson Bowes, Esq., first heard in the Arches*; Foot, p. 51.
55 Biographical details of Elizabeth Craven, née Lady Elizabeth Berkeley, later the Margravine of Brandenburg-Ansbach-Bayreuth, are from Craven, *passim*; and ODNB, vol. 18, pp. 94–5. Background on Craven Cottage is from Fèret, vol. 3, pp. 90–3. The Fulham parish rate book shows rates were first paid on the house in 1779 by Lady Craven. Lady Mary Coke said in 1781 it had been built 'two or three years' earlier. Craven Cottage burnt down in 1888 and the grounds of Fulham Football Club, known as Craven Cottage, were later built on the site. The description by Mary Coke is cited in Lewis, vol. 41, p. 404n.
56 Evidence John Hunter, *The Trial of Andrew Robinson Bowes, Esq., first heard in the Arches*, p. 96.
57 ARB to George Stoney, 14 November 1777, in Stoney, p. 37.
58 Anon, Allegations against the Countess of Strathmore, p. 10 in anon, *The Trial of Andrew Robinson Bowes, Esq., first heard in the Arches.*
59 The parish register states 'baptized 25 Nov 1777 St Mary's Church

Whickham, Mary daughter of Andrew Robinson Bowes Esq & Maria Countess Dowager of Strathmore his wife born Nov 16 privately baptized 25th'. Parish register Whickham Church, DCRO; *Gentleman's Magazine* 47 (1777), p. 555; *Annual Register* 1777, p. 218.

60 Pinchbeck and Hewitt, vol. 2, pp. 582–9.

61 Francis Bennett to MEB, 21 May 1785: SPG, box 185, bundle 2.

62 *A Supplement to the Court of Adultery* (1778) and *A New Song* (1779): DUL BBP Box 71, 239 and 248.

63 Evidence Isabella Filliberti (née Fenton), Consistory Court of London deposition book 1783–90: LMA DL/C/282.

64 Earl of Strathmore v Bowes b. r. [15 June 1777]: NA C12/1057/31.

65 Anne Massingberd to MEB, 30 May 1777; and AM to ARB, 16 July 1777: SPG, volume C. The letter from Scarborough is Judith Noel to Mary Noel (her aunt), 26 August 1777, in Elwin, p. 68. Anne Massingberd married William Maxwell by licence, 6 December 1777, at Ormsby parish church. Marriage register, parish of Ormsby, cited in Massingberd, p. 369.

66 Narrative, pp. 21–3.

67 Narrative, p. 18.

CHAPTER 7: LOATHSOME WEEDS

The main secondary source for Paterson and his travels in the Cape is Forbes and Rourke's book. As well as providing plentiful biographical information, this transcribes the manuscript account of his journeys from his notebook which was discovered in London in 1956. Forbes and Rourke cite the baptism in Kinnettles parish church of 'William Son of David Paterson Gardener in Bridgetoun' on 22 August 1755. Other biographical information on Paterson can be found in Gunn and Codd, pp. 273–5 and Desmond (1994), p. 539.

1 Log book *Houghton*: BL India Office, L/MAR/B/438N. The ship left Plymouth on 9 February 1777 and arrived in False Bay for Cape Town on 15 May.

2 Paterson to William Forsyth, 24 May 1777, in Forbes and Rourke, p. 33. Sadly Paterson's letters to Forsyth are currently missing from Kew Library.

3 Lemmon, p. 64.

4 Paterson (1790), p. 3. This tribute only appears in the second edition of the book. It is entirely omitted from the first edition published in

1789. All information and quotes are from the first edition, 1789, unless specified.
5 Forbes and Rourke, p. 20.
6 Spencer, pp. 108–9.
7 Paterson, p. 9. This plant was later named *Erica patersonia* in Paterson's honour. Forbes and Rourke, p. 66n.
8 Only two paintings bear Paterson's signature and these are from his later visit to India. For discussion of the possible candidates see Forbes and Rourke, p. 38n.
9 The name Gordon's Bay has been transferred to the former Vishoek Bay while Paterson's Bay was later renamed Plettenberg Bay. Forbes and Rourke, p. 63n.
10 Paterson, pp. 29 and 35.
11 MEB, 'Copies and Extracts': SPG, box 243, f. 1; Foot's verdict is Foot, p. 10.
12 Bowes, p. 5. Succeeding quotes are all from Bowes, pp. 12, 89–90 and 46–7.
13 Narrative, p. 16.
14 Narrative, pp. 25–6.
15 John Scott to Henry Scott, 1 May 1778, in Surtees, William, p. 75.
16 Testimonies of Margaret Garret and Ann Bell in anon, *A full and accurate report of the trial*, pp. 13 and 17.
17 Bacon, vol. 1, p. 285; Blackstone, vol. 1, p. 432. For background on the history of domestic violence see Foyster (2005); and Doggett. Doggett has pointed out that there appears to be no legal case in which Justice Buller made this remark. However, the three cartoons produced by Gillray depicting him as 'Judge Thumb' in 1782 make it plain that he did make such a comment, possibly out of court.
18 Judith Noel to Mary Noel (her aunt), 28 June 1778, in Elwin, p. 68.
19 Berry, pp. 120–40. The assembly rooms opened in 1776; ARB is listed in the book of subscribers.
20 Narrative, pp. 33–4.
21 Testimony MEB, 16 December 1784 [in pursuit of Chancery case to regain custody of her children], submitted by ARB in divorce appeal to Delegates: NA, DEL 2/12.
22 Personal accounts of children 1778–9: SPG, box 97, bundle 11.
23 Testimony MEB, 16 December 1784.
24 ARB to anon [William Davis], cited in Foot, p. 63.

25 Evidence Revd Samuel Markham, Consistory Court of London deposition book 1783–90: LMA, DL/C/282.
26 MEB, 'Copies and Extracts': SPG, box 243, f. 3. ARB's abuse of his sister is described here and in Narrative, pp. 26–7.
27 Foot, p. 65. Foot cites a letter from ARB to anon [William Davis], sent on 10 May 1779; the dashes are Foot's. Stanley House was sold to Lewis or Louis Lochee, who is listed in the Chelsea rates book from March 1780. Rates book, Chelsea, 1775–80, Kensington Library, March 1780.
28 Longrigg, pp. 69–99.
29 *Newcastle Chronicle*, 26 July 1777.
30 Foot, p. 66. Bowes later stated that he had paid £750 for the horse but was forced to relinquish her in 1798 at which point she had 'not a single tooth in her head' and was expected to die within weeks. *Newcastle Advertiser*, 8 December 1798. Icelander won £50 at Hexham, £50 at Durham, 100 guineas at Nottingham and £100 at Morpeth. Weatherby, p. 165.
31 Foot, p. 67. The explanation for the term 'stoney-broke' is widely reported in Irish and north-east England circles although I have been unable to ascertain an original source for the link and it may be apocryphal. See, for example, *Gaelport.com*; *http://tinyurl.com/58m88l*; Newcastle City Council/West Newcastle; *http://tinyurl.com/5h7u58*; Sunniside and District Local History Society; *http://tinyurl.com/59cvjs*.
32 Robinson, pp. 171–7.
33 Narrative, p. 105.
34 Narrative, pp. 54–8. For more detail on the letters see Moore (2007).
35 M. Armstrong to ARB, 8 October [c. 1780]: SPG, box 185, bundle 1.
36 For information on the sheriff's role see Gladwin.
37 Wills (1995), p. 78; Day book of Gibside estate receipts and expenditure, 24 May 1776 to 9 July 1782, for October 1780: DCRO SEA D/St/E5/5/22. This volume is the last of the Gibside household accounts to have survived from Bowes's period of ownership. Jessé Foot's quote is from Foot, pp. 81–2.
38 Wills (1995), p. 78.
39 Thunberg, pp. 69 and 94.
40 Paterson, p. 39; Forbes and Rourke, p. 43. The following quotes in this section are from Paterson, pp. 110–2, 113, 124 and 124–7. The plant Paterson describes as of the Pentandria Monogynia class was *Pachy-*

podium namaquanum, see Forbes and Rourke, p. 162n.
41 Lindsay, p. 52.
42 Hickey, pp. 223–7. The later details are from pp. 267–8 and 290–3.
43 James Lind to Joseph Banks, 23 October 1779, in Dawson, p. 542.
44 MEB to Thomas Joplin, 9 January 1781 and 27 August (probably 1782): SPG, box 186, bundle 6.
45 My thanks for advice on the cabinet to Claire Jones, former keeper of furniture at the Bowes Museum. So far no records regarding the design or purchase of the cabinet have been found and its maker has not been identified. It is not known when Mary commissioned the cabinet, conceivably before she married Bowes. The cabinet was sold after the death of John Bowes, Mary's grandson, and only bought back by the museum in 1961.
46 Mary Bowes to John Bowes, October 1854: BM Archives. Some dried plants kept in an album thought to have belonged to MEB may have been the original specimens from the cabinet. Album of Botanical Specimens believed to have been collected by MEB, BM Archives.
47 Aiton, vol. 2, pp. 191 and 412; and vol. 3, pp. 498–9. Several plants were claimed as new species by botanists reading Paterson's narrative and studying the accompanying plates; only a handful, including *Monsonia patersonii* and *Erica patersonii*, were named after him: Forbes and Rourke, p. 38. The 'giant cudweed' is described in *Curtis's Botanical Magazine* (1795), plate 300. Today it is known as the strawberry everlasting or *Syncarpha eximia*. My thanks to Peter Goldblatt and John Manning for botanical advice on the Cape.
48 Moore (2005), pp. 292–3 and 348; Dobson, pp. 124–8; *London Evening Post*, 7 June 1788.
49 Le Vaillant, vol. 1, pp. 32–3.
50 Karsten, pp. 283–310.
51 Forbes and Rourke, p. 28.
52 Forbes and Rourke, p. 43. Masson's account of his earlier travels was published only as an article in the *Philosophical Transactions of the Royal Society* in 1776. Paterson's original manuscript was discovered in 1956 in Swedenborg House, London, and is now preserved in the Brenthurst Library, Johannesburg. The document, a leather-covered notebook, is believed to have been written between 1780 and 1785, since it refers to Gordon as colonel, a rank he only assumed in 1780. Possibly Paterson wrote the document, which forms the basis for his published narrative, on his return journey from the Cape. See Duckworth, pp. 191–7. The

Brenthurst Library also possesses Paterson's three albums of more than 300 watercolours.
53 William Paterson to William Forsyth, 21 December 1783, sent from India, cited in *The Cottage Gardener* vols 8–9 (1852), pp. 364–5.
54 Brown, Robert, pp. 303–4.
55 *Gentleman's Magazine* 98 (1828), II, p. 7.

CHAPTER 8: IMPROPER LIBERTIES

Background information on the 1780 general election in Newcastle and Bowes's term as MP is from Namier and Brooke, vol. 2, pp. 106–8 and 350–1; Dickinson; and Knox (1992), as well as various contemporary newspapers. The result is recorded in the Poll Book, Newcastle Election (Newcastle, 1780). Details of the refreshments Bowes ordered can be gleaned from the Day book of Gibside estate receipts and expenditure, 24 May 1776 to 9 July 1782, 29 November 1780: DCRO SEA D/St/E5/5/22.
1 *General Advertiser and Morning Intelligencer*, 9 February 1780.
2 Foot, p. 70.
3 *Newcastle Courant*, 5 April 1780. The *Courant* supported the government.
4 Foot, p. 71.
5 Narrative, pp. 91–2.
6 *Newcastle Chronicle*, 2 September 1780. The attack, originally in the *Courant*, was cited in the *Chronicle* by Bowes's team.
7 Newspaper cutting, n. d. [c. 1811], BM Album.
8 Namier and Brooke, vol. 2, p. 350.
9 Judith Noel to Mary Noel, 23 September 1780, in Elwin, p. 169.
10 Details of Mary Stoney's escape are from Narrative, p. 27; ARB to Thomas Johnston, 3 July 1781 and MEB to George Stoney, 8 December 1780 in Stoney, pp. 39–43; Mary Lawrenson (née Stoney) to MEB, March [no day] 1785: SPG, box 185, bundle 1.
11 George Stoney's diary, 8 March 1781, in Stoney, p. 45.
12 Mary Lawrenson (née Stoney) to MEB, March [no day] 1785: SPG, box 185, bundle 1.
13 Narrative, p. 60.
14 Copy of Mary Bowes's will, 6 April 1777: SPG, deed box 12.
15 It would be more than forty years before George and Mary Bowes were finally interred together in the mausoleum of the Gibside chapel.
16 Mary Lawrenson (née Stoney) to MEB, March [no day] 1785 and same to same, n. d.: SPG, box 185, bundle 1.

17 Testimony MEB, 16 December 1784 [in pursuit of Chancery case to regain custody of her children], submitted by ARB in divorce appeal to Delegates: NA, DEL 2/12. All the letters quoted are from this document.
18 Biographical information on John Downman can be found in Munro; and Williamson (1907). The nine sketches of the Bowes family are preserved in the Fitzwilliam Museum, numbers 1867, 1868a, b, c and d, 1869a, b, c and d. All the portraits are dated 1781 with the exception of that of young Mary which Downman has dated 1786, plainly erroneously since the sketch obviously shows a much younger child.
19 Narrative, pp. 63–6; depositions of Ann Davis and Sarah Frederick, LCC divorce case: LMA DL/C/282. The 17,000-acre estate of Wemmergill Moor, near Lunedale in County Durham, was sold in 2006 by the current Earl of Strathmore. For historical background on grouse-hunting see Carlisle; for a contemporary account see Thornton, especially pp. 149–52. Beating or driving grouse was only introduced in about 1800. My thanks for advice to the British Association for Shooting and Conservation.
20 Foot, pp. 82 and 72.
21 William's birth is given as 8 May in some sources. However, the *Newcastle Chronicle* of 16 March 1782 reported that he had been born the previous week which tallies with a handwritten note giving his date of birth as 8 March 1782, in SPG, volume C.
22 John Burton, *An Essay towards a Complete New System of Midwifery*, 1751, cited in Hill, Bridget, p. 106.
23 Narrative, p. 67. The following exploits are from Narrative, pp. 32–3, 44, 68–70, and Foot, p. 85.
24 Deposition of Ann Parkes, LCC divorce case: LMA DL/C/282.
25 Bowes to Lord Shelburne, 19 February 1783, cited in Namier and Brooke, vol. 2, p. 107. ARB's comment is from Foot, p. 78.
26 Narrative, p. 70.
27 Judith Noel to Mary Noel (her aunt), 29 July 1783, in Elwin, p. 216.
28 Sarah Angus, sister to the Gibside gardener Thomas Joplin, referred in 1782 to Bowes refusing to pay the 'work people'. Thomas Joplin described Bowes sacking Robert Stephenson and the Gibside groom. Sarah Angus to Thomas Joplin, 7 August 1782; Thomas Joplin to Silas [Angus?] 13 August 1782: DCRO SEA D/St/C2/3/122. Estate accounts for Gibside were not kept or have been destroyed after July 1782.
29 Deposition of Dorothy Stevenson [sic], LCC divorce case: LMA

DL/C/282. Dorothy's parents signed their name Stephenson.
30 Bowes rented 48 Grosvenor Square from a Mrs Wyndham from 1783 to 1785. Parish rates books, St James's Church, Piccadilly, CWAC, 1783–5; Dasent, p. 101.
31 Deposition of Dorothy Stevenson [sic], LCC divorce case: LMA DL/C/282.
32 George Stoney to William Gibson, 18 September 1783, in Stoney, p. 51.
33 Deposition of Dorothy Stevenson [sic], LCC divorce case: LMA DL/C/282; anon, *The Trial of Andrew Robinson Bowes, Esq; first heard in the Arches*, p. 21.
34 Narrative, pp. 67, 31, 104–5 and 15.
35 Deposition of Dorothy Stevenson [sic], LCC divorce case: LMA DL/C/282.
36 Deposition of Susanna Church, LCC divorce case: LMA DL/C/282.
37 MEB to Thomas Joplin, 27 August [n. y. probably 1782]; 10 September 1782; 19 October 1782: SPG, box 186, bundle 6. The new gardener's evidence is given in Testimony of Robert Thompson, NA divorce appeal to Delegates: DEL 2/12. Thompson said Bowes gave him his instructions in summer 1783.
38 Foot, pp. 85–6.
39 Taylor, vol. 1, p. 5; Moore (2005), pp. 199–200.
40 Evidence of Jessé Foot, anon, *The Trial of Andrew Robinson Bowes, Esq; first heard in the Arches*, pp. 90–2.
41 Narrative, pp. 76–8, 72–5 and 83–4; Deposition of Dorothy Stevenson [sic], LCC divorce case: LMA DL/C/282.
42 Deposition of Elizabeth Waite, LCC divorce case: LMA DL/C/282; anon, *The Trial of Andrew Robinson Bowes, Esq; first heard in the Arches*, pp. 1–8. Her letter is recorded in Narrative, p. 79.
43 *Newcastle Chronicle*, 17 April 1784.
44 *Newcastle Chronicle*, 24 April 1784.
45 Namier and Brooke, vol. 2, p. 107.
46 Narrative, pp. 48–50; Deposition of Dorothy Stevenson [sic], LCC divorce case: LMA DL/C/282.
47 Narrative, p. 61.

CHAPTER 9: AN ARTFUL INTRIGUING WOMAN

Mary Morgan related her employment history in court. Deposition of

Mary Morgan, anon, *The Trial of Andrew Robinson Bowes, Esq; first heard in the Arches*, p. 56. It seems that Morgan had a daughter who was aged about ten when she entered service with Mary Eleanor although no mention of her is made in letters or other documents. She was buried in the same grave as her mother, at Priory Church, Christchurch. Although Mary wrote that Morgan arrived on 17 or 18 May, Morgan herself said she began work on 18 May. Chancery suit ARB v MEB, 1 June 1786: NA, C12/608/15.

1 Narrative, p. 85.

2 Testimony MEB, 16 December 1784 [in pursuit of Chancery case to regain custody of her children], submitted by ARB in divorce appeal to Delegates: NA, DEL 2/12. The letters quoted, contained in the testimony, are from Thomas Lyon to MEB, 5 May 1784 and MEB to TL, 10 May 1784. The lack of punctuation is typical of court clerical transcribing, not Mary's normal impeccably grammatical style.

3 Augustus Hare, vol. 1, p. 25.

4 Deposition of Mary Reynett, LCC divorce case: LMA DL/C/282.

5 Transcript of letter Mary Bowes to MEB, 12 May 1784: BM Archives. This letter was erroneously ascribed by Arnold to Maria Jane who had, of course, already left the school by then. The writing style and a reference to not yet being able to dance at balls make clear this could not have been Maria Jane. See also an unpublished tract by Charles Hardy, 'Mary Bowes 1777–1855', BM Archives, 1974.

6 Foot, p. 88–94. Foot describes the kidnap and subsequent stay in France in detail, no doubt briefed by William Davis.

7 NA, Chancery Orders and Decrees, C33/461/part 1, p. 365. The guardians presented their bill on 27 May 1784 according to the Orders and Decrees book. James Menzies having died, only Thomas Lyon and David Erskine remained as guardians. The original petition appears not to have survived.

8 For general information on Paris and France in the eighteenth century see Black (2003). The contemporary accounts cited are Bessborough, p. 18 and Reichel, pp. 265–75. For background on France in the approach to the revolution of 1789 see Price, pp. 57–87; Doyle, *passim*; Schama (2004), *passim*.

9 Sterne, pp. 32 and 149n.

10 Thomas Gray to Thomas Ashton, 21 April 1739, in Toynbee (1915), vol. 1, p. 213.

11 Cole, pp. 40 and 51; Andrews, p. 12.

12 Simpson, Helen, p. 109. Mercier's writings on Paris were first published in 12 volumes between 1782–8.
13 Narrative, pp. 75 and 87.
14 Deposition of Mary Morgan, LCC divorce case: LMA DL/C/282; anon, *The Trial of Andrew Robinson Bowes, Esq; first heard in the Arches*, pp. 39–68.
15 Cole, p. 55.
16 Foot, pp. 96–111. All letters subsequently quoted from ARB to Davis are from these pages.
17 For information on John Scott, Lord Eldon, see Surtees, William; Twiss; and Melikan. Arnold states that it was William Scott, who took on the Chancery case but it was obviously John, who made his career in Chancery. Information on John Lee can be found in Schama (2005), pp. 157–60 and 166–7; and ODNB, vol. 33, pp. 82–3.
18 NA, Chancery Orders and Decrees, C33/461/part 1, p. 365.
19 ARB to William Davis, 13 June 1784, in Foot, p. 97.
20 Narrative, pp. 86, 92, 98 and 94.
21 Narrative, pp. 87–89; Deposition of Mary Morgan, LCC divorce case: LMA DL/C/282; anon, *The Trial of Andrew Robinson Bowes, Esq; first heard in the Arches*, pp. 39–68.
22 Deposition of Lady Anna Maria Bowes, LCC divorce case: LMA DL/C/282.
23 MEB to ARB, 3 February 1785: SPG, box 185, bundle 1.
24 Mary Lawrenson (née Stoney) to MEB, March [no day] 1785: SPG, box 185, bundle 1.
25 Foot, pp. 101 and 110. The outcome is recorded in NA, Chancery Orders and Decrees, C33/461, part 2, p. 562. The case was heard on 3 August 1784.
26 Narrative, p. 99. The succeeding episodes are from Narrative, pp. 101–2 and 95–7.
27 Foot, p. 107.
28 Deposition of William Davis, LCC divorce case: LMA DL/C/282.
29 Deposition of Dorothy Stevenson (sic), LCC divorce case: LMA DL/C/282.
30 Narrative, pp. 103–4; Depositions of Mary Morgan, Ann Parkes and Lady Anna Maria Bowes, LCC divorce case: LMA DL/C/282.
31 Depositions of Susannah Sunderland, Richard Thompson and Dorothy Stevenson [sic], LCC divorce case: LMA DL/C/282. Bowes

himself would suggest Sunderland ran a brothel in the interrogatories, LCC divorce case: LMA DL/C/180.

32 Narrative, pp. 106–16; Testimony of MEB, 16 December 1784, originally produced for Chancery case, Lord Strathmore and others v ARB and MEB, c. 1784, produced by ARB in Delegates case, 9 April 1788: NA DEL 2/12.

33 Todd, pp. 286–7; Wollstonecraft, pp. 147–8. Interestingly, the novel tells the story of an educated woman who is deprived of her daughter and confined to an asylum by her licentious husband.

34 My thanks for advice to Peter Homan, Museum of the Royal Pharmaceutical Society.

35 Venn, vol. 1, p. 342. John was admitted on 9 November 1784; Testimony of MEB, 16 December 1784, originally produced for Chancery case. Accounts 1782–5: SPG, box 146, bundle 3.

36 Testimony of MEB, 16 December 1784, originally produced for Chancery case.

37 Narrative, pp. 90–1.

38 Stone (1995), pp. 167–8; Foyster (2002).

39 Narrative, pp. 120 and 89–90.

40 Deposition of Mary Morgan, LCC divorce case: LMA DL/C/282.

41 Foot, p. 112.

42 Answer MEB, 15 March 1787, ARB v MEB: NA Chancery C12/608/15.

43 Answer ARB, 3 July 1786, MEB v ARB: NA Chancery C12/605/34.

44 Narrative, pp. 127–8; answer of Mary Morgan, 17 March 1787, ARB v MEB: NA Chancery C12/608/15. Morgan describes the arrangements for the escape in this testimony. Charles Shuter was not Morgan's cousin, as suggested by Arnold, but the brother-in-law of her friend Miss Charles.

CHAPTER 10: VILE TEMPTATIONS

The main sources for Mary's escape are Foot, pp. 114–6 ; answer of Mary Morgan, 17 March 1787, ARB v MEB: NA Chancery C12/608/15; affidavit Susanna Church, divorce appeal to Delegates: NA DEL 2/12; and Depositions of Mary Reynett and Anna Maria Bowes, LCC divorce case: LMA DL/C/282. Background information on the history of the English legal system is from Baker.

1 Narrative, pp. 48, 50, 129–30 and 133.

2 Copy of letter MEB to ARB, 3 February 1785: SPG, box 185, bundle 1. The copy was made by MEB herself.

3 HW to Lady Ossory, 5 February 1785, in Lewis, W. S., vol. 33, pp. 459–60.

4 Handwritten copy of Articles of the Peace exhibited by MEB against ARB, 7 February 1785: SPG, Bowes Paper, vol. 41; *Gentleman's Magazine*, 55 (1785), p. 152. Another handwritten copy of the articles exists in SPG, volume C which has a poem, presumably by Mary, on the reverse. It reads: 'Our poets oft have satire tried,/To stop the hideous female rore,/But Bowes his keener pen apply'd,/And woman for a while gave o'er,/Thus may their tongues for ever bleed,/And pens be ne'er employ'd in vain,/Bowes then may glory in the Deed,/And try the experiment again.'

5 *Morning Chronicle*, 8 and 24 February 1785.

6 Narrative, p. 7.

7 Foot, p. 117.

8 Affidavit Dorothy Stephenson, divorce appeal to Delegates: NA DEL 2/12. Dorothy said she left on 25 February 1785.

9 ARB to Charles Harborne and James Seton [MEB's attorneys], 11 February 1785, cited in Answer MEB, ARB v MEB: NA Chancery C12/608/15; ARB to same, 16 February 1785, copy: SPG, box 185, bundle 2.

10 Answer MEB in ARB v MEB: NA Chancery C12/608/15; Foot, p. 119.

11 Bill ARB in ARB v MEB: NA Chancery C12/608/15. The bill says Stephens was 'late under treasurer' of the Middlesex Hospital, now in the East Indies, in December 1786.

12 Dickens (1991, first pub. 1852–3), p. 53.

13 For information on the history of divorce in England see Phillips (1988) and (1991); Stone (1995); and Baker, pp. 490–8.

14 Hay and Rogers, p. 53.

15 Stone (1995), pp. 153–5. Eldon and Kenyon subsequently attempted to abolish private separation deeds.

16 Stone (1995), p. 213; Lord Abergavenny against Richard Lyddel for criminal conversation with Lady Abergavenny, in anon, *A New Collection of Trials for Adultery*, vol. 1, case 7, p.12.

17 Anon, *A New Collection of Trials for Adultery*, vol. 2, p. iii.

18 According to Stone, cases seeking separation which reached the Court of Arches (the appeal court for southern England) rose between

1780 and 1810, while matrimonial litigation at the London Consistory Court, the biggest of the preliminary courts, doubled between 1750 and 1820. Stone provides a breakdown of plaintiffs to the LCC by gender between 1670 and 1857. Stone (1995), pp. 40, 43 and 428.
19 Stone (1995), pp. 309–11.
20 Phillips (1988), p. 65.
21 Campbell, vol. 7, pp. 153–5.
22 Dickens (1938, first pub. 1849–50), p. 320.
23 Foot, p. 120. Mary's libel was lodged on 4 May 1785 and is given in LCC divorce case: LMA DL/C/180. The depositions are collected as LCC divorce case: LMA DL/C/282.
24 MEB to Thomas Johnston, 27 April 1785, in Stoney, appendix to p. 55.
25 Foot, p. 119. Foot meant in financial terms.
26 MEB to Thomas Colpitts, 15 June 1785: SPG, volume C.
27 Mary Lawrenson (née Stoney) to MEB, March 1785, George Stoney to MEB, 31 March 1785: SPG, box 185, bundle 1; George Stoney to General Armstrong, 6 April 1785, cited in Stoney, p. 56.
28 Thomas Lyon to MEB, 27 May 1785: SPG, box 201, bundle 3; TL to MEB, 27 July 1786: SPG, box 69, bundle 4.
29 Elizabeth Parish to Thomas Lyon, 4 May 1785: SPG, box 146, bundle 6; same to same, 3 November 1785: SPG, box 99, bundle 2.
30 Foot, p. 119. William Lyon describes himself as a distant relation in anon, *A full and accurate report of the trial*, p. 32–3.
31 Foot, p. 120; Jessé Foot to MEB, 24 May 1785: SPG, box 185, bundle 1; Jessé Foot to MEB, 24 May 1785: SPG, box 185, bundle 1; deposition of Jessé Foot, LCC divorce case: LMA DL/C/282.
32 John Hunter to MEB, 18 September 1785: DCRO SEA St/C1/9/5. The feud between Foot and Hunter may have been at least partly motivated by their opposing loyalties in the Bowes divorce case. The following year, 1786, when Hunter published his long-awaited treatise on venereal disease, Foot responded with a virulent counter-attack. While Hunter characteristically dismissed the diatribe with the aside that 'every animal has its Lice', Foot would have the last laugh: penning a poisonous biography of the revered surgeon the moment he was safely dead. See Moore (2005), pp. 199–201 and ODNB, vol. 20, pp. 245–6. Depositions of John Hunter and Richard Thompson, LCC divorce case: LMA DL/C/282.
33 *The Times*, 27 April and 9 May 1785. The Stephensons' story is told

in Statement by Mary Stephenson, n.d. [1785/6]: SPG, box 185, bundle 2. Dorothy's statement of her ordeal is given in Affidavit Dorothy Stephenson, 3 May 1785, for divorce appeal to Delegates: NA DEL 2/12.
34 Francis Bennett to MEB, 31 May 1785: SPG, box 185, bundle 2.
35 Depositions of Dorothy Stevenson [sic], LCC divorce case: LMA DL/C/282.
36 Robert Thompson to MEB, 16 March 1785 and 3 April 1785: SPG, box 69, bundle 6 and bundle 4.
37 Letters Francis Bennett to MEB, 12 March to 19 July 1785: SPG, box 185, bundle 2.
38 MEB to Thomas Colpitts, 31 May 1785: SPG, volume C. Colpitts's father and grandfather had worked as agents to the Bowes family.
39 MEB, handbill, 24 December 1785: BBP DUL box 71, 248.
40 William Stephenson to Mary Stephenson, 3 February 1786: SPG, box 185, bundle 3.
41 Various letters Ann and George Arthur to MEB, 7 March to 21 October 1785 and undated: SPG, box 185, bundle 2.
42 MEB to Thomas Colpitts, 2 August 1785: SPG, volume C.
43 MEB, handbill, 24 December 1785: BBP DUL box 71, 248. MEB to Thomas Colpitts, 7 January [the letter is dated 1785 but was definitely 1786]: SPG, volume C.
44 James Farrer and Thomas Lacey are listed in *Browne's General Law-List* for 1780–2 at 8 Bread Street Hill and noted as specialising in the King's Bench. Farrer does not appear in other biographical directories of lawyers and little more information can be found about him beyond his copious correspondence with MEB. His brother Henry Farrer was born in Yorkshire c. 1745. I am grateful for the help of Christopher Jessel of Farrer & Co, the law firm still based in Lincoln's Inn Fields, for ascertaining that Mary's attorney was not the James Farrer who worked there contemporaneously.
45 Mary Morgan to Thomas Colpitts, 19 January 1786: SPG, volume C. The succeeding quotes are from MEB to Thomas Colpitts, 14 February 1786: SPG, volume C, and James Farrer to Thomas Lacey, 9 December 1786: SPG, box 185, bundle 2.
46 Testimony Francis Bennett, 29 July 1788, divorce appeal to Delegates: NA DEL 2/12; Robert Thompson to MEB, 14 December 1785: SPG, box 81, bundle 5.

47 Countess of Strathmore v Bowes, in Brown, William, vol. 2, pp. 345–50.
48 Transcript letter ARB to Mr Langstaff, 2 March 1786 and Thomas Colpitts to James Farrer, 2 February 1786: SPG, box 185, bundle 1.
49 John Hall to MEB, 26 April 1786 and James Smith to MEB, 2 May 1786: SPG, box 69, bundles 4 and 7; *English Chronicle*, 6 May 1786, BM Album.
50 *The Times*, 19 May 1786.

CHAPTER 11: SAY YOUR PRAYERS

Background on Gillray and the Strathmore prints is from Gatrell, pp. 258–74 and 331–44. Also see McCreery, pp. 173–4 and 195–6, and George, vol. 6, nos. 7011, 7013 and 7083. All sources agree that at least the first two prints were probably commissioned by Bowes. The three prints are 'LADY TERMAGANT FLAYBUM going to give her STEP SON a taste of her DESERT after Dinner, a Scene performed every day near Grosvenor Square, to the annoyance of the neighbourhood', 1786; 'The Injured COUNT..S', (undated but most probably 1786); 'The MISER'S Feast', 1786. There seems no apparent reason for Morgan's wasp-waist other than that Gillray was experimenting with such figures at the time. My thanks to Vic Gatrell for advice. The third print was labelled 'Lady Strathmore' by Edward Hawkins, keeper of antiquities at the British Museum from 1826 to 1867, according to Gatrell, p. 340 and 645n. The connection is still unclear, however. The anecdote about the tenth earl appeared in *The Ton Gazette*, 1777, copy in BBP DUL box 71, 248.
1 MEB bill in MEB v ARB, 3 June 1786: NA C12/605/34. Bowes replied on 3 July with a scurrilous attack on Mary, claiming he had cut the trees because they were old. The felled trees were advertised on 3 June 1786, with a counter advertisement from MEB, in the *Newcastle Courant*. The injunction was granted sometime in July.
2 Thomas Colpitts to James Farrer, 14 July 1786: SPG, box 69, bundle 4.
3 Robert Thompson to MEB, 24 July 1786: SPG, box 69, bundle 6. Several authors report Bowes visiting Scandinavia on a tour with Sir Henry Liddell and Matthew Consett at this time. This trip took place between 24 May and 12 August 1786. But as these tenants' letters show Bowes was very much at large in County Durham during those months. The 'Mr Bowes' who accompanied Liddell and Consett was probably

Thomas Bowes of Durham, listed as a subscriber to the book describing the expedition. See Consett. The tenants' letters mentioned below are Robert Thompson to MEB, 24 March 1786; Hannah Dixon to MEB, 17 July 1786; William and Mary Stephenson to MEB, 23 May 1786 and same to Farrer, 26 July 1786: all SPG, box 69, bundle 4. Various eviction notices are mentioned including three in a letter from John Glover to Farrer, 27 April 1786: SPG, box 69, bundle 5, as well as others referred to below.

4 Thompson to MEB, 16 July 1786: SPG, box 69, bundle 4.

5 MEB to Colpitts, 16 July 1786: SPG, volume C.

6 MEB to Colpitts, 16 July 1786: SPG, volume C.

7 Farrington, p. 261; Captain Farrer's divorce bill, *Journal of the House of Lords*, 36 George III, vol. XL (1796), p. 654. Farrer had served a seven-year apprenticeship at sea and worked up the ranks before being given command of the *True Briton* in 1782. The divorce was granted in April 1796. Mary's letter referring to him is MEB to Colpitts, 16 July 1786: SPG, volume C.

8 Miniature of MEB, watercolour on ivory, by J. C. Dillman Engleheart, c. 1800, in the BM. The list of works kept by J. C. Dillman Engleheart shows that he painted MEB's portrait 'for my Aunt W' on 9 August 1800 and it is believed this was copied from an earlier portrait by his uncle George Engleheart, which is since lost. Mary had died a few months prior to the nephew's portrait. Williamson (1902), p. 130; BM catalogue details, record no. 1509.

9 MEB to Colpitts, 22 October 1786: SPG, volume C. The ensuing details are described in Affidavit Mary Morgan, n. d.: SPG, box 69, bundle 5; MEB to Colpitts, 16 August 1786; Morgan to Colpitts, 26 October 1786: SPG, volume C; and Morgan to Colpitts, 26 October and 2 November 1786: SPG, volume C. The two coaches followed Mary's on 22 October 1786.

10 MEB to Colpitts, 7 November 1786: SPG, volume C; Morgan to Colpitts, 7 November 1786: SPG, volume C.

11 Details of the abduction are described in many sources. The principal ones I have referred to are Lady Strathmore's Narrative, vol. 2, Narrative of my journey from Streatlam Castle to the Highlands etc. and my return to Bread Street Hill, hereafter called Narrative, vol. 2.; Information filed for the King's Bench, Hilary term 1787, in the case of abduction on 10 Nov 1787 against ARB and others: SPG, box 186, bundle 1; affidavit of Henry Farrer and Mary Morgan for *habeas corpus* against ARB, 11

November 1786: NA KB/1/25/1, Michaelmas bundle 1. The ironmonger is variously named Edward Foster and Forster, but the former is given in street directories. The shop was at 253 Oxford Street, close to Oxford Circus. *Lowndes's London Directory for the year 1787*, p. 56; *Kent's Directory for the year 1794*.

12 Information filed for the King's Bench: SPG, box 186, bundle 1. Details of Bowes's plans also emerged at the later court case.

13 MEB to Morgan, 10 November 1786: DCRO SEA D/St/C2/11/21.

14 Durham County Council, pp. 18–23; Tipping; Sale catalogues, Streatlam Castle, 1922 and 1927: BM Archives.

15 Events during 11 and 12 November at Streatlam Castle are described in Narrative, vol. 2, pp. 175–88.

16 Horace Walpole to Lady Ossory, 1 December 1786, in Lewis, W. S., vol. 33, pp. 536–40; Duchess of Brunswick to the Duchess of Argyll, 26 December 1786: BL add. MSS 29577.

17 *London Evening Post*, 11 November 1786: BM Album; *The Times*, 16 November 1786; *Gentleman's Magazine* 56 (1786), p. 991; *Madras Courier*, 6 December 1787, cutting in a scrapbook of news cuttings compiled by MEB, entitled 'Paragraphs Etc Pro and Con Concerning Myself & Family', in the possession of the Bowes Lyon family at St Paul's Walden Bury, hereafter called SPWB Album.

18 Affidavit Henry Farrer and Mary Morgan for *habeas corpus* against ARB, 11 November 1786: NA KB/1/25/1, Michaelmas bundle 1. Background on policing is from Hay and Snyder, *passim*. In 1856 it became compulsory for every county in England and Wales to have a police force.

19 *English Chronicle*, 14 November 1786, BM Album.

20 *London Evening Post*, 11 November 1786, BM Album; handbill, 11 November, SPWB Album.

21 Zachary Hubbersty to 'Lacey and Farrer', 13 November 1786: SPG, box 69, bundle 5.

22 Robert Thompson to Morgan, 19 December 1786: SPG, box 69, bundle 6.

23 *English Chronicle*, 21 November 1786, BM Album; *London Chronicle*, 28–30 November 1786.

24 *Rambler's Magazine*, 1786, p. 444; letter, anon to anon: BM Archives; Lady Darlington to her son, 16 November, 1786: BM Archives.

25 Margaret Liddell to Thomas Colpitts, 13 November 1786: SPG, volume C.

26 Edward Whatmore to Frederick Gibson, 13 November 1786: SPG, box 69, bundle 5.
27 Affidavit Thomas Ridgeway, 13 November: NA KB/1/25/1, Michaelmas bundle 1.
28 News cutting, no title or date: BBP DUL box 71, 243; *Gentleman's Magazine* 56 (1786), p. 991.
29 Information filed for the King's Bench: SPG, box 186, bundle 1.
30 Letter, anon to anon: BM Archives.
31 Details of Mary's ordeal from 12 to 20 November differ slightly in dates and locations according to various sources. My main source has been Narrative, vol. 2. Details can also be found in Information filed for the King's Bench: SPG, box 186, bundle 1. The autumn season of 1786 (September, October, November) was not only the coldest of the eighteenth century but also since records first began in 1659 according to the Hadley Centre Central England Temperature Handset, *http://hadobs.metoffice.com/hadcet/*. My thanks to Barry Gromett of the Met Office. Background information on the Pennines is from Smith, *On Foot in the Pennines*, pp. 111–12; Marsh, *passim*; Defoe, vol. 3, pp. 75–6. Access is now restricted in the area Mary crossed since large parts are private grouse moors or artillery ranges.
32 Ridgeway's and Captain Farrer's search efforts are described in Information filed for the King's Bench: SPG, box 186, bundle 1; Thomas Colpitts junior to James Farrer, 18 November 1786: SPG, volume C.
33 Letter, anon to anon, BM Archives.
34 Margaret Liddell to Thomas Colpitts, 19 November 1786: SPG, volume C.
35 Several copies of reward posters with different dates and text survive in SPG, volume C and the SPWB Album. Mrs Liddell refers to a poster in her letter of 19 November.
36 Information filed for the King's Bench: SPG, box 186, bundle 1.
37 Details of the rescue are contained in Narrative, vol. 2; affidavit of Gabriel Thornton, 5 December 1786: NA KB/1/25/1, Michaelmas bundle 2.
38 Thomas Lacey to Thomas Colpitts, 21 November 1786 and Mary Morgan to Thomas Colpitts, 23 November 1786: SPG, volume C.
39 *English Chronicle*, 25 November 1786, BM Album; *Public Advertiser*, 24 November 1786, SPWB Album. Several poems and leaflets are preserved in the SPWB Album with titles such as: 'A True and Particular Account, of the Many Hardships, and Surprizing Escape, of the

Countess of Strathmore Who was rescued from Mr Bowes, by a great Number of Country People in a Field, near Darlington, in the County of Durham'.

CHAPTER 12: THE TAMING OF BAD WIVES

Details of ARB's court appearance are contained in the newspaper articles mentioned as well as numerous others contained in the SPWB Album and BM Album. The scene is pictured in James Gillray, 'Andrew Robinson Bowes Esqr. as he appeared in the Court of Kings Bench...', (London, 1786). See Gatrell, pp. 340–2; McCreery, pp. 174–7; George, vol. 6, no. 7012. His journey to court and time in jail is described in Foot, pp. 138–9.

1 *The Times*, 29 November 1786; *Gentleman's Magazine* 56 (1786), p. 1081; *Morning Chronicle*, 29 November 1786.

2 Foss, vol. 1, pp. 137–8; ODNB, vol. 8, pp. 617–9. Although Buller was heavily backed by Lord Mansfield, eventually Lord Kenyon was appointed Mansfield's successor in 1788.

3 Sureties of between £500 and £1,000 were commonplace for such cases; even Earl Ferrers had been allowed bail totalling £10,000. See Doggett, p. 13. Foot, p. 139; cutting [no title], 29 November 1786, BBP DUL, box 71, 248.

4 *Morning Chronicle*, 29 November 1786; *Newcastle Journal*, 9 December 1786.

5 Anon, 'The Irishman in Limbo, or, Stony Batter's Lamentation for the loss of his Liberty', n. d., BBP DUL, box 71, 248; Anon, 'Who Cries Andrew now?', (London, 12 May 1788), BBP DUL, box 71, 248; Martin Brown, 'Paddy's Progress, or the Rise and Fall of Captain S–y' (Durham, 1808): DCRO SEA D/St/C1/13/16. An earlier version of the latter ballad, published 23 July 1788, is preserved in the SPWB Album.

6 Testimony John Beaumont, apothecary, Information filed for the King's Bench: SPG, box 186, bundle 1; anon, *The Trial of ARB ... for a Conspiracy*, p. 31.

7 MEB to Thomas Colpitts, 28 December 1786: MEB to Thomas Colpitts, 8 January 1787; MEB to Thomas Colpitts junior, 13 December 1786: SPG, volume C.

8 MEB to Thomas Colpitts, 28 December 1786: SPG, volume C.

9 Cokayne, vol. 12, pp. 400–1. Lord Strathmore enrolled as a cornet on 15 November 1786. Mary collected news cuttings on his career in the SPWB Album which she began in 1786.

10 Elizabeth Parish to Thomas Lyon [no day] May 1786: SPG, box 99, bundle 2.
11 MEB to Thomas Colpitts, 8 January 1787: SPG, volume C.
12 Affidavit ARB, 21 November 1786, George III v ARB, King's Bench trial: NA KB/1/25/1.
13 A handwritten note by MEB in the SPWB Album in November 1786 states: 'Mr Bowes bought a share in the Universal Register on purpose to have an opportunity of vilifying my Character in it, & all my Friends as much as he chose.'
14 *The World*, 4 January 1787, SPWB Album; *The Times*, 16 January 1787.
15 Anon, Allegations against the Countess of Strathmore, in anon, *The Trial of Andrew Robinson Bowes, Esq; first heard in the Arches*. The allegations, the customary term for the respondent's reply, were reproduced in several formats at various times before the end of the century.
16 George Walker to anon [Mary Morgan?], 3 February 1787: SPG, box 185, bundle 1.
17 Affidavits Francis Bennett, 29 July 1788, Robert Thompson, 5 February 1787 and James Smith, 27 March 1788, divorce appeal to Delegates: NA DEL 2/12.
18 Narrative, vol. 2, p. 133; Mary Morgan to Thomas Colpitts, 26 January 1787: SPG, volume C.
19 James Farrer to Thomas Lacey, 9 December 1786: SPG, box 185, bundle 2.
20 *Newcastle Journal*, 27 January 1787, BM Album.
21 *The Times*, 24 January 1787. Extract from the *Rover's Magazine*, 1 February 1787, BBP DUL, box 71, 241.
22 George Stoney to General Robinson, 17 February 1787, and George Stoney's will, in Stoney, pp. 59–61.
23 ARB to Duke of Norfolk, 2 March 1787: Arundel Castle Howard Letters 1760–1816, vol. 1, section IV.
24 MEB to Thomas Colpitts, 14 March 1787 and Mary Morgan to Colpitts, 1 April 1787: SPG, volume C. Although Mary thought Bowes had procured bail by 14 March, it was the end of March before the bail was agreed.
25 Affidavit Susannah Church, 25 June 1787, cited in divorce appeal to Delegates: NA DEL 2/12. Since she could not read, it is feasible she had signed the affidavit without understanding its contents.
26 Interrogatories on behalf of MEB to be asked of Revd Henry

Stephens, divorce appeal to Delegates: NA DEL 2/12.

27 *The Times*, 8 May 1787.

28 Bowes's appeal to the High Court of Delegates was lodged on 16 May 1787: NA DEL 2/12.

29 *The Times*, 28 May 1787.

30 George III v ARB, King's Bench trial: NA KB/1/25/1. The details of the case were published in various newspapers and several pamphlets. The quotations are taken from anon, *The Trial of ARB ... for a Conspiracy*.

31 Foss, vol. 1, pp. 235–40; Simpson, A. W., p. 167; ODNB, vol. 18, pp. 567–77. According to Simpson, writing in 1984, Erskine is still regarded by many as 'the greatest advocate ever practising in England'. James Mingay is described in Anon, *Sketches of the Characters*, pp. 63–4; ODNB, vol. 38, pp. 357–8.

32 The sentencing was described in anon, *The Trial of ARB ... for a Conspiracy*. Gowland's and Shields's evidence is from Affidavits Mary Gowland and Matthew Shields, George III v ARB: NA KB/1/25/3.

33 *Morning Post*, 13 October 1788, SPWB Album.

34 Thomas Colpitts junior to Mary Morgan, 16 October 1787: SPG, box 185, bundle 3; James Smith to MM, 20 February 1788: DCRO SEA D/St/C2/11/22.

35 MEB to Thomas Colpitts, 17 December 1787: SPG, volume C.

36 Several sources, including Arnold, pp. 146–7, state that Anna was living with her mother in Fludyer Street when she eloped. She was actually living with Mrs Parish at that address as documented by rate books, letters from Mrs Parish and newspaper reports. Parish rates books, St Margaret's Church, CWAC, 1786 re Fludyer Street; various letters Elizabeth Parish to Thomas Lyon: SPG, box 99, bundle 2; *London Evening Post*, 29 January 1788 and *Newcastle Journal*, 2 February 1788: BM Album. The eventual marriage settlement is cited in Invoice signed J. Ord, paying first instalment of marriage settlement of July 1789 to Henry James Jessop, 29 December 1789: SPG, box 99, bundle 3.

37 Full details of the hearing in the Court of Common Pleas are published in anon, *A full and accurate report of the trial*, which went to three editions in 1788.

38 *Gentleman's Magazine*, 58 (1788), p. 459.

39 Doggett, p. 101.

40 William Watson to Frances Bennett, 24 June 1788: SPG, box 185, bundle 1.

41 Farrer.
42 *The Times*, 16 and 22 December, 1788; Rowe, p. 61.
43 Duncan, *passim*; Stone (1995), p. 183; *Reports of the Commissioners of the Ecclesiastical Courts of England and Wales 1831–2* (1832). According to Stone there were eleven appeals in the thirty years in the mid-eighteenth century while the commissioners' report states there were ninety-five in the first thirty years of the nineteenth century.
44 NA DEL 2/12.
45 *Gentleman's Magazine* 59 (1789), p. 267.
46 *The World*, 7 March 1789: SPWB Album.
47 MEB, An Epitaph, Lady Strathmore's Miscells. Verses & Prose: SPG, vol. 335. Foot says MEB sent the poem to ARB in prison after the divorce victory. Foot, p. 147.

CHAPTER 13: OUT OF THE WORLD

Background details on Newington and Southwark are taken from London County Council, vol. 25, pp. 2–19 and 81–3. MEB's correspondence with Eliza is in Ann (Eliza) Stephens (née Planta) to MEB, 31 October, 20 and 31 December 1789, 3 January and 13 February 1790: SPG, box 185, bundle 3.
1 SPWB Album.
2 Affidavits ARB 30 January 1790 and MEB, 3 February 1790: NA DEL 2/12.
3 Schedule of excommunication, 5 February 1790: NA DEL 2/12.
4 Mary Morgan [on behalf of MEB] to anon [?Lacey], 7 March 1790: SPG, box 185, bundle 3.
5 Mary Bowes to MEB, 5 March 1790, copy: BM Archives.
6 Mary Morgan [on behalf of MEB] to anon [?Lacey], 7 March 1790: SPG, box 185, bundle 3.
7 The *habeas corpus* writ is mentioned in Mary Morgan's letter of 7 March 1790, *ibid*, and referred to in the title of a document at DCRO, 'Brief for Lady Strathmore on a Habeas Corpus to produce the body of Mary Bowes, her daughter, at the suit of Andrew Robinson Bowes, 1790', which is among a number of documents currently closed at the family's request: DCRO SEA D/St/L1/2/16. It must therefore have been served on either 6 or 7 March. However, there appears to be no trace of the writ in King's Bench records at the NA. No record of the decision in Chancery can be found at NA either but agreement must have been reached by the time of the deed of revocation, which granted

allowances for William and Mary, signed on 25 September 1790.
8 MEB to James Farrer, 25 April 1790: SPG, box 185, bundle 3.
9 Deed of revocation and appointment, 25 September 1790: DCRO SEA D/St/D13/4/32.
10 Stone (1993), pp. 35–7. Details on Shelley are from ODNB, vol. 50, p. 206. General information on child custody is from Pinchbeck and Hewitt, vol. 2, p. 370; Stone (1995), p. 173. The remark by Mary Wollstonecraft to Gilbert Imlay, 1 January 1794, is cited in Hill, Bridget, p. 103.
11 Hare, vol. 2, p. 172; Mrs Bland to Miss Heber, 16 February 1793, cited in Arnold, p. 159.
12 *English Chronicle*, 19 May 1789: BM Album.
13 Wills (1995), p. 82. The Gibside household accounts were resumed in 1791.
14 Askham, *passim*; Swinburne, vol. 2, pp. 86–90; Wheatley, vol. 5, pp. 201–2. Swinburne's comments are in Henry Swinburne to Sir T. Gascoigne, March 1791, in Wheatley, vol. 5, pp. 86–90. The earl's activities were reported in *The Bon Ton Magazine*, 1 (1791), p. 400. The Isaac Cruikshank cartoon was 'A Strath Spey or New Highland Reel as Danced at Seaton D–l' (London, 29 December), described in George, vol. 6, 1784–92, no. 7741. Although no year is mentioned on the cartoon, George dates it to 1790 but the sequence of events suggests that it was a year later.
15 *Gazetteer*, August and December 1791; *Star*, 24 January 1792: SPWB Album.
16 Venn, vol. 1, pp. 342–3. George was admitted on 9 May 1791 and Thomas on 13 December 1792.
17 MEB, 'To my son Bowes on his coming of age', Miscellaneous poems of Lady Strathmore's written since 1792: SPG, vol. 336.
18 SPWB Album.
19 Farrington, p. 261; Captain Farrer's divorce bill, *Journal of the House of Lords*, 36 George III, vol. XL (1796), pp. 654 and 709. Captain Farrer died on board the *True Briton* on 21 May 1800 and was buried at sea. Log book *Hindostan*: BL India Office, L/MAR/B/267C.
20 The portrait hangs still in the hall of the house at St Paul's Walden Bury.
21 Foot, pp. 142–56.
22 *The Star*, 1 April 1793: SPWB Album.

23 Letter MEB, 14 April 1793, in the *True Briton* and *Hampshire Chronicle*, 18 April 1793: SPWB Album.
24 Garlick and MacIntyre, vol. 1, p. 176. MEB referred to Mrs Ogilvy in a note in *Miscellaneous poems of Lady Strathmore's written since 1792*: SPG, vol. 336.
25 *Morning Post*, 25 December 1792.
26 *Reading Mercury*, 15 July 1793: SPWB Album.
27 Dale. All quotes during Mary's time at Stourfield are from this booklet unless otherwise stated. Richard Dale was born in the year MEB arrived at Stourfield. His text was first published in *Notes and Queries* in 1876. Stourfield House later became a care home and has since been demolished although its front steps and portico remain, now serving a block of flats, with a blue plaque affixed. The area is now the Southbourne suburb of Bournemouth.
28 Dale, pp. 5–6. My thanks to Dr Donald Stevens, archivist of Priory Church Christchurch, for checking the inscription.
29 House of Lords report, 1796: SPG, volume C; Countess of Strathmore v Bowes in Brown, William, vol. 2, pp. 345–50.
30 MEB to James Farrer, 18 and 20 December 1796: SPG, box 185, bundle 3.
31 News cutting, no title, July 1798: SPWB Album.
32 Funeral fee book 1783–1811, Westminster Abbey, p. 157; Chester, vol. 10, pp. 463–4; Will of MEB, NA, prob/11/1374; Obituary, *Gentleman's Magazine* 70 (1800), p. 488; note in Chester, vol. 10, pp. 463–4.
33 Will of ARB: NA, prob/11/1514.
34 Cokayne, vol. 12, p. 400.
35 Mosley, vol. 3, pp. 3,281–4.
36 Hare, vol. 2, p. 181.
37 Hardy (1970); Wills, pp. 89–92.
38 Thomas married three times and died in 1846. He had an only child, Thomas, by his first wife, who died in 1834 so that his grandson, also Thomas, became the twelfth earl. Cokayne, vol. 12, p. 401.
39 Thackeray stayed at Streatlam Castle in June and July 1841 and after hearing Mary Eleanor's story wrote to his publisher: 'I have in my trip to the country found materials (rather a character) for a story, that I'm sure must be amusing...' He began writing *The Luck of Barry Lyndon* in October 1843 and it was serialised in *Fraser's Magazine* throughout 1844. After a pirated version was published in the US as a book in 1852 it was first published in book form in the UK in Thackeray's *Miscellanies:*

Prose and Verse in 1856 when it was renamed *The Memoirs of Barry Lyndon Esq. of the Kingdom of Ireland*. About two-thirds of the book relates imagined events before the marriage. Ray, pp. 271, 339 and 346.

Bibliography

I. MANUSCRIPT SOURCES

Baker Baker Papers, DUL
Bowes Museum – 'Memoranda relating to A R Bowes and the Countess of Strathmore', cited as BM Album; correspondence and other material in Bowes Museum Archives
Howard Letters 1760–1816, Arundel Castle
Royal Archives, Windsor
Royal Society archives
St Paul's Walden Bury Album, album of newspaper cuttings collected by MEB at St Paul's Walden Bury
Strathmore Estate Archives, Durham County Record Office
Strathmore Papers, Glamis Castle (National Register of Scotland 885)

II. PUBLISHED SOURCES

Anon, *The British Code of Duel, a reference to the laws of honour, and the character of gentleman* (London, 1824)
Anon, *A full and accurate report of the trial between the Reverend John Stephens, trustee to E. Bowes, commonly called Countess of Strathmore, and Andrew Robinson Stoney Bowes, Esq. her second husband, in the Court of Common Pleas, before the Right Hon. Alexander Lord Loughborough and a special jury, on Monday, May 19th, 1788* (London, 1788, third edition)
Anon, *The Irish Register, or a list of the Duchess Dowagers, Countesses, Widow Ladies, Maiden Ladies, Widows, and Misses of large fortunes in England* (London, 1742)
Anon, *The Monthly Chronicle of North-Country Lore and Legend* (Newcastle upon Tyne, 1887)
Anon, *A New Collection of Trials for Adultery* (London, 1799)
Anon, *Sketches of the Characters of the Hon. Thomas Erskine, and James*

Mingay, Esq. interspersed with anecdotes and professional strictures (London, 1794)

Anon, *The Stoniad* (Newcastle, 1777)

Anon, *The Trial of Andrew Robinson Bowes, Esq. Edward Lucas, Francis Peacock, Mark Prevot, John Cummins, otherwise called Charles Chapman, William Pigg, John Bickley, Henry Bourn, and Thomas Bowes, Attorney at Law, on Wednesday, the 30th day of May, 1787 . . . for a Conspiracy against the Right Hon. Mary Eleanor Bowes, commonly called Countess of Strathmore* (London, 1787)

Anon, *The Trial of Andrew Robinson Bowes, Esq; first heard in the Arches Court of Doctors Commons; and, in consequence of an Appeal, determined in a Court of Delegates . . . when the Right Hon. the Countess of Strathmore obtained a divorce* (London, 1789)

Anon, *Trials for Adultery, or the history of divorces, being select trials at Doctors Commons, for adultery, fornication, cruelty, impotence, &c. from the year 1760, to the present time* (London, 1779–80)

Anon, *A Turkish Tale* (London, 1770)

Aiton, William, *Hortus Kewensis* (London, 1789)

Allan, G. C., *The Adelphi, Past and Present: A History and A Guide* (London, 2001)

Andrews, John, *Letters to a Young Gentleman on his Setting Out for France* (London, 1784)

Angerstein, Reinhold, *R. R., Angerstein's Illustrated Travel Diary 1753–55*, translated by Torsten and Peter Berg (London, 2001)

Arnold, Ralph, *The Unhappy Countess and her Grandson John Bowes* (London, 1957, reprinted 1993)

Askham, Francis, *The Gay Delavals* (London, 1955)

Aspinall, Arthur, *Politics and the Press c. 1780–1850* (Brighton, 1973)

Astell, Mary, *Some Reflections upon marriage* (London, 1700)

Atkinson, Frank, *The Great Northern Coalfield 1700–1900* (Newcastle, 1966)

Atkinson, John A., *The British Duelling Pistol* (London, 1978)

Attwater, Aubrey, *Pembroke College, Cambridge: A Short History* (Cambridge, 1936)

Bacon, Matthew, *A New Abridgment of the Law* (London, 1778, first pub. 1736)

Baker, J. H., *An Introduction to English Legal History* (London, 2002)

Baldick, Robert, *The Duel: A History of Duelling* (London, 1965)
Barker, Hannah, *Newspapers, Politics, and Public Opinion in late Eighteenth-century England* (Oxford, 1998)
Barlow, Frederick, *The Complete English Peerage* (London, 1775)
Beaglehole, J. C., *The Life of Captain James Cook* (London, 1974)
Bence-Jones, Mark, *Clive of India* (London, 1974)
Berry, Helen, 'Creating Polite Space: the organisation and social function of the Newcastle Assembly Rooms', in Berry, Helen and Gregory, Jeremy (eds), *Creating and Consuming Culture in North-East England, 1660–1830* (Aldershot, Hants, 2004)
Lord Bessborough (ed.), *Lady Bessborough and Her Family Circle* (London, 1940)
Black, Jeremy, *The British Abroad: The Grand Tour in the Eighteenth Century* (London, 1992)
—*France and the Grand Tour* (Basingstoke, 2003)
Blackstone, William, *Commentaries on the Laws of England* (Oxford, 1765–9)
Blunt, Reginald (ed.), *Mrs. Montagu, 'Queen of the Blues,' Her Letters and Friendships from 1762 to 1800* (London, 1923)
Boswell, James, *The Life of Samuel Johnson* (Oxford, 1980)
Bowes, Mary Eleanor, *Confessions of the Countess of Strathmore, written by herself. Carefully copied from the original lodged in Doctor's Commons* (London, 1793)
Brand, John, *The History and Antiquities of the Town and County of the Town of Newcastle upon Tyne* (London, 1789)
Brown, Robert, *Prodromus Flora Novae Hollandiae* (London, 1810)
Brown, William, *Reports of Cases argued and determined in the High Court of Chancery . . . from 1778 to 1794* (London, 1819)
Bullough, Vern L. (ed.), *Encyclopedia of Birth Control* (Santa Barbara, California, 2001)

Campbell, J., *Lives of the Lord Chancellors and Keepers of the Great Seal of England* (London, 1868)
Carlisle, G. L., *Grouse and Gun* (London, 1983)
Chapman, Caroline, *Elizabeth and Georgiana* (London, 2002)
Chester, Joseph Lemuel, (ed.), *The Marriage, Baptismal and Burial Registers of the Collegiate Church or Abbey of St. Peter, Westminster* (London, 1875)
Clark, Alice, *Gleanings from an Old Portfolio, containing some cor-*

respondence between Lady Louisa Stuart and her sister Caroline, Countess of Portarlington (Edinburgh, 1895–8)
Climenson, Emily J. (ed.), *Elizabeth Montagu, The Queen of the Blue-Stockings, her correspondence from 1720 to 1761* (London, 1906)
Cokayne, George E., *The Complete Peerage of England, Scotland, Ireland* (London, 1910–59)
Cole, William, *A Journal of My Journey to Paris in the Year 1765* (London, 1931)
Colman, George and Garrick, David, *The Clandestine Marriage* (London, 1770)
Consett, Matthew, *A Tour through Sweden, Swedish-Lapland, Finland and Denmark in a series of letters* (London, 1789)
Cowper, J. M. and L. I. (eds), *The King's Own: The Story of a Royal Regiment* (Oxford, 1939)
Craven, Elizabeth (afterwards Margravine of Brandenburg-Anspach-Bayreuth), *The Beautiful Lady Craven* (London, 1914)

Dale, Richard, *Reminiscences of Stourfield in the 19th Century* (Bournemouth, 1975)
Dasent, Arthur Irwin, *A History of Grosvenor Square* (London, 1935)
Dawson, Warren R. (ed), *The Banks Letters: A Calendar of the Manuscript Correspondence of Sir Joseph Banks* (London, 1958)
Defoe, Daniel, *A Tour Thro' the Whole Island of Great Britain* (London, 1724)
Desmond, Ray, *Dictionary of British and Irish Botanists and Horticulturalists* (London, 1994)
—*Kew: The History of the Royal Botanic Gardens* (London, 1995)
Dickens, Charles, *The Adventures of Oliver Twist* (London, 2004)
—*Bleak House* (London, 1991)
—*David Copperfield* (London, 1938)
Dickinson, H. T., *Radical Politics in the North-East of England in the Later Eighteenth Century* (Durham, 1979)
Dobrée, Bonamy (ed.), *The Letters of Philip Dormer Stanhope, 4th Earl of Chesterfield* (London, 1932)
Dobson, Jessie, 'John Hunter's giraffe', in *Annals of the Royal College of Surgeons of England*, 24 (1959), pp. 124–8
Doggett, Maeve E., *Marriage, Wife-Beating and the law in Victorian England: 'Sub Virga Viri'* (London, 1992)
Doran, John (ed.), *A Lady of the Last Century* (London, 1873)

Doyle, William, *Origins of the French Revolution* (Oxford, 1999)

Duckworth, Dennis, 'The Log-book of William Paterson' in *Africana Notes and News*, 12 (1957), pp. 191–97

Duncan, G. I. O., *The High Court of Delegates* (Cambridge, 1971)

Durham County Council, *Streatlam and Gibside, the Bowes and Strathmore Families in County Durham* (Durham, 1980)

Ellis, Joyce, 'The "Black Indies", the economic development of Newcastle, c. 1700–1840', in Colls, Robert and Lancaster, Bill (eds), *Newcastle upon Tyne, A Modern History* (Chichester, 2001), pp. 1–26

Elwin, Malcolm, *The Noels and the Milbankes: Their Letters for Twenty-five Years, 1767–1792* (London, 1967)

Ewing, J. C. and MacCallum, Andrew, *Robert Graham, Twelfth of Fintry, Patron of Robert Burns* (Glasgow, 1931)

Farrer, Mary, *The Appeal of an Injured Wife against a Cruel Husband* (London, 1788)

Farrington, Anthony, *A Biographical Index of East India Company Maritime Service Officers 1600–1834* (London, 1999)

Faulkner, Thomas, *An Historical and Topographical Description of Chelsea and its Environments* (London, 1829)

Fèret, Charles, *Fulham Old and New* (London, 1900)

Flinn, Michael W. and Stoker, David, *The History of the British Coal Industry, vol. 2, 1700–1830: The Industrial Revolution* (Oxford, 1984)

Foot, Jessé, *The Lives of Andrew Robinson Bowes, Esq., and the Countess of Strathmore, written from Thirty-Three Years Professional Attendance, from Letters and other Well Authenticated Documents* (London, 1812)

Foote, Samuel, *The Nabob* (London, 1778)

Forbes, Vernon S. and Rourke, John, *Paterson's Cape Travels 1777 to 1779* (Johannesburg, 1980)

Foreman, Amanda, *Georgiana, Duchess of Devonshire* (London, 1998)

Fortescue, John (ed.), *The Correspondence of George III from 1760 to December 1783* (London, 1927)

Foss, Edward, *Biographical Dictionary of the Judges of England 1066–1870* (London, 1870)

Foyster, Elizabeth, *Marital Violence: An English Family History, 1660–1857* (Cambridge, 2005)

—'At the limits of liberty: married women and confinement in

eighteenth-century England' in *Continuity and Change*, 17 (1), (2002), pp. 39–62
Fyvie, John, *Noble Dames and Notable Men of the Georgian Era* (London, 1910)

Garlick, Kenneth and MacIntyre, Angus (eds), *The Farington Diary* (New Haven and London, 1978)
Gatrell, Vic, *City of Laughter: Sex and Satire in Eighteenth-Century London* (London, 2006)
John Gay, *The Beggar's Opera*, Lewis, Peter Elfed (ed.), (Edinburgh, 1973)
George, M. Dorothy, *London Life in the Eighteenth Century* (London, 1976)
—*Catalogue of Political and Personal Satires preserved in the Department of Prints and Drawings in the British Museum, vols 5–11* (London, 1952)
Gladwin, Irene, *The Sheriff: The Man and his Office* (London, 1974)
Græme, Louisa, *Or and Sable: a book of Græmes and Grahams* (Edinburgh, 1903)
Grosley, Pierre Jean, *A Tour to London; or New Observations on England, and its Inhabitants* (London, 1772)
Gunn, Mary and Codd, L. E., *Botanical Exploration of Southern Africa* (Cape Town, 1981)

Habakkuk, John, *Marriage, Debt, and the Estates System: English Landownership 1650–1950* (Oxford, 1994)
Halsband, Robert (ed.), *The Complete Letters of Lady Mary Wortley Montagu*, (Oxford, 1965)
—*The Life of Lady Mary Wortley Montagu* (Oxford, 1956)
Hardy, Charles, *John Bowes and the Bowes Museum* (Newcastle upon Tyne, 1970)
Hare, Augustus J. C., *The Story of My Life* (London, 1896)
Hay, Douglas and Rogers, Nicholas, *Eighteenth-Century English Society* (Oxford, 1997)
Hay, Douglas and Snyder, Francis (eds), *Policing and Prosecution in Britain 1750–1850* (Oxford, 1989)
Hicks, Carola, *Improper Pursuits: The Scandalous Life of Lady Di Beauclerk* (London, 2001)
Hill, Bridget, *Eighteenth-Century Women: An Anthology* (London, 1984)

Hill, G. B. (ed.), *Boswell's Life of Johnson* (Oxford, 1964)
Hindle, Wilfrid, *The Morning Post, 1772–1937: Portrait of a Newspaper* (London, 1937)
Home, J. A. (ed.), *The Letters and Journals of Lady Mary Coke* (Bath, Somerset, 1970)
Hudson, Margaret, 'Pillar of Patriotism', in *Country Life*, 156 (1979), pp. 2,460–1

Lady Ilchester and Lord Stavordale (eds), *The Life and Letters of Lady Sarah Lennox, 1745–1826* (London, 1901)
Ingamells, John, *A Dictionary of British and Irish Travellers in Italy, 1701–1800* (New Haven, London, 1997)
Innes-Smith, Robert, *Glamis Castle* (Derby, 2000)

Karsten, Mia C., 'Francis Masson, a gardener-botanist who collected at the Cape', in *Journal of South African Botany*, 25 (1959), pp. 283–310
Khan, Abdul Majed, *The Transition in Bengal 1756–1775* (Cambridge, 1969)
Knowles, W. H., 'Benwell Tower, Newcastle', in *Archaeologia Aeliana*, 19 (3), (1922), pp. 89–98
Knox, Thomas R., '"Bowes and Liberty": The Newcastle by-election of 1777', in *Durham University Journal*, 77 (1985), pp. 149–64
—'"Peace for Ages to come": the Newcastle elections of 1780 and 1784', in *Durham University Journal*, 84 (1992), pp. 3–19

Landale, James, *Duel: A True Story of Death and Honour* (Edinburgh, 2005)
Lemmon, Kenneth, *The Golden Age of Plant Hunters* (London, 1968)
Lewis, Judith Schneid, *In the Family Way: Childbearing in the British Aristocracy, 1760–1860* (New Brunswick, New Jersey, 1986)
Lewis, W. S. (ed.), *The Yale Edition of Horace Walpole's Correspondence* (New Haven, 1937–61)
Lindsay, Ann, *Seeds of Blood and Beauty: Scottish Plant Explorers* (Edinburgh, 2005)
Litta, Pompeo, *Famiglie celebri Italiane* (Milan, 1819–74)
Lady Llanover (ed.), *The autobiography and correspondence of Mary Granville, Mrs Delany* (London, 1862)
Lomas, S. C., 'The manuscripts in the possession of Sir John James

Graham, of Fintry, KCMG,' in *Royal Commission on Historical Manuscripts, First Report, Report on Manuscripts in Various Collections* (MC55) (Hereford, 1909), vol. 5, pp. 185–269

London County Council joint publishing committee (various eds), *Survey of London* (London, 1909–)

Longrigg, Roger, *The History of Horse Racing* (London, 1972)

Mack, Robert L., *Thomas Gray: A Life* (New Haven, London, 2000)

Marsh, Terry, *The Pennine Mountains* (London, 1989)

Massingberd, William Oswald, *History of the Parish of Ormsby-cum-Ketsby* (Lincoln, 1893)

Matthew, H. C. G, and Harrison, Brian, *Oxford Dictionary of National Biography* (Oxford, 2004)

McCreery, Cindy, *The Satirical Gaze: Prints of Women in Later Eighteenth-Century England* (Oxford, 2004)

Melikan, Rose A., *John Scott, Lord Eldon, 1751–1838* (Cambridge, 1999)

Melville, Lewis and Hargreaves, Reginald, *Famous Duels and Assassinations* (London, 1929)

Middlebrook, Sydney, *Newcastle upon Tyne, its Growth and Achievement, etc* (Yorkshire, 1968, first pub. 1950)

Millan, J., *Annual Army List* (London, 1763)

Millingen, John Gideon, *The History of Duelling: including, narratives of the most remarkable personal encounters that have taken place from the earliest period to the present time* (London, 1841)

Moore, Wendy, *The Knife Man: The Extraordinary Life and Times of John Hunter, Father of Modern Surgery* (London, 2005)

—'The surgeon, the countess, her husband and his lover: John Hunter (1728–93) and the Countess of Strathmore (1749–1800)' in *Journal of Medical Biography*, 15 (2007), pp. 131–3

Mosley, Charles (ed.), *Burke's Peerage, Baronetage, and Knightage* (Stokesley, 2003)

Mudie, Sir Francis and Walker, David, *Mains Castle and the Grahams of Fintry* (Dundee, 1964)

Munro, Jane, *John Downman, 1750–1824* (Cambridge, 1996)

Myers, Sylvia Harcstark, *The Bluestocking Circle: Women, Friendship, and the Life of the Mind in Eighteenth-Century England* (Oxford, 1990)

Namier, Lewis and Brooke, John (eds), *The History of Parliament: The House of Commons 1754–90* (London, 1964)

O'Brian, Patrick, *Joseph Banks* (London, 1989)
Osborn, Emily (ed.), *Political and Social Letters of a Lady of the Eighteenth-Century (the Hon. Mrs Osborn), 1721–1771* (London, 1890)

Paine, James, *Plans, Elevations and Sections, of Noblemen and Gentlemen's Houses* (London, 1767)
Papendiek, Charlotte, *Court and Private Life in the Time of Queen Charlotte, being the Journals of Mrs Papendiek, Assistant-Keeper of the Wardrobe and Reader to Her Majesty* (London, 1887)
Paterson, William, *A Narrative of Four Journeys into the Country of the Hottentots, and Caffraria, in the years 1777, 1778, 1779* (London, 1789, first ed.) and (London, 1790, second ed.)
Perry, Ruth, *The Celebrated Mary Astell: An Early English Feminist* (Chicago, 1986)
Phillips, Roderick, *Putting Asunder: A History of Divorce in Western Society* (Cambridge, 1988)
—*Untying the Knot: A Short History of Divorce* (Cambridge, 1991)
Pinchbeck, Ivy and Hewitt, Margaret, *Children in English Society* (London, Toronto, 1969)
Pottle, Frederick A. (ed.), *Boswell's London Journal 1762–1763* (Edinburgh, 2000)
Price, Roger, *A Concise History of France* (Cambridge, 1993)

Ray, Gordon N., *Thackeray, The Uses of Adversity, 1811–1846* (London, 1955)
Reichel, Oswald J. (ed.), 'Extracts from a Devonshire Lady's Notes of Travel in France in the Eighteenth Century', reprinted from *Transactions of the Devonshire Association for the Advancement of Science, Literature, and Art*, 34 (1902), pp. 265–75
Rhodes, R. Crompton, *Harlequin Sheridan: The Man and Legends* (Oxford, 1933)
Riddle, John M., *Eve's Herbs: A History of Contraception and Abortion in the West* (Cambridge, Mass., London, 1997)
Robinson, John Martin, *The Dukes of Norfolk* (Chichester, West Sussex, 1995)
Rowe, Nicholas, *Tamerlane* (London, 1784)

de Salignac, François de la Mothe-Fénelon, *Instructions for the Education of a Daughter*, trans. by George Hickes (London, 1713)

Savile, George, Marquis of Halifax, *The Lady's New-years Gift: or, advice to a daughter* (London, 1688)
Schama, Simon, *Citizens: A Chronicle of the French Revolution* (London, 2004)
—*Rough Crossings: Britain, the Slaves and the American Revolution* (London, 2005)
Sheridan, Richard Brinsley, *The School for Scandal and other plays* (Oxford, 1998)
Sherwen, Russell, 'Mary Eleanor Bowes, Countess of Strathmore, John Lyon, Ninth Earl of Strathmore, and George Gray', in *Durham Local History Society Bulletin*, 43 (1989), pp. 25–34
Shorter, Edward, *A History of Women's Bodies* (London, 1982)
Shteir, Ann B., *Cultivating Women, Cultivating Science: Flora's Daughters and Botany in England, 1760–1860* (Baltimore, London, 1996)
Simpson, A. W. (ed.), *Biographical Dictionary of the Common Law* (London, 1984)
Simpson, Helen (ed.), *The Waiting City, Paris 1782–88* (London, 1933)
Slade, Harry Gordon, *Glamis Castle* (London, 2000)
Smith, Roland, *On Foot in the Pennines* (Newton Abbot, 1994)
Spencer, Alfred (ed.), *Memoirs of William Hickey* (London, 1913–25)
Sterne, Laurence, *A Sentimental Journey through France and Italy* (London, 1977)
Stone, Lawrence, *Broken Lives: Separation and Divorce in England, 1660–1857* (Oxford, 1993)
—*The Family, Sex and Marriage in England, 1500–1800* (London, 1977)
—*Road to Divorce: A History of the Making and Breaking of Marriage in England, 1530–1987* (Oxford, 1995)
Stoney, Major F. S., *Some Old Annals of the Stoney Family* (London, 1879)
Surtees, Robert, *The History of Antiquities of the County Palatine of Durham* (London, 1816–1840)
Surtees, William, *A Sketch of the Lives of Lords Stowell and Eldon* (London, 1846)
Swinburne, Henry, *The Courts of Europe at the Close of the Last Century* (London, 1895)
Sykes, John, *Local Records or Historical Records of Northumberland and Durham, Newcastle-upon-Tyne, and Berwick-upon-Tweed* (Stockton-on-Tees, 1973)

Taylor, John, *Records of My Life* (London, 1832)
Thackeray, William Makepeace, *The Memoirs of Barry Lyndon, Esq.* (Oxford, 1999)
Thornton, Colonel T., *A Sporting Tour through Northern Parts of England, and great part of the Highlands of Scotland* (London, 1804)
Thunberg, Carl Peter, *Travels in Europe, Africa, and Asia made between the years 1770 and 1779* (London, 1796)
Tipping, H. Avray, 'Streatlam Castle, Durham, a seat of the Earl of Strathmore', in *Country Life*, 38 (1915), pp. 836–43
Todd, Janet, *Mary Wollstonecraft: A Revolutionary Life* (London, 2000)
Toynbee, Paget (ed.), *The Correspondence of Gray, Walpole, West and Ashton, 1734–1771* (Oxford, 1915)
Toynbee, Paget and Whibley, Leonard (eds), *Correspondence of Thomas Gray* (Oxford, 1935)
Turberville, A. S., *A History of Welbeck Abbey and its Owners* (London, 1938)
Twiss, Horace, *The Public and Private Life of Lord Chancellor Eldon* (London, 1846)

le Vaillant, François, *Travels into the Interior Parts of Africa by the way of the Cape of Good Hope* (Dublin, 1790)
Venn, J. A., *Alumni Cantabrigienses* (Cambridge, 1951)
Vickers, Hugo, *Elizabeth, the Queen Mother* (London, 2005)
Vincent, Benjamin (ed.), *Haydn's Dictionary of Dates* (London, 1871)

Wadd, William, *Mems. Maxims and Memoirs* (London, 1827)
Weatherby, James, *Racing Calendar 1779* (London, 1779)
Wheatley, Henry B. (ed.), *The Historical and Posthumous Memories of Sir Nathaniel William Wraxall, 1772–1784* (London, 1884)
Williamson, George C., *George Engleheart, 1750–1829* (London, 1902)
—*John Downman, ARA* (London, 1907)
Wills, Margaret, *Gibside and the Bowes Family* (Chichester, 1995)
Wills, Margaret, and Garnett, Oliver, *Gibside* (London, 1999)
Willson, E. J., *James Lee and the Vineyard Nursery Hammersmith* (London, 1961)
Wollstonecraft, Mary, *Maria* in Todd, Janet (ed.), *Mary and Maria, Matilda* (London, 2004)
Young, Arthur, *A Six Months Tour through the North of England* (London, 1770)

Index

Not
The End